ADVANCING POSITIVE ORGANIZATIONAL BEHAVIOUR

This comprehensive book provides an overview of the present status of positive organizational behaviour, offering insights on the growing body of research and scholarship, as well as suggestions for future directions in the field. Recent times have seen phenomenal and unprecedented changes in work settings, with many transitioning to hybrid or fully remote arrangements. In addition, unwarranted and unscrupulous application of technology, detrimental ramifications of work stress, and impaired well-being at work are posited to create an unsustainable work environment.

Bringing together leading experts from around the world, this collection synthesizes and captures the advancements within the discipline of positive organizational behaviour. It covers topics such as psychological capital, work engagement interventions, self-efficacy, emotions and positive work behaviour, free will, resilience, work well-being, evolutionary psychology and positive workplace, cross-cultural positive organizational behaviour, common-good HRM practices, and methodological advances and challenges in positivity assessments.

This book offers a valuable resource for students and scholars of work/organizational psychology, organizational behaviour, and applications of positive psychology. It is also a useful reference for organizations looking to understand and implement positive organizational policies in their workplaces.

Professor Sir Cary L. Cooper, CBE, is the 50th Anniversary Professor of organizational psychology and health at the ALLIANCE Manchester Business School, University of Manchester, UK.

Subhendu Patnaik is an Assistant Professor of organizational behaviour and human resource management at the Management Development Institute, Gurgaon, India. He previously held the Sir Cary Cooper Professorship of organizational psychology and was the Chair at the Centre for Management Research (CMR), School of Business, Woxsen University, India.

Raul Villamarin Rodriguez is the Vice President at Woxsen University, India, and holds the Steven Pinker Professor of cognitive psychology and Classavo Chair Professorship in integrative research and digital learning.

Current Issues in Work and Organizational Psychology

Series Editor: Cary L. Cooper

Current Issues in Work and Organizational Psychology is a series of edited books that reflect the state-of-the-art areas of current and emerging interest in the psychological study of employees, workplaces and organizations.

Each volume is tightly focused on a particular topic and consists of seven to ten chapters contributed by international experts. The editors of individual volumes are leading figures in their areas and provide an introductory overview.

Example topics include digital media at work, work and the family, workaholism, modern job design, positive occupational health and individualised deals.

Burnout at Work: A Psychological Perspective
Edited by Michael P. Leiter, Arnold B. Bakker, and Christina Maslach

New Frontiers in Work and Family Research
Edited by Joseph G. Grzywacz, and Evangelia Demerouti

The Psychology of Digital Media at Work
Edited by Daantje Derks, and Arnold B. Bakker

A Day in the Life of a Happy Worker
Edited by Arnold B. Bakker and Kevin Daniels

Advancing Positive Organizational Behaviour
Edited by Cary L. Cooper, Subhendu Patnaik, and Raul V. Rodriguez

For more information about this series, please visit: https://www.routledge.com/Current-Issues-in-Work-and-Organizational-Psychology/book-series/CURRENTISSUES

ADVANCING POSITIVE ORGANIZATIONAL BEHAVIOUR

Edited by
Cary L. Cooper, Subhendu Patnaik, and Raul V. Rodriguez

Routledge
Taylor & Francis Group
LONDON AND NEW YORK

Designed cover image: Getty Images © ipopba

First published 2025
by Routledge
4 Park Square, Milton Park, Abingdon, Oxon OX14 4RN

and by Routledge
605 Third Avenue, New York, NY 10158

Routledge is an imprint of the Taylor & Francis Group, an informa business

British Library Cataloguing-in-Publication Data
A catalogue record for this book is available from the British Library

ISBN: 9781032619378 (hbk)
ISBN: 9781032612416 (pbk)
ISBN: 9781032619385 (ebk)

DOI: 10.4324/9781032619385

Typeset in Times New Roman
by codeMantra

CONTENTS

ABOUT THE EDITORS

Cary L. Cooper is the 50th Anniversary Professor of organizational psychology and health at the Alliance Manchester Business School, University of Manchester, UK. Previously, he was Pro Vice-Chancellor and Distinguished Professor of organizational psychology and health at Lancaster University. He is the immediate past President of the Chartered Institute of Personnel and Development, President of the Institute of Welfare, past Chair of the Academy of Social Sciences, and past President of the British Association of Counselling and Psychotherapy and the British Academy of Management. He is the author/editor of over 250 books and over 450 scholarly articles and a regular contributor to radio and TV. He was knighted by the Queen in 2014 for his contribution to the social sciences.

He is the Editor-in-Chief of the *Wiley-Blackwell Encyclopedia of Management* (14 volumes), editor of *Who's Who in Management*, editor of the Wiley-Blackwell *Wellbeing* volumes (six), Founding Editor of the *Journal of Organizational Behavior*, Founding and Former Chair of the UK government think tank, The Sunningdale Institute, and lead scientist on the UK Government Office for Science Foresight project on Mental Capital and Wellbeing and was Chair of the Global Agenda Council on Chronic Diseases and Mental Health of the World Economic Forum. He has also worked closely with the European Commission, the European Council, the European Central Bank, and the UN's World Health Organisation and ILO in the health and well-being arena. Over a number of years, he was voted by *HR Magazine* as the Most Influential HR Thinker and was elected to the HR Hall of Fame. He is an Honorary Fellow of the British Psychological Society, Royal College of Physicians, The Royal College of Physicians of Ireland (Occupational Medicine), and many more and has Honorary Doctorates from a number of universities (e.g., Sheffield, Bath, Aston, Heriot-Watt, Middlesex, Wolverhampton, Chester, and Bolton). Professor Cooper created, and is Co-Chair, the National Forum for Health and Wellbeing at Work, an employer's organization of over 40 global employers (e.g., BP, Microsoft, BT, Shell, Rolls Royce, GSK, NHS Employers, UK Government (Wellbeing Lead), John Lewis Partnership, Fujitsu, and Aon), and represented by HR Directors, Chief Medical Officers, and Directors of Health & Wellbeing of these organizations.

Subhendu Patnaik is an Assistant Professor of organizational behaviour and HRM at the Management Development Institute, Gurgaon, India. He previously worked with the Institute of Management Technology, Ghaziabad, India, as a faculty member in the organizational behaviour and HRM area. He was also the co-chairperson for the PGDM-ExP programme (full-time executive MBA). He is an expert panel member for HR and IR in the Confederation of Indian Industry (CII), Delhi. He is co-chair of the International Common Good HRM Network (CIG- CGHRM & Health and Well-being) based at Vienna University of Economics and Business (WU Vienna), Austria. He obtained an MBA from Cardiff University, UK, and a Ph.D. in positive organizational behaviour. He has over a decade of industry and teaching experience. He has published papers in ABDC "A" and ABS "3" ranked journals. He has taught at the University of Pecs, Hungary. He held a Chair Professorship for "*Sir Cary Cooper, Professor of Organizational Psychology*" and was the Center for Management Research Chair at the School of Business, Woxsen University. He has conducted Management Development Programs for working executives from UNICAM, Brazil, Universidad Externado de Colombia, and NTPC Limited, and similar programs for other Indian corporations. He was the project lead for a joint Brand Trust Ranking Project in collaboration with the Gustavson School of Business, University of Victoria, Canada, and Woxsen University. His current research interests are in positive organizational behaviour and work outcomes.

Raul Villamarin Rodriguez, Vice President of Woxsen University, is a Cognitive Technologist and an Adjunct Professor at Universidad del Externado, Colombia. He serves as a member of the International Advisory Board at IBS Ranepa, Russian Federation, and holds positions on the Advisory Boards of PUCPR; Johannesburg Business School, South Africa; Milpark Business School, South Africa; PetThinQ Inc.; and SpaceBasic, Inc. Additionally, Dr. Rodriguez is a Visiting Professor at Uni. del Rosario, an Expert at UNESCO, and an Editorial Board member at World Summit AI.

As a Steering Committee Member for the Annual Conference at EFMD Global and an Indian Business Council Founding Member, Dr. Raul is deeply involved in shaping the future of education. He is honoured with a scholarship in his name at ZIBS, China, and represents India in the PRME i5 Expert Pedagogy Group. Further, he holds two prestigious titles: Steven Pinker Professor of cognitive psychology and Classavo Chair Professorship in integrative research and digital learning.

Dr. Rodriguez specializes in the convergence of cognitive psychology with cutting-edge technologies such as machine learning, deep learning, natural language processing, computer vision, robotic process automation and quantum artificial intelligence. Registered as an expert in artificial intelligence, intelligent systems, and multi-agent systems at the European Commission, he has been nominated for the Forbes 30 Under 30 Europe 2020 list.

A sought-after keynote speaker and panel moderator, Dr. Raul contributes significantly to national and international conferences, including the Web Summit (Lisbon and Rio), ASQ, PMI, AI Summit, and South Summit, among others. He actively participates in the ETS Business School Advisory Council (BSAC) in India and the Institute for Robotics Process Automation & Artificial Intelligence. Committed to responsible research, he aligns his efforts with RRBM, GRLI, and PRME. He has authored over 12 books and 55 practitioner articles along with his usual academic research.

ABOUT THE CONTRIBUTORS

Jafar Akbari is a Ph.D. candidate and researcher at the Centre for Work, Organisation and Wellbeing at Griffith University in Brisbane, Australia. His research focuses on occupational health and safety, psychosocial hazards in the workplace, safety leadership styles, occupational risks for mental health, and well-being at work. Before his current role, Jafar spent over ten years in various positions, including researcher, inspector, specialist, and director, primarily in the oil and gas industries, addressing occupational health, safety, and ergonomic issues. He received the Best Researcher Award while working in these industries. He has authored over 35 journal articles and three books, significantly contributing to the field of occupational health and safety.

Neal M. Ashkanasy is an Emeritus Professor of management at the UQ Business School at The University of Queensland, Australia. He studies emotion in organizations, leadership, culture, ethical behaviour, and the physical environment of work. He has published in journals such as the *Academy of Management Journal*, *Academy of Management Review*, *Academy of Management Learning & Education*, *The Journal of Management*, and *the Journal of Applied Psychology*. He served as Editor-in-Chief of the *Journal of Organizational Behavior* and Associate Editor for the *Academy of Management Review* and *Academy of Management Learning & Education*. He is currently Associate Editor for the *Journal of Management Education*, *Management Teaching Review*, and *Emotion Review* and Series Editor for *Research on Emotion in Organizations*. He is the founder and administrator of the Emonet Listserv. Ashkanasy is a fellow of the International Association for Applied Psychology, the US Society of Industrial and Organizational Psychology, the Academy of the Social Sciences in Australia and the UK, and the British Academy of Management and is a Life Fellow of ANZAM. In 2017, he was awarded a Medal of the Order of Australia (OAM), and in 2019, he was named the US Academy of Management's Managerial and Organizational Cognition Division Distinguished Scholar. He retired from full-time employment in 2023.

Arnold B. Bakker is a Professor of work and organizational psychology at Erasmus University Rotterdam, The Netherlands. He is the Chair of the Center of Excellence for Positive Organizational Psychology and (Distinguished) Visiting Professor at North-West University and the University of Johannesburg (both in South Africa). He is a visiting professor at the University of Vaasa, Finland. He is a fellow of the Association for Psychological Science, the International Association of Applied Psychology, and the European Academy of Occupational Health Psychology. He is an expert in positive organizational psychology, and his research interests include JD-R theory, job crafting, playful work design, the work–family interface, burnout, and work engagement. He is one of the most-cited scientists in the world. Since 2014, he is included in Thomson Reuters' list of "The World's Most Influential Scientific Minds".

Anmol Basant is a doctoral student in the organizational behaviour area at IIM Ahmedabad. He holds a Bachelor's degree and a Master's degree in exploration geophysics from IIT Kharagpur. Before joining IIMA, he worked as Market Analyst at Futures First, Kolkata, and as Product Development Engineer at Phenom People, Hyderabad. He has presented his research work at prestigious conferences such as the Academy of Management and the Indian Academy of Management conferences. His areas of research include stress management, well-being and happiness at the workplace, mindfulness, positive psychology, and technology and organizations.

Thomas Britt is a Professor of psychology at Clemson University and the Editor-in-Chief for *Military Psychology*. He has published many academic articles in leading journals and is also the author of two books in the fields of organizational psychology and employee stress. He has also been the editor for two books and a four-volume series in the field of military psychology. His current research programmes investigate the determinants of resilience and mental health treatment seeking among employees in high-risk occupations. His research has been funded by multiple grants and contracts from the Department of Defense, Intelligence Community, and NASA.

Julie Dyrdek Broad is the Founder and President of The Positive Organizational Behavior Institute (POBI) where she conducts research on positive organizational behaviour and multi-level psychological capital. Based in the Washington, DC, metro area, Broad has consulted globally on the emergence, measurement, sustainment, and replenishment of core psychological capital assets that are causal and predictive of well-being and performance in the workplace. Broad's research has involved the adaptation, development, and validation of a collective psychological capital intervention (*c*PCI) focusing on groups and teams, both static and dynamically formed. She is a staunch supporter of transitioning the workplace from the primary source of 21st-century epidemic stress to the primary source of well-being and performance.

Paula Brough is a Professor of organizational psychology and Director of the Centre for Work, Organisation and Wellbeing at Griffith University in Brisbane, Australia. Paula's primary research areas are occupational stress and coping, employee mental health and well-being, work engagement, work–life balance, workplace conflict (bullying, harassment, toxic leadership), and the psychosocial work environment. Paula is listed in the top 2% of scientists in her field and is identified as one of the top 50 work–family scholars globally. She has received $6m in competitive external research grant funding. She has authored over 60 industry reports and over 150 journal articles and book chapters and has produced 12 scholarly books based on her research. She is an Associate Editor of *Work & Stress* and the Deputy Editor of *Stress & Health* and is a board member of the *Journal of Organizational Behaviour*, *International Journal of Stress Management*, and the *BPS Work-Life Balance Bulletin.*

Kim Cameron is William Russell Kelly Professor Emeritus of management and organizations in the Ross School of Business and Professor of higher education in the School of Education. His past research on organizational virtuousness, downsizing, effectiveness, corporate quality culture, and the development of leadership excellence has been published in more than 130 academic articles and 15 scholarly books. His current research focuses on virtuousness in and of organizations – such as forgiveness, gratitude, kindness, and compassion – and on positively energizing leadership. He is one of the co-founders of the Center for Positive Organizations at the University of Michigan and has served as Dean at the Weatherhead School of Management at Case Western Reserve University, Associate Dean in the Marriott School of Management at Brigham Young University, and Associate Dean and Department Chair at the University of Michigan. He was recognized as among the top ten organizational scholars in the world whose work has been most frequently downloaded on Google.

Mable E. Clark is a doctoral student in industrial/organizational psychology at Central Michigan University. She is interested in the ways that evolutionary mechanisms apply to social systems and their implications for decision-making.

Stephen M. Colarelli is a Professor of psychology at Central Michigan University. He is interested in applications of evolutionary psychology to industrial and organizational psychology.

Scott I. Donaldson is an Assistant Professor of general internal medicine in the Rutgers Robert Wood Johnson Medical School and a core faculty member of the Rutgers Institute for Nicotine & Tobacco Studies. He also works as a faculty member at the University of Connecticut in Research Methods, Measurement, and Evaluation. His research uses quantitative and qualitative methodologies, such as psychometrics, meta-analysis, content analysis, and advanced statistical approaches, to examine organizational and commercial determinants of health and well-being. He has published in top peer-reviewed journals like *JAMA Pediatrics*, *JAMA Network Open*, *International Journal of Management Reviews*, and *The Journal of Positive Psychology*. Professor Donaldson's research has garnered media attention from many news and policy outlets, such as the U.S. News & World Report, NBC Los Angeles, and the World Health Organization.

Stewart I. Donaldson is a Distinguished University Professor and Executive Director of the Claremont Evaluation Center (CEC) and the Evaluators' Institute (TEI) at Claremont Graduate University. He is deeply committed to improving lives through positive organizational psychology research, evaluation, and education. He is the Co-Founder of the first Ph.D. and research-focused master's programmes in positive psychology at Claremont Graduate University and mentors many graduate students specializing in positive organizational psychology and evaluation science. Professor Donaldson has been honoured with many career achievement awards for his research and evaluation contributions and published hundreds of peer-reviewed articles, chapters, evaluation reports, and more than 20 books on positive psychology and evaluation science topics including PERMA+4: Building Blocks for Human Flourishing (2025); Flow 2.0: Optimal Experience in a Complex World (2025); Well-being and Success for University Students: Apply PERMA+4 (2024); Introduction to Theory-Driven Program Evaluation: Culturally Responsive and Strengths-Focused Applications (2022); Positive Organizational Psychology Interventions: Design and Evaluation (2021); Positive Psychological Science (2020); Toward a Positive Psychology of Relationships (2018); Scientific Advances in Positive Psychology (2017); and Applied Positive Psychology (2011).

Sharon Glazer is the Program Director of the Organizational PsyD program in the Graduate School of Applied & Professional Psychology at Rutgers, The State University of New Jersey. She is a fellow of SIOP, International Academy for Intercultural Research, and International Association of Applied Psychology. Her research focuses on occupational health and stress across cultures and organizations. Most recently, she has been focusing on validating a measure on meaningfulness in life across cultures and co-authoring the fourth edition of *Cross-Cultural Psychology*. Sharon has taught and conducted research as Visiting Professor in a dozen universities across the globe. Currently, in service to her profession, she is Secretary General for the Alliance for Organizational Psychology. In 2021, Sharon was recognized with The University of Baltimore's President's Faculty Award, the Yale Gordon College of Arts & Sciences Distinguished Scholarship Award, and the ISMA Federation International Award from the International Stress Management Association.

Vishal Gupta is a Professor in the organizational behaviour area at the Indian Institute of Management (IIM) Ahmedabad. He was chosen as one of the *India's 25 Young HR Leaders* in 2013 by People Matters and as an *Emerging Psychologist* by the Indian National Academy of Psychology in 2014 and was conferred the *Young Scientist* Award by the Indian National Academy of Sciences in 2016. He served as the President of the Indian Academy of Management, an affiliate of the Academy of Management, from 2020 to 2022. His research has been published in reputed international journals such as the *Academy of Management Journal, Human Resource Management, Journal of Leadership & Organizational Studies, International Journal of Human Resource Management*, and *Personnel Review* and has been covered by the top Indian dailies. His areas of research and teaching include leadership, mindfulness, emotional intelligence, R&D management, and ethics.

Andy Jiang is an undergraduate student specializing in psychology at the University of Toronto. He worked as a research assistant for Behaviourally Informed Organizations, where he worked on consulting projects involving redesigning the customer service process to streamline operations and optimize client satisfaction. Furthermore, he helped to conduct comprehensive assessments of team dynamics within the client organization, furnishing insights to facilitate strategic restructuring initiatives. He has volunteered as a research assistant in many areas of psychology, including personality in the workplace, workplace well-being, decision-making styles, and social media's impact on mental health. His research interests include motivation, well-being, assessment methodologies, job performance, and recruitment.

Tom L. Junker is an Assistant Professor in human resource studies at Tilburg University, The Netherlands. Prior to starting his appointment at Tilburg University, Junker completed his doctoral dissertation "Working in Agile Teams – On the Edge of Chaos" at Erasmus University Rotterdam, which was awarded with cum laude. In his current work, Junker investigates proactive and relational approaches to improving well-being and performance at work. In most of his projects, he adopts quantitative multi-level research designs and analyses. Junker's research has appeared in *Human Relations*, the *European Journal of Work and Organizational Psychology*, and *Career Development International.*

Momo D. Kromah is a registered psychologist who holds a Ph.D. in Management at the UQ Business School, The University of Queensland. His dissertation focused on the role, process, and consequences of workspace territoriality in the context of organizational change. He is passionate about understanding human motivations, attitudes and behaviours in the workplace. His research interests include territoriality, organizational change, psychological ownership, career management competencies, onboarding and cybersecurity. Momo Kromah has published in peer-reviewed journals such as *Human Resource Management Review* and national and international conferences including the Academy of Management, Australian and New Zealand Academy of Management, Society of Industrial and Organizational Psychology, and International Association of Conflict Management.

Catherine T. Kwantes is a Professor of psychology, industrial, and organizational psychology at the University of Windsor in Canada. Her area of focus is on societal culture's impact on employee attitudes and behaviours as well as cross-cultural interactions in the workplace. Most recently, her work has focused on methods for organizations to create more inclusive workplaces for members of minoritized social groups. Her work has appeared in numerous journals such as the *Journal of International Management*, the *International Journal of Cross-Cultural Management*, and *Equality, Diversity and Inclusion: An International Journal.*

Chelsea LeNoble is an Assistant Professor in the industrial–organizational (I–O) psychology doctoral programme at the University of Central Florida. Her research focuses on issues at the intersection of work and societal resilience. Dr. LeNoble studies the implications of burnout in occupations critical to society, developing theory and interventions designed to advance human resilience in work and non-work domains. Her work has been funded by organizations including the National Science Foundation and the National Institute of Occupational Safety and Health. Dr. LeNoble earned her Ph.D. in I–O Psychology at Florida Institute of Technology, followed by a post-doctoral fellowship at Clemson University.

Gloria Liou is a Ph.D. student in industrial–organizational psychology at Purdue University and an NSF Graduate Research Fellow. She is also a faculty member in computer science at Rose-Hulman Institute of Technology. Gloria received her Bachelor's degree in computer science and cognitive science from Pomona College, after which she worked as a software engineer and product manager at Google. There, she developed the first fully machine learning-based personalized ranking system at Google, drove technology and process changes to improve equity in their hiring process, and served as a Google.org fellow. Her research interests include well-being, relationships, machine learning, and big data.

Fred Luthans is a Distinguished Professor of management, Emeritus, University of Nebraska. A former President of the Academy of Management, he received the Academy's Distinguished Educator Award, Publications Hall of Fame, OB Lifetime Achievement Award, and recently the Career Distinguished Scholarly Contributions to Management Award. He has also received the University of Iowa Distinguished Alumni Award, an Honorary Doctorate from De Paul University, and Harvard Medical School's Award for Leadership in Behavioral Health. He authored multiple editions of several well-known books and over 300 academic articles and chapters. His work has over 175,000 citations and was named to Top 1% Citations for all researchers in the world and was ranked #1 cited in OB textbooks.

James E. Maddux is a Distinguished University Professor Emeritus (Psychology) and Senior Scholar at the Center for the Advancement of Well-Being at George Mason University (Fairfax, Virginia, USA). Maddux has a Ph.D. in clinical psychology from the University of Alabama. His research interests include self-efficacy theory, the social construction of psychological disorders, and subjective well-being. He is the co-editor (with Barbara Winstead) of the sixth edition of *Psychopathology: Foundations for a Contemporary Understanding* and editor of the second edition of *Social Psychological Foundations of Subjective Well-Being.* He is a fellow of the American Psychological Association and the Association for Psychological Science.

Brian Matthews is a post-doctoral researcher and lecturer in Human Resource Management at the Institute of Human Resource Management at Vienna University of Economics and Business (WU) with a special focus on Sustainable HRM (SustHRM). Brian introduced with his colleagues Ina Aust and Michael Muller-Carmen in 2020 the influential concept of Common-Good HRM (CGHRM). Since then, he has been engaged in researching how this "outside-in", pro-welfare perspective with an increased focus on common-good values, democratic governance, employee participation and wider stakeholder inclusion influences the attempt of HRM to address the multi-level challenge of sustainability.

His research is strongly influenced by Institutional theory and Stakeholder theory but also embedded in the tradition of Critical Theory, characterized by increased reflexivity and the critique of established assumptions, with the declared goal of human emancipation and societal transformation. He, however, holds a pluralistic mindset which attempts to integrate both explanatory and normative narratives and which recognizes the value of multi-disciplinary dialogue, collaboration, and diversity of viewpoints. His research and teaching are therefore critically positioned around the central question: *How can HRM policy, strategies and practices be reframed in terms of increasing workplace democracy, stakeholder participation and ultimately in changing behaviour for common-good impact?*

Thisali Mendis is a student in the doctoral programme in industrial–organizational psychology at George Mason University (Fairfax, Virginia, USA). She holds a BS in psychology from Northern Arizona University and a BSc in applied sciences from the University of Sri Jayewardenepura, Sri Lanka. Her research interests include work stress, recovery, meaningful work, work–nonwork life balance, employee well-being, and the use of artificial intelligence for work. To maintain her own work–nonwork life balance, Thisali enjoys taking walks and engaging in activities that demonstrate her appreciation for music, cooking, and humour.

Michael Muller-Camen is the Chair of human resource management and Full Professor at Vienna University of Economics and Business (WU Vienna). Michael's main areas of research are sustainable HRM, green HRM, and common-good HRM.

He has published extensively in journals such as *Human Resource Management*, *Human Resource Management Review*, and *Human Resource Management Journal*.

Ken Sheldon is a Curator's Distinguished Professor of social-personality psychology at the University of Missouri. His primary research interests concern goals, motivation, creativity, and psychological well-being. He is also a founder of the "positive psychology" movement, having received a Templeton Prize in 2002 for his contributions to the field. Ken's most recent book is *Freely Determined: What the New Psychology of the Self Teaches Us about How to Live* (2022), and he has also authored *Self-Determination Theory in the Clinic* (2003) and *Optimal Human Being: An Integrated Multi-level Perspective* (2004). Furthermore, he was the lead editor of the 2011 book *Designing Positive Psychology: Taking Stock and Moving Forward* and the 2014 book *Stability of Happiness: Theories and Evidence on Whether Happiness Can Change*. Ken is married with three children and pursues stained-glass making, backpacking, river-running, and tennis in his spare time.

Louis Tay is the William C. Byham Professor in industrial–organizational psychology at Purdue University. His research interests are in well-being, character, measurement, and data science. He has co-edited multiple books, including *Big Data in Psychological Research* (APA Books) and *Technology and Measurement Around the Globe*. He is the founder of the tech startup, ExpiWell (www.expiwell.com), which advances the science of daily life experiences through experience sampling methodology.

Carter Vespi is a doctoral student of industrial/organizational psychology at Central Michigan University. His interests are in evolutionary psychology and individual differences.

Jennifer Wieland is a doctoral candidate at the Chair of Corporate Management at the Technical University of Munich. Her research explores how growth mindsets impact a wide range of workplace outcomes, including job attitudes such as employee engagement, commitment, openness to change, and the adoption of new technologies, such as Generative AI. In addition to her academic work, she brings practical experience from her role as a Strategy Consultant, where she focuses on people and organization topics. This combination of research and real-world experience enables her to bridge theory and practice, enriching her perspective on how mindset shifts can drive both personal and organizational developments.

1

EDITORS' INTRODUCTION

Advances in Positive Organizational Behavior

Cary L. Cooper, Subhendu Patnaik,
and Raul Villamarin Rodriguez

The positive psychology movement provided the impetus for a surge of research and applications of positive psychology principles and concepts in the workplace beyond the scope of traditional psychology. Seligman (1999), in his presidential address at the American Psychological Association, laid out a renewed vision for research and practice in positive psychology. Seligman pointed out that scientific studies on human strengths have been largely neglected, and the central focus of psychology has been on studying psychopathology. To address this imbalance, Seligman and Csikszentmihalyi (2000) called for a paradigm shift in psychology and propagated that the primary focus of positive psychology should be to build on the strength of human beings rather than focusing only on what was wrong with people and treating psychopathological conditions. However, it is important to note that Seligman and his colleagues did not assert that they were the first to recognize the significance of positivity, which has a very long and rich history rooted in the humanistic school of psychology championed by Carl Rogers and Abraham Maslow in the 1950s. In contemporary times, Seligman (1999) and Snyder and Lopez (2002) urged psychologists to renew their focus to study positive subjective experiences, positive individual traits, and positive institutions. They advocated for more research and scholarship focused on identifying and fostering individuals' positive traits, which would enhance human wellbeing, decrease negativity, and assist in the treatment of psychological disorders. Drawing on this paradigm over the past decades, organizational scholars have devoted significant attention to exploring positive phenomena in work contexts, resulting in a growing body of research and scholarship on positive organizational behavior (POB) at the micro level and positive organizational scholarship at the macro level (Cameron & Spreitzer, 2012; Luthans et al., 2015; Luthans & Youssef-Morgan, 2017).

DOI: 10.4324/9781032619385-1

A brief history over the past few decades illustrates how the concept of "work" has changed and the reasons for our current unsustainable, hypercompetitive, and chaotic workplace scenarios across the globe (Cooper, 2009, 2011). The 1980s marked the emergence of an "enterprise culture" in developed nations, where workplaces began adopting American practices. This era saw the privatization of the public sector, a rise in cross-national mergers and acquisitions, and a shift in the psychological contract between employees and employers, indicating that jobs were no longer guaranteed for life. During the 1990s and much of the early 2000s, a culture of "short-term contracts" emerged, characterized by job insecurity, outsourcing of various organizational functions, downsizing, flattening organizational structures, an endemic long-hours working culture, and a focus on bottom-line results along with micro-management styles have become prominent. The shift toward what is often referred to as the "flexible workforce" began in Britain and Ireland, gradually spreading throughout Western Europe. While it was initially adopted more enthusiastically in the United Kingdom, it eventually gained significant traction in both Western and Eastern Europe.

The changing nature of the psychosocial work environment has immensely contributed to the increase in workplace stress and poor wellbeing, affecting society as a whole. These issues have seriously affected individuals, organizations, and overall social health. Globally, poor mental health at work is increasing rapidly. Worldwide, around 12 billion working days are lost annually due to depression and anxiety, resulting in a loss of productivity valued at $1 trillion per year (World Health Organization [WHO], 2024). The UK Government's Foresight Report on Mental Capital and Wellbeing (Cooper et al., 2010) presents comprehensive evidence regarding the economic and social costs associated with mental health problems, stress, and lack of wellbeing in Britain. This report examines the entire lifespan, from birth to old age, and highlights the factors that can both hinder and promote our mental wellbeing. In England alone, the cost of diminished mental health and wellbeing is estimated at £77 billion annually (Cooper et al., 2010). Specific costs include work-related absenteeism, which results in 10–14 million lost workdays and costs around £750 million per year; presenteeism, where employees are present but not fully productive, costing approximately £900 million annually; and reduced profitability when workers lose their jobs due to work-related mental health issues, estimated at £82 million per year. Additionally, incapacity benefits exceed £12 billion, with 40% attributed to stress and mental health issues. Some other studies suggest that these figures may be underestimations, with the total costs of mental health issues and workplace stress reaching £25.9 billion due to absenteeism, presenteeism, and employee turnover (Sainsbury Centre for Mental Health, 2007). Further, globally, common mental disorders, such as anxiety and depression, affect about one in six individuals (Cooper, 2009).

Further, advances in artificial intelligence have brought prospects in generating various efficiencies but have also posed severe job insecurity challenges for the world population. *The New York Times* reports that 300 million full-time jobs could be affected by artificial intelligence (Kessler, 2023). McKinsey's report states that "technologies could automate 45% of the activities people are paid to perform and that about 60% of all occupations could see 30% or more of their constituent activities automated, again with technologies available today" (Chui et al., 2016). Additionally, the onset of the pandemic has caused phenomenal and unprecedented changes in work settings; workplaces around the globe have transitioned to hybrid or fully remote work arrangements, people have lost their loved ones, and the virtual mode of work is increasingly causing monotony and boredom. These increasingly turbulent mental health scenarios, hypercompetitive employment relations, the relentless and blinded pursuit of high-performing work systems, unwarranted and unscrupulous application of technology, detrimental ramifications of work stress, and impaired wellbeing warrant urgent and genuine attention both from academic and policy-formulating bodies.

Positive organizational approaches offer a wide range of benefits, as research has demonstrated holistic advantages for organizations, leaders, and employees. These benefits include increased positive emotions, enhanced creativity, more effective coping strategies, reduced stress, improved resilience, heightened work engagement, and a greater sense of meaning in daily tasks. Additionally, these approaches boost motivation, happiness, and life satisfaction, while also improving performance and staff morale. In essence, employees who participate in positive psychology-based programs and interventions at work tend to "flourish." Flourishing leads to thriving, learning, engagement, and an overall sense of happiness (Cameron & Spreitzer, 2012; Day et al., 2014; Luthans et al., 2015; Luthans & Youssef-Morgan, 2017). Therefore, insights on the application of *human strength-based positive psychology principles and concepts* can help facilitate coping mechanisms with stress and adversities, foster a culture of thriving, and augment individual and societal wellbeing at large.

Given the rise of empirical scholarship on POB (Cameron & Spreitzer, 2012; Luthans et al., 2015; Luthans & Youssef-Morgan, 2017), this book is an attempt to synthesize and capture the advances made in POB by *pioneering and senior leading* scholars, involving contributions from the *United States, Canada, The Netherlands, Australia, Europe, South Africa, and India.* This book covers classic and contemporary topics on POB, which include:

Psychological capital: Founding POB scholar Fred Luthans and Julie Dyrdek Broad have contributed a brilliant review on the need for POB and psychological capital (PsyCap). They have extensively discussed the PsyCap construct along with its work correlates.

Positive organizational scholarship: Kim Cameron, one of the pioneering scholars of positive organizational scholarship, has written a brilliant chapter on positivity and its importance in the macro workplace context. He highlights the saliency of positive energy, virtuous collective action, and positive leadership.

Work engagement interventions: Leading organizational behavior scholar Arnold B. Bakker and Tom L. Junker have contributed a great piece on work engagement interventions and its applications. They have provided a review on the promising aspect of work engagement interventions and have discussed five different levels of intervention: organizational level, team level, job level, person level, and activity level.

Self-efficacy: James E. Maddux and Thisali Mendis have written an overview of self-efficacy theory and the role of self-efficacy beliefs in the performance of employees, including leaders and managers in the workplace. They narrate interesting positive and negative outcomes of self-efficacy beliefs in work context. They also address leadership self-efficacy and the collective efficacy of groups and teams.

Emotions and positive work behavior: Neal M. Ashkanasy and Momo D. Kromah examine the relationship between POB and emotions. They have articulated the *FLMEW model* which includes five levels of analysis of emotions in work settings: within-person temporal variation in emotions; between-persons individual differences in experiencing and expressing emotions; perception and communication of emotions in interpersonal relationships; emotions in groups and teams; and emotional culture and climate at the organizational level of analysis.

Free will: One of the founders of the "positive psychology" movement Kennon M. Sheldon contributed a brilliant and an innovative scholarly work on free will in the work context. He discussed the goal breakthrough model, which explains how people can discover satisfying new goals to pursue, and more broadly, how people can best operate their own "free will" in organizational context.

Resilience in organizational settings: Thomas W. Britt and Chelsea LeNoble have narrated an exhaustive account of research on resilience in organizational settings and provide recommendations for future research to better understand the attributes and processes required in organizations for successful coping and bouncing back from adversities.

Work wellbeing: Paula Brough and Jafar Akbari have contributed by documenting contemporary emerging work wellbeing challenges. They have discussed four major changes to our working lives as a result of the COVID-19 pandemic. This work suggests longer-term implications for fostering wellbeing at work.

Evolutionary psychology and positive workplace: Stephen M. Colarelli and colleagues have contributed innovative and cutting-edge perspectives on evolutionary psychology for a positive workplace. They have written an outstanding overview of evolutionary psychology perspectives and identified concepts that are relevant to building a more positive workplace. They have discussed four evolutionary-based interventions that contribute to a positive workplace.

Cross-cultural POB: Sharon Glazer and Catherine T. Kwantes discuss on the importance of studying positive OBs in relation to recent policies from international organizations. They have written a brief review of the cultural tools that can be used to test hypotheses about organizational behavior constructs across cultures. They have wonderfully identified the blind spots that hinder the full understanding of the relationship between societal culture and POB.

New POB construct (HEAL): Vishal Gupta and Anmol Basant based on the principles of POB have conceptualized a new POB construct (HEAL). They have proposed a set of three positive capacities of harmony (H), equanimity (E) and authentic living (AL). This construct has the potential to act as a positive resource for managing stress, foster wellbeing and higher performance.

Common-good HRM (CGHRM) practices: Brian Matthews and colleagues have written on the contemporary importance of POB, growth mindset, and common-good HRM practices to foster sustainability in the workplace. They discuss on the new CGHRM perspective and discuss how organizational sustainability is inherently linked to the broader communal good. They propose that a common-good HRM mindset equates personal wellbeing with societal flourishing or collective happiness (eudaimonia).

Methodological advances and challenges in positivity assessments: Gloria Liou and colleagues have written a brief review on positive trait measures, including the Values in Action Inventory of Strengths (VIA-IS) and the Comprehensive Inventory of Virtuous Instantiations of Character (CIVIC). They have discussed the recent developments, challenges, and strategies to overcome positive trait assessment.

PERMA+4 and positive organizational psychology 2.0: Stewart I. Donaldson and Scott I. Donaldson have developed a chapter that aims to explore methodological and technological opportunities for improving the next wave of positive organizational psychology (POP) research and practice. They suggest that POP 2.0 is posited to expand our understanding and improve the applications of the PERMA+4 holistic framework for enhancing wellbeing and positive functioning at work.

References

Cameron, K. S., & Spreitzer, G. M. (Eds.). (2012). *The Oxford handbook of positive organizational scholarship*. Oxford University Press, New York (USA).

Chui, M., Manyika, J., & Miremadi, M. (2016). Where machines could replace humans—and where they can't (yet). Digital McKinsey. Retrieved from https://www.mckinsey.com/capabilities/mckinsey-digital/our-insights/where-machines-could-replace-humans-and-where-they-cant-yet Accessed 11 January 2025.

Cooper, C. L. (2009). The changing nature of work: Enhancing the mental capital and well-being of the workplace. *Twenty-First Century Society*, 4(3), 269–275.

Cooper, C. L. (2011). Editor's introduction: Organizational health and well-being. In C. L. Cooper (Ed.), *Organizational health and well-being* (Vol. 1, pp. xxi–xxxii). Sage, London (UK).

Cooper, C. L., Field, J., Goswami, U., Jenkins, R., & Sahakian, B. J. (Eds.). (2010). *Mental capital and wellbeing*. Wiley Blackwell, West Sussex (UK).

Day, A., Gilbert, S., & Kelloway, K. (2014). Positive psychology and the healthy workplace. In A. Day, E. K. Kelloway, & J. J. Hurrell, Jr. (Eds.), *Workplace well-being: How to build psychologically healthy workplaces* (pp. 50–71). Wiley-Blackwell, West Sussex (UK).

Kessler, S. (2023). The A.I. revolution will change work. Nobody agrees how. *The New York Times*: June. Retrieved from https://www.nytimes.com/2023/06/10/business/ai-jobs-work.html# Accessed 02 October 2024.

Luthans, F., & Youssef-Morgan, C. M. (2017). Psychological capital: An evidence-based positive approach. *Annual Review of Organizational Psychology and Organizational Behavior*, 4, 339–366.

Luthans, F., Youssef-Morgan, C. M., & Avolio, B. J. (2015). *Psychological capital and beyond.* Oxford University Press, New York (USA).

Sainsbury Centre for Mental Health (2007). *The costs of mental health.* Sainsbury Centre for Mental Health. London.

Seligman, M. E. P. (1999). The president's address. *American Psychologist*, 54(8), 559–562.

Seligman, M. E. P., & Csikszentmihalyi, M. (2000). Positive psychology: An introduction. *American Psychologist*, 55(1), 5–14.

Snyder, C. R., & Lopez, S. J. (Eds.). (2002). *Oxford Handbook of positive psychology.* Oxford University Press, New York (USA).

World Health Organization (WHO) (2024, September 2). *Mental health at work.* Retrieved from https://www.who.int/news-room/fact-sheets/detail/mental-health-at-work Accessed 15 October 2024.

2

POSITIVE ORGANIZATIONAL BEHAVIOR AND PSYCHOLOGICAL CAPITAL

An Evidence-Based 20-Year Journey

Fred Luthans and Julie Dyrdek Broad

Introduction

In 1999, first author Dr. Fred Luthans conceptualized positive organizational behavior (POB), and subsequently shortly after its core construct of psychological capital, or simply PsyCap. During this time, workplaces faced challenges related in large part to globalization, accelerated competition, a decreasing middle class in all parts of the world, and economic downturns leading to increasing stress and massive downsizing (Luthans & Youssef-Morgan, 2017). In other words, a turbulent global environment had emerged. Luthans defined POB as "the study and application of positively oriented human resource strengths and psychological capacities that can be measured, developed, and effectively managed for performance improvement in today's workplace" (Luthans, 2002b, p. 59). It's core construct used in the research and application of POB is PsyCap, defined as

> An individual's positive psychological state of development that is characterized by (1) having confidence (efficacy) to take on and put in the necessary effort to succeed at challenging tasks; (2) making a positive attribution (optimism) about succeeding now and in the future; (3) persevering toward goals and, when necessary, redirecting paths to goals (hope) in order to succeed; and (4) when beset by problems and adversity, sustaining and bouncing back and even beyond (resiliency) to attain success.
>
> *(Luthans, Youssef-Morgan, & Avolio, 2015, p. 2)*

Scholars and practitioners worldwide wrestling with turbulent global environments quickly embraced and began researching and applying Luthans and colleagues POB and PsyCap within a number of domains (workplaces, schools,

DOI: 10.4324/9781032619385-2

families, universities, communities, societies, and even nations), occupational sectors (service, financial, healthcare, government including defense and intelligence, academia, for profit, non-profit, NGO, and even NASA), and levels (beyond individual to extend from micro to macro, individual to societal) with exponential success on every continent. Fast forward to 2024, and Luthans' POB and PsyCap with its overt focus on human strengths, human potential, and positivity in general, are needed now more than ever, and perhaps are more important than ever as we face unprecedented and further amplified turbulent global environments and challenges that are even more complex.

Today, the world faces accelerated breakthroughs in science and technology, the broadening and blurring of geopolitical lines with associated global conflicts, climate and sustainability challenges, global political and social unrest, challenges with diversity, equity, inclusion, and accessibility (DEIA), geographical and demographical disparities, and fractured mental and physical health systems as global workforce shortages threaten every continent (World Economic Forum [WEF], 2022). The world is recovering from the unprecedented novel coronavirus (COVID-19), leaving millions who are facing new elevated levels of stress and anxiety, declared as the epidemic of the 21st century by the World Health Organization prior to the pandemic (World Health Organization [WHO], 1999, 2020a, 2020b) and now further exacerbated. Some scholars have even classified the present and foreseeable future as continuous cascading traumas, highlighting the constellation of multiple, consecutive traumatic events experienced globally (Silver, Holman, & Garfin, 2021; Igic et al., 2017).

For example, the WEF even predicts a bleaker future characterized by a deteriorating global outlook that includes economic (e.g., inflation and economic downturns), environmental (e.g., extreme weather events, pollution, critical damage to Earth systems, biodiversity loss and ecosystem collapse, natural resource shortages), geopolitical (e.g., interstate armed conflict, blurring geographical and geopolitical lines), societal (e.g., societal polarization, lack of economic opportunity, involuntary migration), and technological risks (e.g., misinformation and disinformation, cyber insecurity, adverse outcomes of AI technologies) (WEF, 2024).

Given this bleak context and the projected future challenges ahead, scholars and practitioners globally *now* need POB and PsyCap inquiry, research, and evidence-based application more than ever as focus is aimed at strengthening the human element, to include the identification and development of human strengths and positivity. Now backed by multiple decades of rigorous evidence-based scientific research leveraging the most advanced and sophisticated research designs and methodologies available (see Avey et al., 2011; Newman et al., 2014; Ertosun et al., 2015; Loghman et al., 2023), POB and PsyCap provide a *part* of the solution that will be required to navigate the cascading traumas, challenges, setbacks, and obstacles that we have and will continue to face globally. We believe that the workplace will play an essential role in the strengthening of this human element globally.

It is estimated that individuals spend a third of their lifetimes in the workplace, making non-stigma and open to development POB and PsyCap an invaluable tool for organizations to implement as they face unprecedented volatility, uncertainty, complexity, and ambiguity (often referred to as VUCA contexts, Luthans & Broad, 2022). The good news is that POB and PsyCap scholars and practitioners have been fine tuning how to leverage human strengths and expand human potential within extreme VUCA contexts for some time now. Examples many of which we have been directly involved include the Department of Defense (pre-during-post deployments), NASA, intelligence communities, first responders, healthcare (surgery teams, nurses, oncology, and with terminally ill patients), active shooters, suicide, workplace and school violence (also see Roberts, Scherer, & Bowyer, 2011) making this non-stigma approach to well-being and performance critical during the most uncertain of times. What's even more exciting to us is that when individuals and groups and teams learn about POB and PsyCap at work, research consistently demonstrates that this is predictive and causal to increases in both health and relationships outside of the workplace (to include immediate families), contributing in part to improvements in overall general population health. As the next ten years predict staggering shortages and challenges in the global workforce, to include especially nurses, mental health professionals, and teachers, non-stigma interventions that are evidence-based, scientifically validated, and highly effective will become increasingly important and valuable, and worth their weight in gold as organizations try to effectively cope with today's most turbulent and accelerating global challenges.

POB and PsyCap – A Brief History

Over 20 years ago, POB was conceptualized by Fred Luthans, a member of the first generation of organizational behavior scholars, and recently recognized as a top 1% scholar across all sciences, during a time when his field was becoming increasingly sophisticated in terms of research methodology and analysis (Luthans, 2002a). Concerned with the lack of development of core concepts (see Steers, Mowday, & Shapiro, 2004 describing the precipitous decline of work motivation theories by the early 1990s) and even more disturbed by the enthusiastic reception of popular press books (all dealing with OB topics, but without the necessary academic, peer reviewed theoretical development or research back-up[1]). He became passionate about increasing scientific theory and rigor in the study of positivity in the workplace (see Luthans, 2002a, 2002b, 2002c). He was also committed to addressing the chasm between OB theory and research and real-world applications, as evidenced by the extreme popularity of the popular press books that lacked the scientifically evidence-based rigor he knew was available within the OB field. Luthans himself describes this period as a time when he was "swirling in his own negativity" as it related to his field. As a result, time was ripe for the development of his awareness of the just emerging positive psychology movement (Seligman,

1998; Seligman & Csikszentmihalyi, 2000) that would in part answer the call to his search for theory driven, rigorous, scientific approaches to positive phenomena, particularly in the workplace, and causal and predictive of at first targeted performance, and later simultaneously, and very importantly, well-being.

In 1999, besides being an organizational behavior professor at the University of Nebraska, Luthans was also a senior research scientist/advisor at the Gallup Organization. Based on their organizational culture created by majority owner – President Don Clifton and their positive, strength-based consulting practice, Gallup sponsored the first Positive Psychology Conference held in Luthans' University of Nebraska home of Lincoln. At this initial academically oriented Positive Psychology Conference, papers were presented by internationally recognized research psychologists such as Martin Seligman, Ed Diener, Mike Csikszentmihalyi, and Barb Frederickson. Although not presenting at this initial conference, as a participant, Luthans noted it was a "eureka" moment for him in considering how this positive psychology approach could be taken to organizational behavior and the workplace. Although the presentations were focused on applying positive psychology to mental health and developmental applications, this positive pathway was precisely what he had been searching for – a theory and research-driven new perspective and approach to OB concepts and some new and exciting first-order concepts such as confidence, hope, optimism, happiness, and resiliency (Luthans, 2002a) applied within the organizational behavior field and applied to the workplace. However, interestingly, POB and PsyCap have recently been widely researched and applied to mental health and developmental issues not only in the workplace but also a wide range of domains from the most extreme of nonorganizational environments (see Krasikova, Lester, & Harms, 2015) and to health care, education, the military, intelligence, first responder professionals (see Broad, 2023), and to everyday citizens worldwide.

While many may consider Luthans' seminal literature on POB (Luthans, 2002a, 2002b, 2002c) to represent the beginning of his interest in POB, the fact is his research interest in positivity began at the onset of his career, and long before the turn of the century. This is evidenced by his positive reinforcement theory-based research and highly cited academic publications on what he termed Organizational Behavior Modification (O.B. Mod) (e.g., see Luthans & Kreitner, 1975; Luthans, Paul, & Baker, 1981; Stajkovic & Luthans, 1997, 2003), positive leadership (Luthans, Hodgetts, & Rosenkrantz, 1988; Luthans et al., 2001), and the highly cited meta-analysis of the impact self-efficacy has on work-related performance (see Stajkovic & Luthans, 1998).

After serving as an Army Captain teaching psychology and leadership to cadets at the U.S. Military Academy at West Point (1965–1967), Luthans joined the faculty of the Department of Management at the University of Nebraska, where he remained his entire academic career. As a management scholar with a strong background in psychology from his doctoral studies at the University of Iowa, he was one of the first business school management professors to draw heavily from behavioral science for the purpose of managing human behavior in organizations (See Luthans, 1973). As indicated above, his initial research applied theories of reinforcement and positive behaviorism to improving employee performance. O.B. Mod provided one of the first positivity-based interventions demonstrating a strong relationship between Luthans' concept of "organizational behavior modification" and improved employee performance across multiple domains (Luthans & Kreitner, 1975; Stajkovic & Luthans, 1997). Thus, from the beginning of his career, Luthans' interests and research have focused on positivity and its impact on attitudes, behaviors, performance, and then later simultaneously improvements in well-being as well (Luthans & Stajkovic, 1999).

Given this history, Luthans conceptual introduction of POB in the academic literature in 2002 was a natural progression that complemented and added to his lifetime career of research and knowledge creation around positivity and its impact in the workplace and beyond.

POB Scientific Inclusion Criteria

From the beginning, for a positive psychological capacity to qualify for inclusion in POB and PsyCap, Luthans (2002a) required that it must be positive, with extensive theory and research foundations, and include valid measures published in the academic literature. In addition, Luthans required that it must be state-like (as opposed to trait-like), open to development and therefore manageable for performance improvement (and later well-being). Inherently, POB has focused on human strengths across multiple organizational levels that operate synergistically and parsimoniously in building the best workplace, with the ability to proactively measure, develop, sustain, and replenish resources in a whole-system organizational behavior approach. Luthans research integrating positivity in organizational settings led him after years of research to the introduction of POB and PsyCap, tapping into human strengths and potential as opposed to his field's historical overemphasis on deficits, weaknesses, and dysfunction.

POB's Core Construct – PsyCap

Following the conceptualization of POB at the turn of the century, Luthans and his colleagues began rigorously evaluating the existing positive psychology constructs against the established strict PsyCap inclusion criteria. These inclusion criteria would later pay exponential dividends on impact and effectiveness within the workplace, a constant focus throughout Luthans' academic career.

Research from POB identifying the four positive psychological resources of hope, efficacy, resilience, and optimism which best met the inclusion criteria led to the discovery and introduction of POB's core construct of PsyCap. PsyCap, defined above and drawn from the seminal articles by Luthans, Luthans, and Luthans (2004) and Luthans and Youssef (2004) and books by Luthans, Youssef-Morgan, and Avolio (2007, 2015), is a positive state of development that is characterized by hope (the ability to set goals, maintain motivation toward the accomplishment of those goals, and develop multiple pathways around obstacles during goal pursuit, to include re-goaling); efficacy, or self-efficacy (confidence, or belief in one's ability to succeed with perseverance and effort); resilience (the ability to bounce back and, importantly, beyond, tapping into human potential); and optimism (positive attributions and beliefs about the past, present, and future). Since its introduction in the academic literature, PsyCap research has demonstrated that as a second-order construct (comprised of the four first-order constructs of hope, efficacy, resiliency, and optimism or simply the **HERO** within), PsyCap is additive and exponential in value, meaning that PsyCap is greater than the sum of each of its individual components (Avey, Luthans, & Youssef, 2010; Luthans et al., 2007). This is largely attributed to the four first-order constructs sharing more in common than in variance (Avey, 2014).

PsyCap has been distinguished from other forms of *people-related capital*, namely human and social capital (Luthans & Youssef, 2004). Human capital, with its intellectual origins lying in economics, refers to an individual's stock of knowledge, skills, and abilities that can be increased by experience and/or investment in education and training (Becker, 1993; Newman et al., 2014). Social capital emerged from sociology and is related to the aggregate of the actual or potential resources that are linked to the possession of a durable network of relationships of mutual acquaintance and recognition (Newman et al., 2014).

PsyCap is differentiated as concerned with "who you are" and, of importance, "who you are becoming" tapping into future human potential (Dawkins et al., 2015). Said differently, Luthans, Youssef-Morgan, and Avolio (2015) highlighted that although it is important to hire the right people and develop their human and social capital, these organizational expenditures can only be turned into "investments" by employees themselves and with the help from their leaders, both of whom are the *agents* in control of this "capital." They additionally point out that as scientific and technological breakthroughs accelerate, so too does the need for knowledge development and acquisition (i.e., the human and social capital an employee possesses today may or may not be valuable tomorrow, making human and social capital a moving target). PsyCap, related to "who we are" carries greater stability across multiple turbulent global environments.

This is especially pertinent in today's global VUCA environment. The rate and velocity of change in VUCA contexts requires dynamic capabilities that extend well beyond one individual or leader, and well beyond traditional human capital (i.e., competency models, knowledge, skills, abilities) and social capital (i.e., volatile globalization context where relationship value can shift quickly). PsyCap augments and optimizes (it does not substitute or replace) all other forms of competitive capital advantage and, as a developmental state, can interact with and foster the optimization of all capital resources, inclusive of economic capital (e.g., tangible plant, equipment, technology, facilities). Because PsyCap optimizes the investment and use of other forms of capital, its additive and exponential value results in a high return on dollars of investment (Luthans, Youssef-Morgan, & Avolio, 2015).

PsyCap Hope

PsyCap hope is derived from the late Rick Snyder's extensive theory building and research (see Snyder's *Handbook of Hope*, 2000), defined as "a positive motivational state that is based on an interactively derived sense of successful (1) agency (goal-directed energy), and (2) pathways (planning to meet goals)" (Snyder et al., 1991, p. 287). Practical approaches for developing hope include setting challenging "stretch" goals; proactively engaging in contingency planning (i.e., ability to develop multiple pathways around obstacles during goal pursuit); and re-goaling when appropriate (e.g., adjusting sales targets amid a global pandemic) when necessary, to avoid false hope (Snyder, 2000).

PsyCap Efficacy

Efficacy is based on the work of Albert Bandura (1982, 1986, 1991, 2000) and refers to one's self-efficacy, or confidence in one's abilities to attain goals or complete courses of action successfully. Confident people engage in challenging tasks, are persistent, and are accepting of improvement feedback when they get off track (Peterson et al., 2008). Of all the PsyCap psychological resources, efficacy, or simply confidence has the largest positive impact on well-being and especially performance (see Luthans & Stajkovic, 2000; Stajkovic & Luthans, 1998; Luthans & Stajkovic, 1999), and is therefore the most important PsyCap resource. In addition, efficacy as a construct has been validated and measured as both an individual and a collective construct, providing an example for the development of individual PsyCap to the collective (cPsyCap).

PsyCap Resilience

PsyCap resilience is defined as "the developable capacity to rebound or bounce back from adversity, conflict, and failure, or even positive events, progress, and increased responsibility" (Luthans, 2002a, p. 702). Seminal research from clinical and positive psychology has been found to contribute to or hinder resilience, including one's inventory of physiological, cognitive, affective, and social assets; the nature, intensity, and frequency of risks encountered; adaptational processes utilized to balance the use of psychological assets in the face of adversity and/or risk; and underlying value systems (Coutu, 2002; Masten, 2001; Masten et al., 2009). While resilience is perhaps more important than ever as we recover from the global pandemic and resultant global mental health fallout (see Broad & Luthans, 2020), PsyCap interventions expand on general resilience to also include the critical self-reliant resource development of hope, efficacy, and optimism as well, adding to the exponential value that can be gained by individuals, groups and teams, leaders, organizations, communities/societies, and even countries overall (see Avey, 2014; Luthans, Vogelgesang, & Lester, 2006). Additionally, PsyCap resilience extends "bouncing back" from adversity, tapping into human potential to not only bounce back but also beyond.

PsyCap Optimism

Optimism is commonly portrayed as a generalized positive outlook or expectancy (Carver et al., 2009). Seligman (1998) also defined optimism as an attributional style that explains positive events in terms of personal, permanent, and pervasive causes, and negative events in terms of external, temporary, and situation specific. Particularly relevant to the workplace is that optimism be realistic (Schneider, 2001) and flexible (Peterson, 2000). As such, organizational leaders and employees must be flexible in discerning when to use optimistic versus pessimistic explanatory styles, as well as develop and maintain the capacity to adapt these styles realistically to the situation at hand. Luthans has consistently emphasized the importance of "realistic" optimism that is rooted firmly in reality.

Theoretical Underpinnings of Individual PsyCap

The theoretical underpinnings of individual-based PsyCap are based largely upon Hobfoll's (2002) Conservation of Resources (COR) Theory and Fredrickson's (2001) broaden-and-build theory of positive emotions, as well as individual agentic and conative motivations (Youssef-Morgan & Luthans, 2015). COR is a collection of stress theories that describes the motivation that drives humans to both maintain their current resources and pursue new resources. COR states that loss of resources will drive individuals to certain levels of stress; however, resources can also be accrued positively to reduce levels of stress (such as those positive psychological resources found in PsyCap), leading to the development of what Hobfoll (1989) referred to as "resource caravans." Resource caravans emphasize that personal, social, and material resources tend to develop and exist in aggregate. As a result, when PsyCap is developed, its constituent resources of hope, efficacy, resilience, and optimism are proposed to form such aggregate resource caravans that serve to protect individuals from loss of resources and resultant stress. COR further suggests that people "seek to obtain, retain, and protect resources and that stress occurs when resources are threatened with loss or are lost or when individuals fail to gain resources after substantive resource investment" (Hobfoll, 2002, p. 312). COR as a theoretical framework for POB's PsyCap emphasizes the means for positive adaptation under circumstances of loss (Avey, 2014) through the simultaneous development of the individual's HERO within.

Together, the four positive PsyCap resources that collectively form a "resource caravan" assist individuals in buffering the impact and effect of stress, while promoting well-being and performance (Youssef-Morgan & Luthans, 2015). Hobfoll has suggested a number of corollaries that can be applied to resource changes, specifically that (a) individuals with higher resources will be set up for gains in resources, while, similarly, individuals with fewer resources are more likely to experience resource losses; (b) initial resource loss will lead to resource loss in the future; (c) initial resource gains will lead to gains in the future; and (d) a lack of resources will invariably lead to defensive attempts to conserve remaining resources. Because all of the individual PsyCap resources are open to development and lead to positive adaptations in goal setting, pathways development, navigating obstacles (hope), self-belief in one's ability (efficacy), the ability to bounce back and beyond from adversity, or even extremely positive events that require adaptation (resilience) and positive attributions about the past, present, and future (optimism), these positive psychological resources in turn provide a buffer against stress. As a result, individuals with higher PsyCap are expected to leverage these "resource caravans" to foster positive adaptations, especially within high-stress and now escalating and cascading VUCA contexts.

COR theory highlights the importance of *motivation* for decisions involving "how employees acquire, maintain, and foster the necessary resources to both meet their current work demands and to help guard against further resource depletion" (Wright & Hobfoll, 2004, p. 390). As pointed out earlier, it is one thing to invest in human capital, but human capital alone does not tap into individual employee motivation to act on their human capital assets.

Additionally, in fast-paced VUCA contexts, the targets of human and social capital shift quickly with the environment, making PsyCap potentially a more stable form of competitive capital to leverage and optimize across economic, human, and social capitals, by fundamentally altering "who we are" and, perhaps more importantly, "who we can become" in expanding human potential.

Fredrickson's (2004) broaden-and-build theory of positive emotions provides further theoretical underpinnings for PsyCap. The broaden-and-build theory describes the form and function of a subset of positive emotions that have been found to broaden an individual's momentary thought-action repertoire. As an example, joy sparks the urge to play, interest sparks the urge to explore, contentment sparks the urge to savor and integrate, and love sparks a recurring cycle of each of these urges within safe, close relationships (Fredrickson, 2001). Fredrickson's research has evaluated how broadened mindsets arising from these positive emotions are contrasted to the narrowed mindsets sparked by negative emotions (e.g., anger, threat, fear, disgust). Additionally, as positive broadened mindsets are developed, positive emotions promote creativity and innovation, ideas, and social bonds, which in turn build that individual's personal resources. These resources range from physical and intellectual resources to social and psychological resources, which can be drawn on later as "reserves" that increase our odds of successful coping and survival (Fredrickson, 2001). This ultimately additionally increases human resilience, or the ability to bounce back, following adversity or challenges (Fredrickson, 2001; Fredrickson et al., 2003).

The broaden-and-build theory of positive emotions also refers to the development of both "upward" and "downward" spirals. Within the context of PsyCap, the positive emotions that are developed within the PsyCap Interventions (PCIs)[2] create upward spirals where positive emotions beget more positive emotions (also consistent with Hobfoll's explanation of resource gains), while providing a "buffering" or protective factor against downward spirals or resource loss. Further evidence of broaden-and-build is found in the synergistic commonality of positively oriented hope, efficacy, resilience, and optimism, recalling that these resources share more in common than in variance. Individuals with high levels of PsyCap, consistent with Fredrickson's research, demonstrate increases in creativity, innovation, well-being, and performance (Avey, Luthans, & Youssef, 2010; Avey et al., 2010, 2011; Newman et al., 2014).

The "how" of PsyCap is largely attributed to agentic conation, cognitive appraisals, positive emotions, and social mechanisms (Youssef-Morgan & Luthans, 2015). Conation is the personal, intentional, planful, deliberate, goal-oriented, or striving component of motivation. This touches on the proactive rather than reactive aspect of behavior. Conation is closely associated with the concept of volition, defined as the use of will, or the freedom to make choices about what to do (Huitt, 1999). Conation facilitates agency, sense of control, and intentionality, all of which are critical in the development of PsyCap (Luthans & Youssef-Morgan, 2017; Youssef-Morgan & Luthans, 2013). This conation also facilitates goal-directed energy (hope), which can trigger the motivation and resource deployment necessary for goal pursuit, and promote a positive (i.e., challenge) versus negative (i.e., threat) reaction when obstacles are encountered.

Positive cognitive appraisals serve as an important mechanism through which potentially negative or neutral situations are "reframed" and reinterpreted more positively. As a result, more challenging goals, when reframed, can become more appealing and worthy of time, energy, and resource investment. It also serves to shield positive individuals from prevalent negativity biases (Baumeister et al., 2001; Cameron, 2008). Negativity bias is the notion that even when of equal intensity, things of a more negative nature (e.g., unpleasant thoughts, emotions, social interactions, or even harmful or traumatic events) have a greater effect on one's psychological state and processes than neutral or positive emotions. Positive emotions tend to be more "fleeting" than negative emotions that tend to linger for longer, drawing upon psychological resources. Because PsyCap HERO shares the common theme of "positive appraisal of circumstances and probability for success based upon motivated effort and perseverance" (Luthans et al., 2007, p. 55), PsyCap supports more positive cognitive appraisals, while combatting inherent tendencies toward negativity biases (Youssef-Morgan & Luthans, 2013).

PsyCap is also directly related to positive emotions (Avey, Wernsing, & Luthans, 2008). Positive emotions in this case are a by-product of PsyCap. As a result, the positive nature of PsyCap can trigger positive affective states that can facilitate broadening one's thought-action repertories (based on Fredrickson's broaden-and-build theory), leading to higher levels of creativity (Luthans, Youssef-Morgan, & Rawski, 2011) and a broader range of pathways development in hope (Snyder, 2000). As PsyCap generates positive emotions, these facilitate the building and restoration of previously depleted resources (Fredrickson, 2001, 2009), such as hope, efficacy, resilience, and optimism. As a result, positive emotions can serve as both a by-product and source for PsyCap.

PsyCap's Additive Exponential Value and Causal Links to Positive Well-Being and Performance

Over the past two decades plus, PsyCap has been researched on every continent, demonstrating cross-cultural and generalized *causal* links to increases in well-being and performance simultaneously. Avey et al.'s (2011) PsyCap meta-analysis of 51 independent samples (representing a total of N = 12,567 employees) indicated the expected significant positive relationships between PsyCap and desirable employee attitudes (job satisfaction, organizational commitment, psychological well-being), desirable employee behaviors (citizenship), and multiple measures of performance (self, supervisor evaluations, and objective). There was also a significant negative relationship between PsyCap and undesirable employee attitudes (e.g., cynicism, turnover intentions, job stress, and anxiety) and undesirable employee behaviors (e.g., deviance, counterproductive work behaviors, absenteeism (see Avey, Patera, & West, 2006).

Latent profile analysis, shifting the focus from overall variable centered PsyCap measure approaches to individual latent profiles, has empowered researchers with a deeper understanding of how PsyCap profiles may vary across individuals and impact causal and predictive outcomes of PsyCap in the workplace. For example, Bouckenooghe, De Clercq, and Raja (2019) found five distinct PsyCap profiles (Low PsyCap, Low/Moderate PsyCap, Moderate PsyCap, High/Moderate PsyCap, and High PsyCap) across multiple industries (government, consulting, financial services, transportation/shipping, tourism, manufacturing, and retail). If PsyCap develops differently across individuals leading to the identification of latent PsyCap profiles, more customized evidence-based interventions can then be targeted and customized for individual (and higher levels) of PsyCap development and sustainment.

Latent growth modeling applied by Peterson et al. (2011) demonstrated the longitudinal and causal impact of the development of PsyCap across $n = 179$ financial services employees' supervisor-rated performance as well as sales revenue. Individuals with higher PsyCap had more positive performance ratings by supervisors, and this was causal in relation to sales revenue performance. In addition, increases in PsyCap were also associated with increased well-being, and PsyCap seems to hold over time; once employees learn the skills that support the PsyCap developmental resources and state, interventions are effective up to 12 months-plus in supporting well-being and performance; however, boosters provide additive value in building and sustaining PsyCap assets (Avey, Luthans, & Youssef, 2010; Krasikova, Lester, & Harms, 2015).

Neuroscientific implications of PsyCap have demonstrated that the brains of optimistic, hopeful, confident, and resilient leaders are different (Peterson et al., 2008), and that the state-like nature of PsyCap provides plasticity, malleability, and openness to development through targeted micro-interventions. PsyCap is positively correlated with positive organizational change (Avey, Wernsing, & Luthans, 2008), and effective in web-based training interventions (Luthans et al., 2008). Importantly, demographics such as age, gender, tenure, or work experience are often controlled but rarely related to PsyCap (see Avey, 2014).

Newman et al.'s (2014) review of 66 PsyCap studies for performance, attitudinal, behavioral, and well-being outcomes at the individual, team, and organizational levels provided a more expansive meta-analytic review, with similar positive outcomes in attitudes, behaviors, and performance. Computer-aided text analysis elevating the construct of PsyCap to the organizational level of analysis (McKenny, Short, & Payne, 2013) provided valuable insights about organizational PsyCap over time in a ten-year sample of large, publicly traded organizations (reviewing, among others, CEO letters to shareholders and internal communications). Cassidy, Mclaughlin, and McDowel (2014) found evidence of the mediating role that PsyCap plays in reducing bullying and promoting health at work, while Luthans et al. (2013) found extended causal links of PsyCap development to Health PsyCap and Relationship PsyCap. In essence, PsyCap development at work crosses domains positively impacting employee health and relationships outside of the workplace. Roche, Haar, and Luthans (2014) found the role of mindfulness and PsyCap in the well-being of leaders, demonstrating negative relationships with various dysfunctional outcomes such as anxiety, depression, negative affect, and burnout of managerial leaders. As it relates to DEIA, Waldman and Sparr (2023) offer POB and its rigorous ability to unite as part of a solution that simultaneously increases well-being and performance of participants.

Recently, the American Psychological Association (APA) has supported evidence-based POB and its multi-level PsyCap construct as a gold standard evidence-based intervention in creating "healthy workplaces" (see American Psychological Association, 2023; Donaldson & Chen, 2021) and in support of the broader U.S. Surgeon General's Framework for Workplace Mental Health & Well-being (see U.S. Department of Health and Human Services, Office of the U.S. Surgeon General, 2022). Gone are the days where organizations can throw employee well-being and performance to now well-established employee assistance programs (EAPs). Today's organizations are taking a much more proactive and self-reliant approach where organizational health, well-being, and healthy workplaces are owned at all levels, top-down-and-bottom-up within the workplace. What's more, POB and PsyCap scientific inquiry linking workplace well-being and performance to the outside domains of health and relationships provide important levers in positively impacting general population health.

A review of PsyCap's development through PCI and accompanying meta-analyses provides expansive and rigorous global support across every continent that as PsyCap increases, significant and veritable positive outcomes increase (e.g., job satisfaction, intentions to stay, overall subjective well-being, performance, etc.), while negative outcomes decrease (e.g., stress, anxiety, depression, harassment, counterproductive work behaviors, addictions, substance abuse, mental health diagnoses, etc.) (see Avey et al., 2011; Loghman et al., 2023; Lupsa et al., 2020).

Loghman et al. (2023) presented the most rigorous meta-analysis undertaken to date of empirical literature examining antecedent and outcomes related to PsyCap and moderators of these relationships. This meta-analysis of 244 studies (254 independent samples of over 96,000 participants, twice as large as previous meta-analyses) investigated seven leadership styles as antecedents of PsyCap (authentic, ethical, servant, empowering, transactional, transformational, and abusive leadership); five outcomes (burnout, turnover intentions, work engagement, performance, and satisfaction); and the impact of four moderators (country of sample origin, cultural characteristics, industry type, and research design). Cultural characteristics (e.g., power distance, masculinity, long-term orientation, and uncertainty avoidance) moderated several conceptual relationships, offering new and extended insights into the antecedents, outcomes, and moderators related to PsyCap beyond previous meta-analyses. These findings also provide valuable insights into how PCIs may be adjusted, or personalized, to cultural contexts and industries, as well as extend our knowledge on the impact of leadership styles with causal links to PsyCap.

As it relates to the PCI, Lupsa et al. (2020) found in their meta-analysis (n = 3,911) that the overall effect of interventions on all PsyCap variables, the PCI, was the best evidence-based gold standard approach, and the most effective and efficient intervention above and beyond the development of individual HERO. This further demonstrated the additive value of PsyCap as a second-order construct above and beyond the summation of its individual components. This research confirmed the effectiveness and power of the evidence-based PCI in increasing multi-level PsyCap, and the importance of the omnibus PsyCap perspective. Within this omnibus perspective, the first-order constructs of hope, efficacy, resilience, and optimism are additive, leading to exponential gains in PsyCap that are causal to simultaneous positive improvements in well-being and performance (Lupsa et al., 2020; Luthans et al., 2007). Luthans et al.'s (2007) work on positive PsyCap and its measurement and relationship with performance and satisfaction confirmed positive causal relationships with both, respectively; it also provided validation of PsyCap as a distinctive second-order construct. PsyCap and each of its four first-order constructs were confirmed in this research to have conceptual independence and empirically based discriminant validity. By the same token, although distinct, the four HERO constructs share more in common than in variance, providing an underlying link that runs between them and ties them together as higher-order PsyCap.

Because PsyCap is more state-like than trait-like, it is open to management development and has been broadly successful globally in motivational propensities in today's workplace (Avey, 2014; Luthans et al., 2007; Youssef-Morgan & Luthans, 2015). As a result, employees who demonstrate higher PsyCap may be more likely to "weather the storm" of the type of dynamic, global environmental contexts confronting most organizations today better than their counterparts with lower PsyCap (Luthans et al., 2007). Employees who demonstrate higher PsyCap are also expected to "weather the storm" of VUCA contexts better than their lower PsyCap counterparts (Broad, 2023; Krasikova et al., 2015; Lester et al., 2011).

PsyCap has been applied within the mental health space as a non-stigma approach to developing well-being and performance among the terminally ill (such as cancer patients at the Dana Farber Cancer Institute at Harvard), and even in health outcomes in homeless female youths targeting the reduction of health-risk behaviors, while promoting the achievement of short-term behavioral goals (Rew et al., 2017). Krasikova, Lester, and Harms (2015) found strong effects of PsyCap in predicting and protecting soldiers in combat from mental health and substance abuse diagnoses. They demonstrated in a population of 1,889 U.S. Army soldiers that soldiers with higher levels of PsyCap prior to deployment were less likely to receive diagnoses for mental health problems and substance abuse post deployment, confirming PsyCap's causal and buffering effect on well-being and performance within VUCA contexts, and even within cascading VUCA contexts such as combat and/or multiple deployments.

PsyCap has also been applied within educational settings, demonstrating strong causal links between PsyCap development and academic performance as well as a mediational role in relationship to grit (Luthans, Luthans, & Chaffin, 2019). Sweet and Swayze (2017) identified PsyCap as a novel approach to freshman retention, demonstrating PsyCap as *causal and predictive* of retention between freshman and sophomore years of university. As a result, PsyCap is *causal and predictive* of academic performance, providing promising pathways to young students globally, from elementary to collegiate populations.

PsyCap has been found to reduce depression among adolescents, mediated by positive coping and perceived social support within Chinese teenagers clinically diagnosed with depression; thus, clinicians are urged to be attentive to and target the development of positive PsyCap resources as part of treatment protocols (Song & Song, 2021). Lastly, as it relates to adolescents, PsyCap was found to influence social anxiety during the COVID-19 pandemic outbreak, largely attributed to the coping styles that are used as PsyCap increases (cognitive reappraisals, positive emotions, social interactions) (see Li et al., 2022).

Ertosun et al. (2015) conducted a field study of PsyCap by the Solomon Four Group Design, adding rigor to the empirical research around PsyCap. The Solomon Four Group Design is one of the most powerful research designs available and is rarely used because of its difficulty to administer, especially for training intervention programs. This study design involved an experimental group receiving a pre-test, training intervention (PCI), then post-test; a control group receiving a pre-test and a post-test; another experimental group receiving training and only a post-test; and a last control group only taking a post-test. As a result, the Solomon Four Group Design contained two experimental and two control groups. This research provided in-depth, rigorous evidence that positive PsyCap provides new perspective for understanding and potentially managing negative and stressful organizational circumstances, such as those found in our current cascading VUCA contexts.

PsyCap has also been studied within nursing and midwifery, unarguably stressful endeavour's requiring high levels of PsyCap and associated coping strategies (such as cognitive reappraisals, positive emotions) (Luthans & Jensen, 2005). Workplace stress has a direct impact on safety, and PsyCap in this study was found to have a direct effect on both caregivers and, importantly, perceptions of safety by patients and actual safety measure performance improvements. Since the novel coronavirus, PsyCap has also been found to play mediational roles related to the undue fear of COVID-19 among nurses (Mubarek et al., 2020).

Vilariño del Castillo and Lopez-Zafra (2021) addressed systematically the existing research on PsyCap as a mediating and moderating variable in the workplace and found the importance of PsyCap within the fields of creativity, psychological health, performance, job satisfaction, organizational climate, leadership, and other emerging issues, such as human resources policies and practices. In this research, the authors propose the inclusion of job characteristics as a category of PsyCap antecedents and point out that there is a direct relationship between job characteristics and the level of PsyCap in general and/or for each component. They expand this work further through example. When a task is extraordinarily complex (like today's environment of cascading traumas and VUCA contexts), an employee will be more likely to fail, affecting their sense of mastery and their level of self-efficacy. Employee's emotional state will likely be negative if this situation is frequently repeated, developing a pessimistic outlook about the future in the workplace. In the same way, each key job characteristic (i.e., skill variety, task identity, task significance, autonomy, and feedback from the job itself) yields similar consequences because each one affects internal motivation (Bonanno, 2004; Hackman & Oldham, 1980).

Alternatively, resource caravans and the development of PsyCap HERO assets allow employees to foster the development of new resources in the presence of other new ones, which helps keep resources available to employees, teams, or organizations overall (Hobfoll, 2011). As such, caravans of resources can be used by employees as they face job demands, such is the case of PsyCap as a personal resource in the presence of meaningful work. Vilariño del Castillo and Lopez-Zafra (2021) expand the great variety of antecedents, which they classify according to three levels of influence (i.e., background of the employee, background of the team, and background of the organization), which collectively and aggregated, all significantly predict PsyCap.

Empirically Validated Measures of PsyCap

Over the past 20 plus years, several empirically validated measures of PsyCap have been developed. The most widely used instrument to assess PsyCap is the Psychological Capital Questionnaire (PCQ) developed by Luthans et al. (2007). This 24-item questionnaire drew from well-established, validated measures of each of the four HERO resources contained in the core, second-order construct of PsyCap and contained six items for each first-order construct (hope [Snyder, 2000], efficacy [Parker, 1998], resilience [Wagnild & Young, 1993], and optimism [Scheier & Carver, 1985]). Items were adapted to the workplace and measured on a 6-point Likert scale ranging from 1 – strongly disagree to 6 – strongly agree. Examples of items include: "I feel confident in representing my work area in meetings with management" (efficacy); "Right now I see myself as being pretty successful at work (hope); "I can be "on my own" so to speak at work if I have to (resilience); and "I'm optimistic about what will happen to me in the future as it pertains to work" (optimism) (Luthans et al., 2007).

This was followed by the empirical testing and validation of a shorter and more pragmatic twelve-item measure (PCQ-12) on the same 6-point Likert scale for hope (four items), efficacy (three items), resilience (three items), and optimism (two items) (Avey et al., 2011). Research has also demonstrated that the PCQ-12's structure was invariant across cultures, countries, and sex (Caza et al., 2010; Rus et al., 2012; Wernsing, 2014; Luthans & Youssef-Morgan, 2017).

To address methodological concerns with social desirability and faking common to all self-report measures, but especially those purporting to measure one's positive characteristics, such as PsyCap, an implicit PCQ (I-PCQ) was empirically tested and validated (see Harms & Luthans, 2012). McKenney, Short, and Payne (2013) measured PsyCap through computer-aided text analysis that involved analysis of historical communications such as that from chief executive officers, annual reports, and company press releases. In Japan, Dr. Yano Kazuo has developed artificial intelligence and machine learning algorithms that accurately measure PsyCap based upon biometric data (see Bernstein & Marton, 2017; Tsuji et al., 2019). Most recently, an open source publicly available short 5-item measure (PCQ-5) has been introduced for quick PsyCap pulse checks (Szerdahelyi et al., 2024).

Continuing a more macro level of analysis, work correlating multi-level PsyCap with biometric data (Bernstein & Marton, 2017; Tsuji et al., 2019) offers much to workplaces, such as Hitachi in Japan, where Dr. Kazuo Yano is conducting rigorous scientific research correlating biometric data to multi-level PsyCap. Today, and more broadly in the future, we will be empowered to predict PsyCap through biometrics, providing immense capabilities in proactive measurement, development, and management.

As evidenced above, there are now multiple empirically validated measures of PsyCap, and more are certain to come as we enter the AI revolution, which we believe will significantly accelerate our ability to measure, and perhaps more importantly, proactively intervene in building and sustaining PsyCap. Because PsyCap is a state of development, it is less trait-like and more state-like, thus open to fluctuation, which is normal and expected. This also means that it is open for development, especially following natural declines in PsyCap. For example, following a high op-tempo assignment, individuals, teams, and even organizations can expect to see declines in PsyCap resources. When measured regularly and proactively, organizations can lean in sooner to identify when resources have declined, and proactively work with individuals, groups and teams, leaders, and the enterprise overall to engage in evidence-based approaches to replenish and re-fuel essential PsyCap resources with resulting desirable outcomes.

POB as an Ecosystem Supported by Multi-Level PsyCap

Several studies have demonstrated a significant increase in well-being and performance for intact groups and teams that demonstrate higher levels of collective PsyCap (*c*PsyCap) (Broad, 2023; Clapp-Smith, Vogelgesang, & Avey, 2009; Dawkins et al., 2013; Mathe-Soulek et al., 2014; McKenny, Short, & Payne, 2013; Memili, Welsh, & Luthans, 2014; Peterson & Zhang, 2011; Rego et al., 2019; Roche, Haar, & Luthans, 2014), along with psychometric analysis of referent-shift PsyCap to the group and team. Elevated to the group and team level of analysis, Peterson & Zhang (2011) defined collective PsyCap as a team's shared positive appraisal of their circumstances and their probability of success based on their combined effort and perseverance.

*c*PsyCap has been empirically validated to increase organizational citizenship behaviors, while reducing counterproductive work behaviors (Luthans & Youssef-Morgan, 2017), as well to increase team performance (planning, coordination, positive conflict management, communication, trust, and cohesion) (see West, Patera, & Carsten, 2009).

In a recent comprehensive study, Broad introduced and validated a *c*PsyCap Intervention (*c*PCI) targeting group and team development. Using a mixed methods approach, Broad developed and empirically validated a new *c*PCI aimed at the group and team, and demonstrated that *c*PsyCap can emerge, or be developed, through evidence-based intervention (Broad, 2023). Additionally, this research provided a rich qualitative case study and grounded theory research methods teasing apart "how" *c*PsyCap is developed at the collective level, and expanded to other domains (such as health, relationships, and families) outside of the workplace. This research provides explicit examples of the theoretical underpinnings of social cognitive theory (Bandura, 1982, 1986, 1991, 2000) and social contagion (Christakis & Fowler, 2013) in action. Essentially, as groups and teams learn how to develop, manage, and sustain *c*PsyCap, they rely upon theoretical foundations of social cognitive theory (whereby team members observe, learn vicariously or model one another, and develop self-efficacy (confidence) through mastery experiences, social persuasion, and physiological and psychological arousal (see Luthans, Luthans, & Luthans, 2004), and social contagion (whereby team members positive *c*PsyCap attitudes and behaviors become contagious across the group; that is it was shown positivity begets positivity. To even the keel on positivity, POB and PsyCap scholars consistently emphasize the importance of being rooted across the development of all psychological resources (providing guidance on the risks of "blind hope," "over confidence," or "Pollyanna Optimism" that are not based in reality).

Why is understanding how *c*PsyCap is measured and developed important? Because how individuals feel about their most immediate team is predictive of how they feel about the organization overall. If an employee's team has high *c*PsyCap, we can expect to see that team set more aggressive stretch goals (hope), take on more challenging tasks (efficacy), bounce back from adversity and beyond when setbacks (or even extremely positive events) occur, and positive expectations about the past, present and future, with leniency for the past. Alternatively, low *c*PsyCap teams are sure to establish fewer stretch goals, demonstrate less confidence in their collective ability to achieve goals, take longer to bounce back following an adversity to an extremely positive event, and demonstrate more pessimism than optimism about their collective past, present, and future, with less leniency for the past.

The Critical Importance of Leader PsyCap

It's no surprise that leader PsyCap has a significant impact on followers (Chen et al., 2019; Hackman, 1992; Luthans, 2003; Luthans, Luthans, & Avey, 2014; Luthans & Youssef-Morgan, 2017). In fact, leader PsyCap is predictive and causal of follower PsyCap. Luthans understood this from the onset of his scholarly career while serving in the Army teaching leadership to the cadets at West Point. Thus, it seems fitting that his work and that of his colleagues (e.g., Avey, Avolio, Hannah, Harms, Lester, B. Luthans, K. Luthans, Paterson, Peterson, Vogelgesang, and Youssef-Morgan, to name just a few) have confirmed this predictive and causal relationship. This makes leadership an essential component to engage when it comes to the development and sustainment of well-being, performance, and ultimately healthy workplaces organization wide. Extant research informs us that PsyCap is a predictor of promotability to leadership (Lester et al., 2011), within neuroscience, the brains of high PsyCap leaders look differently than their peers (Peterson et al., 2008). Given that PsyCap is more state-like than trait-like, it can be developed and measured, and as it is developed, the neuroplasticity in our brains causes material changes in leader brain structure (Peterson et al., 2008). Leaders themselves need to be transformed, through PsyCap development, to become more authentic, transparent, and trustworthy, to model PsyCap to their employees, and facilitate the climate and resources necessary for them to lead their own PsyCap development journey (Luthans, 2003; Petersen & Youssef-Morgan, 2018). As Youssef-Morgan and Stratman (2016) note, leaders need to be "all in" on the value of positivity and Luthans, Luthans, and Avey (2014) further add this leader positivity requires a mindset of openness and inquiry rather than advocacy.

Fast forward to today, and scholars further understand the importance of leader PsyCap, and the significant role that leaders play not only in the well-being and performance of their employees but also the immense power and influence leaders have in fostering healthy workplaces that carry trickle down effects to general population health through positive impacts on health and relationships outside of work (Luthans et al., 2013; American Psychological Association, 2023).

Radical Changes in the Workplace

At the turn of the century, Luthans and his colleagues began conceptualizing POB and multi-level PsyCap to meet turbulent global environments that have now become cascading VUCA contexts that have accelerated, escalated, and been further amplified. The result is radical changes globally, not the least of which is radical changes in the workplace, again where we spend an estimated third of our lifetimes. The pandemic catalyzed us to think about work in different ways, especially as it relates to space and flexibility, and dealt a serious blow to the five-day, 9-to-5, in-office workweek that has underpinned work life for nearly a century (Agovino, 2020; Foss, 2021). Flexibility had been seeping into the workplace, but it's now flooding organizations globally as companies have discovered that remote work didn't slash productivity and employees valued the arrangement. Workplaces such as hospitals, hotels, retailers, and manufacturing plants have a limited ability to let employees work remotely, and in some cases, this is forcing global workforce shortages. For example, it is expected that we will see a shortage of ten million nurses in the next ten years, sounding off alarm bells worldwide as healthcare demands increase, and were further exacerbated by the global pandemic.

The Society for Human Resource Management (SHRM) estimates that 70% of employed Americans would prefer to work remotely on a full-time or part-time basis if given the option, and 35% would accept a salary reduction in return for that flexibility. SHRM further finds that nearly 20% of employed Americans who would prefer to work from home in some capacity would start looking for a remote position elsewhere, and 7% would quit their job if their employer did not give them the option to work remotely (SHRM, 2021). As a result, century old paradigms on how work gets done have been shattered as we make our foray into the new future of work that represents a significant paradigm shift for organizations globally. What's more, as DEIA, and geographical and demographical disparities widen, variances in where and how work gets done threaten to limit the flexibility and freedoms of the most vulnerable, potentially contributing further to societal unrest and distrust of large organizations, to include governments. This also means that the previous century of organizational behavior research and practice must consider this radical shift in the global workplace.

The Future of Work

As a result of the cascading VUCA contexts and traumas described above and the radical shifts in how work is done following the global pandemic, organizations are transforming as they adopt new technologies and use new sources of data, changing the experiences of employees and pushing organization researchers to respond (Polzer, 2023). Today, as employees perform work activities, they generate digital data that in some ways are equivalent to a digital footprint of daily activities. In the previous century, such access to how and where work gets done was simply not available outside laboratory and field experimentation. Today, there are massive amounts of data that are creating unprecedented opportunities for studying human behavior at work. Essentially, this will open a whole new perspective on the practices of individuals, groups and teams, and how organization's function, to include how decision-making processes and work procedures are accomplished, to communication and collaboration, and even attempts to monitor and control employees. Organizational behavior scholars are optimally positioned to stay at the forefront of research on the next century of workplace scientific research and development. Accordingly, top organizational behavior journals and their editors today are pursuing topics related to spanning traditional boundaries (Gruber & Bliese, 2024), when and how AI augments employee creativity (Jia et al., 2023), understanding intra-individual conflict and task performance in a multi-team context (Park et al., 2024), or diversity, equity, and inclusion through the lens of structural power (To, Sherf, & Kouchaki, 2024) and crafting meaningful roles for fieldworkers operating in poverty (Barkema et al., 2024).

The Next 20 Years of POB and PsyCap Research and Beyond

What does the next 20 plus years of POB and PsyCap research look like? The need for POB and PsyCap is *now* as we witness first-hand the volatility of accelerated, intensified, and cascading VUCA contexts globally, and an environmental context where the value of human, social, and economic capital can shift quickly, leading to vast global instabilities. What is within our control is the state of development that we approach these cascading VUCA contexts from, and how we combat the massive influx of newly available data as we protect our attention spans, focus on what is important, and ultimately the protection, sustainment, and further development of our well-being and performance individually and collectively.

Gone are the days that organizations can outsource healthy workplaces to simplistically targeted EAPs placing well-being and performance in the laps of employees. Today and in the future, organizations will be more focused and engaged proactively in building their own POB organizational "ecosystems" where they take on more ownership and engagement of employee and enterprise-wide well-being and performance.

In our own work, the application of POB and PsyCap within organizations globally has changed substantially in just the past decade, and even more so significantly when we compare today to the beginning of the century. POB and PsyCap provide the ability to measure, sustain, and develop critical POB and multi-level PsyCap resources, that act as resource caravans in proactively protecting us individually and as collectives from the accelerated and intensified VUCA contexts that are becoming our new normal.

The use of AI in research design and methods will rapidly expand our capabilities as scholars and practitioners, opening entirely new pathways of investigation and inquiry. For example, as we face threats of extreme shortages in professions such as teaching, nursing, and mental health, we stand to gain much by further understanding how we create states of development through leadership and employee engagement that proactively protect our well-being and performance during times of unprecedented stress and anxiety (WHO, 2019, 2020a, 2020b).

Within the workplace, we now have the capability and are deploying the use of organizational wide well-being and performance dashboards where real-time dynamic access to snapshots of population well-being and performance are available. The positivity and proactivity of this approach empowers organizations who are taking on and embracing more ownership of enterprise-wide well-being and performance. What are the implications?

To be clear, POB and PsyCap alone will not provide a silver bullet solution, but they do provide a rigorous scientifically evidence-based approach to the science of organizations, and how organizations can develop, sustain, and stabilize POB and multi-level PsyCap. As the radical changes in the workplace continue to unfold in the next 20-years and beyond, alongside unprecedented access to data previously unfathomable, our ability to access and proactively engage with organizational well-being and performance is certain to play an important role in fostering and developing healthy workplaces, while also contributing to positive improvements in general population health. The workplace, and the people that support it, are more important than ever to our collective well-being, performance, and even health and relationships outside of the workplace.

Advancing Positive Organization Behavior and PsyCap Conclusion

Obviously, it was unfathomable at the beginning of the 21st century to predict the radical changes workplaces have and will experience. What is certain is that the human element of workplaces is the most valuable asset within any organization. Within this human dimension of work, research on POB and PsyCap have made clear the critical importance of workplaces on well-being and performance. The crises and adversities that we face today and in our collective futures have taken a toll on mental health globally. The workplace represents rich, fertile, and accessible ground in measuring, building, sustaining, and replenishing PsyCap assets that not only improve well-being and performance but also contribute meaningfully to general population physical and mental health, and touching domains outside the workplace. Longitudinally, the science of POB and PsyCap offers much to organizations globally as their workforces face unprecedented cascading VUCA challenges at accelerated rates of change. We see a future where POB and multi-level PsyCap become important tools and a part of the solution required to develop, manage, and sustain healthy workplaces. We see a future that transforms the workplace from the primary source of stress to the primary source of well-being and performance globally.

Notes

1 Popular press books lacking evidence-based rigor during this time (yet enthusiastically received) include Ken Blanchard's *One Minute Manager*, Steven Covey's *Seven Habits*, and Spencer Johnson's *Who Moved My Cheese* as examples (see Luthans, 2002a).
2 PCIs refer to evidence-based scientifically validated interventions where PsyCap is measured and strategically developed for predictive, causal, and positive well-being and performance improvements (see Luthans et al., 2006, 2010, Luthans, Youssef-Morgan, & Avolio, 2007, 2015).

References

Agovino, T. (2020, May 22). *The new world of work.* The Society for Human Resource Management (SHRM): Alexandria, VA. Retrieved from https://www.shrm.org/topics-tools/news/all-things-work/new-world-work

American Psychological Association. (2023). Psychological capital: What it is and why employers need it now (Healthy Workplaces). Retrieved from https://www.apa.org/topics/healthy-workplaces/psychological-capital

Avey, J. B., Patera, J. L., & West, B. J. (2006). The implications of positive psychological capital on employee absenteeism. *Journal of Leadership and Organizational Studies, 13*, 42–60. https://doi.org/10.1177/10717919070130020401

Avey, J. B., Wernsing, T. S., & Luthans, F. (2008). Can positive employees help positive organizational change? *Journal of Applied Behavioral Science, 44*, 48–70. https://doi.org/10.1177/0021886307311470

Avey, J. B., Luthans, F., & Youssef, C. M. (2010). The additive value of positive psychological capital in predicting work attitudes and behaviors. *Journal of Management, 36*(2), 430–452. https://doi.org/10.1177/0149206308329961

Avey, J. B., Luthans, F., Smith, R. M., & Palmer, N. F. (2010). Impact of positive psychological capital on employee well-being over time. *Journal of Occupational Health Psychology, 15*, 17–28. https://digitalcommons.unl.edu/managementfacpub/55

Avey, J. B., Avolio, B., & Luthans, F. (2011). Experimentally analysing the impact of leader positivity on follower positivity and performance. *The Leadership Quarterly, 22*, 282–294. https://doi.org/10.1016/j.leaqua.2011.02.004

Avey, J. B., Reichard, R. J., Luthans, F., & Mhatre, K. H. (2011). Meta-analysis of the impact of positive psychological capital on employee attitudes, behaviors, and performance. *Human Resources Development Quarterly, 22*(2), 127–152. https://doi.org/10.1002/hrdq.20070

Avey, J. B. (2014). The left side of psychological capital: New evidence on the antecedents of PsyCap. *Journal of Leadership & Organizational Studies, 21*(2), 141–149. https://doi.org/10.1177/1548051813515516

Bandura, A. (1982). Self-efficacy mechanism in human agency. *American Psychologist, 37*,122–147. https://doi.org/10.1037/0003-066X.37.2.122

Bandura, A. (1986). *Social foundations of thought and action.* Prentice-Hall: Upper Saddle River, NJ.

Bandura, A. (1991). Social cognitive theory of self-regulation. *Organizational Behavior and Human Decision Processes, 50*(2), 248–287. https://doi.org/10.1016/0749-5978(91)90022-L

Bandura, A. (2000). Cultivate self-efficacy for personal and organizational effectiveness. In E. A. Locke (Ed.), *The Blackwell handbook of principles of organizational behavior* (pp. 120–136). Blackwell: Oxford, UK.

Baumeister, R. F., Bratslavsky, E., Finkenauer, C., & Vohs, K. D. (2001). Bad is stronger than good. *Review of General Psychology, 5*, 323–370. https://doi.org/10.1037/1089-2680.5.4.323

Becker, G. S. (1993). *Human capital: A theoretical and empirical analysis, with special reference to education.* University of Chicago Press: Chicago.

Barkema, H. G., Coyle-Shapiro, J. A-M., le Grand, E. M. (2024). How do fieldworkers in poverty craft meaningful roles to achieve social impact? Female teachers in slums in India. *Academy of Management Journal, 67*(1). https://doi.org/10.5465/amj.2021.1244

Bernstein, E., & Marton, S. (2017). *Sensing (and monetizing) happiness at Hitachi.* HBS No 418–019. Harvard Business School Publishing: Cambridge, Mass.

Bonanno, G. A. (2004). Loss, trauma, and human resilience: Have we underestimated the human capacity to thrive after extremely aversive events? *American Psychologist, 59*, 20–28. https://doi.org/10.1037/0003-066X.59.1.20

Bouckenooghe, D., De Clercq, D., & Raja, U. (2019). A person-centered, latent profile analysis of psychological capital. *Australian Journal of Management, 44*(1), 91–108. https://doi.org/10.1177/0312896218775153

Broad, J. D., & Luthans, F. (2020). Positive resources for psychiatry in the fourth industrial revolution: Building patient and family focused psychological capital (PsyCap). *International Review of Psychiatry, 32*(7–8), 542–554. https://doi.org/10.1080/09540261.2020.1796600

Broad, J. D. (2023). The emergence of collective psychological capital (*c*PsyCap) in volatile, uncertain complex, and ambiguous (VUCA) environments – A mixed methods case study dissertation within law enforcement and non-law enforcement professions. George Washington University. Retrieved from https://eric.ed.gov/?q=law&ff1=dtySince_2020&ff2=subLaw+Enforcement&id=ED6 37984

Cameron, K. S. (2008). Paradox in positive organizational change. *Journal of Applied Behavioral Science, 44*(1), 7–24. https://doi.org/10.1177/0021886308314703

Carver, C., Scheier, M., Miller, C., & Fulford, D. (2009). Optimism. In S. J. Lopez & C. R. Snyder (Eds.), Oxford handbook of positive psychology (2nd Ed., pp. 303–311). Oxford University Press.

Cassidy, T., Mclaughlin, M., & McDowel, E. (2014). Bullying and health at work: The mediating roles of psychological capital and social support. *Work and Stress, 28*. https://doi.org/10.1080/02678373.2014.927020

Caza A., Bagozzi R. P., Woolley L., Levy L., & Caza B. (2010). Psychological capital and authentic leadership: Measurement, gender, and cultural extension. *Asia-Pacific Journal of Business Administration, 2*, 53–70. https://doi.org/10.1108/17574321011028972

Chen, Q., Kong, Y., Niu, J., Gao, W., Li, J., & Li, M. (2019). How leaders' psychological capital influence their followers' psychological capital: Social exchange or emotional contagion. *Frontiers in Psychology, 10*. https://doi.org/10.3389/fpsyg.2019.01578

Christakis, N. A., & Fowler, J. H. (2013). Social contagion theory: Examining dynamic social networks and human behavior. *Statistics in Medicine, 32*(4), 556–577. https://doi.org/10.1002/sim.5408

Clapp-Smith, R., Vogelgesang, G. R., & Avey, J. B. (2009). Authentic leadership and positive psychological capital: The mediating role of trust at the group level of analysis. *Organizational Studies, 15*, 227–240. https://doi.org/10.1177/1548051808326596

Coutu, D. L. (2002). How resilience works. *Harvard Business Review, 80*(3), 46–55.

Dawkins, S., Martin, A., Scott, J., & Sanderson, K. (2013). Building on the positives: A psychometric review and critical analysis of the construct of psychological capital. *Journal of Occupational and Organizational Psychology, 86*(3), 348–370. https://doi.org/10.1111/joop.12007

Dawkins, S., Martin, A., Scott, J., & Sanderson, K. (2015). Advancing conceptualization and measurement of psychological capital as a collective construct. *Human Relations, 68*(6), 925–949. https://doi.org/10.1177/0018726714549645

Donaldson, S. I., & Chen, C. (2021). *Positive organizational psychology interventions: Design and evaluation*. John Wiley & Sons Ltd.: Hoboken, NJ.

Ertosun, O. Z., Erdil, O., Deniz, N., & Lutfihak, A. (2015). Positive psychological capital development: A field study by the Solomon four group design. *International Business Research, 8*(10), 102–111. https://doi.org/10.5539/ibr.v8n10p102

Foss, N. J. (2021). The impact of the Covid-19 pandemic on firms' organizational designs. *Journal of Management Studies, 58*(1), 270–274. https://doi.org/10.1111/joms.12643

Fredrickson, B. L. (2001). The role of positive emotions in positive psychology: The broaden-and-build theory of positive emotions. *American Psychologist: Special Issue, 56*, 218–226. https://doi.org/10.1037//0003-066x.56.3.218

Fredrickson, B. L., Tugade, M. M., Waugh, C. E., & Larkin, G. R. (2003). What good are positive emotions in crisis? A prospective study of resilience and emotions following the terrorist attacks on the United States on September 11th, 2001. *Journal of Personality and Social Psychology, 84*(2), 365–376. https://doi.org/10.1037//0022-3514.84.2.365

Fredrickson, B. L. (2004). The broaden-and-build theory of positive emotions. *Philosophical Transactions of the Royal Society of London Series B, Biological Sciences, 359*(1449), 1367–1378. https://doi.org/10.1098/rstb.2004.1512

Fredrickson, B. L. (2009). *Positivity: Groundbreaking research reveals how to embrace the hidden strength of positive emotions, overcome negativity, and thrive*. Crown Publishers/Random House: New York.

Gruber, M., & Bliese, P. (2024). Expanding AMJ's manuscript portfolio: Research methods articles designed to advance theory and span boundaries. *Academy of Management Journal, 67*(1), 1–4. https://doi.org/10.5465/amj.2024.4001

Hackman, J. R., & Oldham, G. R. (1980). *Work redesign*. FT Press: London.

Hackman, J. R. (1992). Group influences on individuals in organizations. In M. D. Dunnette, & L. M. Hough (Eds.), Handbook of industrial and organizational psychology (pp. 199–267). Consulting Psychologists Press: Washington, DC.

Harms, P. D., & Luthans, F. (2012). Measuring implicit psychological constructs in organizational behavior: An example using psychological capital. *Journal of Organizational Behavior, 33*(4), 589–594. https://doi.org/10.1002/job.1785

Hobfoll, S. (1989). Conservation of resources: A new attempt at conceptualizing stress. *American Psychologist, 44*, 513–524. https://doi.org/10.1037//0003-066x.44.3.513

Hobfoll, S. (2002). Social and psychological resources and adaptation. *Review of General Psychology, 6*, 307–324. https://doi.org/10.1037/1089-2680.6.4.307

Hobfoll, S. E. (2011). Conservation of resources theory: Its implication for stress, health, and resilience. In S. Folkman (Ed.), *The Oxford handbook of stress, health, and coping* (pp. 127–147). Oxford University Press.

Huitt, W. (1999). Conation as an important factor of mind. *Educational Psychology Interactive.* Valdosta State University. Retrieved from https://www.edpsycinteractive.org/topics/conation/conation.html

Igic, I., Keller, A. C., Elfering, A., Tschan, F., Kälin, W., & Semmer, N. K. (2017). Ten-year trajectories of stressors and resources at work: Cumulative and chronic effects on health and well-being. *Journal of Applied Psychology, 102*(9), 1317–1343. https://doi.org/10.1037/apl0000225

Jia, N., Luo, X., Fang, Z., & Liao, C. (2023). When and how artificial intelligence augments employee creativity. *Academy of Management Journal, 67*(1), 5–32. https://doi.org/10.5465/amj.2022.0426

Krasikova, A., Lester, P. B., & Harms, P. D. (2015). Effects of psychological capital on mental health and substance abuse. *Journal of Leadership and Organizational Studies, 22*(3), 280–291. https://doi.org/10.1177/1548051815585853

Lester, P. B., Harms, P. D., Herian, M. N., Krasikova, D. V., & Beal, S. J. (2011). *The comprehensive soldier fitness program evaluation report #3: Longitudinal analysis of the impact of master resilience training on self-reported resilience and psychological health data.* U.S. Department of Defense.

Li, N., Fan, L., Wang, Y., Wang, J., & Huang, Y. (2022). Risk factors of psychological distress during the COVID-19 pandemic: The roles of coping style and emotional regulation. *Journal of Affective Disorders, 299*, 326–334. https://doi.org/10.1016/j.jad.2021.12.026

Loghman, S., Quinn, M., Dawkins, S., Woods, M., Om Sharma, S., & Scott, J. (2023). A comprehensive meta-analyses of the nomological network of psychological capital (PsyCap). *Journal of Leadership and Organizational Studies, 30*(1), 108–128. https://doi.org/10.1177/15480518221107998

Lupsa, D., Virga, D., Maricutoiu, L., & Rusu, A. (2020). Increasing psychological capital: A preregistered meta-analysis of controlled interventions. *Applied Psychology: An International Review, 69*(4), 1506–1556. https://doi.org/10.1111/apps.12219

Luthans, F. (1973). *Organizational behavior.* McGraw-Hill: New York.

Luthans, F., & Kreitner . R. (1975). *Organizational behavior modification.* Scott, Foresman: Glenview, IL.

Luthans, F., Paul, R., & Baker, D. (1981). An experimental analysis of the impact of contingent reinforcement on salespersons' performance behavior. *Journal of Applied Psychology, 66*, 314–323. https://doi.org/10.1037/0021-9010.66.3.314

Luthans, F., Hodgetts, R. M., & Rosenkrantz, S. A. (1988). *Real managers.* Ballinger: Boston.

Luthans, F., & Stajkovic, A. D. (1999). Reinforce (not necessarily pay) for performance. *Academy of Management Executive, 13*(2), 49–57. https://doi.org/10.5465/AME.1999.1899548

Luthans, F., & Stajkovic, A. D. (2000). Provide recognition for performance improvement. In E. A. Locke (Ed.), *Handbook of principles of organizational behavior* (pp. 166–180). Blackwell: Oxford, UK.

Luthans, F., Luthans, K. W., Hodgetts, R. M., & Luthans, B. C. (2001). Positive approach to leadership (PAL) – Implications for today's organizations. *Journal of Leadership Studies, 8*(2), 3–20. https://doi.org/10.1177/107179190100800201

Luthans, F. (2002a). The need for and meaning of positive organizational behavior. *Journal of Organizational Behavior, 23*, 695–706. https://doi.org/10.1002/job.165

Luthans, F. (2002b). Positive organizational behavior: Developing and managing psychological strengths. *Academy of Management Executive, 16*, 57–72. https://www.jstor.org/stable/4165814

Luthans, F. (2002c). Positive psychology approach to OB. In F. Luthans (Ed.), Organizational behavior (9th ed., pp. 286–322). McGraw-Hill/Irwin: New York.

Luthans, F. (2003). Positive organizational behavior (POB): Implications for leadership and HR development and motivation. In R. M. Steers, L. W. Porter, & G. A. Begley (Eds.), *Motivation and leadership at work.* (pp. 187–195). McGraw-Hill/Irwin: New York.

Luthans, F., & Youssef, C. M. (2004). Human, social, and now positive psychological capital management: Investing in people for competitive advantage. *Organizational Dynamics, 33*(2), 143–160. https://doi.org/10.1016/j.orgdyn.2004.01.003

Luthans, F., Luthans K. W., & Luthans, B. C. (2004). Positive psychological capital: Beyond human and social capital. *Business Horizons, 47*(1), 45–50. https://doi.org/10.1016/j.bushor.2003.11.007

Luthans, K. W., & Jensen, S. M. (2005). The linkage between psychological capital and commitment to organizational mission: A study of nurses. *Journal of Nursing Administration, 35*(6), 304–310. https://doi.org/10.1097/00005110-200506000-00007

Luthans, F., Vogelgesang, G. R., & Lester, P. B. (2006). Developing the psychological capital of resiliency. *Human Resource Development Review*, *5*(1), 25–44. https://doi.org/10.1177/1534484305285335

Luthans, F., Avey, J. B., Avolio, B. J., Norman, S. M., & Combs, G. M. (2006). Psychological capital development: Toward a micro-intervention. *Journal of Organizational Behavior: The International Journal of Industrial, Occupational and Organizational Psychology and Behavior, 27*(3), 387–393. https://doi.org/ 10.1002/job.373

Luthans, F., Youssef-Morgan, C., & Avolio, B. J. (2007). *Psychological capital: Developing the human competitive edge*. Oxford University Press.

Luthans, F., Avolio, B. J., Avey, J. B., & Norman, S. M. (2007). Positive psychological capital: Measurement and relationship with performance and satisfaction. *Personnel Psychology, 60*(3), 541–572. https://doi.org/10.1111/j.1744-6570.2007.00083.x

Luthans, F., Avey, J. B., & Patera, J. L. (2008). Experimental analysis of a web-based training intervention to develop positive psychological capital. *Academy of Management Learning and Education, 7*(2), 209–221. https://doi.org/10.5465/amle.2008.32712618

Luthans, F., Avey, J. B., Avolio, B. J., & Peterson, S. (2010). The development and resulting performance impact of positive psychological capital. *Human Resource Development Quarterly, 21*(1), 41–67. https://doi.org/10.1002/hrdq.20034

Luthans, F., Youssef-Morgan, C. M., & Rawski, S. L. (2011). A tale of two paradigms: The impact of psychological capital and reinforcing feedback on problem solving and innovation. *Journal of Organizational Behavior Management, 31*(4), 333–350. https://digitalcommons.unl.edu/managementfacpub/130

Luthans, F., Youssef-Morgan, C. M., Sweetman, D., & Harms, P. (2013). Meeting the leadership challenge of employee well-being through relationship PsyCap and health PsyCap. *Journal of Leadership and Organizational Studies, 20,* 114–129. https://doi.org/10.1177/1548051812465893

Luthans, B. C., Luthans, K. W., & Avey, J. B. (2014). Building the leaders of tomorrow: The development of academic psychological capital. *Journal of Leadership and Organizational Studies, 21*(2), 191–199. https://doi.org/10.1177/1548051813517003

Luthans, F., Youssef-Morgan, C. M., & Avolio, B. J. (2015). *Psychological capital and beyond.* Oxford University Press.

Luthans, F., & Youssef-Morgan, C. (2017). Psychological capital: An evidence-based positive approach. *Annual Review of Organizational Psychology and Organizational Behavior, 4*, 339–366. https://doi.org/10.1146/annurev-orgpsych-032516-113324

Luthans, K. W., Luthans, B. C., & Chaffin, T. D. (2019). Refining grit in academic performance: The mediational role of psychological capital. *Journal of Management Education, 43*(1), 35–61. https://doi.org/10.1177/1052562918804282

Luthans, F., & Broad, J. D. (2022). Positive psychological capital to help combat the mental health fallout from the pandemic and VUCA environment. *Organizational Dynamics, 51*(2), 1–13. https://doi.org/10.1016/j.orgdyn.2020.100817

Masten, A. S. (2001). Ordinary magic: Resilience processes in development. *American Psychologist, 56*, 227–239. https://doi.org/10.1037//0003-066x.56.3.227

Masten, A. S., Cutuli, J. J., Herbers, J. E., & Reed, M. G. J. (2009). Resilience in development. In S. J. Lopez & C. R. Snyder (Eds.), *Oxford handbook of positive psychology* (2nd ed., pp. 117–131). Oxford University Press.

Mathe-Soulek, K., Scott-Halsell, S., Kim, S., & Krawczyk, M. (2014). Psychological capital in the quick service restaurant industry: A study of unit level performance. *Journal of Hospitality and Tourism Research, 41*(7), 823–845. https://doi.org/10.1177/1096348014550923

McKenny, A. F., Short, J. C., & Payne, T. (2013). Using computer-aided text analysis to elevate constructs: An illustration using psychological capital. *Organizational Behavior Methods, 16*, 152–184. https://doi.org/10.1177/1094428112459910

Memili, E., Welsh, D., & Luthans, F. (2014). Going beyond research on goal setting: A proposed role for organization psychological capital of family firms. *Entrepreneurship Theory and Practice, 37*, 1289–1296. https://doi.org/10.1111/etap.12066

Mubarek, N., Safdar, S., Faiz, S., Khan, J., & Jaafar, M. (2020). Impact of public health education on undue fear of COVID-19 among nurses: The mediating role of psychological capital. *International Journal of Mental Health Nursing, 30*(2), 544–552. https://doi.org/10.1111/inm.12819

Newman, A., Ucbasaran, D., Zhu, F., & Hirst, G. (2014). Psychological capital: A review and synthesis. *Journal of Organizational Behavior, 35*, S120–S138. https://doi.org/10.1002/job.1916

Park, S., Luciano, M. M., Mathieu, J. E., & Fenters, V. W. (2024). Intra-individual conflict and task performance in a multi-team context: Examining the structural elements of conflict experience. *Academy of Management Journal, 67*(1), 33–60. https://doi.org/10.5465/amj.2021.0285

Parker, S. K. (1998). Enhancing role breadth self-efficacy: The roles of job enrichment and other organizational interventions. *Journal of Applied Psychology, 83*, 835–852. https://doi.org/10.1037/0021-9010.83.6.835

Petersen, K., & Youssef-Morgan, C. M. (2018). The "left side" of authentic leadership: Contributions of climate and psychological capital. *Leadership and Organization Development Journal, 39*(3), 436–452. https://doi.org/10.1108/LODJ-06-2017-0171

Peterson, C. (2000). The future of optimism. *American Psychologist, 55*(1), 44–55. https://doi.org/10.1037/0003-066X.55.1.44

Peterson, S. J., Balthazard, P. A., Waldman, D. A., & Thatcher, R. W. (2008). Neuroscientific implications of psychological capital: Are the brains of optimistic, hopeful, confident, and resilient leaders different? *Organizational Dynamics, 37*(4), 342–353. https://doi.org/10.1016/j.orgdyn.2008.07.007

Peterson, S. J., & Zhang, Z. (2011). Examining the relationships between top management team psychological characteristics, transformational leadership, and business unit performance.

In M. A. Carpenter (Ed.), Handbook of top management research (pp. 127–149). Edward Elgar: North Hampton, Mass.

Peterson, S. J., Luthans, F., Avolio, B. J., Walumbwa, F., & Zhang, Z. (2011). Psychological capital and employee performance: A latent growth modelling approach. *Personnel Psychology*, *64*, 427–450. https://digitalcommons.unl.edu/managementfacpub/14

Polzer, J. T. (2023). The rise of people analytics and the future of organizational research. *Research in Organizational Behavior, 42*, Supplement. https://doi.org/10.1016/j.riob.2023.100181

Rego, A., Owens, B., Yam, K. C, Bluhm, D., Pina e Cunha, M., Silard, A., Gonçalves, L., Martins, M., Simpson, A. V., & Liu, W. (2019). Leader humility and team performance: Exploring the mediating mechanisms of team PsyCap and task allocation effectiveness. *Journal of Management, 45*(3), 1009–1033. https://doi.org/10.1177/0149206316688941

Rew, L., Powell, T., Brown, A., Becker, H., & Slesnick, N. (2017). An intervention to enhance psychological capital and health outcomes in homeless female youths. *Western Journal of Nursing Research, 39*(3), 356–373. https://doi.org/10.1177/0193945916658861

Roberts, S. J., Scherer, L. L., & Bowyer, C. J. (2011). Job stress and incivility: What role does psychological capital play? *Journal of Leadership and Organizational Studies, 18*(4), 449–458. https://doi.org/10.1177/1548051811409044

Roche, M., Haar, J. M., & Luthans, F. (2014). The role of mindfulness and psychological capital on the well-being of leaders. *Journal of Occupational Health Psychology, 19*(4), 476–489. https://doi.org/10.1037/a0037183

Rus, C., Băban, A., de Jesus, S., & Andrei, D. (2012). An analysis of the psychometric properties of the Psychological Capital Questionnaire-12. *Journal of Educational Psychology, 2*, 110–122.

Scheier, M. F., & Carver, C. S. (1985). Optimism, coping, and health: Assessment and implications of generalized outcome expectancies. *Health Psychology. 4*, 219–247. https://doi.org/10.1037//0278-6133.4.3.219

Schneider, S. L. (2001). In search of realistic optimism. *American Psychologist, 56*, 250–263.

Seligman, M. E. P. (1998). *Learned optimism*. Pocket Books: New York.

Seligman, M. E. P., & Csikszentmihalyi, M. (2000). Positive psychology: An introduction. *American Psychologist, 55*(1), 5–14. https://doi.org/10.1037/0003-066X.55.1.5

Silver, R. C., Holman, A. E., & Garfin, D. R. (2021). Coping with cascading collective traumas in the United States. *Nature Human Behaviour*, *5*, 4–6. https://doi.org/10.1038/s41562-020-00981-x

Snyder, C. R., Harris, C., Anderson, J. R., Holleran, S. A., Irving, L. M., Sigmon, S. T., Yoshinobu, L., Gibb, J., Langelle, C., & Harney, P. (1991). The will and the ways: Development and validation of an individual-differences measure of hope. *Journal of Personality and Social Psychology, 60*(4), 570–585. https://doi.org/10.1037/0022-3514.60.4.570

Snyder, C. R. (Ed.). (2000). *Handbook of hope: Theory, measures, and applications.* Academic Press: Cambridge, Mass.

Society for Human Resource Management (SHRM). (2021). SHRM Report: Radical inequity persists, costs American workplaces billions annually. SHRM: Alexandria, VA. Retrieved from https://www.shrm.org/about/press-room/shrm-report-racial-inequity-persists-costs-american-workplaces-billions-annually

Song, R. J., & Song, L. J. (2021). The dampen effect of psychological capital on adolescent depression: A moderated mediation model. *Current Psychology, 40*(1), 56–64. https://doi.org/10.1007/s12144-020-00626-2

Stajkovic, A. D., & Luthans, F. (1997). A meta-analysis of the effect of organizational behavior modification on task performance. *Academy of Management Journal*, *40*, 1122–1149.

Stajkovic, A. D., & Luthans, F. (1998). Self-efficacy and work-related performance: A meta-analysis. *Psychological Bulletin, 124*(2), 240–261.

Stajkovic, A. D., & Luthans, F. (2003). Behavioral management and task performance in organizations. *Personnel Psychology, 56*, 155–194

Steers, R. M., Mowday, R. T., & Shapiro, D. L. (2004). Introduction to special topic forum: The future of work motivation theory. *The Academy of Management Review, 29*(3), 379–387. https://doi.org/10.2307/20159049

Sweet, J., & Swayze, S. (2017). The multi-generational nursing workforce: Analysis of psychological capital by generation and shift. *Journal of Organizational Psychology, 17*(4). https://articlegateway.com/index.php/JOP/article/view/1661

Szerdahelyi, M., Paterson, T. A., Huang, L., Martos, T., & Komlósi, L. (2024). Validation of the PCQ-5: A short form to measure state positive psychological capital. *Group and Organization Management, 49*(1), 215–245. https://doi.org/10.1177/10596011221127383

To, C., Sherf, E. N., & Kouchaki, M. (2024). How much inequity do you see? Structural power, perceptions of gender and racial inequity, and support for diversity initiatives. *Academy of Management Journal, 67*(1), 126–149. https://doi.org/10.5465/amj.2022.0253

Tsuji, S., Sato, N., Yano, K., Broad, J., & Luthans, F. (2019). Employees wearable measure of face-to-face communication relates to their positive psychological capital, well-being. IEEE/WIC/ACM International Conference on Web. https://doi.org/10.1145/3358695.3360923

U.S. Department of Health and Human Services, Office of the U.S. Surgeon General. (2022). *U.S. Surgeon General's framework for workplace mental health & well-being.* Retrieved from https://www.hhs.gov/sites/default/files/workplace-mental-health-well-being.pdf

Vilariño del Castillo, D., & Lopez-Zafra, E. (2021). Antecedents of psychological capital at work: A systematic review of moderator-mediator effects and a new integrative proposal. *European Management Review, 19*(1), 154–169. https://doi.org/10.1111/emre.12460

Wagnild, G. M., & Young, H. M. (1993). Development and psychometric evaluation of the Resilience Scale. *Journal of Nursing Measurement, 1*(2), 165–178.

Waldman, D. A., & Sparr, J. L. (2023). Rethinking diversity strategies: An application of paradox and positive organization behavior theories. *Academy of Management Perspectives, 37*(2), 174–192. https://doi.org/10.5465/amp.2021.0183

Wernsing, T. (2014). Psychological capital: A test of measurement invariance across 12 national cultures. *Journal of Leadership and Organizational Studies, 21*, 179–190. https://doi.org/10.1177/1548051813515924

West, B. J., Patera, J. L., & Carsten, M. K. (2009). Team level positivity: Investigating positive psychological capacities and team level outcomes. Journal of Organizational Behavior, 30(2), 249–267. https://doi.org/10.1002/job.593

World Economic Forum (WEF). (2022, July). *Risk proof: A framework for building organizational resilience in an uncertain future.* Retrieved from https://www3.weforum.org/docs/WEF_A_Framework_for_Building_Organizational_Resilience_in_an_Uncertain_Future_2022.pdf

World Economic Forum (WEF). (2024). *World Economic Forum Global Risks Perception Survey* 2023–2024. Retrieved from https://www3.weforum.org/docs/WEF_The_Global_Risks_Report_2024.pdf

World Health Organization (WHO). (2019). *The WHO Special Initiative for Mental Health (2019–2023): Universal health coverage for mental health.* Retrieved from https://www.who.int/publications/i/item/WHO-MSD-19.1

World Health Organization (WHO). (2020a, April 29). *Doing what matters in times of stress.* Retrieved from https://www.who.int/publications/i/item/9789240003927

World Health Organization (WHO). (2020b, October 7). *Global challenge for movement on mental health kicks off as lack of investment in mental health leaves millions without access to services.* Retrieved from https://www.who.int/news/item/07-10-2020-global-challenge-for-movement-on-mental-health-kicks-off-as-lack-of-investment-in-mental-health-leaves-millions-without-access-to-services

Wright, T. A., & Hobfoll, S. E. (2004). Commitment, psychological well-being, and job performance: An examination of conservation of resources (COR) theory and job burnout. *Journal of Business and Management, 9*(4), 375–400.

Youssef-Morgan, C. M., & Luthans, F. (2013). Psychological capital theory: Toward a positive holistic model. In A. B. Bakker (Ed.), *Advances in positive organizational psychology* (pp. 145–166). Emerald Group: Leeds, England. https://doi.org/10.1108/S2046-410X(2013)0000001009

Youssef-Morgan, C. M., & Luthans, F. (2015). Psychological capital and well-being. *Stress and Health: Journal of the International Society for the Investigation of Stress, 31*(3), 180–188. https://doi.org/10.1002/smi.2623

Youssef-Morgan, C.M., & Stratman, J. (2016). Psychological capital: Developing resilience by leveraging the 'Hero' within leaders. In M. Crane (Ed.), *Managing for resilience: A practical guide to individual well-being and organizational performance* (pp. 53–68). Taylor & Francis: Milton Park, UK.

3

POSITIVE ORGANIZATIONAL SCHOLARSHIP

An Introduction

Kim Cameron

Key Concepts

Positive organizational scholarship (POS) is an umbrella concept used to unify a variety of approaches in organizational studies, each of which incorporates the notion of "the positive".[1] In previously published work, POS has been associated with life-giving dynamics, optimal functioning, collective strengths, human flourishing, especially positive outcomes of organizations and their members. Concepts such as excellence, thriving, flourishing, abundance, resilience, and virtuousness are associated with the processes, dynamics, and outcomes of organizations (Cameron, 2022; Cameron & Spreitzer, 2012; Cameron, Dutton, & Quinn, 2003).

The three concepts that denote the focus of POS were deliberately selected and are important in elucidating the uniqueness of POS as a field of study. The "O" (organizational) and the "S" (scholarship) are relatively noncontroversial concepts. The "P" (positive), however, is more contentious and requires more explanation.

Organizational

POS differs from the bulk of positive psychological research in that it explicitly focuses on *organizational* dynamics, or on the work context in which people operate. It examines positive phenomena within organizations as well as positive organizational contexts themselves. POS draws from the full spectrum of organizational theories to understand, explain, and predict the occurrence, causes, and consequences of positivity not so much within individuals' psyches as in the organizational milieu.

POS expands the boundaries of traditional organizational theories to make visible positive states, positive processes, and positive relationships that are typically

DOI: 10.4324/9781032619385-3

ignored within organizational studies. For example, POS research spotlighted how the virtuousness of organizations is associated with financial performance in the context of downsizing, in contrast to a more typical focus on how organizations try to mitigate the harmful effects of downsizing (Cameron, Mora, Leutscher, & Calarco, 2011). POS research examined organizational practices that enable work meaningfulness through crafting a sense of calling in contrast to a more typical focus on employee productivity or morale (Berg, Wrzesniewski, & Dutton, 2010). And, POS research highlighted how building collective efficacy accounts for more positive outcomes in educational institutions than do demographic, ethnic, or socio-economic factors (Goddard & Salloum, 2012).

As this sampling of studies implies, a POS lens exposes new or different mechanisms through which positive organizational dynamics and positive organizational processes produce extraordinarily positive or unexpected outcomes. At the same time, POS purposely illuminates how contexts and processes, and their interactions, are related to positive states in individuals, groups, and organizations.

Scholarship

There is no lack of self-help resources that advocate relatively simplistic and uncomplicated prescriptions for achieving happiness, fulfillment, or effectiveness. A variety of books describing parables, inspirational stories, personal experiences, and commonsense principles for success have become best-sellers. What is lacking in most of these contributions, however, is empirical credibility and theoretical explanations for how and why the prescriptions work. Further, these more prescriptive accounts do not speak to the contingencies regarding when the directives will produce the desired results and when they won't. Having a foundation in the scientific method is the basis upon which most concepts, relationships, and prescriptions develop staying power. Intellectual fads come and go, and usually it is the scientific foundation that creates longevity and continuing impact.

POS does not stand in opposition to the array of self-help publications, but it extends beyond them in its desire to develop rigorous, systematic, and theory-based foundations for positive phenomena. POS requires careful definitions of terms, a rationale for prescriptions and recommendations, consistency with scientific procedures in drawing conclusions, and grounding in previous related work. It is also important to point out that an interest in POS implies a commitment to the full spectrum of activities involved in scholarship. This includes the practical application of this knowledge in organizations, interventions to help organizations achieve extraordinary success, and the dissemination of knowledge in classrooms and training facilities.

Positive

The most controversial concept associated with POS is the "P"—*positive.* Most of the misunderstandings and criticisms of POS have centered on this concept, creating controversy in organizational studies and spawning both skeptics and advocates. A review of dictionary definitions of "positive" reveals that the concept has such a wide range of connotations and so many applications that it defies establishing precise conceptual boundaries (e.g., *Webster's*, *Oxford*, *American Heritage*, *Dictionary.com*). Literally scores of meanings are offered. Experiencing the positive—like experiencing love or leadership—often serves as the basis for its meaning.

On the other hand, some convergence on the meaning of "positive" has begun to emerge as the term has been employed in organizational scholarship over the past decade. The convergence can be summarized in four approaches which help specify the domain of "positive" as applied to organizational phenomena. Identifying these themes helps provide a conceptual explanation of what "positive" means in the context of POS.

One approach to "positive" is adopting *a unique lens or an alternative perspective*. Adopting a POS lens means that the interpretation of phenomena is altered. For example, challenges and obstacles are reinterpreted as opportunities and strength-building experiences rather than as tragedies or problems. Variables not previously recognized or seriously considered in organizational scholarship become central, such as positive energy, moral capital, flow, inspiration, compassion, elevation, and callings (see Cameron & Spreitzer, 2012). Adopting a POS lens means that adversities and difficulties reside as much in the domain of POS as do celebrations and successes, but a positive lens focuses attention on the life-giving elements or generative processes associated with these phenomena. It is the positive perspective—not the nature of the phenomena—that draws an issue into the POS domain.

A second consensual approach to the concept of "positive" is *a focus on extraordinarily positive outcomes or positively deviant performance*. This means that outcomes are investigated that dramatically exceed common or expected performance. Investigating spectacular results, surprising outcomes, and extraordinary achievements have been the focus of several investigations with each treating "positive" as synonymous with exceptional performance. Reaching a level of positive deviance, in other words, extends beyond achieving effectiveness or ordinary success. For example, the closure and clean-up of the Rocky Flats Nuclear arsenal exceeded federal standards by a factor of 13, 60 years ahead of schedule, and $30 billion under budget (Cameron & Lavine, 2006).

A third area of convergence regarding the term "positive" is its focus on *an affirmative bias that fosters resourcefulness*. POS accepts the premise that positivity unlocks and elevates resources in individuals, groups, and organizations, so that capabilities are broadened and capacity is built and strengthened (Fredrickson, 2009). "Resourcefulness" means that individuals and organizations experience an amplifying effect when exposed to positivity, such that resources and capacity expand (Fredrickson & Joiner, 2002). All living systems have a heliotropic inclination toward positive energy (Cameron, 2021), so that, indeed, positivity is life-giving. Adopting an affirmative bias, therefore, prioritizes positive energy, positive climate, positive relationships, positive communication, and positive meaning in organizations (Cameron, 2021), as well as the value embedded in difficult challenges or negative events (Cameron & Lavine, 2006).

POS is unapologetic in emphasizing affirmative attributes, capabilities, and possibilities more than problems, threats, and weakness, so that strengths-based activities and outcomes are highlighted (Clifton & Harter, 2003). Again, an affirmative approach does not exclude considering negative events. Rather, these are incorporated in accounting for life-giving dynamics, generating resources, and flourishing outcomes (e.g., Dutton, Worline, Frost, & Lilius, 2006; Dutton & Glynn, 2007).

A fourth area of convergence regarding the concept of the positive is *the examination of virtuousness or the best of the human condition.* POS is based on a eudemonic assumption—that is, the postulation that an inclination exists in all human systems toward achieving the highest aspirations of humankind. POS research examines the development and the effects associated with virtuousness and eudemonism (Bright, Cameron, & Caza, 2006; Cameron, 2021), or "that which is good in itself and is to be chosen for its own sake" (Aristotle, *Metaphysics XII*, p. 3). Studies of virtuousness *in* organizations focus, for example, on individuals' behaviors in organizational settings that help others flourish, including investigating character strengths, gratitude, wisdom, forgiveness, hope, and courage (Grant & Schwartz, 2011). Studies of virtuousness *through* organizations focus on practices and processes in organizations that represent and perpetuate what is good, right, and worthy of cultivation (Park & Peterson, 2003). This includes, for example, investigating profound purpose and transcendent objectives, healing routines, institutionalized forgiveness, and human sustainability (Cameron, Dutton, & Quinn, 2003; Cameron & Spreitzer, 2012).

These four convergent uses of the concept of "positive"—adopting a positive lens, investigating extraordinarily positive performance, espousing an affirmative bias, and exploring virtuousness—do not precisely *define* the term "positive" per se, but they do identify the scholarly domain that POS scholars are attempting to map. Like other concepts in organizational science that do not have precisely bounded definitions (e.g., culture, innovation, core competence), this mapping provides the conceptual boundaries required to locate POS as an area of inquiry.

Emergence

Unlike positive psychology, POS did not emerge as an attempt to rebalance the prodigious emphasis on illness and languishing in organizations. Organizational research has not been focused overwhelmingly on failure, damage, and demise. In fact, studying organizational decline was first introduced in organizational studies in 1980 because most organizational theories focused almost exclusively on growth. Big was assumed to be better than small; getting more was preferable to getting less. Negative phenomena did not dominate organizational studies literature as it did in psychology, even though plenty of attention had been paid to alienation, stress, injustice, and the evils of bureaucracy in traditional organizational studies (e.g., Weber, 1997).

Rather, POS arose because an array of organizational phenomena was being ignored; consequently, such phenomena were neither systematically studied nor valued. It was usually not considered legitimate in scientific circles, for example, to discuss the effects of virtues in organizations or to use terms such as "flourishing" or "positive deviance" to describe outcomes. Studies of organizational compassion, forgiveness, energy, gratitude, courage, and kindness certainly diverged from the mainstream of organizational science.

POS also arose because the outcome variables that dominated the organization literature focused mainly on profitability, competitive advantage, problem solving, and economic efficiency. Granted, outcomes such as job satisfaction, justice, and teamwork have appeared frequently in the organizational studies literature, but alternative outcomes such as psychological, social, and eudemonic well-being (Keyes, 2005)—including social integration, social contribution, social coherence, social actualization, and social acceptance—as well as human sustainability, were largely outside the purview of mainline organizational science. The best of the human condition—what people care about deeply and profoundly—was almost invisible in organizational scholarship.

Criticisms

The legitimacy of POS as a field of scientific study is by no means universally accepted, and three primary criticisms of POS have been promoted: (a) POS ignores negative phenomena, (b) POS adopts an elitist (managerial) viewpoint, and (c) POS may not be the same for everyone, and the concepts and phenomena associated with POS are fuzzy terms that lack construct and discriminant validity and careful measurement.

One criticism is that POS ignores issues such as conflict, poverty, exploitation, unemployment, war, and other negative circumstances that are typical of the human condition and are commonplace in organizational functioning. Positivity is equated with being Pollyannaish and simply "putting on a happy face" in the midst or serious problems and challenges. Some authors, such as Ehrenreich (2009), for example, find little that is positive in POS, claiming that positivity unrealistically assumes unremitting growth and guaranteed success in organizations, excuses excess and folly, denies reality, mitigates against hard work, implies pride and boastfulness, avoids difficult questions, invites unpreparedness, assumes that all success is deserved, and leads to "reckless optimism" and "delusional thinking" (Ehrenreich, 2009, p. 13). Little evidence exists, according to its critics, that positivity fosters success (Ehrenreich, 2009; Hackman, 2009).

To be sure, empirical evidence exists that individually bad is stronger than good (Baumeister, Bratslavsky, Finkenauer, & Vohs, 2001), that is, human beings react more strongly and more quickly to negative phenomena than to positive phenomena because existence is threatened. When equal measures of good and bad are present, the psychological effects of the bad outweigh those of the good. It is inaccurate, however, to argue that POS ignores negative phenomena inasmuch as some of the greatest triumphs, most noble virtues, and highest achievements have resulted from the presence of the negative (e.g., Cameron & Lavine, 2006). Common human experience and abundant scientific evidence supports the idea that negativity has an important place in investigating positive processes and outcomes. Developing positive identities in negative environments, organizational healing after trauma, and achieving virtuous outcomes in the face of trials exemplify cases in which negative conditions have been investigated with a POS lens (Powley & Cameron, 2006). POS does not ignore the negative; instead, it seeks to investigate the positive processes, outcomes, and interpretations embedded in negative phenomena.

A second criticism of POS is that it adopts an elitist perspective. Critics claim that POS is oriented toward exploiting human beings in favor of corporate profits and productivity and maintaining power for the advantaged over the disadvantaged. Perpetuating the positive for the sake of organizational success, to make managers look good, to manipulate the workforce, or to reinforce unequal employment status are common criticisms (e.g., Ehrenreich, 2009; Fineman, 2006). These critiques fundamentally center on the claim that POS narrowly focuses on managers rather than on the exploited underclass. Detractors accuse POS of not asking the question, "Positive for whom?" and suggest that unexamined assumptions are biased toward Western philosophies and toward power elites.

On the other hand, this criticism seems to miss the unequivocally stated focus of POS on life-giving dynamics, generating resources, and flourishing outcomes whether for workers or managers, the underclass or the upper class, the individual or the organization (e.g., Cameron, Dutton, & Quinn, 2003; Cameron & Spreitzer, 2012). The fundamental assumption of POS is a eudaemonic one: all human systems are biased toward achieving the highest aspirations of humankind or excellence and goodness for its own sake. Adopting an affirmative bias prioritizes positive energy, positive climate, positive relationships, positive communication, and positive meaning for individuals and for organizations. Indeed, exploitation that allows one party to achieve advantage over another is inconsistent with the fundamental assumptions of POS. Thus, the answer to "Positivity for whom?" is not exclusive.

Positive energy, flourishing relationships, empowerment, and virtuousness all represent non-zero-sum dynamics that benefit all parties. Moreover, abundant research has examined cultural differences regarding positive phenomena, including employee well-being in more than 50 countries and has identified universal attributes and predictors, as well as unique cultural differences across a wide variety of cultures. Non-Western cultures are well-represented in POS research (see Cameron, 2021).

A third criticism of POS is that a precise definition of the term "positive" is lacking. Positive is experienced subjectively, such that what may be positive for one person is not necessarily positive for another. What is defined as "good" or "ennobling" may be individualistic. Imposing a definition of positive on others is an act of power and, therefore, is, by definition, non-positive (Caza & Carroll, 2012). Moreover, other related terms used in POS research lack precise definition and scientific validity.

Of course, many core scientific terms are the subjects of investigation, measurement, and theory-building without precise definitions. Well-used and frequently discussed terms such as "life", "effectiveness", and "quality" are examples, none of which has been precisely and consensually defined. These terms are considered to be "constructs", meaning they are terms constructed to capture the meaning of something that is ambiguous and difficult to circumscribe precisely. In such circumstances, investigators artificially constrain the meaning or dimensions of the construct in order to examine certain aspects of it. The key is to be precise about what is and is not included in measuring the construct. Individualistic definitions are addressed, therefore, by defining the term scientifically and precisely in scholarly investigations.

Constructs such as "thriving", "virtuousness", "positive emotions", "meaningfulness", "energy", "best-self", "resilience", "positive deviance", and others have been defined quite carefully in POS investigations. Thus, mapping the conceptual terrain of "positive" is not so much an act of exclusion, therefore, as a scientific necessity in order for cumulative work to be conducted and for the nomological network surrounding the constructs to expand. Some progress has been made in this regard, although much is left to be done.

Advances

The progress or advancements in POS research can be highlighted by a review of a small sampling of empirical studies that have been published. No summary of POS research can capture the breadth and core themes of all the work being done, of course, but an examination of the empirical literature has uncovered a set of themes that describe several of the main thrusts.

The irony in many of these findings is that, by definition, positive practices do not need to produce traditionally pursued organizational outcomes in order to be of worth. An increase in profitability, for example, is not the criterion for determining the value of positivity in organizations. Positivity is inherently valued because it is eudemonic and heliotropic. Nevertheless, studies have shown that organizations in several industries (including financial services, health care, manufacturing, education, and government) that implemented and improved their positive practices over time also increased their performance in desired outcomes such as profitability, productivity, quality, customer satisfaction, and employee retention.

Positive practices that were institutionalized in organizations—including providing compassionate support for employees, forgiving mistakes and avoiding blame, fostering the meaningfulness of work, expressing frequent gratitude, showing kindness, and caring for colleagues—led organizations to perform at significantly higher levels on desired outcomes than most organizations. Examples of these studies are briefly summarized below.

Positive Management Practices

Aggregating data from 182 companies in Germany, Becker (2024) measured eight positive management practices (PMP) and their associations with firm profitability. The PMP were derived from 14,722 written reviews of employees' descriptions of their own supervisors, and eight clusters emerged: respectful interaction (gratitude, humility), open communication (truthfulness, forgiveness), interpersonal support (compassion, friendliness), reasonable instructions (meaning, inspiration), intellectual support (caring, wisdom), managerial competence (courage, prudence). Profitability was defined as operating profit (earning divided by sales) in the 182 firms. Several statistical tests were conducted to investigate not only the predictive associations among variables but also to ensure a causal relationship rather than a mere association.

The results of the analyses revealed that PMP was a significant predictor of firm profitability, with respectful interactions being the most powerful dimension. "Overall, the findings indicate that PMP and respectful have an effect on operating profitability rather than vice versa" (p. 297). A direct impact of PMP was also found on employee emotions and satisfaction.

Individual Virtue and Social Concern

A survey study of white-collar workers examined the relationship linking hope, gratitude, and responsibility (Andersson, Giacalone, & Jurkiewicz, 2007). Hope was defined as a motivational state of felt agency, as the belief that one could achieve a desirable effect. Gratitude was a moral affective state, in which the individual feels motivated toward prosocial behavior, to "give back" in return for whatever caused the feeling of gratitude. In this study, the researchers found that gratitude led to greater feelings of responsibility for employees and social issues if high hope was present. That is, if individuals felt both grateful and hopeful, then they also felt greater responsibility for other members of the organization and for extra-organizational social matters.

Leadership

There have been several investigations of the role of POS phenomena in explaining leadership. Bono and Ilies (2006) described a series of studies showing that leaders who express more positive emotions engender the same emotions in followers, who then perceive that leader as more charismatic and effective. Similarly, another study found that Army leaders who expressed more vision and love for their troops foster greater well-being, commitment, and productivity among followers (Fry, Vitucci, & Cedillo, 2005). In the fast-food industry, leader hope has been linked to follower satisfaction and retention (Peterson & Luthans, 2003).

Organizational Virtuousness

A number of studies have examined virtuousness as an organizational phenomenon. For example, one study described how members of a business school were able to redirect existing organizational systems to support compassionate responses to individual tragedy (Dutton, Worline, Frost, & Lilius, 2006). One study within a health care network showed how units that were supportive of their members' spirituality produced higher levels of customer satisfaction (Duchon & Plowman, 2005). Another study, among Dutch sales staff, found that pride was a source of self-worth, motivation, creativity, and altruism, and thus led to higher levels of adaptive selling, individual effort, self-efficacy, and citizenship behavior (Verbeke, Belschak, & Bagozzi, 2004). Consistent with both of these studies, Cameron and colleagues (2004, 2011) used organizational forgiveness, trust, optimism, compassion, and integrity to predict measures of innovation, quality, turnover, customer retention, and profitability. They found that virtuous practices in two different industries—financial services firms and health care organizations—strongly predicted desired outcomes. In financial services, firms that improved the most in virtuous practices also achieved the highest levels of profitability, productivity, engagement, and employee and customer retention two years later compared to firms that did not improve or that improved the least. A similar result was detected among health care organizations. Double-digit improvement was produced on a dozen dimensions of health care effectiveness in units that scored highest in virtuous practices and that improved the most in implementing these practices. In a related paper, Bright and colleagues (2006) found that leaders who took responsibility for the disruptive effects of downsizing received more forgiveness from followers, and this forgiveness reduced the performance losses usually created by downsizing. These studies all suggest that virtuous behaviors were manifest as a collective, organizational phenomenon.

Positive Relationships and Performance

Relationships are another important source of potential performance benefits investigated by POS. A study of the airline industry found that carriers with better interpersonal relations showed greater resilience in the post-9/11 economy. Airlines with better internal relations had lower costs, fewer layoffs, and quicker recovery to pre-9/11 stock prices (Gittell, Cameron, Lim, & Rivas, 2006). Similarly, an ethnographic study of a midwifery practice showed how that practice's emphasis on social relationships and humanistic values benefited patient service and staff development (Wooten & Crane, 2004). And in a study of management teams, Losada and Heaphy (2004) found that the highest performing teams on unit profitability, customer satisfaction, and 360-degree evaluations were characterized by more positive communication and interpersonal connection among members.

Energy

Owens, Baker, and Cameron (2012) investigated the positive energy displayed by unit leaders in a variety of business units. Several forms of energy exist, such as physical energy, emotional energy, and mental energy. With each of these forms of energy, their use creates a diminishing of energy. People become exhausted after expending physical or emotional energy, for example. This study assessed relational energy, defined as the uplifting, motivational, and life-giving influence leaders have on employees. The study showed that positively energizing leaders had a significant, positive impact on individuals—including their performance, engagement, well-being, satisfaction, and even family life—as well as on the organization's performance, teamwork, innovation, and learning orientation. Positive energy in leaders was a far more predictive factor than power position or information centrality in the organization.

Application

Unfortunately, there has been relatively little formal study of the effect of POS interventions in organizations. This is primarily due to the constraints of detecting effects from planned organizational interventions while controlling for possible confounds. However, some reports have been made, with results suggesting that POS in practice is associated with higher levels of performance.

For example, Cameron and Lavine (2006) studied the exceptional performance of a company that cleaned up and closed a nuclear production facility 60 years ahead of schedule, $30 billion under budget, and to standards 13 times greater than the federal standard. This was arguably the most remarkable example of organizational success in recent memory. More than three million square feet of buildings had to be decontaminated and removed, over 100 tons of plutonium residues had to be neutralized and disposed of, and numerous protesters had to be converted into supporters and advocates. During the clean-up, union members were motivated to work themselves out of a job as quickly as possible, an approach contradictory to traditional union priorities, while maintaining levels of morale and safety that exceeded industry averages by a factor of two. Cameron and Lavine (2006) explained this remarkable performance as a product of 21 different positive organizational practices.

A set of POS interventions is described in an interview with the CEO of one of the Prudential Financial Services companies. This senior executive reported that his entire business strategy was driven by a reliance on the principles and practices associated with POS, and his business turned around from a $140 million loss to a $20 million profit in a period of just over a year (Cameron & Plews, 2012).

Another study reported by Grant (2007) found that the perceived meaningfulness of work could be enhanced by personal interaction with recipients of services. Workers who had direct contact with the beneficiaries of their work subsequently displayed almost three times more task persistence. These workers also had significantly greater productivity in routine tasks, producing more than one and a half times the output of those who did not have contact with beneficiaries.

This small sample of applications provides support for the benefits of POS-related practices in real-world work settings. As yet, however, not enough is known to draw firm conclusions regarding the what, how, or when of such interventions, but there is growing evidence that practices based on POS benefit individuals and organizations.

Summary

To repeat, POS is not value-neutral. It advocates the position that the desire to improve the human condition is universal and that the capacity to do so is latent in most systems. The means by which this latent capacity is unleashed and organized, the extent to which human possibilities are enabled, and the extent to which systems produce extraordinarily positive outcomes are of special interest. POS does not exclude phenomena that are typically labeled negative in organizational studies—such as competitive pressures, downsizing, stressful circumstances, or financial losses—but it has a bias toward life-giving, generative, and ennobling human conditions and addresses traditional negative phenomena with a positive lens.

POS offers a unique conceptual foundation for understanding how and why organizational strategies have their effects on human behavior in the workplace, and why some strategies and practices are more generative than others. An important function of POS, therefore, is to provide more attention to the processes and practices that unleash heliotropic effects and elevate resourcefulness. Empirical evidence suggests that when positive factors are given greater emphases than negative factors, individuals and organizations tend to flourish.

Research on POS has begun to explain variance that has largely been ignored in previous investigations of organizations. Processes and attributes are highlighted that have received little attention in previous organizational research—including virtuousness, positive energy networks, and high-quality connections. Adopting a positive lens illuminates research questions and relationships that have been under-investigated and frequently ignored. Thus, POS provides fertile territory for understanding the mechanisms and the outcomes associated with the naturally occurring but seldom examined inclination toward the positive in organizations.

Note

1 This chapter borrows from other works by the author, including Cameron (2022), Cameron and Spreitzer (2012), Caza and Cameron (2008).

References

Andersson, L. M., Giacalone, R. A., & Jurkiewicz, C. L. (2007). On the relationship of hope and gratitude to corporate social responsibility. *Journal of Business Ethics, 70*, 401–409.

Aristotle, Metaphysics XII, 7, 3–4. (written 350 BC.) Translated by Ross, W.D.

Baumeister,R.F.,Bratslavsky,E.,Finkenauer,C.,&Vohs,K.D.(2001).Badisstrongerthangood. *Review of General Psychology, 5*(4), 323–370.

Becker, M. (2024). The effect of positive management practices in firm profitability: Evidence from text mining. *Journal of Applied Behavioral Science, 60*, 280–309.

Berg, J. M., Wrzesniewski, A., & Dutton, J. E. (2010). Perceiving and responding to challenges in job crafting at different ranks: When proactivity requires adaptivity. *Journal of Organizational Behavior, 31*, 158–186.

Bono, J. E. & Ilies, R. (2006). Charisma, positive emotion and mood contagion. *Leadership Quarterly, 17*, 317–334.

Bright, D. S., Cameron, K. S., & Caza, A. (2006). The amplifying and buffering effects of virtuousness in downsized organizations. *Journal of Business Ethics, 64*, 249–269.

Cameron, K. S. (2021). *Positively energizing leadership*. San Francisco: Berrett Koehler.

Cameron, K. S. (2022). Responsible leadership as virtuous leadership. In N. M. Pless & T. Maak (Eds.), *Responsible leadership*. (2nd edition, Chapter 8: pp. 133–153). New York: Routledge.

Cameron, K. S., Bright, D. S., & Caza, A. (2004). Exploring the relationships between organizational virtuousness and performance. *American Behavioral Scientist, 47*, 766–790.

Cameron, K. S., Dutton, J. E., & Quinn, R. E. (2003). *Positive organizational scholarship: Foundations of a new discipline*. San Francisco: Berrett-Koehler.

Cameron, K. S. & Lavine, M. (2006). *Making the impossible possible: Leading extraordinary performance—The Rocky Flats story*. San Francisco: Berrett-Koehler.

Cameron, K. S., Mora, C. E., Leutscher, T., & Calarco, M. (2011). Effects of positive practices on organizational effectiveness. *Journal of Applied Behavioral Science, 47*, 266–308.

Cameron, K. S. & Plews, E. (2012). Positive leadership in action: Applications of POS by Jim Mallozzi. *Organizational Dynamics, 41*, 99–105.

Cameron, K. S. & Spreitzer, G. M. (2012.) *Oxford handbook of positive organizational scholarship*. New York: Oxford University Press.

Caza, A. and Cameron, K.S., 2008. Positive organizational scholarship: What does it achieve. In Cary L. Cooper & Stewart Clegg (Eds.), *Handbook of macro-organizational behavior* (pp. 99-116) New York: Sage.

Caza, A. & Carroll, B. (2012). Critical theory and positive organizational scholarship. In K. S. Cameron & G. M. Spreitzer (Eds.), *Oxford handbook of positive organizational scholarship* (pp. 965–978). New York: Oxford University Press.

Clifton, D. O. & Harter, J. K. (2003). Investing in strengths. In K. S. Cameron, J. E. Dutton & R. E. Quinn (Eds.), *Positive organizational scholarship: Foundations of a new discipline* (pp. 111–121). San Francisco: Berrett-Koehler.

Duchon, D. & Plowman, D. A. (2005). Nurturing the spirit at work: Impact on work unit performance. *Leadership Quarterly, 16*, 807–833.

Dutton, J. E. & Glynn, M. (2007). Positive organizational scholarship. In C. Cooper & J. Barling (Eds.), *Handbook of organizational behavior* (pp. 1–28). Thousand Oaks: Sage.

Dutton, J. E., Worline, M. C., Frost, P. J., & Lilius, J. M. (2006). Explaining compassion organizing. *Administrative Science Quarterly, 51*, 59–96.

Ehrenreich, B. (2009). *Bright-sided: How positive thinking is undermining America*. New York: Henry Holt.

Fineman, S. (2006). On being positive: Concerns and counterpoints. *Academy of Management Review, 31*(2), 270–291.

Fredrickson, B. M. (2009). *Positivity*. New York: Crown.

Fredrickson, B. L. & Joiner, T. (2002). Positive emotions trigger upward spirals toward emotional well-being. *American Psychologist, 13*, 172–175.

Fry, L. W., Vitucci, S., & Cedillo, M. (2005). Spiritual leadership and army transformation: Theory, measurement, and establishing a baseline. *Leadership Quarterly, 16*, 835–862.

Gittell, J. H., Cameron, K., Lim, S., & Rivas, V. (2006). Relationships, layoffs, and organizational resilience: Airline industry responses to September 11. *The Journal of Applied Behavioral Science, 42*(3), 300–328.

Goddard, R. D. & Salloum, S. J. (2012) Collective efficacy beliefs, organizational excellence, and leadership. In K. S. Cameron & G. M. Spreitzer (Eds.), *Oxford handbook of positive organizational scholarship* (pp. 642–650). New York: Oxford University Press.

Grant, A. M. (2007). Relational job design and the motivation to make a prosocial difference. *Academy of Management Journal, 32*(2), 393–417.

Grant, A. M., & Schwartz, B. (2011). Too much of a good thing: The challenge and opportunity of the inverted U. *Perspectives on Psychological Science, 6*(1), 61–76. https://doi.org/10.1177/1745691610393523

Hackman, J. R. (2009). The perils of positivity. *Journal of Organizational Behavior, 30*, 309–319.

Keyes, C. L. M. (2005). Mental illness and/or mental health? Investigating axioms of the complete state model of health. *Journal of Consulting and Clinical Psychology, 73*, 539–548.

Losada, M. & Heaphy, E. (2004). The role of positivity and connectivity in the performance of business teams: A nonlinear dynamics model. *American Behavioral Scientist, 47*(6), 740–765.

Owens, B., Baker, W., & Cameron, K. (2012). Relational energy at work: Establishing construct, nomological, and predictive validity. Working paper, Ross School of Business, University of Michigan.

Park, N. & Peterson, C. M. (2003). Virtues and organizations. In K. S. Cameron, J. E. Dutton & R. E. Quinn (Eds.), *Positive organizational scholarship: Foundations of a new discipline* (pp. 33–47). San Francisco: Berrett Koehler.

Peterson, S. J. & Luthans, F. (2003). The positive impact and development of hopeful leaders. *Leadership and Organization Development Journal, 24*(1), 26–31.

Powley, E. H. & Cameron, K. S. (2006). Organizational healing: Lived virtuousness amidst organizational crisis. *Journal of Management, Spirituality, and Religion, 3*, 13–33.

Verbeke, W., Belschak, F., & Bagozzi, R. P. (2004). The adaptive consequences of pride in personal selling. *Academy of Marketing Science Journal, 32*(4), 386–402.

Weber, M. (1997). *The theory of social and economic organization*. New York: Free Press.

Wooten, L. P. & Crane, P. (2004). Generating dynamic capabilities through a humanistic work ideology: The case of a certified-nurse midwife practice in a professional bureaucracy. *American Behavioral Scientist, 47*(6), 848–866.

4

WIND OF CHANGE

Promising Work Engagement Interventions

Arnold B. Bakker and Tom L. Junker

When employees are engaged, they feel active, full of energy, are dedicated toward their tasks, and are often completely immersed in their work activities (Schaufeli & Bakker, 2023). This motivational state prepares workers to invest considerable physical, emotional, and mental effort in their work. Indeed, reviews and meta-analyses indicate that work engagement is positively related to creativity, prosocial behavior, task performance, and productivity (Bakker et al., 2023; Christian et al., 2011). Moreover, work engagement is negatively related to safety incidents, medical mistakes, and absenteeism (Prins et al., 2009; Schaufeli et al., 2009; Wachter & Yorio, 2014). Since work engagement is such an important determinant of employee functioning, it is crucial that we try to promote engagement among employees who struggle and sustain engagement among those who flourish.

In the present chapter, we discuss promising work engagement interventions. While some of these interventions have received considerable empirical support, other interventions are potentially promising but need further validation. This is an emerging field, in which engagement scholars have just started to develop and evaluate theory-based interventions. We discuss five different levels of intervention: (a) organizational level, (b) team level, (c) job level, (d) person level, and (e) activity level. Next to top-down job design approaches, these interventions include agile work practices, and focus on job crafting, personal resources, strengths use, proactive vitality management, and playful work design. We position each of these approaches in Job Demands–Resources (JD-R) theory (Bakker et al., 2023; Demerouti & Bakker, 2023) and discuss how the interventions and their blends can blow a wind of organizational change.

DOI: 10.4324/9781032619385-4

Work Engagement in JD-R Theory

Work engagement was introduced in the organizational and management literatures at the turn of the century (Schaufeli & Bakker, 2023). Although various definitions of work engagement exist, most definitions include a physical component (vigor, energy), an affective-motivational component (dedication, enthusiasm), and a cognitive component (concentration, absorption) (e.g., Rothbard, 2001; May et al., 2004). The work engagement concept quickly became popular since it was found to be a better predictor of job performance than job satisfaction (Christian et al., 2011; Mackay et al., 2017). Scholars have used various frameworks to predict engagement, but the most popular framework is arguably JD-R theory. For recent overviews and extensions, we refer to Bakker et al. (2023) and Demerouti and Bakker (2023). JD-R theory can predict a range of well-being indicators (ranging from strain to motivation), but for the purpose of the present chapter we focus on work engagement. Accordingly, work engagement is most likely when employees face challenging job demands and have access to a large pool of job and personal resources.

Challenge job demands are all facets of the job that cost considerable effort, but also offer opportunities for mastery and performance. Examples are task complexity, high responsibility, and deadlines. On the days employees are challenged, they stretch their skills and invest themselves fully in their work – fostering work engagement. Whether job demands are challenging is often influenced by subjective interpretation (Bakker & Sanz-Vergel, 2013). Job resources are all facets of the job that have motivating potential, facilitate learning and help deal with job demands (Bakker et al., 2023). Examples are social support and skill variety. When employees can collaborate well with their colleagues and use a variety of their skills and talents, they are more likely to feel energized and enthusiastic about their work. Finally, personal resources refer to employees' own cognitions – subjective beliefs regarding how much control they have over their external environment. Examples are optimism and self-efficacy. JD-R theory predicts, for instance, that employees who face a deadline are most likely to be engaged when they have a strong sense of self-efficacy or when there is ample support from others (e.g., Hakanen et al., 2005). It is the combination of job demands and resources that is essential for employee work engagement.

JD-R theory also proposes that employees can proactively influence their job demands and (job and personal) resources (Bakker & Demerouti, 2014). Bindl and Parker (2011) argue that proactive behavior involves self-initiated, anticipatory action aimed at changing either the situation or oneself. Some examples are taking charge to improve work methods, proactive problem solving, and proactive feedback seeking. Employees may also proactively optimize their job design by actively seeking job challenges and job resources. They may commence a new project, start networking, or ask colleagues for feedback and support. Such proactive behaviors are called job crafting – behaviors that can increase person-job fit and facilitate meaningfulness and work engagement (Demerouti & Bakker, 2024). Employees may also identify their personal strengths so that they can start to do what they are naturally good at (Van Woerkom et al., 2016). In this way, they can increase their personal resources, including their self-efficacy, resilience, and optimism (Virga et al., 2023). Personal resources, in turn, help to deal with job demands and foster work engagement (e.g., Bakker et al., 2023; Bakker & Sanz-Vergel, 2013).

Although the focus in this chapter is on work engagement and performance, it is important to also consider that employees may feel stressed and unwell. According to the health impairment hypothesis in JD-R theory (Demerouti & Bakker, 2011), repeated exposure to (severe) job demands will lead to increased levels of strain (e.g., exhaustion, anxiety), which may first lead to minor (e.g., neck pain, stomach aches), and then to more serious health complaints (e.g., Type-2 diabetes, cardiovascular disease). Moreover, based on the theory, employees may enter a loss cycle in which the strain caused by job demands leads to maladaptive and self-undermining behaviors (e.g., making mistakes, creating conflicts) that result in even higher job demands. It is under these unfavorable conditions that employees are most in need of but are least inclined to proactively mobilize their job and personal resources (Bakker & De Vries, 2021; Roczniewska & Bakker, 2021). This is a paradox with important implications for work engagement interventions – as will be discussed in more detail later.

Organizational Level Interventions

Since job design is so important for employee work engagement, several attempts have been made to use organization-level interventions to optimize job demands and resources. A top-down job redesign approach necessitates a collaborative effort from organizational leaders who advocate the intended change and human resources (HR) professionals who enable the change. The redesign project ideally starts with an organization-wide assessment of job characteristics and levels of work engagement (Bakker & Demerouti, 2014). Comparing the mean levels of specific job demands and resources in departments and teams will help identify specific targets for job redesign. HR professionals may discuss job demands and resources in workshops with department and team leaders, and facilitate a discussion of relatively low, medium, or high levels of workload, emotional demands, social support, autonomy, and other demands and resources (Bakker & Demerouti, 2024). In this way, leaders are supported in making an accurate diagnosis of their own teams' job design, which forms the basis for possible interventions.

Holman and Axtell (2016) investigated the impact of a participative job redesign intervention in a call center. Representatives identified the most important tasks and obstacles and generated ideas about how to optimize job demands and resources. Results showed that the experimental job redesign intervention influenced a range of important organizational outcomes (i.e., employee well-being, psychological contract fulfillment, and supervisor-rated job performance) through a change in job characteristics. This study is one of 55 promising organization-led work redesign interventions that were included in the systematic review of Knight and Parker (2021). This review concluded that work design interventions can lead to improvements in job resources, with strong evidence for the effectiveness of participative work redesign interventions (e.g., Holman & Axtell, 2016) and relational interventions (e.g., increasing structural social support; Parker et al., 2013).

Another interesting observation in Knight and Parker's (2021) review is that almost none of the organization-led interventions aimed to reduce job demands. However, in line with JD-R theory, the review suggests that the effects of work redesign interventions are stronger when job demands are high. This was particularly the case for interventions that aimed to increase job autonomy. For example, Cordery and colleagues (2010) found that an intervention that provided teams with more autonomy was especially useful for teams working on tasks with high operational uncertainty. Thus, it appears that organizations can expect larger benefits from work redesign when these interventions consider both job demands and job resources.

Team Level Interventions

A handful of studies have offered support for JD-R theory at the team level. These studies show that higher levels of collective work engagement can be found in groups that provide access to various job resources such as psychological safety (Peeters et al., 2022), psychological contract fulfillment (Laulié et al., in press), or psychological ownership (Martinaityte et al., 2020). Yet, because these studies are correlational and relate team engagement to other emergent psychological states it is unclear whether they can inform interventions to increase work engagement in teams. What could be more useful is to examine collective practices that can be implemented in teams and transform members' shared work experiences in ways that promote energy, enthusiasm, and absorption at work.

To fill this void in the current body of knowledge, Junker et al. (in press) investigated how agile work practices (AWPs) relate to team engagement. They sampled 110 teams at different stages of an agile transformation program in the digital service division of a German railway company. Their findings indicate that when teams make use of AWPs by planning tasks in short "sprint" cycles and approaching goals iteratively, team members experience work engagement more frequently. Agile taskwork practices were particularly useful for teams working on complex assignments (e.g., software development or consulting). Approaching tasks in short iterative goal cycles helps to mobilize cognitive-attentional resources (Lieberum et al., 2022), encourage proactive work behavior (Junker et al., 2022), and establish learning routines within teams (Annosi et al., 2020).

The study of Junker and colleagues (in press) also found that agile teamwork practices such as daily stand-up meetings and retrospective meetings can promote team engagement, albeit only when team role conflict is absent. In addition, the effects of such team reflexivity interventions may be conditional on whether they lead to improvements in resources such as colleague support and job control. This is what an intervention study among 73 manufacturing teams in a Chinese factory suggests. In their nine-week quasi-experimental study, Chen and colleagues (2018) demonstrated that team reflexivity interventions can help to reduce burnout via changes in job resources. Although the study of Chen et al. (2018) did not include work engagement as an outcome, JD-R theory suggests we may find similar effects (i.e., job resources predict work engagement). In sum, AWPs and other reflexive team practices (Junker et al., 2023, 2025) represent promising team-based work engagement interventions, but more research is needed to validate the generalizability of their effects.

Job Level Interventions

Job crafting refers to the proactive changes employees make in their tasks or social relationships at work (Wrzesniewski & Dutton, 2001). Task crafting refers to changing the content of one's tasks or the order in which tasks are carried out. Relational crafting refers to actively changing with whom one interacts at work, for example, spend more time with colleagues one gets along with well. According to Wrzesniewski and Dutton, employees may also change their perspective of their job (i.e., cognitive crafting). However, to date, most research has used the JD-R approach of job crafting, which proposes that employees can proactively optimize their job demands and resources (Tims & Bakker, 2010). Thus, employees who experience a misfit between their abilities or preferences and the requirements of work may optimize their job demands or try to seek new challenges (e.g., start a new project, take more responsibilities). In a similar vein, employees who want to satisfy their basic psychological needs of autonomy and relatedness may negotiate decision latitude and proactively ask for feedback and social support (Bakker & Oerlemans, 2019). Studies using the JD-R approach of job crafting have shown that job crafting is related to improved job demands and resources (Holman et al., 2024). By improving their job demands and resources, individuals increase their own work engagement, creativity, and performance (Demerouti & Bakker, 2024). Vogt et al. (2016) also found that job crafting is prospectively related to increases in personal resources (i.e., psychological capital).

Intervention studies have provided further evidence for these effects and indicate that job crafting has a causal impact on work design and work engagement. For example, Gordon et al. (2018) conducted two intervention studies in a Dutch hospital and found that nurses and medical specialists were more likely to use job crafting after the training intervention. Consequently, they increased their well-being (work engagement, health, reduced exhaustion), and job performance (i.e., adaptive, task, and contextual performance) relative to the control groups. In a similar vein, Van Wingerden et al. (2016, 2017a, 2017b) showed in a series of studies among teachers that job crafting interventions had a positive impact on personal resources, basic need satisfaction, work engagement, and job performance. A recent meta-analysis of 14 job crafting intervention studies (Oprea et al., 2019) showed that employees can learn to proactively increase their own job challenges and resources and reduce their hindrance job demands. The job crafting behaviors, in turn, contributed to higher levels of work engagement and improved contextual performance.

Person Level Interventions

Personal Resources

Personal resources encompass the individual beliefs individuals hold regarding how much control they can exercise over their work environment (Hobfoll et al., 2003). These personal resources include optimism, self-efficacy, resilience, and self-esteem (Xanthopoulou et al., 2009). When employees are optimistic, they expect that the best will happen, and they are more likely to use an approach orientation to job demands. When employees feel resilient and self-efficacious, they feel that they can effectively handle complex work problems and requests of demanding clients – they have the psychological resources to turn these job demands into a challenge.

Several studies have shown that personal resources can be increased through training interventions. For example, while the effect size was modest, a study by Luthans et al. (2008) demonstrated that a brief two-hour web-based training could enhance personal resources like hope, self-efficacy, optimism, and resilience, collectively referred to as "psychological capital." Employing a more intense approach, Demerouti et al. (2011) revealed that a personal effectiveness intervention involving four 3-hour group training sessions improved self- and other-assessments of psychological capital and assertiveness. In a comparable vein, Van Wingerden et al. (2017b) showed that a personal resources intervention comprising three 3-hour group training sessions enhanced employees' psychological capital.

JD-R theory proposes that personal resources can be used to deal with job demands (e.g., Bakker & Sanz-Vergel, 2013). Personal resources can also generate new job resources and indirectly foster work engagement. Xanthopoulou et al. (2009) found that employees with higher levels of personal resources reported more job resources over time (e.g., social support and opportunities for growth). Employees who feel confident are more likely to seek job resources and negotiate with their supervisor regarding their training opportunities and the timing of their work. Resourceful employees are therefore more likely to be engaged at work (Knight et al., 2017).

Interventions that directly build personal resources foster work engagement, as individual self-evaluations become more positive. When individuals have a more positive view of themselves, they believe they are able to meet work demands and achieve their goals despite adversity (Bakker et al., 2023). Individuals who have developed a sense of self-efficacy and resilience will persevere and continue to invest themselves in work to achieve their goals (Xanthopoulou et al., 2009).

Moreover, personal resources training enables employees to leverage their strengths and better cope with emotional demands. In this way, they can maintain their work engagement over time (Bakker & Van Wingerden, 2021).

Strengths Use

JD-R theory proposes that employees can also try to discover and more often use their strengths at work (Bakker & Van Woerkom, 2018). Character strengths refer to all the things people are really good at – their natural talents (Wood et al., 2011), such as social skills, creativity, or bravery. When employees use their talent to be creative – also when there are no creativity requirements, they will be better able to solve complex work problems and deal with other demands. An employee who is highly skilled socially could try to more often engage in work tasks that involve interacting with others. In this way, employees can do what they are naturally good at. Strength use implies that one chooses tasks that are a good fit with personal strengths, in this way optimizing job demands and generating personal resources. Using a weekly diary study among engineers, Van Woerkom et al. (2016) found that when engineers used their signature strengths, they were more proactive and self-efficacious, and consequently experienced higher work engagement. Moore et al. (2024) found that when employees used their strengths in the morning, they generated more momentary personal resources (e.g., relatedness, competence) at noon, and consequently performed better in the afternoon.

Many individuals lack self-awareness regarding their inherent strengths, consequently failing to fully realize their potential. Moore et al. (2022) found that employees were more likely to use their strengths when their organization supported strengths use and offered opportunities for professional development. Strengths use, in turn, was related to vitality and learning – particularly when colleagues recognized employees' strengths. Recent studies have shown that employees can learn to make better use of their strengths. Harzer and Ruch (2016) used a web-based intervention to instruct participants to use their four highest character strengths more often and in new ways at work for four weeks. Relative to a placebo control group, the intervention group reported increased levels of calling and life satisfaction. The participants started to see their work as a vocation and thus increased the purpose and meaning of their work. In a similar vein, Tobias et al. (2023) found that older (but not younger) employees who learned to use their strengths through an intervention training reported increased vitality and job performance (compared to a control group). Taken together, this literature suggests that strengths use generates personal resources with which employees can craft their tasks to stay engaged at work.

Proactive Vitality Management

Proactive vitality management is an individual strategy that employees use to proactively optimize their own energetic, affective, and cognitive resources

(Op den Kamp et al., 2018). Thus, a person may intentionally take a walk in the park to feel energized or take the initiative to meet inspiring others to test new ideas. Whereas job crafting is about changing the job, proactive vitality management is about changing aspects of the self. By taking anticipatory action to manage their psychological and physical energy, employees can become more capable and productive in their work. Proactive vitality management is different from work recovery in that the latter is *reactive*: in response to work-related strain, individuals may try to *rebuild* energetic and affective resources through psychological detachment, relaxation, or mastery experiences. In contrast, when using proactive vitality management, employees take preemptive measures to conserve and optimize their energetic, affective, and cognitive resources (e.g., their cognitive flexibility, physical energy) (Op den Kamp et al., 2023).

Op den Kamp and colleagues (2018) found that employees working in finance, health care, hospitality industry, and other sectors who proactively managed their vitality were more creative, particularly when they had good self-insight and when the organization supported creative ideas. Expanding this study, Bakker et al. (2020) argued and showed that weekly proactive vitality management was predictive of creativity through weekly work engagement, particularly for employees with a high (vs. low) learning goal orientation. Moreover, Op den Kamp et al. (2023) found that proactive vitality management facilitated a state of mindfulness, which, in turn, facilitated creativity (originality, and fluency). Thus, the proactive regulation of one's energy helps paying careful attention to work activities, which in turn fosters creative work performance.

Employees may trigger their own proactive attempts to be physically active by using *self-nudging*. According to nudge theory (Thaler & Sunstein, 2008), individuals often make their choices on the basis of heuristics. This suggests that by adjusting the choice architecture of their immediate work or home environment, individuals may influence their own physical activity (and other relevant behaviors). In an unpublished ten-day diary study among employees working at a real estate company, To and Bakker (2018) found that self-nudging was positively related to physical activity. Employees who reminded themselves to walk, use the stairs, or proactively talked about their fitness goals with others experienced higher levels of daily energy and reported better mental health. Interventions to increase proactive vitality management through training efforts have started but still need to be empirically evaluated.

Activity Level Interventions

Even with optimized job design, certain daily stressors or events can undermine employee work engagement. Consider Dr. Brandao, a pediatric surgeon, who found separating children from their parents before surgery emotionally taxing (The Sun, 2023). To alleviate distress, he introduced superhero costumes, empowering the young patients to embrace their inner heroes by "flying" into the operating room carried by him. This playful approach positively impacted children's experiences while bringing joy to medical staff, demonstrating how a creative approach to work activities can enhance engagement despite challenging circumstances.

Playful work design involves employees proactively introducing elements of fun and competition into their work activities (Scharp et al., 2023). Through this strategy, employees intentionally alter how tasks are approached and executed, leveraging play to regulate cognitions and emotions and foster active learning (Celestine & Yeo, 2021). Essentially, playful work design is a proactive cognitive-behavioral strategy to enhance the interest and meaning derived from work itself. Playful work design differs from job crafting which operates at a higher-order level (considering the job as a whole and in relation to the organization; Bindl et al., 2019). In contrast, playful work design involves behaviors and thoughts that directly facilitate task execution (by making specific tasks more interesting, playful, challenging, and entertaining). Research has indeed shown that job crafting and playful work design have unique effects on performance (Bakker & Scharp, in press).

Scharp et al. (2021) showed that on the days employees designed their work-tasks to be more fun, they were better able to cope with emotionally demanding social interactions, and protect their level of work engagement. In addition, on the days employees playfully designed their work to be more challenging or competitive, they were better able to deal with monotonous, simple, or repetitive tasks. In another daily diary study, Scharp et al. (2019) showed that playful work design facilitated daily work engagement and creativity. Moreover, they found that trait openness and trait playfulness strengthened the impact of designing fun and competition on work engagement (and indirectly on creative performance), indicating that some individuals are better able to benefit from playful work design than others.

Playful work design is a strategy that can be used to increase work engagement during work episodes, and can be used at the activity level. Consistent with JD-R theory, recent research has indicated that employees are most engaged and least exhausted on the days they *combine* the strategies of designing fun and designing competition (see, Bakker & Scharp, in press). The reason for this is that one these days, employees optimize their episodic demands and resources.

Discussion

In this chapter, we presented several possible strategies to increase work engagement. While some of these strategies have received considerable empirical support, other strategies are promising but need further testing in experimental intervention research. We distinguished five levels of intervention: (a) organizational level, primarily top-down job design; (b) team level – use of agile work practices; (c) job level – job crafting, (d) person level – including personal resources, strengths use, and proactive vitality management; and (e) activity level – playful word design. We positioned these approaches in JD-R theory (Bakker et al., 2023; Demerouti &

Bakker, 2023) and described how the various interventions contribute to work engagement, performance, and other individual and organizational outcomes. We will now use this section to discuss how a tailored approach and *blends* of interventions from different levels may facilitate work engagement.

An important starting point for our discussion is that employees who work in the same organization usually have different abilities, needs, personalities, and (starting) levels of work engagement. In most interventions, such differences are largely ignored. Top-down job redesign interventions ideally start with assessing the overall levels of job demands and resources to make an adequate diagnosis of the work design of teams, departments, and the organization at large (Bakker & Demerouti, 2014, 2018). On the basis of such an assessment, it can be determined which job demands and resources in different parts of the organization need to be optimized. The top-down intervention could take the form of participative job redesign, in which employees, leaders, and experts identify the most important events, tasks, and obstacles and generate ideas about how to optimize job demands and resources in the organization. Research has shown that such an intervention can be effective (Holman & Axtell, 2016). However, this approach overlooks possible differences *within* teams and departments. It is well conceivable that in the same department some employees are highly engaged and have access to an abundance of job resources such as social support, feedback, and skill variety, whereas others are less engaged because they hardly have access to these resources. By looking at team averages, such differences cannot be observed. Differences within teams and departments could be due to the existence of subgroups of workers in the same team. There may be low vs. high interdependency between team members, low vs. high frequency of contact (e.g., depending on agile teamwork), or differential treatment by the team leader, to name only a few possible reasons. Thus, even when a top-down intervention is based on a robust diagnosis (validated questionnaires, reliable indicators), a one-size-fits-all approach may only be effective to a limited extent. We argue that top-down interventions should always be combined with bottom-up interventions to maximize their effectiveness in improving work engagement (cf. Kompier et al., 2000).

Blends Are Better

Although bottom-up interventions such as job crafting are typically tailored to individual participants' needs, abilities, and preferences (Demerouti & Bakker, 2024), individual participants' levels of work engagement are usually not taken into account when designing the intervention. Thus, an employee who participates in a job crafting training may learn how to identify the personally most important job demands and resources, and then set personal goals regarding how to optimize those demands and resources through job crafting. As another example, a participant in a strengths use intervention may learn to recognize and actively use their character strengths, for example frequently use their creativity and social skills in new ways in order to feel self-efficacious and be engaged. However, when considering the starting level of work engagement, one will find out that some employees are highly engaged, others show average levels of work engagement, and a third group may be low on engagement. Accounting for beseline levels of work engagement is crucial, because job crafting and strengths use do cost effort and energy (Bakker & Oerlemans, 2019). Moreover, disengaged employees are less likely to benefit from the proactive work behaviors they learn in a training (Bakker, 2018; Bakker & De Vries, 2021).

Some previous studies have suggested that combining multiple proactive work behaviors can produce synergistic benefits for well-being. For example, Seppälä et al. (2020) discovered that while decreasing hindrance job demands alone led to decreased engagement over time, this negative impact was counterbalanced when employees simultaneously increased their challenge job demands. This finding suggests that a blend of proactive strategies, such as minimizing hindrances while actively seeking challenges, can have a complementary effect on sustaining high levels of work engagement. In a similar vein, Zacher et al. (2014) found that prioritizing important work goals (selection) was especially predictive of daily work engagement when employees simultaneously invested resources to attain those goals (optimization). Additionally, Dysvik et al. (2013) found that simultaneously satisfying multiple basic psychological needs yielded the highest level of intrinsic motivation. These findings further highlight how integrating complementary proactive strategies can amplify positive outcomes like engagement through their mutually reinforcing effects.

Conclusion

In this chapter, we discussed various strategies to improve work engagement. We argued that organizational scholars and practitioners should use a combination of top-down and bottom-up interventions, and may use a blend of interventions to foster work engagement and reap other benefits. We have theory and validated instruments to find out which interventions will be most beneficial for which employees. Now it is time to use this knowledge to effectively foster engagement in the workplace.

References

Annosi, M. C., Martini, A., Brunetta, F., & Marchegiani, L. (2020). Learning in an agile setting: A multilevel research study on the evolution of organizational routines. *Journal of Business Research, 110*, 554–566.

Bakker, A. B. (2018). Job crafting among health care professionals: The role of work engagement. *Journal of Nursing Management, 26*, 321–331.

Bakker, A. B., & Demerouti, E. (2014). Job demands-resources theory. In P. Y. Chen & C. L. Cooper (Eds.), *Wellbeing: A complete reference guide* (Volume III: pp. 37–64). Hoboken, New Jersey: Wiley-Blackwell.

Bakker, A. B., & Demerouti, E. (2018). Multiple levels in job demands-resources theory: Implications for employee well-being and performance. In E. Diener, S. Oishi, & L. Tay (Eds.), *Handbook of well-being*. Salt Lake City: DEF Publishers. DOI:nobascholar.com

Bakker, A. B., & Demerouti, E. (2024). Job demands–resources theory: Frequently-asked questions. *Journal of Occupational Health Psychology. 29*(3), 188–200. https://doi.org/10.1037/ocp0000376

Bakker, A. B., Demerouti, E., & Sanz-Vergel, A. (2023). Job demands–resources theory: Ten years later. *Annual Review of Organizational Psychology and Organizational Behavior, 10*, 25–53.

Bakker, A. B., & Oerlemans, W. G. M. (2019). Daily job crafting and momentary work engagement: A self-determination and self-regulation perspective. *Journal of Vocational Behavior, 112*, 417–430.

Bakker, A. B., Petrou, P., Op den Kamp, E. M., & Tims, M. (2020). Proactive vitality management, work engagement, and creativity: The role of goal orientation. *Applied Psychology: An International Review, 69*, 351–378.

Bakker, A. B., & Sanz-Vergel, A. I. (2013). Weekly work engagement and flourishing: The role of hindrance and challenge demands. *Journal of Vocational Behavior, 83*, 397–409.

Bakker, A. B., & Scharp, Y. S. (in press). It pays to play: Playful work design. In S. Parker, F. Klonek, C. Knight, & F. Zhang (Eds.), *Transformative work design: Synthesis and new directions*. SIOP Frontier Series.

Bakker, A. B., & van Wingerden, J. (2021). Do personal resources and strengths use increase work engagement? The effects of a training intervention. *Journal of Occupational Health Psychology, 26*(1), 20–30.

Bakker, A. B., & Van Woerkom, M. (2018). Strengths use in organizations: A positive approach of occupational health. *Canadian Psychology, 59*, 38–46.

Bindl, U. K., & Parker, S. K. (2011). Proactive work behavior: Forward-thinking and change-oriented action in organizations. In S. Zedeck (Ed.), *APA handbook of industrial and organizational psychology, Vol. 2. Selecting and developing members for the organization* (pp. 567–598). American Psychological Association.

Bindl, U. K., Unsworth, K. L., Gibson, C. B., & Stride, C. B. (2019). Job crafting revisited: Implications of an extended framework for active changes at work. *Journal of Applied Psychology, 104*(5), 605–628.

Celestine, N. A., & Yeo, G. (2021). Having some fun with it: A theoretical review and typology of activity-based play-at-work. *Journal of Organizational Behavior, 42*(2), 252–268.

Chen, J., Bamberger, P. A., Song, Y., & Vashdi, D. R. (2018). The effects of team reflexivity on psychological well-being in manufacturing teams. *Journal of Applied Psychology, 103*(4), 443–462.

Christian, M. S., Garza, A. S., & Slaughter, J. E. (2011). Work engagement: A quantitative review and test of its relations with task and contextual performance. *Personnel Psychology, 64*, 89–136.

Cordery, J., Morrison, D., Wright, B., & Wall, T. (2010). The impact of autonomy and task uncertainty on team performance: A longitudinal field study. *Journal of Organizational Behavior, 31*, 240–258.

Demerouti, E., & Bakker, A. B. (2011). The Job demands–resources model: Challenges for future research. *South African Journal of Industrial Psychology, 37*, 1–9.

Demerouti, E., & Bakker, A. B. (2023). Job demands-resources theory in times of crises: New propositions. *Organizational Psychology Review, 13*, 209–236.

Demerouti, E., & Bakker, A. B. (2024). Job crafting: A powerful job redesign approach. In M. C. W. Peeters, J. de Jonge, & T. Taris (Eds.), *An introduction to contemporary work psychology*. (pp. 524–543). Hoboken, New Jersey: Wiley.

Demerouti, E., Van Eeuwijk, E., Snelder, M., & Wild, U. (2011). Assessing the effects of a "personal effectiveness" training on psychological capital, assertiveness and self-awareness using self-other agreement. *The Career Development International, 16*, 60–81.

Dysvik, A., Kuvaas, B., & Gagné, M. (2013). An investigation of the unique, synergistic and balanced relationships between basic psychological needs and intrinsic motivation. *Journal of Applied Social Psychology, 43*, 1050–1064.

Gordon, H. J., Demerouti, E., LeBlanc, P. M., Bakker, A. B., Bipp, T., & Verhagen, M. A. (2018). Individual job redesign: Job crafting interventions in health care. *Journal of Vocational Behavior, 104*, 98–114.

Hakanen, J. J., Bakker, A. B., & Demerouti, E. (2005). How dentists cope with their job demands and stay engaged: The moderating role of job resources. *European Journal of Oral Sciences, 113*, 479–487.

Harzer, C., & Ruch, W. (2016). Your strengths are calling: Preliminary results of a web-based strengths intervention to increase calling. *Journal of Happiness Studies, 17*, 2237–2256.

Hobfoll, S. E., Johnson, R. J., Ennis, N., & Jackson, A. P. (2003). Resource loss, resource gain, and emotional outcomes among inner city women. *Journal of Personality and Social Psychology, 84*(3), 632.

Holman, D., & Axtell, C. (2016). Can job redesign interventions influence a broad range of employee outcomes by changing multiple job characteristics? A quasi-experimental study. *Journal of Occupational Health Psychology, 21*(3), 284.

Holman, D., Escaffi-Schwarz, M., Vasquez, C. A., Irmer, J. P., & Zapf, D. (2024). Does job crafting affect employee outcomes via job characteristics? A meta-analytic test of a key job crafting mechanism. *Journal of Occupational and Organizational Psychology, 97*(1), 47–73.

Junker, T. L., Bakker, A. B., Derks, D., & Pletzer, J. L. (in press). Work engagement in agile teams: Extending multilevel JD-R theory. *Journal of Organizational Behavior,* DOI: 10.1002/job.2860

Junker, T. L., Bakker, A., & Derks, D. (2024). Toward a theory of team resource mobilization: A systematic review and model of sustained agile team effectiveness. *Human Resource Management Review, 2021*(1), 15727.

Junker, T. L., Bakker, A. B., Derks, D., & Molenaar, D. (2023). Agile work practices: Measurement and mechanisms. *European Journal of Work and Organizational Psychology, 32*(1), 1–22.

Junker, T. L., Bakker, A. B., Gorgievski, M. J., & Derks, D. (2022). Agile work practices and employee proactivity: A multilevel study. *Human Relations, 75*(2), 2189–2217.

Knight, C., & Parker, S. K. (2021). How work redesign interventions affect performance: An evidence-based model from a systematic review. *Human Relations, 74*(1), 69–104.

Knight, C., Patterson, M., & Dawson, J. (2017). Building work engagement: A systematic review and meta-analysis investigating the effectiveness of work engagement interventions. *Journal of Organizational Behavior, 38*(6), 792–812.

Kompier, M. A. J., Cooper, C. L., & Geurts, S. A. E. (2000). A multiple case study approach to work stress prevention in Europe. *European Journal of Work & Organizational Psychology, 9*, 371–400.

Laulié, L., Tekleab, A. G., & Rousseau, D. M. (in press). Psychological contracts at different levels: The cross-level and comparative multilevel effects of team psychological contract fulfillment. *Group & Organization Management,* 10596011231203365.

Lieberum, T., Schiffels, S., & Kolisch, R. (2022). Should we all work in Sprints? How Agile Project Management improves performance. *Manufacturing & Service Operations Management, 24*(4), 2293–2309.

Luthans, F., Avey, J. B., & Patera, J. L. (2008). Experimental analysis of a web-based training intervention to develop positive psychological capital. *Academy of Management Learning and Education, 7*, 209–221.

Mackay, M. M., Allen, J. A., & Landis, R. S. (2017). Investigating the incremental validity of employee engagement in the prediction of employee effectiveness: A meta-analytic path analysis. *Human Resource Management Review, 27*, 108–120.

Martinaityte, I., Unsworth, K. L., & Sacramento, C. A. (2020). Is the project 'mine' or 'ours'? A multilevel investigation of the effects of individual and collective psychological ownership. *Journal of Occupational and Organizational Psychology, 93*(2), 302–327.

May, D. R., Gilson, R. L., & Harter, L. M. (2004). The psychological conditions of meaningfulness, safety and availability and the engagement of the human spirit at work. *Journal of Occupational and Organizational Psychology, 77*(1), 11–37.

Moore, H. L., Bakker, A. B., & van Mierlo, H. (2022). Using strengths and thriving at work: The role of colleague strengths recognition and organizational context. *European Journal of Work and Organizational Psychology, 31*(2), 260–272.

Moore, H. L., Bakker, A. B., Van Mierlo, H., & Van Woerkom, M. (2024). Daily strengths use and work performance: A self-determination perspective. *Journal of Organizational and Occupational Psychology, 97*, 190–208.

Op den Kamp, E., Tims, M., Bakker, A. B., & Demerouti, E. (2018). Proactive vitality management in the work context: Development and validation of a new instrument. *European Journal of Work and Organizational Psychology, 27*, 493–505.

Op den Kamp, E., Tims, M., Bakker, A. B., & Demerouti, E. (2023). Creating a creative state of mind: Promoting creativity through proactive vitality management and mindfulness. *Applied Psychology: An International Review, 72*, 743–768.

Oprea, B. T., Barzin, L., Vîrgă, D., Iliescu, D., & Rusu, A. (2019). Effectiveness of job crafting interventions: A meta-analysis and utility analysis. *European Journal of Work and Organizational Psychology, 28*, 723–741.

Parker, S. K., Johnson, A., Collins, C., & Nguyen, H. (2013). Making the most of structural support: Moderating influence of employees' clarity and negative affect. *Academy of Management Journal, 56*(3), 867–892.

Peeters, T., Van De Voorde, K., & Paauwe, J. (2022). The effects of working agile on team performance and engagement. *Team Performance Management: An International Journal, 28*(1), 61–78.

Prins, J. T., van der Heijden, F. M., Hoekstra-Weebers, J. E., Bakker, A. B., van de Wiel, H. B., Jacobs, B., & Gazendam-Donofrio, S. M. (2009). Burnout, engagement and resident physicians' self-reported errors. *Psychology, Health & Medicine, 14*, 654–666.

Roczniewska, M., & Bakker, A. B. (2021). Burnout and self-regulation failure: A diary study of self-undermining and job crafting among nurses. *Journal of Advanced Nursing, 77*, 3424–3435.

Rothbard, N. P. (2001). "Enriching or depleting?" The dynamics of engagement in work and family roles. *Administrative Science Quarterly, 46*, 655–684.

Scharp, Y., Bakker, A. B., Breevaart, K., Kruup, K., & Uusberg, A. (2023). Playful work design: Conceptualization, measurement, and validity. *Human Relations, 76*, 509–550.

Scharp, Y. S., Breevaart, K., & Bakker, A. B. (2021). Using playful work design to deal with hindrance job demands: A quantitative diary study. *Journal of Occupational Health Psychology, 26*, 175–188.

Scharp, Y. S., Breevaart, K., Bakker, A. B., & Van der Linden, D. (2019). Daily playful work design: A trait activation perspective. *Journal of Research in Personality, 82*, 103850.

Schaufeli, W. B., & Bakker, A. B. (2023). Work engagement: A critical assessment of the concept and its measurement. In W. Ruch, A. B. Bakker, L. Tay, & F. Gander (Eds.), *Handbook of positive psychology assessment* (pp. 273–295). Amsterdam, The Netherlands: Hogrefe.

Schaufeli, W. B., Bakker, A. B., & Van Rhenen, W. (2009). How changes in job demands and resources predict burnout, work engagement and sickness absenteeism. *Journal of Organizational Behavior, 30,* 893–917.

Seppälä, P., Harju, L., & Hakanen, J. J. (2020). Interactions of approach and avoidance job crafting and work engagement: A comparison between employees affected and not affected by organizational changes. *International Journal of Environmental Research and Public Health, 17*, 9084.

Thaler, R. H., & Sunstein, C. R. (2008). *Nudge: Improving decisions about health, wealth, and happiness*. Yale University Press.

The Sun (2023). Brazilian doctor dresses children in superhero costumes to ease surgical anxiety. Retrieved on 13 May 2024 from https://thesun.my/style-life/going-viral/brazilian-doctor-dresses-children-in-superhero-costumes-to-ease-surgical-anxiety-BN11499811.

Tims, M., & Bakker, A. B. (2010). Job crafting: Towards a new model of individual job redesign. *South African Journal of Industrial Psychology, 36*, 1–9.

To, F., & Bakker, A. B. (2018). *Self-initiated nudging for physical activity: A diary study.* Internal report. Center of Excellence for Positive Organizational Psychology. Erasmus University Rotterdam.

Tobias, V. Y., van Woerkom, M., Meyers, M. C., Runhaar, P., & Bakker, A. B. (2023). Thriving on strengths: Effects of a strengths intervention for younger and older teachers. *Journal of Happiness Studies*, *24*(3), 1121–1144.

Van Wingerden, J., Bakker, A. B., & Derks, D. (2016). A test of a job demands–resources intervention. *Journal of Managerial Psychology, 31*, 686–701.

Van Wingerden, J., Bakker, A. B., & Derks, D. (2017a). The longitudinal impact of a job crafting intervention. *European Journal of Work and Organizational Psychology, 26*, 107–119.

Van Wingerden, J., Derks, D., & Bakker, A. B. (2017b). The impact of personal resources and job crafting interventions on work engagement and performance. *Human Resources Management, 56*, 51–67.

Van Woerkom, M., Oerlemans, W., & Bakker, A. B. (2016). Strengths use and work engagement: A weekly diary study. *European Journal of Work and Organizational Psychology, 25*, 384–397.

Virga, D., Rusu, A., Pap, Z., Maricuțoiu, L., & Tisu, L. (2023). Effectiveness of strengths use interventions in organizations: A pre-registered meta-analysis of controlled trials. *Applied Psychology*, *72*, 1653–1693.

Vogt, K., Hakanen, J. J., Brauchli, R., Jenny, G. J., & Bauer, G. F. (2016). The consequences of job crafting: A three-wave study. *European Journal of Work and Organizational Psychology*, *25*(3), 353–362.

Wachter, J. K., & Yorio, P. L. (2014). A system of safety management practices and worker engagement for reducing and preventing accidents: An empirical and theoretical investigation. *Accident Analysis and Prevention, 68*, 117–130.

Wood, A. M., Linley, P. A., Maltby, J., Kashdan, T. B., & Hurling, R. (2011). Using personal and psychological strengths leads to increases in well-being over time: A longitudinal study and the development of the strengths use questionnaire. *Personality and Individual Differences, 50*, 15–19.

Wrzesniewski, A., & Dutton, J. E. (2001). Crafting a job: Revisioning employees as active crafters of their work. Academy of Management Review, 26(2), 179–201.

Xanthopoulou, D., Bakker, A. B., Demerouti, E., & Schaufeli, W. B. (2009). Reciprocal relationships between job resources, personal resources, and work engagement. *Journal of Vocational Behavior*, *74*(3), 235–244.

Zacher, H., Chan, F., Bakker, A. B., & Demerouti, E. (2014). Selection, optimization, and compensation strategies: Interactive effects on daily work engagement. *Journal of Vocational Behavior*, *87*, 101–107.

5

SELF-EFFICACY[1]

James E. Maddux and Thisali Mendis

Self-Efficacy

The basic premise of self-efficacy theory is that "people's beliefs in their capabilities to produce desired effects by their own actions" – self-efficacy expectancies or beliefs (Bandura, 1997, p. vii) – are the most important determinants of the behaviors people choose to engage in and how much they persevere in their efforts in the face of obstacles and challenges. A self-efficacy expectancy is not simply the belief that "I can successfully perform X behavior" but that "I can successfully perform X behavior under these particular challenging circumstances." Thus, a self-efficacy expectancy includes the broader belief about one's ability at self-regulation in the execution of the behavior in particular situations where challenges are inevitable.

Interest in beliefs about personal control and perceived competence has a long history in psychology, but Bandura's 1977 *Psychological Review* article formalized the notion of perceived competence (or confidence) as a behavior-specific and situation-specific belief about one's ability to execute specific behaviors under specific conditions and to manage challenges in executing those behaviors – a *self-efficacy expectancy* – and embedded it in a theory of how it develops and influences human behavior.[2] Self-efficacy expectancies are distinguished from *outcome expectancies* (Bandura, 1977) or *behavior–outcome expectancies* (Maddux, 1999), which is the belief that a specific behavior may lead to a specific outcome in a specific situation.

Self-efficacy theory was originally developed to explain the mechanisms of successful psychological interventions for clinically dysfunctional anxiety and avoidant behaviors, not the performance of employees, leaders, and managers in the workplace. The early studies of self-efficacy beliefs found that they were highly effective at what self-efficacy theory was developed to do (e.g., Bandura, 1977; Bandura & Adams, 1977). Because of the appeal and potential of the concept, the

DOI: 10.4324/9781032619385-5

study of self-efficacy beliefs rapidly spread to a wide variety of other problems of concern to clinical psychologists such as depression, eating disorders, and addictions, as well as problems, behaviors, and settings in other subfields of psychology, including health psychology, educational psychology, and industrial–organizational (I–O) psychology.

The goal of this chapter is to provide a relatively brief overview of the role of self-efficacy beliefs (or expectancies) on the performance of employees, including leaders and managers, in the workplace and in organizations. The limitation placed on the length of the chapters in this volume does not allow for the exploration of every topic related to self-efficacy in I–O psychology nor for in-depth exploration of any. For such in-depth explorations, the reader is encouraged to consult the sources cited in this chapter.

Self-efficacy overlaps conceptually and empirically with several other constructs in I–O psychology. For example, self-efficacy is one of four components of what are called ***core self-evaluations***, along with internal locus of control, self-esteem, and emotional stability that share considerable theoretical overlap and are substantially correlated with each other (Judge et al., 1997). In addition, along with *hope, optimism,* and *resilience*, self-efficacy is a component of what has been called ***core confidence*** (Stajkovic, 2006) or ***positive psychological capital*** (Luthans et al., 2004; Chapter 7, this volume) that has been shown to be predictive of work-related motivation, performance and well-being. Self-efficacy also has been integrated into theories goal-setting and motivation (e.g., Locke & Latham, 1990) . Self-efficacy also figures prominently in theories of career and vocational choice (e.g., Lent et al., 2022), although a discussion of why people choose the work they choose is beyond the scope of this chapter.

General Self-Efficacy Versus Task-Specific or Job-Specific Self-Efficacy

Although self-efficacy, by definition, is not a personality trait, several measures of general or trait-like self-efficacy have been developed and have been used extensively in research (e.g., Chen et al., 2001; Jerusalem & Schwarzer, 1995; Sherer et al., 1982).

Generally, measures of general self-efficacy are not as useful as more specific self-efficacy measures in predicting what people will do under specific circumstances, most likely because the relationship between general self-efficacy and the performance of specific behaviors in specific situations is usually mediated by self-efficacy for those specific behaviors in those specific situations – in I–O psychology otherwise known as *job-specific* or *task-specific self-efficacy expectancies* (Chen et al., 1999, 2001, 2004; Eden, 1988; Gardner & Pierce, 1998; Kanfer & Heggestad, 1997; Yao & Neal, 2006).

This chapter, unless otherwise noted, is concerned exclusively with research that has examined the factors influencing ***task-specific*** or ***job-specific*** self-efficacy expectancies and the influence of these expectancies on work-related behavior.

How Self-Efficacy Beliefs Develop

Personality Predispositions

Research suggests that personality predispositions can influence the development of self-efficacy beliefs. For example, perhaps 50%–75% of individual variations in *general self-efficacy* is due to genetic factors (Instinske & Kandler, 2023; Waaktaar & Torgersen, 2013). Research on the five-factor model of personality (the Big Five) suggests that people high in ***conscientiousness*** (which includes the components of deliberation, organization, and achievement orientation) are likely to set more explicit and more challenging goals, less likely to procrastinate, more likely to persist in the face of challenges, and are better able to delay gratification, all of which are associated with goal attainment and the development of stronger self-efficacy beliefs (McCrae & Löekenhoff, 2010). Because **neuroticism** (generally a predisposition to experience depression and anxiety) is associated with rumination, including a focus on threats to the self (McCraie & Löekenhoff, 2010, people higher in neuroticism may be more likely to become critically ***self-diagnostic*** ("What's wrong with me?!") rather than ***task-diagnostic*** ("What do I need to do now?") when encountering self-regulatory challenges and setbacks. Negative self-diagnostic reactions are more likely to lead to discouragement and disengagement from the goal and therefore likely to undermine self-efficacy beliefs (Bandura & Wood, 1989; Wood & Bandura, 1989). (See also Maddux, 2008.)

Situational and Contextual Influences

Self-efficacy beliefs about various domains and situations develop throughout the life span as people continually integrate information from five primary sources: performance experiences, vicarious experiences, imagined experiences, verbal persuasion, and physiological/emotional states (Bandura, 1997).

Performance Experiences

One's own attempts to achieve one's goals are the most powerful source of self-efficacy information. Successful attempts at goal-striving that one attributes to one's own efforts will strengthen self-efficacy expectancies for that behavior or domain. Likewise, perceptions of failure that one attributes to lack of ability usually weaken self-efficacy beliefs.

Vicarious Experiences

People observe the behavior of others and the consequences of those behaviors and use this information to form expectancies about their own behavior and its consequences, depending partly on the extent to which they believe that they are similar to the person they are observing. Vicarious experiences generally have weaker effects on self-efficacy expectancy than do performance experiences.

Imagined Experiences

People can influence their self-efficacy beliefs, for better or worse, by imagining themselves or others behaving effectively or ineffectively in hypothetical situations. Such images may be derived from actual or vicarious experiences with situations similar to the one anticipated, or they may be induced by verbal persuasion.

Verbal Persuasion

Self-efficacy beliefs are influenced by what others say to a person about what they believe that person can or cannot do. The potency of verbal persuasion as a source of self-efficacy expectancies will be influenced by such factors as the expertness, trustworthiness, and attractiveness of the source.

Physiological and Emotional States

Physiological and emotional states influence self-efficacy when people learn to associate poor performance or perceived failure with aversive physiological arousal and success with pleasant feeling states. A person who becomes aware of unpleasant physiological arousal is more likely to doubt their competence in that situation than if their physiological state were pleasant or neutral. Likewise, comfortable physiological sensations are likely to lead someone to feel confident in their ability in the situation at hand.

Self-Efficacy and Self-Regulation

One of the most important ways that self-efficacy beliefs influence behavior is through the role that they play in self-regulation. Self-efficacy beliefs figure prominently in two major theories of self-regulation – ***social cognitive theory*** (Bandura, 1986) and ***control theory*** (Powers, 1973; Vancouver, 2005).

According to Bandura's version of social-cognitive theory, self-efficacy beliefs influence self-regulation in several ways. ***First***, they influence the goals that people choose and the level of those goals. People with stronger self-efficacy expectancies in a specific situation or achievement domain are likely to set more difficult goals. ***Second***, they influence a person's choices of goal-directed activities, expenditure of effort, and perseverance in the face of challenge and obstacles (Bandura, 1997; Locke et al., 1984). A person with strong efficacy beliefs will be more resistant to the disruptions in self-regulation that can result from difficulties and setbacks and, therefore, is more likely to persevere. ***Third***, they influence the efficiency and effectiveness of problem solving and decision making. In the face of difficulty, a person with strong self-efficacy beliefs is likely to remain ***task-diagnostic*** and focus on finding solutions to the problems they encounter. A person with weaker self-efficacy, however, is more likely to become ***self-diagnostic*** and reflect on their inadequacies, which can lead to discouragement and perhaps eventually to disengagement from the goal (Bandura, 1997; Hoffman & Schraw, 2009).

Control theory also proposes that self-efficacy influences the goals people choose to pursue and the difficulty of those goals. A major difference, however, is that control theory proposes (and research has found) that self-efficacy can have a *negative* effect on motivation and effort when feedback about performance is either absent or ambiguous. This can occur because people with stronger self-efficacy beliefs are more likely to miscalculate the effort needed to perform the task at hand and therefore reduce their efforts (Vancouver et al., 2014; Vancouver & Purl, 2017). This finding has been replicated by research on the related notion of ***performance ambiguity*** – that is, having clear versus ambiguous information about how well one is performing on a task. When such information is ambiguous, self-efficacy may be negatively related to subsequent performance but positive related when this information is clear and unambiguous (Schmidt & DeShon, 2010). Feedback on one's performance seems to be necessary for self-efficacy to have a positive relationship with performance (Beattie et al., 2016). (For a more detailed comparison of social cognitive theory and control theory, see Vancouver, 2005.) (See also Yeo & Neal, 2006.)[3]

Self-Efficacy and Work Performance

Do self-efficacy beliefs predict the performance of employees in work settings? The answer to this question is a qualified "yes." Qualified because one must consider (1) the difference in the relationship between self-efficacy beliefs and performance in lab studies that simulate work-related tasks and studies of work-related behavior in actual work settings (field studies) and (2) the conditions under which self-efficacy beliefs might not be positively related to performance or might actually be negatively related to performance.

Simulation Lab Studies Versus Field Studies

Generally, the relationship between self-efficacy expectancies and work performance is much stronger in simulation laboratory studies than in studies conducted in real-life settings (r corrected for sampling error = 0.60 and 0.34 respectively; Sadri & Robertson, 1993). This occurs for at least three reasons. *First,* in simulation studies it is easier to match self-efficacy measures more closely with the tasks that subjects are asked to perform, referred to as *point-to-point correspondence. Second*, simulation studies, as opposed to field studies, typically involve strong outcome expectancies for clearly specified outcomes, which will enhance the influence of self-efficacy expectancies. *Third*, in simulation studies, time lag between measures of self-efficacy and actual performance is generally much shorter than in field studies, this minimizing the impact of uncontrollable extraneous influences on performance (Sadri & Robertson, 1993).

Self-Efficacy and Work Performance: Empirical Evidence

The first meta-analysis of research on self-efficacy and work-related task performance (114 studies) found a significant weighted average correlation between self-efficacy and work-related performance [G(r+) = .38]. In addition, the relationship between self-efficacy and performance varied with levels of task complexity and type of study (simulation versus field). The correlation between self-efficacy and task performance was strongest for low-complexity tasks in simulation studies and weakest for high-complexity tasks in field studies. Overall, the relationship between performance and self-efficacy revealed by the meta-analysis was stronger than the relationship between performance and goal-setting, feedback interventions, and modifying organizational behavior, as well as between performance many trait-based constructs (Stajkovic & Luthans, 1998). A later longitudinal field study found an even stronger effect of.47 between self-efficacy and job performance (Carter et al., 2018).

A later meta-analysis (Judge et al., 2007), however, found that the contribution of task-specific self-efficacy beliefs to the prediction of work-related performance was relatively small when added to what can be predicted from personality (the Big Five noted previously), intelligence, and experience with the job or task at hand. Consistent with the earlier meta-analysis, this meta-analysis also revealed that self-efficacy beliefs predicted performance for low-complexity tasks but not for medium- and high-complexity tasks (Judge et al., 2007).

Another meta-analysis of within-person studies (versus between-persons studies) found that the relationship between past performance and current self-efficacy was stronger than the relationship between current self-efficacy and future performance even under conditions that produced the strongest relationship between self-efficacy and performance (Sitzman & Yeo, 2013).

Some research has found that performance predicts self-efficacy beliefs better than self-efficacy beliefs predict future performance (e.g., Locke et al., 1984) and that self-efficacy does not always predict performance (Richard et al., 2006). In fact, some research suggests that when past performance is controlled statistically, the relationship between self-efficacy beliefs and subsequent performance is greatly reduced and that self-efficacy does not predict performance beyond what is predicted by past performance – most likely because self-efficacy beliefs are a ***result*** of past performance (Heggestad & Kanfer, 2005). Perhaps self-efficacy beliefs predict performance only because past performance influences and predicts self-efficacy beliefs (e.g., Sitzman & Yeo, 2013).

The vast majority of the studies included in the above meta-analyses were conducted in offices, factories, and other traditional work settings. More recently, studies have been examining the role that self-efficacy beliefs play in ***remote virtual*** work settings. For example, a study of employees in Germany who worked remotely for at least 50% of the time found that feelings of autonomy and remote-work experience were positively associated with self-efficacy beliefs for working remotely and that stronger self-efficacy beliefs for working remotely were associated with reduced work-related stress and work–family conflict (Lange & Kayser, 2022). A study of remote employees in China found self-efficacy for remote work predicted remote-work effectiveness (Qi et al., 2023). Similar results were found in a study of employees at a large multinational technology company (Adamovic et al., 2021).

Although strong self-efficacy beliefs are generally seen as helpful, in some situations they can be "too strong" and actually diminish rather than enhance motivation and performance?. As noted previously regarding research on control theory, the answer is "yes." The results of a series of six simulation and field studies suggests that inexperienced newcomers to a task typically do not start out feeling overly confident but that a little experience at the new task can lead to an inflated sense of confidence as a result of "faulty but forcefully held theories about how to approach the task based on the shards of experience they have gained" (Sanchez & Dunham, 2018, p. 25). Additional experience can lead to a leveling off of confidence, but confidence may rise again after even more experience (Sanchez & Dunham, 2018).

Self-Efficacy and Other Organizational Variables

Worker Well-Being

Research suggests that employees with stronger self-efficacy beliefs experience less ***anxiety*** while performing their jobs and that lower anxiety leads to better performance (De Clercq et al., 2018). Research also suggests that employees with weaker work-related self-efficacy beliefs experience greater work-related ***stress*** under stressful working conditions (Fida et al., 2015). For this reason, employees with weaker self-efficacy may benefit more greatly from anxiety-management and stress-management programs than employees with stronger self-efficacy beliefs, although this appears to be true only if the low-self-efficacy employees display relatively high levels of work-related intrinsic motivation (Lloyd et al., 2017). (See also Chapter 6, this volume.)

Engagement, Commitment, and Job Satisfaction

Work engagement has been defined as "a positive, fulfilling, work-related state of mind that is characterized by vigor, dedication, and absorption" (Schaufeli et al., 2002, p. 74). A related construct, ***organizational commitment*** refers to one's psychological attachment to an organization job consisting of a desire, a need, and an obligation to maintain employment in an organization (Meyer & Allen, 1991). Research suggests that employees with strong work-related self-efficacy beliefs are likely be more highly engaged in their work and more committed to their organizations, which then leads to greater work performance (e.g., Song et al. 2018; Liu & Huang, 2019; Lisbona et al. 2018).

Feedback-Seeking

As noted previously, research suggests that the relationship between self-efficacy beliefs and performance is strongest when people receive clear and substantial feedback on how they are doing during the learning of a task or acquisition of a skill. Are people with higher self-efficacy more or less likely to seek feedback concerning their performance? One factor that seems to influence the relationship between self-efficacy and feedback-seeking is ***perspective taking,*** which occurs when employees "step outside of their usual mental routines and default tendencies to consider alternative viewpoints and possibilities and process information more deeply" (Sherf & Morrison, 2020, p. 148). Research suggests that the more employees engage in perspective taking, the more positive is the relationship between their self-efficacy beliefs for job performance and seeking feedback concerning job performance, possibly because perspective-taking makes it more likely that employees will view feedback as valuable (Sherf & Morrison, 2020). In addition, research suggests that receiving feedback enhances self-efficacy for improvement, which leads to subsequent feedback-seeking (Dimotakis et al., 2017).

Seeking Additional Knowledge and Skills

Self-efficacy beliefs can also influence the motivation of employees to seek opportunities to enhance their skills. Employees with stronger self-efficacy beliefs may be more likely to seek out formal and informal ***work-related learning experiences*** (Grosemans et al., 2020). In addition, decreases in job-related self-efficacy beliefs over time can lead to diminished motivation to seek out new job-related knowledge and skills over time (Van Hootegem et al., 2022).

Creativity on the Job

Self-efficacy beliefs can also predict ***job-crafting***, an employee's proactive initiation of changes in their jobs toward the end of aligning their job with their personal needs and abilities (Tims et al., 2014; Wrzesniewski & Dutton, 2001). Job crafting predicts both work enjoyment and performance, partly because people who enjoy their work perform better (Tims et al., 2014, Ingusci et al., 2019). In addition, employees with stronger self-efficacy beliefs for dealing with job and organizational changes are more likely to be innovative and creative in their jobs (Ng & Lucianetti, 2016).

Job Autonomy

Job autonomy refers to employees' beliefs about how much control they have over how, when, and where they do their jobs. Research suggests that feelings of job autonomy and self-efficacy beliefs are strongly related, although the direction of the relationship (which precedes which) remains to be determined because the relationship is likely bi-directional.

As noted previously, a study of employees in Germany who worked remotely for at least 50% of the time found that feelings of autonomy and remote-work experience were positively associated with self-efficacy beliefs for working remotely

(Lange & Keyser, 2022). Similar results were found in a study of employees in Portugal (Sousa et al., 2012) and a study of school principals in Norway (Federici, 2013). A study of teachers in Norway found that measures of job autonomy and job-related self-efficacy were highly correlated and were independent predictors of engagement, job satisfaction, and burnout (Skaalvik & Skaalvik, 2014).

Social and Emotional Self-Efficacy

In advanced economies, most people work as part of a team. Teams work more effectively when its members get along with each other. Belief in one's abilities to get along with others at work, to understand the emotions of other people, and to manage one's emotions effectively at work is known as *social and emotional self-efficacy.*

Research suggests that beliefs about social and emotional self-efficacy can predict work performance, worker well-being, job satisfaction, and burnout. For example, a study of Swedish and German employees found that a measure of social self-efficacy predicted team climate beyond what was predicted by a measure of general occupational self-efficacy and that a measure of self-oriented emotional self-efficacy predicted irritation and exhaustion beyond what was predicted by the measure of general occupational self-efficacy (Loeb et al., 2016).

A study of flight attendants found that those who were higher in self-efficacy for emotion work such as dealing with difficult passengers coped more effectively with these situations (Heuven et al., 2006). A study of military academy cadets in Italy found that self-efficacy for managing negative emotions mediated the relationship between emotional stability and job burnout (Alessandri et al., 2018). Studies of emergency dispatchers and police officers in Canada found that self-efficacy for managing one's emotions, managing the emotions of other people, and using one's emotions predicted workplace psychological well-being (Emeriau-Farges et al., 2019; Huard et al., 2021).

Leadership Self-Efficacy

Effective organizations require good leaders and managers who have confidence in their ability to lead and manage. Early analyses of the important components of effective leadership noted that confidence or self-efficacy is likely an important quality of effective leaders (Chemers et al., 2000; McCormick, 2001). ***Leadership self-efficacy*** has been defined as a leader's "beliefs in their perceived capabilities to organize the positive psychological capabilities, motivation, means, collective resources, and courses of action required to attain effective, sustainable performance across their various leadership roles, demands, and contexts" (Hannah et al., 2008, p. 2). Some research suggests that leadership self-efficacy consists of three dimensions: ***direction-setting, gaining the commitment of followers***, and ***overcoming obstacles to change*** (Paglis & Green, 2002).

Effects of Leadership Self-Efficacy

Most research has found that higher leadership self-efficacy is positively associated with leader effectiveness and group performance (Dwyer, 2019; Hannah et al., 2008), including enhancing the self-efficacy of the people they lead and manage (Hannah et al., 2016). Some studies suggest that the association between leadership self-efficacy and group performance is mediated partly by the positive influence of leadership self-efficacy on ***group collective efficacy*** (Dwyer, 2019). (See section below on collective efficacy.) One study using both real-world and simulated situations found that managers higher in managerial self-efficacy are more likely to solicit input from employees and to positively evaluate employees who voice their opinions (Fast et al., 2014). As with individual self-efficacy, although strong leadership self-efficacy beliefs are generally positive, research suggests that unrealistically high leadership self-efficacy (leader overconfidence) may be detrimental to the long-range effectiveness of groups (Hannah et al., 2008).

Predictors of Leadership Self-Efficacy

Certain personality traits are positively associated with leadership self-efficacy, especially conscientiousness and extraversion, but also to a lesser extent, openness to experience (Dwyer, 2019; Hannah et al., 2008; Ng et al., 2008). In addition, leadership self-efficacy is positively associated with cognitive ability, emotional intelligence, self-esteem, internal locus-of-control, and having a learning goal orientation (that is, seeing good leadership as a skill that can be enhanced through practice) (Dwyer, 2019; Hannah et al., 2008). Previous leadership experience also predicts leadership self-efficacy, and people with higher leadership self-efficacy are more likely to seek out and accept leadership roles, which in turn is likely to lead to stronger leadership self-efficacy (McCormick et al., 2002).

Collective Efficacy

Accomplishing important goals in organizations depends on the ability of individuals to identify the abilities of other individuals and to harness these abilities to accomplish common goals. This idea is captured in the notion of ***collective efficacy*** defined as "a group's shared belief in its conjoint capabilities to organize and execute the courses of action required for producing given levels of attainments" (Bandura, 1997, p. 477; Zaccaro et al., 1995). As does individual self-efficacy, collective efficacy influences the goals set by groups or teams, how hard they work at the tasks, and their resilience on the face of challenges (Tasa et al., 2007). Collective efficacy can be measured at both the level of the groups that comprise an organization and at the level of the larger organization (Borgogni et al., 2009). In addition, research suggests that collective efficacy can be viewed as having three dimensions: collective efficacy for group task management, collective efficacy for managing relationships among group members, and collective efficacy for managing emotions of group members (Petitta et al., 2015).

As with individual self-efficacy, collective efficacy has been measured as both task-specific or job-specific and as a more general or trait-like and enduring quality of the group, sometimes referred to as ***group potency.*** As with individual general self-efficacy, the relationship between group potency (general collective efficacy) and performance is mediated by task-specific collective efficacy (Stajkovic et al., 2009).

A meta-analysis (96 studies) found that collective efficacy was a significant predictor of group performance (.35) and that the strength of the relationship depended on the interdependence of the group's tasks – the greater the interdependence of the tasks, the stronger the relationship between collective efficacy and group performance. A measure of group potency also predicted group performance, but this relationship was fully mediated by collective efficacy (Stajkovic et al., 2009). Collective efficacy was a strong indicator of performance in a study of air traffic controllers (Mathieu et al., 2009). Collective efficacy is also important for the effective functioning of virtual teams (McLarnon & Woodley, 2021).

Another meta-analysis (67 studies) found that both group potency (general collective efficacy) and task-specific collective efficacy (or team efficacy) predicted team/group performance. A measure of team interdependence (combined measure of goal, task, and outcome interdependence) moderated the relationship between collective efficacy and performance (but not between potency and performance) such that the relationship was stronger when interdependence was higher (Gully et al., 2002).

Interventions to Enhance Self-Efficacy in the Workplace

As noted previously, actual performance experiences have the most powerful effect (both positive and negative) on self-efficacy beliefs. Consistent with this notion. reviews of the training literature indicate that training interventions aimed at enhancing job-related skills can enhance both self-efficacy and job performance (Colquitt et al., 2000; Salas & Cannon-Bowers, 2001). Some attempts have been made to enhance self-efficacy beliefs in the workplace by means other than directly targeting job skills.

For example, an intervention designed to increase emotional flexibility of knowledge employees in the Netherlands significantly elevated general self-efficacy (task-specific self-efficacy was not assessed), and particularly benefited individuals with lower starting levels of general self-efficacy (Brassey et al., 2020). A study of professionals caring for individuals with intellectual disabilities in Spain highlighted the pivotal role of emotional intelligence, specifically the adept use of emotions, in mediating general self-efficacy and job engagement (job performance was not assessed) (Guerrero-Barona et al., 2019). Another study in the Netherlands involving employees from a variety of organizations in the demonstrated the effectiveness of a self-administered online intervention to enhance general workplace-related self-efficacy beliefs (Ouweneel et al., 2013). In a study of nurses at risk for burnout at a Chinese hospital, a six-month-long app-based program that encouraged them to record daily positive experiences and reflect on their role in these events enhanced both general self-efficacy and job performance (Guo et al., 2020). A study of rehabilitation professionals in Canada comparing face-to-face training with virtual training found that these modalities were equally effective in enhancing self-efficacy for using outcome measures in their work (Szekeres & MacDermid, 2021).

As noted previously, self-efficacy can be enhanced via vicarious or observational learning – that is, watching other perform a task competently. Observing high performers, however, does not always have a positive impact on self-efficacy and performance. If the observers' main goal is to display his or her competence at task (and avoid appearing incompetent), then observing high performing others can have a detrimental impact on both self-efficacy beliefs and performance (Downes et al., 2021), consistent with research on the distinction between learning goals and performance goals and their differential impact on motivation and performance (Dweck, 2006). Another study on increasing motivation for leadership among women found that women with lower levels of leadership self-efficacy were less inspired to become leaders by highly success women leader role models and that such role models may actually discourage women lower in leadership self-efficacy from aspiring to leadership positions (Hoyt, 2012).

Summary

Self-efficacy is one of the most studied psychological constructs over the past almost-half-century, and I–O psychology has been one of the most fertile fields for the study of self-efficacy. Taken as a whole, the relationship between self-efficacy beliefs and performance in work settings is weaker and more complicated than what is predicted by self-efficacy theory. Although job-related self-efficacy beliefs are generally good predictors of job performance, they probably are better predictors of performance on simpler tasks than of performance on more complex tasks. Consistent with control theory, self-efficacy beliefs may actually predict poorer performance when a person receives no or weak feedback on the task.

In addition to predicting job performance, job-related self-efficacy beliefs are also negatively related to workplace anxiety and stress and positively related to employee engagement and commitment, all of which have been linked to job performance. Self-efficacy beliefs may also influence job performance due to their influence on motivation to learn new job-related knowledge and skills and motivation to seek performance-related feedback, be more proactive and creative in "crafting" their jobs, and seek job-enhancing feedback. Self-efficacy beliefs also can be "too high" when confidence increases quickly with a little experience at a new task which can lead to inaccurate beliefs about how to go about the task. This applies to leaders as well as to employees.

Although effects of self-efficacy beliefs on performance may be relatively small, they may be nonetheless important, because unlike personality and cognitive ability, self-efficacy beliefs are relatively malleable (Judge et al., 2007). However, interventions designed to directly raise the strength of self-efficacy beliefs that do not involve clear feedback about performance during the intervention run the risk of failing or even back-firing.

There is little doubt that self-efficacy beliefs are, under most conditions, important predictors of behavior and performance in work settings, including the behavior of leaders and managers. Whether self-efficacy beliefs actually ***cause*** rather than simply ***predict*** future performance remains in doubt. Some research suggests that measures of self-efficacy beliefs do not significantly predict future performance above and beyond what can be predicted by measures of past performance, personality (broadly defined), and cognitive ability. However, even if measures of self-efficacy do not predict future performance better than measures of past performance, they can still be useful because self-report measures of self-efficacy are much easier to administer than are measures of actual past performance. Apparently, one of the best and easiest ways to predict if someone is going to be successful at something in the workplace is to ask them how confident they are that they will be. It's not fool-proof, but considerable research indicates that it's a pretty good bet.

Notes

1 The authors are grateful to Seth Kaplan and Nathan Bowling for their helpful comments on an earlier version of this chapter.

2 This chapter will use the terms *self-efficacy belief* and *self-efficacy expectancy* interchangeably. Sometimes the term *self-efficacy* will be used, but these terms will always refer to a set of beliefs or expectancies.

3 The authors are grateful to Jeffrey Vancouver for his helpful comments on this section. Any misinterpretations of his comments are entirely the fault of the authors!

References

Adamovic, M., Gahan, P., Olsen, J., Gulyas, A., Shallcross, D., & Mendoza, A. (2021). Exploring the adoption of virtual work: The role of virtual work self-efficacy and virtual work climate. *The International Journal of Human Resource Management*, 1–34. https://doi.org/10.1080/09585192.2021.1913623

Alessandri, G., Perinelli, E., De Longis, E., Schaufeli, W. B., Theodorou, A., Borgogni, L., Caprara, G. V., & Cinque, L. (2018). Job burnout: The contribution of emotional stability and emotional self-efficacy beliefs. *Journal of Occupational and Organizational Psychology*, *91*(4), 823–851. https://doi.org/10.1111/joop.12225

Bandura, A. (1977). Self-efficacy: Toward a unifying theory of behavioral change. *Psychological Review*, *84*, 191–215.

Bandura, A. (1986). *Social foundations of thought and action: A social cognitive theory* (pp. xiii, 617). Prentice-Hall, Inc.

Bandura, A. (1997). *Self-efficacy: The exercise of control*. Freeman.

Bandura, A., & Adams, N. E. (1977). Analysis of self-efficacy theory of behavioral change. *Cognitive Therapy and Research*, *1*(4), 287–310. https://doi.org/10.1007/BF01663995

Bandura, A., & Wood, R. (1989). Effect of perceived controllability and performance standards on self-regulation of complex decision making. *Journal of Personality and Social Psychology*, *56*(5), 805–814. https://doi.org/10.1037/0022-3514.56.5.805

Beattie, S., Woodman, T., Fakehy, M., & Dempsey, C. (2016). The role of performance feedback on the self-efficacy–performance relationship. *Sport, Exercise, and Performance Psychology*, *5*(1), 1–13. https://doi.org/10.1037/spy0000051

Borgogni, L., Dello Russo, S., Petitta, L., & Latham, G. P. (2009). Collective efficacy and organizational commitment in an Italian City Hall. *European Psychologist*, *14*(4), 363–371. https://doi.org/10.1027/1016-9040.14.4.363

Brassey, J., van Witteloostuijn, A., Huszka, C., Silberzahn, T., & van Dam, N. (2020). Emotional flexibility and general self-efficacy: A pilot training intervention study with knowledge workers. *PLoS One*, *15*(10), e0237821. https://doi.org/10.1371/journal.pone.0237821

Carter, W. R., Nesbit, P. L., Badham, R. J., Parker, S. K., & Sung, L.-K. (2018). The effects of employee engagement and self-efficacy on job performance: A longitudinal field study. *The International Journal of Human Resource Management*, *29*(17), 2483–2502. https://doi.org/10.1080/09585192.2016.1244096

Chemers, M. M., Watson, C. B., & May, S. T. (2000). Dispositional affect and leadership effectiveness: A comparison of self-esteem, optimism, and efficacy. *Personality and Social Psychology Bulletin*, *26*(3), 267–277. https://doi.org/10.1177/0146167200265001

Chen, G., Goddard, T. G., & Casper, W. J. (1999). Be specific! The role of context in core evaluations of the world and the self. *Paper Presented at the 59th Annual Meeting of the Academy of Management*. Chicago.

Chen, G., Gully, S. M., & Eden, D. (2001). Validation of a new general self-efficacy scale. *Organizational Research Methods*, *4*, 62–83.

Chen, G., Gully, S. M., & Eden, D. (2004). General self-efficacy and self-esteem: Toward theoretical and empirical distinction between correlated self-evaluations. *Journal of Organizational Behavior*, *25*(3), 375–395. https://doi.org/10.1002/job.251

Colquitt, J., LePine, J., & Noe, R. (2000). Toward an integrative theory of training motivation: A meta-analytic path analysis of 20 years of research. *The Journal of Applied Psychology*, *85*, 678–707. https://doi.org/10.1037//0021-9010.85.5.678

De Clercq, D., Haq, I. U., & Azeem, M. U. (2018). Self-efficacy to spur job performance: Roles of job-related anxiety and perceived workplace incivility. *Management Decision*, *56*(4), 891–907. https://doi.org/10.1108/MD-03-2017-0187

Dimotakis, N., Mitchell, D., & Maurer, T. (2017). Positive and negative assessment center feedback in relation to development self-efficacy, feedback seeking, and promotion. *Journal of Applied Psychology*, *102*(11), 1514–1527. https://doi.org/10.1037/apl0000228

Downes, P. E., Crawford, E. R., Seibert, S. E., Stoverink, A. C., & Campbell, E. M. (2021). Referents or role models? The self-efficacy and job performance effects of perceiving higher performing peers. *Journal of Applied Psychology*, *106*(3), 422–438. https://doi.org/10.1037/apl0000519

Dweck, C. S. (2006). *Mindset: The new psychology of success*. Random House Publishing Group.

Dwyer, L. P. (2019). Leadership self-efficacy: Review and leader development implications. *Journal of Management Development*, *38*(8), 637–650. https://doi.org/10.1108/JMD-03-2019-0073

Eden, D. (1988). Pygmalion, goal setting, and expectancy: Compatible ways to raise productivity. *Academy of Management Review*, *13*, 639–652.

Emeriau-Farges, C. V., Deschênes, A.-A., & Dussault, M. (2019). Emotional self-efficacy and psychological health of police officers. *Policing: An International Journal, 42*(4), 598–610. https://doi.org/10.1108/PIJPSM-06-2018-0076

Fast, N. J., Burris, E. R., & Bartel, C. A. (2014). Managing to stay in the dark: Managerial self-efficacy, ego defensiveness, and the aversion to the employee voice. *Academy of Management Journal, 57*(4), 1013–1034.

Federici, R. A. (2013). Principals' self-efficacy: Relations with job autonomy, job satisfaction, and contextual constraints. *European Journal of Psychology of Education, 28*(1), 73–86. https://doi.org/10.1007/s10212-011-0102-5

Fida, R., Paciello, M., Tramontano, C., Barbaranelli, C., & Farnese, M. L., (2015). "Yes I Can": The protective role of personal self-efficacy in hindering counterproductive work behavior under stressful conditions. *Anxiety, Stress, & Coping: An International Journal, 28*(5), 479–499.

Gardner, D. G., & Pierce, J. L. (1998). Self-esteem and self-efficacy within the organizational context: An empirical examination. *Group & Organization Management, 23*(1), 48–70. https://doi.org/10.1177/1059601198231004

Grosemans, I., Coertjens, L., & Kyndt, E. (2020). Work-related learning in the transition from higher education to work: The role of the development of self-efficacy and achievement goals. *British Journal of Educational Psychology, 90*(1), 19–42. https://doi.org/10.1111/bjep.12258

Guerrero-Barona, E., Rodríguez-Jiménez, M., & Chambel, M. J. (2019). Engagement in careers of persons with intellectual disabilities: The role of self-efficacy and emotional intelligence. *Disability and Rehabilitation, 42*(10), 1397–1405. https://doi.org/10.1080/09638288.2018.1526976

Gully, S. M., Incalcaterra, K. A., Joshi, A., & Beaubien, J. M. (2002). A meta-analysis of team-efficacy, potency, and performance: Interdependence and level of analysis as moderators of observed relationships. *Journal of Applied Psychology, 87*(5), 819–832. https://doi.org/10.1037/0021-9010.87.5.819

Guo, Y.-F., Lam, L., Plummer, V., Cross, W., & Zhang, J.-P. (2020). A WeChat-based "Three Good Things" positive psychotherapy for the improvement of job performance and self-efficacy in nurses with burnout symptoms: A randomized controlled trial. *Journal of Nursing Management, 28*(3), 480–487. https://doi.org/10.1111/jonm.12927

Hannah, S. T., Avolio, B. J., Luthans, F., & Harms, P. D. (2008). Leadership efficacy: Review and future directions. *The Leadership Quarterly, 19*(6), 669–692. https://doi.org/10.1016/j.leaqua.2008.09.007

Hannah, S. T., Schaubroeck, J. M., & Peng, A. C. (2016). Transforming followers' value internalization and role self-efficacy: Dual processes promoting performance and peer norm-enforcement. *Journal of Applied Psychology, 101*(2), 252–266. https://doi.org/10.1037/apl0000038

Heggestad, E. D., & Kanfer, R. (2005). The predictive validity of self-efficacy in training performance: Little more than past performance. *Journal of Experimental Psychology: Applied, 11*, 84–97.

Heuven, E., Bakker, A. B., Schaufeli, W. B., & Huisman, N. (2006). The role of self-efficacy in performing emotion work. *Journal of Vocational Behavior, 69*(2), 222–235. https://doi.org/10.1016/j.jvb.2006.03.002

Hoffman, B., & Schraw, G. (2009). The influence of self-efficacy and working memory capacity on problem-solving efficiency. *Learning and Individual Differences, 19*, 91–100.

Hoyt, C. L., (2012). Inspirational or self-deflating: The role of self-efficacy in elite role model effectiveness. *Social Psychological and Personality Science, 4*(3), 290–298.

Huard, C., Deschênes, A.-A., & Rioux, C.-A. (2021). Emotional self-efficacy and workplace psychological health in emergency dispatchers. *International Journal of Emergency Services, 10*(2), 276–287. https://doi.org/10.1108/IJES-03-2020-0011

Ingusci, E., Callea, A., Cortese, C. G., Zito, M., Borgogni, L., Cenciotti, R., Colombo, L., Signore, F., Ciavolino, E., & Demerouti, E. (2019). Self-efficacy and work performance: The role of job crafting in middle-age workers. *International Journal of Business and Society, 20*(2), 533–551.

Instinske, J., & Kandler, C. (2023). Structure and sources of core self-evaluations: Construct validation using multi-rater and genetically informative designs. *European Journal of Personality, 38*(3), 516–533. https://doi.org/10.1177/08902070231176690

Jerusalem, M., & Schwarzer, R. (1995). General self-efficacy scale–revised–English Version (Gse-R) [Database record]. *APA PsycTests*. https://doi.org/10.1037/t18916-000

Judge, T. A., Jackson, C. L., Shaw, J. C., Scott, B. A., & Rich, B. L. (2007). Self-efficacy and work-related performance: The integral role of individual differences. *Journal of Applied Psychology, 92*(1), 107–127. https://doi.org/10.1037/0021-9010.92.1.107

Judge, T. A., Locke, E. A., & Durham, C. C. (1997). The dispositional causes of job satisfaction: A core evaluations approach. *Research in Organizational Behavior, 19*, 151–188.

Kanfer, R., & Heggestad, E. D. (1997). Motivational traits and skills: A person centered approach to work motivation. In L. L. Cummings & B. M. Staw (Eds.), *Research in organizational behavior* (Vol. 19, pp. 1±56). JAI Press, Inc.

Lange, M., & Kayser, I. (2022). The role of self-efficacy, work-related autonomy and work-family conflict on employee's stress level during home-based remote work in Germany. *International Journal of Environmental Research and Public Health, 19*(9), 4995. https://doi.org/10.3390/ijerph19094955

Lent, R. W., Morris, T. R., Wang, R. J., Moturu, B. P., Cygrymus, E. R., Yeung, J. G. (2022). Test of a social cognitive model of proactive career behavior. *Journal of Career Assessment, 30*(4), 756–775.

Lisbona, A., Palaci, F., & Salanova, M. (2018). The effects of work engagement and self-efficacy on personal initiative and performance. *Psicothema, 30*(1), 89–96. https://doi.org/10.7334/psicothema2016.245

Liu, E., & Huang, J. (2019). Occupational self-efficacy, organizational commitment, and work engagement. *Social Behavior and Personality: An International Journal, 47*(8), 1–7. https://doi.org/10.2224/sbp.8046

Lloyd, J., Bond, F. W., & Flaxman, P. E. (2017). Work-related self-efficacy as a moderator of the impact of a worksite stress management training intervention: Intrinsic work motivation as a higher order condition of effect. *Journal of Occupational Health Psychology, 22*(1), 115–127. https://doi.org/10.1037/ocp0000026

Locke, E. A., & Latham, G. P. (1990). *A theory of goal setting and performance*. Englewood Cliffs, NJ: Prentice-Hall.

Loeb, C., Stempel, C., & Isaksson, K. (2016). Social and emotional self-efficacy at work. *Scandinavian Journal of Psychology, 57*(2), 152–161. Luthans, F., Luthans, K. W., & Luthans, B. C. (2004). Positive psychological capital: Beyond human and social capital. *Business Horizons, 47*(1), 45–50. https://doi.org/10.1016/j.bushor.2003.11.007

Maddux, J. E. (1999). Expectancies and the social–cognitive perspective: Basic principles, processes, and variables. In I. Kirsch (Ed.), *How expectancies shape experience* (pp. 17–39). American Psychological Association. https://doi.org/10.1037/10332-001

Maddux, J. E. (2008). Positive psychology and the illness ideology: Toward a positive clinical psychology. *Applied Psychology, 57*(s1), 54–70. https://doi.org/10.1111/j.1464-0597.2008.00354.x

Mathieu, J. E., Rapp, T. L., Maynard, M. T., & Mangos, P. M. (2009). Interactive effects of team and task shared mental models as related to air traffic controllers' collective efficacy and effectiveness. *Human Performance*, *23*(1), 22–40. https://doi.org/10.1080/08959280903400150

McCormick, M. J. (2001). Self-efficacy and leadership effectiveness: Applying social cognitive theory to leadership. *Journal of Leadership Studies*, *8*(1), 22–33. https://doi.org/10.1177/107179190100800102

McCormick, M. J., Tanguma, J., & López-Forment, A. S. (2002). Extending self-efficacy theory to leadership: A review and empirical test. *Journal of Leadership Education*, *1*(2), 34–49.

McCrae, R. R., & Löckenhoff, C. E. (2010). Self-regulation and the five-factor model of personality traits. In *Handbook of personality and self-regulation* (pp. 145–168). John Wiley & Sons, Ltd. https://doi.org/10.1002/9781444318111.ch7

McLarnon, M. J. W., & Woodley, H. J. R. (2021). Collective efficacy in virtual teams: Emergence, trajectory, and effectiveness implications. *Canadian Journal of Behavioural Science/Revue Canadienne Des Sciences Du Comportement*, *53*(2), 187–199. https://doi.org/10.1037/cbs0000233

Meyer, J. P., & Allen, N. J. (1991). A three-component conceptualization of organizational commitment. *Human Resource Management Review*, *1*(1), 61–89. https://doi.org/10.1016/1053-4822(91)90011-Z

Ng, K.-Y., Ang, S., & Chan, K.-Y. (2008). Personality and leader effectiveness: A moderated mediation model of leadership self-efficacy, job demands, and job autonomy. *Journal of Applied Psychology*, *93*(4), 733–743. https://doi.org/10.1037/0021-9010.93.4.733

Ng, T. W. H., & Lucianetti, L. (2016). Within-individual increases in innovative behavior and creative, persuasion, and change self-efficacy over time: A social–cognitive theory perspective. *Journal of Applied Psychology*, *101*(1), 14–34. https://doi.org/10.1037/apl0000029

Ouweneel, E., Le Blanc, P. M., & Schaufeli, W. B. (2013). Do-it-yourself: An online positive psychology intervention to promote positive emotions, self-efficacy, and engagement at work. *Career Development International*, *18*(2), 173–195. https://doi.org/10.1108/CDI-10-2012-0102

Paglis, L. L., & Green, S. G. (2002). Leadership self-efficacy and managers' motivation for leading change. *Journal of Organizational Behavior*, *23*(2), 215–235. https://doi.org/10.1002/job.137

Petitta, L., Jiang, L., & Palange, M. (2015). The differential mediating roles of task, relations, and emotions collective efficacy on the link between dominance and performance: A multilevel study in sport teams. *Group Dynamics: Theory, Research, and Practice*, *19*(3), 181–199. https://doi.org/10.1037/gdn0000031

Powers, W. T. (1973). Feedback: Beyond behaviorism. *Science*, *179*(4071), 351–356. https://www.science.org/doi/abs/10.1126/science.179.4071.351.

Qi, L., Xu, Y., & Liu, B. (2023). Work out of office: How and when does employees' self-control influence their remote work effectiveness? *Frontiers in Psychology*, *14*. https://doi.org/10.3389/fpsyg.2023.1265593

Richard, E. M., Diefendorff, J. M., & Martin, J. H. (2006). Revisiting the within-person self-efficacy and performance relation. *Human Performance*, *19*(1), 67–87. https://doi.org/10.1207/s15327043hup1901_4

Sadri, G., & Robertson, I. T. (1993). Self-efficacy and work-related behaviour: A review and meta-analysis. *Applied Psychology: An International Review*, *42*(2), 139–152. https://doi.org/10.1111/j.1464-0597.1993.tb00728.x

Sanchez, C. & Dunham, D. (2018). Overconfidence among beginners: Is a little learning a dangerous thing? *Journal of Personality and Social Psychology, 114*(1), 10–28.

Salas, E., & Cannon-Bowers, J. A. (2001). The science of training: A decade of progress. *Annual Review of Psychology, 52*(1), 471–499. https://doi.org/10.1146/annurev.psych.52.1.471

Schaufeli, W. B., Salanova, M., González-romá, V., & Bakker, A. B. (2002). The measurement of engagement and burnout: A two sample confirmatory factor analytic approach. *Journal of Happiness Studies, 3*(1), 71–92. https://doi.org/10.1023/A:1015630930326

Schmidt, A. M., & DeShon, R. P. (2010). The moderating effects of performance ambiguity on the relationship between self-efficacy and performance. *Journal of Applied Psychology, 95*(3), 572–581. https://doi.org/10.1037/a0018289

Sherer, M., Maddux, J. E., Mercandante, B., Prentice-Dunn, S., Jacobs, B., & Rogers, R. W. (1982). The self-efficacy scale: Construction and validation. *Psychological Reports, 51*, 633–671.

Sherf, E. N., & Morrison, E. W. (2020). I do not need feedback! Or do I? Self-efficacy, perspective taking, and feedback seeking. *Journal of Applied Psychology, 105*(2), 146–165. https://doi.org/10.1037/apl0000432

Sitzman, T., & Yeo, G. (2013). A meta-analytical investigation of the within-person self-efficacy domain: Is self-efficacy a product of past performance or a driver of future performance? *Personnel Psychology, 66*(3), 531–568. https://doi.org/10.1111/peps.12035

Skaalvik, E. M., & Skaalvik, S. (2014). Teacher self-efficacy and perceived autonomy: relations with teacher engagement, job satisfaction, and emotional exhaustion. *Psychological Reports, 114*, 68–77.

Song, J. H., Jeong, Y., Kim, S. J., Lim, H. J., Roh, T., & Lee, J. (2018). Statistics of the educational welfare priority support project in 2018. Central Educational Welfare Research Support Center. Seoul, Korea.

Sousa, C. M. P., Coelho, F., & Guillamon-Saorin, E. (2012). Personal values, autonomy, and self-efficacy: Evidence from frontline service employees. *International Journal of Selection and Assessment, 20*(2), 159–170. https://doi.org/10.1111/j.1468-2389.2012.00589.x

Stajkovic, A. D. (2006). Development of a core confidence-higher order construct. *Journal of Applied Psychology, 91*(6), 1208–1224. https://doi.org/10.1037/0021-9010.91.6.1208

Stajkovic, A. D., Lee, D., & Nyberg, A. J. (2009). Collective efficacy, group potency, and group performance: Meta-analyses of their relationships, and test of a mediation model. *Journal of Applied Psychology, 94*(3), 814–828. https://doi.org/10.1037/a0015659

Stajkovic, A. D., & Luthans, F. (1998). Self-efficacy and work-related performance: A meta-analysis. *Psychological Bulletin, 124*(2), 240–261. https://doi.org/10.1037/0033-2909.124.2.240

Szekeres, M., & MacDermid, J. C. (2021). Online learning versus workshops: A rank minimized trial comparing the effect of two knowledge translation strategies designed to alter knowledge, readiness to change, and self-efficacy with respect to rehabilitation outcome measures. *Disability and Rehabilitation, 44*(21), 1–8. https://doi.org/10.1080/09638288.2021.1965227

Tasa, K., Taggar, S., & Seijts, G. H. (2007). The development of collective efficacy in teams: A multilevel and longitudinal perspective. *Journal of Applied Psychology, 92*(1), 17–27. https://doi.org/10.1037/0021-9010.92.1.17

Tims, M., B. Bakker, A., & Derks, D. (2014). Daily job crafting and the self-efficacy – Performance relationship. *Journal of Managerial Psychology, 29*(5), 490–507. https://doi.org/10.1108/JMP-05-2012-0148

Vancouver, J. B. (2005). The depth of history and explanation as benefit and bane for psychological control theories. *Journal of Applied Psychology*, *90*(1), 38–52. https://doi.org/10.1037/0021-9010.90.1.38

Vancouver, J. B., Gullekson, N. L., Morse, B. J., & Warren, M. A. (2014). Finding a between-person negative effect of self-efficacy on performance: Not just a within-person effect anymore. *Human Performance*, *27*(3), 243–261. https://doi.org/10.1080/08959285.2014.913593

Vancouver, J. B., & Purl, J. D. (2017). A computational model of self-efficacy's various effects on performance: Moving the debate forward. *Journal of Applied Psychology*, *102*(4), 599–616. https://doi.org/10.1037/apl0000177

Van Hootegem, A., Sverke, M., & De Witte, H. (2022). Does occupational self-efficacy mediate the relationships between job insecurity and work-related learning? A latent growth modelling approach. *Work & Stress*, *36*(3), 229–250. https://doi.org/10.1080/02678373.2021.1891585

Waaktaar, T., & Torgersen, S. (2013). Self-efficacy is mainly genetic, not learned: A multiple-rater twin study on the causal structure of general self-efficacy in young people. *Twin Research and Human Genetics*, *16*(3), 651–660. https://doi.org/10.1017/thg.2013.25

Wood, R., & Bandura, A. (1989). Social cognitive theory of organizational management. *The Academy of Management Review*, *14*(3), 361–384. https://doi.org/10.2307/258173

Wrzesniewski, A., & Dutton, J. E. (2001). Crafting a job: Revisioning employees as active crafters of their work. *Academy of Management Review*, *26*(2), 179–201.

Yeo, G. B., & Neal, A. (2006). An examination of the dynamic relationship between self-efficacy and performance across levels of analysis and levels of specificity. *Journal of Applied Psychology*, *91*(5), 1088–1101. https://doi.org/10.1037/0021-9010.91.5.1088

Zaccaro, S. J., Blair, V., Peterson, C., & Zazanis, M. (1995). Collective efficacy. In J. E. Maddux (Ed.), *Self-efficacy, adaptation, and adjustment: Theory, research, and application* (pp. 305–328). Springer US. https://doi.org/10.1007/978-1-4419-6868-5_11

6

A FIVE-LEVEL MODEL OF POSITIVE ORGANIZATIONAL BEHAVIOR AND EMOTIONS

Neal M. Ashkanasy and Momo D. Kromah

Over the years, the movement of positive psychology catalyzed a wave of change in psychology with the aim of shifting scholars' focus from preoccupation with repairing the worst things in life to building positive qualities (Seligman & Csikszentmihalyi, 2000). This change inspired organizational behavior scholars to study and emphasize the value of the "positive aspects" of organizational behaviors in organizations. Consequently, Luthans (2002) proposes a positive approach to organizational behavior: Positive organizational behavior (POB). Luthans defined POB as "the study and application of positively oriented human resource strengths and psychological capacities that can be measured, developed, and effectively managed for performance improvement in today's workplace" (p. 59).

POB includes the development of human resource strengths and psychological capacities of efficacy, hope, optimism, subjective wellbeing, and emotional intelligence. Researchers (e.g., see Youssef & Luthans, 2007) found that employees who have positive psychological capacities (e.g., self-concept, hope, optimism, resilience) tend to perform better, more satisfied and motivated in their work (Luthans, 2002). We also draw on Ashkanasy's (2003a) five-level model of emotions (FLMEW) in the workplace. In the model (see Ashkanasy & Dorris, 2017, for more recent update), the authors sets out five distinct but overlapping levels of analysis: Level 1 (within-person temporal variability) is concerned with employees' experience of in-the-moment affect and emotion. Level 2 (between-person individual differences) focuses on how emotions are enacted and experienced by different employees. Level 3 (interpersonal interactions) addresses the ways employees communicate and perceive emotions in interpersonal exchanges. Level 4 (groups and teams) focus on the concepts of group affective tone, emotional contagion, and emotional leadership (George, 2000). Level 5 (organization-wide) address emotional climate and organizational culture (Ashkanasy & Härtel, 2014).

DOI: 10.4324/9781032619385-6

It is important to note, and as Ashkanasy (2003a, 2003b) suggests, emotional behaviors and attitudes at each level, although conceptually distinct, cross the different levels of analysis, results in a complex and inter-connected picture of organizational functioning. In effect, emotions at the different levels "cascade throughout the organization, subsequently impacting key organizational variables that underpin organizational performance" (Ashkanasy et al., 2020, p. 375). In the following sections, we propose a multilevel model of POB and emotions based on the FLMEW model. We conclude with a discussion of how the components of the model fit together at each level of analysis and suggest some directions for future research on POB and emotions in organizations (Figure 6.1).

A Multilevel Model of POB and Emotions

At the core of the multilevel model (i.e., at Level 1) is affective events theory (AET). Weiss and Cropanzano (1996) suggest that employees react to events (e.g., unfair dismissal, interpersonal conflict) at work. These workplace events in turn influence employees' affective states (i.e., discrete emotions or moods) which may vary over time. Finally, both environmental features (e.g., noise, pollution, interest rates, e.g., see Norton et al., 2021) and dispositions (e.g., positive or negative affectivity at Level 2) influence employees' affective reactions and work-related outcomes (e.g., job satisfaction, behaviors). We use AET as the underlying theory of the multilevel model.

We theorize about employees' momentary experiences at Level 1 based on AET and suggest that the temporal nature and effects of moment-by-moment emotion in individual employees. We also consider key variables of POB (e.g., trait optimism and trait resilience) and emotion processes and outcomes at Level 2 (individual differences). At Level 3 (interpersonal relationships), we shift our focus to interpersonal emotional exchanges and communication of emotion, as well as situational moderators (e.g., leadership) at Level 4 (groups and teams) and Level 5 (organizational climate and culture). In the following sections, we discuss in detail each of these characteristics in turn.

Level 1: Within-Person Temporary Variability

AET (Weiss & Cropanzano, 1996) is the framework that underpins Level 1 in the FLMEW model. Weiss and Cropanzano (1996) suggest that, at the core of AET are "affective experiences" that are driven by environmental (e.g., economic, political events) and affective workplace events (e.g., organizational change events). Affective reactions in turn determine organizational members' work-related attitudes and behaviors (Ashkanasy & Dorris, 2017).

In other words, "affective events" that are caused by external or organizational environments (e.g. organizational change, leader behavior) influence employees' affective reactions which might be discrete *emotions* (such as fear, anger,

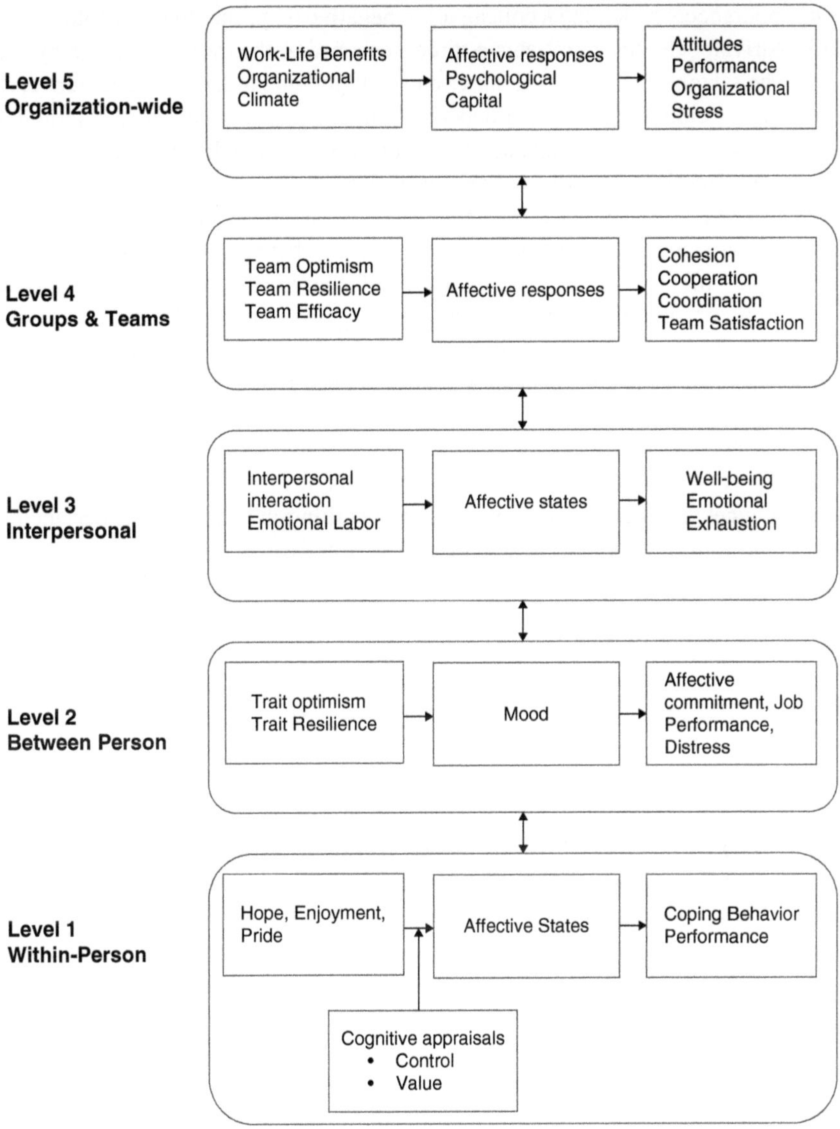

FIGURE 6.1 A Multilevel Model of Positive Organizational Behavior and Emotions

happiness, or sadness) that are acute and object-oriented (e.g., fear of a threat or anger when goals are thwarted). These reactions become *moods* which may not be object-oriented and last longer than emotions (Ashkanasy & Kay, 2023). According to Weiss and Cropanzano (1996), the resulting emotional reactions (e.g., fear, anger, happiness, sadness, and moods) have both attitudinal and behavioral consequences fall into two categories: (a) "Affect-driven" behavior that may be positive (e.g., spontaneously helping a colleague) or negative (e.g., shouting at a colleague). Affect-driven behavior represents a direct response to the event, mediated by the employee's emotional or mood state; and (b) "judgment-driven" behavior (e.g., quitting or deciding to be more productive, which come about because of attitudes (e.g., job commitment, job satisfaction, anomie) result from the affective event and subsequent emotional reactions (Ashkanasy, 2003c).

Finally, we propose that employees' cognitive appraisals of *control* of events and *value* attributed to events mediate relationship between affective events and employees' affective states. The inclusion of cognitive appraisal in our model has both theoretical and empirical support. Cognitive appraisal theory researchers (e.g., Pekrun, 2006) assume that emotional reactions begin with an appraisal of an event. Weiss and Cropanzano (1996) suggest that emotional reaction process begins with an event which employees might initially evaluate for affective relevance to their wellbeing in positive and negative terms. Employees' initial evaluation of events (positive or negative) leads to further specific appraisal of consequences, attributions, coping; thereby resulting in employees experiencing discrete emotions such as anger, sadness, or joy (Weiss & Cropanzano, 1996; Pekrun, 2006).

Evidence for our model is found in the work of Goetz et al. (2009); Bieg et al. (2013), and Hall et al. (2016). For example, in their study of positive emotions and critical appraisals, Goetz and his colleagues found among 50 university students that, emotions of enjoyment, pride, and contentment were positively related to control and value appraisals. Further, control and value interacted to predict positive emotions. The strength of appraisal/positive emotion relations was equivalent across achievement vs. non-achievement settings. These findings are consistent across appraisal–emotions research. In other research, Bieg and her team explored relations between cognitive appraisal antecedents (i.e., control and value) and trait and state emotions (e.g., pride, anxiety, and boredom). Their findings showed that, control, value, and their interaction predicted emotions in the expected direction. Furthermore, results revealed that appraisal–emotion relationships were similar in trait and state data.

Similarly, Hall et al. (2016) examined mediators (i.e., control, value, and perceived progress) of effects of achievement goals on learning-related emotions. These researchers found that perceived progress mediated relationship between mastery-approach goal and positive emotions (enjoyment, hope). In addition, perceived control mediated relationship between mastery- and performance-approach goals and outcome-related emotions (hope, anxiety). Finally, perceived value mediated relationship between mastery- and performance-approach goals and emotion of anxiety, with higher value levels predicting greater anxiety. Taken together, these research findings provide support for control-value theory of emotions (Pekrun, 2006) which posits that perceptions of control and value mediate the relationship between achievement goals and achievement emotions, whereas perceived progress mediates this relationship.

Level 2: Between-Persons Individual Differences

According to Ashkanasy and Kay (2023), Level 2 of the FLMEW concerns the role of individual differences. For example, employees may be angry or sad and these affective reactions will result in *different* attitudinal and behavioral consequences at work (Weiss & Cropanzano, 1996). Over the years, many researchers (e.g., Watson & Tellegen, 1985; Mayer & Salovey, 1997) examine important individual differences constructs that have affective significance at Level 2 of the FLMEW model including personality, temperament, trait affect, trait mindfulness and emotional intelligence (see Ashkanasy & Dorris, 2017 for a review).

From AET perspective, employees react differently to affective events at work (e.g., receiving performance feedback, a lack of promotion, an employee of the month award). These work events in turn influence employees' affective experiences (e.g., emotional states, mood) which vary over time and result in different employees' attitudes (e.g., satisfaction) and behavioral consequences (e.g., performance) (Weiss & Cropanzano, 1996).

Ashkanasy (2003a; see also Ashkanasy & Dorris, 2017) examined two emotion-related individual differences: (1) emotional intelligence (Mayer & Salovey, 1997) and (2) trait affect (Watson & Tellegen, 1985). In line with AET theory (Weiss & Cropanzano, 1996), Ashkanasy and his colleagues argue that such individual differences serve to moderate the effect of affective events on employees' subsequent emotional reactions. That is, compared to low emotional intelligence employees, high emotional intelligence employees should better perceive, assimilate, understand, and ultimately manage their emotions.

Similarly, Jordan et al. (2002) also argue that high emotional intelligence employees are less reactive to affective events (such as job loss) than their low emotional intelligence colleagues. With regards to trait affect, it is axiomatic that high positive affect (PA) individuals are more likely to experience positive affect in response to positive affective events than their low PA peers, while high negative affect (NA) individuals are more reactive to negative affective events than their low NA colleagues. Regarding POB, there is continuous debate in the literature about whether psychological resource capacities of hope, efficacy, resilience, and optimism are state-like constructs or trait-like constructs (Youssef & Luthans, 2007).

For our purposes, we argue that psychological resource capacities of hope, efficacy, resilience, and optimism (Luthans, 2002) are *both* state-like and trait-like; albeit they operate at different levels of the FLMEW model. State-like POB behaviors are suitable at Level 1 while trait-like POB operate appropriately at Level 2 (Ashkanasy, 2003a). In addition, there are evidence for both state-like and trait-like POB behaviors and their relationships to several work-related and organizational outcomes (e.g., performance, job satisfaction, work happiness, organizational commitment) (Youssef & Luthans, 2007). In sum, POB researchers have demonstrated that, differences in affective tendencies are associated with differences in work-related outcomes.

For example, Kluemper et al. (2009) studied state optimism and trait optimism among students (N = 772) and employees (N = 106). These researchers found that state optimism (but not trait optimism) is potentially a powerful indicator of organizational outcomes (e.g., job satisfaction, affective commitment, burnout, job performance, distress) even after controlling for effects of positive and negative affect. Relatedly, Ong et al. (2006) investigated the functional role of psychological resilience and positive emotions in the stress process in a sample of bereaved widows. These authors found that occurrence of daily positive emotions serves to moderate stress reactivity and mediate stress recovery. In addition, differences in psychological resilience accounted for variation in daily emotional responses to stress. Moreover, higher levels of trait resilience predicted a weaker association between positive and negative emotions, particularly on days characterized by heightened stress. Finally, Ong and his colleagues found that, over time, the experience of positive emotions functions to assist high-resilient individuals in their ability to recover effectively from daily stress. We argue that these findings suggest that state-like POB constructs and, by extension, trait-like POB constructs are related to positive emotions and important work-related and organizational outcomes.

Level 3: Interpersonal Relationships

The Level 3 in FLMEW model is largely concerned with *emotional labor*, defined by Hochschild (1983) as "management of feeling to create a publicly observable facial and bodily display" (p. 7). Ashkanasy (2003a) looks at this construct as a means by which organizational employees communicate emotions to others within and out of the organization. Grandey (2000) also made the case that emotional labor is, in essence, a special case of impersonal emotional regulation, insofar as employees seek to communicate emotions according to their perception of organization's mandated display rules (Diefendorff & Richard, 2003).

Subsequently, Zaki and Williams (2013; see also Troth et al., 2018) developed the idea of *organizational interpersonal emotion regulation* by recognizing that emotional regulation is either intrinsic (self-focused) or extrinsic (other-focused), and response independent or dependent. According to these authors, interpersonal emotion regulation can take one of four forms: (1) A purely extrinsic process; (2) a process that differentiates extrinsic from intrinsic regulation; (3) co-occurring emotional regulation; and (4) interpersonal emotional co-regulation.

The first form involves classic emotional labor (Hochschild, 1983), which can mean either surface acting (where the actor follows organizational display rules and displays emotions that may not represent her or his true feelings) or deep acting (where the actor summons up emotional memories to display the mandated emotional expression). The question arises here, however, as to whether an employee needs to engage in POBs to undertake emotional labor appropriately.

From AET perspective, incidents of emotional labor (e.g., hotel staff serves a customer with a smile or police officer displays negative emotions to enforce the law) constitute affective events at work (Ashkanasy, 2003a). We propose that, these affective events in turn affect employees' emotional reactions and thus personal and organizational outcomes (Weiss & Cropanzano, 1996; Ashkanasy & Dorris, 2017). At the personal level, the consequences of affective events are both attitudinal (e.g., job satisfaction, affective commitment) and behavioral (e.g., coping behavior, turnover, extra-role behavior).

For instance, Cheung et al. (2011) investigated the relationship between POB component of psychological capital, emotional labor, burnout, and job satisfaction among 264 Chinese school teachers. The authors found that, psychological capital was related to emotional labor, burnout, and job satisfaction in the hypothesized directions. In addition, psychological capital moderated the relationship between emotional labor and outcome variables. Specifically, Cheung and her team found that when psychological capital was high, the positive relationship between surface acting and depersonalization became weaker. This was also true for the negative relationship between surface acting and job satisfaction. Furthermore, the positive relationship between deep acting and job satisfaction was found to be reinforced for schoolteachers with high psychological capital than schoolteachers who reported low psychological capital. Finally, the authors found that the relationships between psychological capital, depersonalization and job satisfaction were salient for schoolteachers who reported infrequent expression of naturally felt emotion. The findings of this research demonstrate that employees do not necessarily have to engage in POBs to undertake emotional labor but that POB (especially psychological capital) may serve as important resources to amplify or lessen the effects of emotional labor on employees' work-related outcomes.

We argue further that another aspect where POB could play a role at Level 3 concerns the role of interpersonal interactions at work (e.g., interpersonal treatment from a supervisor or co-worker). The work of Dimotakis et al. (2010) is an important consideration at this level. Specifically, these researchers investigated the within-individual effects of workplace interpersonal interaction characteristics (positive or negative) on affect at work and employees' daily wellbeing (i.e., job satisfaction).

Although, workplace interpersonal interaction characteristics were not explicitly defined in the study, the authors measured the construct by modifying the "Recent interaction" section of the "Diary of Ambulatory Behavioral States" Scale which measures participants' recent interactions (i.e., last 30 minutes prior to completing the survey) with supervisor or co-workers. About 60 employees completed the interpersonal interaction characteristics measures as well as other measures on affective states (positive affect or negative affect) and job satisfaction. The researchers found that interpersonal interaction characteristics were associated with affective states and job satisfaction. Moreover, the effects of workplace interpersonal interactions on job satisfaction were mediated by affective states. Finally, results showed that positive affect mitigated the detrimental association between negative affect and job satisfaction (Dimotakis et al., 2010). Although, this study was conducted at the within-individual level, researchers (e.g., Ashkanasy & Dorris, 2017) have suggested that the levels of the FLMEW interact and overlap with each other. Indeed, Ashkanasy (2003b) argued that interactions at Level 3 serve as links between micro levels (i.e., Levels 1 and 2) and macro levels (i.e., Levels 4 and 5).

Level 4: Groups and Teams

The fourth level in the FLMEW encompasses group processes and especially team leadership. Organizational scholars (e.g., George, 2000; Ashkanasy, 2003a) suggest that leaders play a central role in setting the group's *affective tone*, which is also enabled by processes of positive group emotions including emotional contagion and emotional crossover (Sy et al., 2005; Krzeminska et al., 2018). For instance, Sy and his colleagues found that leaders have a special role to play in engendering a positive emotional tone in a group. Similarly, Gooty et al. (2010) argue, groups whose leaders foster a positive emotional tone become both cohesive and effective.

More recently, Krzeminska et al. (2018) found in a study of emergency services teams that leaders who encourage and achieve a positive workgroup emotional tone reduce team members' occupational stress and enhance their psychological capital. Relatedly, Härtel and Page (2009) introduced the idea of *discrete emotional crossover*, which they define as "the transmission of discrete emotions such as anger, joy, contentment, and fear from one individual to another in the same social environment" (p. 238). According to these authors, such crossover is a product of emotional contagion and involves importation of emotional experiences from outside the workplace (e.g., at home or in social activities). Organizational behavior scholars have extended this notion of discrete emotional crossover. For example, Ashkanasy and associates (2020) observe that "teams with important and frequent intra-group and leader interactions are likely to "catch" each other's emotions, while teams whose interactions do not meet these criteria may not" (p. 378).

Petitta et al. (2017) also theorize that the frequency and intensity of social interactions act as precursors of emotional contagion and in this regard, Petitta and her team argue that contagion in work-teams can be a double-edged sword. In other words, positive emotions act as positive resource likely to improve team performance, while contagion of negative emotions represent negative burden on the team likely to result in reduced team performance. Finally, Druskat and Wolff (2001) introduced the notion of *group emotional intelligence* and suggested that this phenomenon represents a form of emotional intelligence (like individual emotional intelligence).

Thus, a team that possesses high group emotional intelligence perceive, assimilate, understand, and manage emotions within the group. In this regard, Jordan et al. (2002) found that high emotional intelligence groups tend to demonstrate higher performance and better interpersonal communication than groups whose emotional intelligence was low. With regards to POB at the team level, West et al. (2009) studied the emergence of team level positive psychological capacities (e.g., team optimism, team resilience, team efficacy) and their relationship with team outcomes (e.g., cohesion, cooperation, coordination, and conflict and team satisfaction) during two team sessions. These authors found that among 101 teams, the positive psychological capital of team optimism was a predictor of team outcomes when teams were newly formed, whereas team resilience and team efficacy show greater explanatory power after several team interactions.

These findings represent another instance of interaction and integration among levels of the FLMEW model (Ashkanasy, 2003). Seen from the perspective of AET and the FLMEW model, West et al. (2009) expanded conceptualization of individual-level POB constructs (e.g., self-efficacy, resilience, optimism) to Level 4 of the FLMEW model (i.e., group and team level)s. These authors showed that, Levels 1 and 2 variables can function effectively as team level POB capacities such as team efficacy, team optimism and team resilience with significant relationships to various team outcomes including cohesion, coordination, conflict, cooperation, and team satisfaction. Although, West and colleagues did not explicitly study time, they however noted that the tenure and amount of time teams spent interacting may have implications for team level positive capacities and team level outcomes.

In other words, the more time teams spend together, the more likely the nature of teams' interactions will develop and change over time (West et al., 2009). While tenure and amount of time may seem important for team level positive capacities and team outcomes, we propose from AET perspective, the *addition* of team level affect (e.g., emotional contagion). Weiss and Cropanzano (1996) suggest that time is an important parameter for affect-satisfaction studies because affect levels fluctuate over time and the patterns of their fluctuations are predictable. Thus, we extend West et al. (2009) conceptualization of relationships between team level positive POB capacities (e.g., team optimism, team efficacy, team resilience) and team outcomes (e.g., team satisfaction) to propose that patterns of team affective reactions (e.g., emotion contagion) influence team members' levels of positive capacities and outcomes (Petitta et al., 2017).

Level 5: The Organization as a Whole

The focus at Level 5 of the FLMEW is on the organization and its climate and culture. Schneider (2000) defines *organizational climate* as the employees' immediate collective conscious perceptions of their work environment. De Rivera (1992, p. 2) also describes climate as "an objective (emotional) phenomenon that can be palpably sensed." In contrast, *organizational culture* is derived from the organization's founder and then evolves from the collective experiences of organizational members (Schein, 1992). Organizational culture is analogous to a "fossil record" (Härtel & Ashkanasy, 2011) and determines the organization's rules and norms of emotional expression (or *display rules*, see Diefendorff & Richard, 2003) and social interactions between organizational members.

Although, organizational culture and climate are distinctly different constructs, both contain an affective component (Ashkanasy, 2007). Thus, while organizational culture sets the norms for display of affect, the actual manifestation of affective climate is reflected in the organization's climate. Thus, as Virtanen (2000) notes, "climate is … more manifest than culture, and culture more latent than climate" (p. 349). In other words, how organizational members experience the emotional climate of their organization daily is derived from the organization's culture (Pizer & Härtel, 2005). For example, Ashkanasy and Nicholson (2003) examined the "climate of fear" in organizations and found that such climate was determined by the way organizational units were managed on a day-by-day basis. Furthermore, Ashkanasy and Daus (2002) suggest that culture and climate typically combine to determine whether the organization is a source of "toxic emotions" to its employees (cf. Frost, 2007).

In this regard, Härtel (2008) coined the term *positive work environment* (PWE) to describe the nature of organizational climate and culture needed to facilitate employee flourishing. According to Härtel (2008), employees in a PWE view their organization to be "respectful, inclusive and psychologically safe; leaders and co-workers as trustworthy, fair and open to diversity; and characterized by ethical policies and decision-making" (p. 584). The question that arises at this point is how do PWEs come about? Fujimoto et al. (2005) argue that it comes down to leadership and development of human resource management (HRM) practices that result in a healthy organizational culture and a PWE.

In an empirical test of this notion, Fujimoto and her colleagues (2005) found that HRM policies and practices underlie employees' individual and collective positive (versus negative) attitudes to diversity. Ashkanasy et al. (2020) argue further that HRM policies and practices play a key role in facilitating a PWE via managing and monitoring the affective experiences of employees, and especially though ensuring that managers are appropriately educated and trained in this regard. Ashkanasy and his team conclude (p. 379) this is achieved via, "facilitating positive workplace relationships and outcomes such as constructive conflict management, trust, diversity openness and organizational justice" (Krzeminska et al., 2018). Our discussion so far about organizational climate, culture and positive work environment has implications for understanding POB at Level 5 in the FLMEW model.

For instance, Muse et al. (2008) explored the relationship between organization provided benefit programs (i.e., work–life balance package) and POB. Using social exchange theory and the norm of reciprocity as theoretical anchors, Muse and her colleaguesz developed and tested a model identifying differential relationships of work–life balance benefit use and perceived benefit value with employee attitudinal and performance outcomes. These authors found support for their model and hypotheses that providing work-life benefits employees use and/or value was part of a positive exchange between employees and their employers. In addition, they found this exchange to be positively related to employees' feelings of perceived organizational support and affective commitment to the organization and reciprocation in the form of higher levels of task and contextual performance behaviors. Moreover, the authors found that, employees' perceptions of benefit program value play a critical role regardless of actual program use in influencing attitudes and behaviors.

Taken together, these findings confirm the crucial role of POB and of valuing employees and investing in their well-being inside as well as outside the workplace. Finally, in another study, Luthans and colleagues (2008) investigated the mediating role of positive psychological capital (i.e., hope, resilience, optimism, and efficacy) in the relationship between supportive organizational climate and employees' work-related outcomes (e.g., performance, satisfaction, commitment). These authors found that employees' positive psychological capital was related positively to their performance, satisfaction, and commitment. In addition, supportive organizational climate was related to both satisfaction and commitment. Lastly, Luthans and his team found support for their mediating hypothesis: that, psychological capital mediates the relationship between supportive organizational climate and employees' performance.

Discussion and Future Research

Theoretical Implications

First, the theoretical anchor we present in this chapter for the multilevel model of POB and emotions is AET (Weiss & Cropanzano, 1996). As we discussed earlier, AET posits that affective experiences at work are influenced by three factors: environmental features, work events and employees' dispositions. Moreover, affective reactions result in both attitudinal and behavioral outcomes. In this chapter, we applied AET to the multilevel model of POB and emotions and argue that positive psychological capacities are evident at each level of analysis of the FLMEW model.

At each level of the FLMEW: Level 1 (hope, enjoyment, pride, contentment), Level 2 (trait optimism, trait resilience), Level 3 (emotional labor, interpersonal interactions), Level 4 (team optimism, team resilience, team efficacy), and Level 5 (work–life benefits, psychological capital). Furthermore, we argue that these positive psychological capacities influence several work-related outcomes for individuals (coping behaviors, performance, job satisfaction, wellbeing), groups and teams (cohesion, cooperation, coordination, and team satisfaction) and organizations (organizational stress and performance).

Finally, we argue that, at the core of the multilevel model of POB and emotions is the role that affective experiences (i.e., affective states, moods, positive affectivity, negative affectivity) play as mediators of the relationships between positive psychological capacities and work-related outcomes at each level of analysis of the FLMEW model. In the following sections, we present some intriguing ideas for future research on the FLMEW model and POB in organizations.

Future Research Ideas

A potential area for future research is exploring additional theoretical perspectives of the FLMEW model. Most researchers (see Ashkanasy & Dorris, 2017 for a good review) have examined the FLMEW model in organizations and employed the AET as anchor (Ashkanasy, 2003). In this chapter, we explored cognitive appraisal theory (Bieg et al., 2013) at Level 1 of the multilevel model while maintaining AET as our overarching theoretical framework. We suggest future researchers would do well to consider other relevant theoretical perspectives including motivational theories, evolutionary theories, psychoanalytic theories with(out) emotions theories in understanding the FLMEW model in organizations. For example, Locke and Latham's (2002) Goal setting theory can be use in tandem with AET to understand employees' motivation as one possible cause of affective experiences at work. Organizational scholars of territoriality in the workplace suggest that, when employees' goals are thwarted, individuals may response emotionally (e.g., anger, fear, sadness) and behave territorially (e.g., reactionary defensive behaviors) (e.g., see Brown & Robinson, 2011).

Dynamic and Interactive Nature of the FLMEW Model

Several researchers (e.g., Ashkanasy, 2003; Ashkanasy & Dorris, 2017; Ashkanasy & Kay, 2023) suggest the dynamic and interactive nature of the FLMEW model. For example, as Ashkanasy (2003b) and Ashkanasy and Dorris (2017) stress that, the levels in the FLMEW model do not act completely independent of each other; and nor are they static. Instead, processes within the FLMEW model are inherently interactive and dynamic. Thus, just as affect varies moment-by-moment and day-by-day at Level 1, affective climate at Level 5 can likewise be variable (Ashkanasy & Härtel, 2014). Similarly, as we discussed earlier POB processes and emotions at each level interact with each other in a complex fashion (Ashkanasy & Dorris, 2017). Thus, as Ashkanasy (2003) suggests,

> while theorizing at Level 1 is based on AET and is intended to describe the nature and effects of moment-by-moment emotion in individual employees, it nonetheless incorporates processes at Level 2 (individual differences), Level 3 (interpersonal communication), as well as situational moderators at Level 4 (groups and teams) and Level 5 (organizational climate and culture).
>
> *(p. 16)*

Future researchers should consider the dynamic and interactive nature of the FLMEW model as they study POB and emotions in organizations.

References

Ashkanasy, N. M. (2003a). Emotions in organizations: A multi-level perspective. In F. Dansereau & F. J. Yammarino (Eds.), *Research on multi-level issues* (vol. 2, pp. 9–54). Bingley: Emerald Group Publishing. https://doi.org/10.1016/s1475-9144(03)02002-2

Ashkanasy, N. M. (2003b). Emotions at multiple levels: An integration. In F. Dansereau & F. J. Yammarino (Eds.), *Research in multi-level issues, volume 2: Multilevel issues in organizational behavior and strategy* (pp. 71–81). Bingley: Emerald/Elsevier/JAI Press. https://doi.org/10.1016/s1475-9144(03)02005-8

Ashkanasy, N. M. (2003c). Emotions in organizations: A multi-level perspective. In *Multi-level issues in organizational behavior and strategy* (pp. 9-54). Bingley: Emerald Group Publishing Limited. https://doi:10.1016/S1475-9144(03)02002-2

Ashkanasy, N. M. (2007). Organizational climate. In S. R. Clegg & J. R. Bailey (Eds.), *International encyclopedia of organization studies* (vol. 3, pp. 1028–1030). Thousand Oaks, CA: Sage.

Ashkanasy, N. M., & Daus, C. S. (2002). Emotion in the workplace: The new challenge for managers. *Academy of Management Perspectives, 16*, 76–86. https://doi.org/10.5465/ame.2002.6640191

Ashkanasy, N. M., & Dorris, A. D. (2017). Emotion in the workplace. *Annual Review of Organizational Psychology and Organizational Behavior*, *4*, 67–90. https://doi.org/10.1146/annurev-orgpsych-032516-113231

Ashkanasy, N. M., & Härtel, C. E. (2014). Positive and negative affective climate and culture: The good, the bad, and the ugly. In B. Schneider & K. Barbera (Eds.), *Oxford handbook of organizational climate and culture* (pp. 136–152). New York: Oxford University Press. https://doi.org/10.1093/oxfordhb/9780199860715.013.0008

Ashkanasy, N. M., Härtel, C. E. J., & Bialkowski, A. (2020). Affective climate and organization-level emotion management. In L.-Q. Yang, R. S. Cropanzano, V. Martinez-Tur, & C. A. Daus (Eds.), *The Cambridge handbook of workplace affect* (pp. 375–385). New York: Cambridge University Press. https://doi.org/10.1017/9781108573887.029

Ashkanasy, N. M., & Kay, A. A. (2023). Mindfulness and emotion: A five-level analysis. *Journal of Management & Organization, 29*(3), 406–424. https://doi.org/10.1017/jmo.2023.22

Ashkanasy, N. M., & Nicholson, G. J. (2003). Climate of fear in organisational settings: Construct definition, measurement, and a test of theory. *Australian Journal of Psychology, 55*, 24–29. https://doi.org/10.1080/00049530412331312834

Bieg, M., Goetz, T., & Hubbard, K. (2013). Can I master it and does it matter? An intraindividual analysis on control–value antecedents of trait and state academic emotions. *Learning and Individual Differences, 28,* 102–108. https://doi.org/10.1016/j.lindif.2013.09.006

Brown, G., & Robinson, S. L. (2011). Reactions to territorial infringement. *Organization Science*, *22*(1), 210–224. https://doi.org/10.1287/orsc.1090.0507

Cheung, F., Tang, C. S., & Tang, S. (2011). Psychological capital as a moderator between emotional labor, burnout, and job satisfaction among schoolteachers in China. *International Journal of Stress Management, 18*(4), 348–371. https://doi.org/10.1037/a0025787

De Rivera, J. (1992). Emotional climate: Social structure and emotional dynamics. *International Review of Studies in Emotions.* 2, 197 – 218. John Wiley & Sons.

Diefendorff, J. M., & Richard, E. M. (2003). Antecedents and consequences of emotional display rule perceptions. *Journal of Applied Psychology*, *88*, 284–294. https://doi.org/10.1037/0021-9010.88.2.284

Dimotakis, N., Scott, B. A., & Koopman, J. (2010). An experience sampling investigation of workplace interactions, affective states, and employee well-being. *Journal of Organizational Behavior*, *32*(4), 572–588. Portico. https://doi.org/10.1002/job.722

Druskat, V. U., & Wolff, S. B. (2001). Group emotional intelligence and its influence on group effectiveness. In C. Cherniss & D. Goleman (Eds.), *The emotionally intelligent workplace* (pp. 132–155). San Francisco, CA: Jossey-Bass. https://doi.org/10.4337/9781848443778.00038

Frost, P. J. (2007). *Toxic emotions at work and what you can do about them*. Cambridge, MA: Harvard Business Review Press.

Fujimoto, Y., Härtel, C. E. J., & Panipucci, D. (2005). Emotional experience of individualist-collectivist workgroups: Findings from a study of 14 multinationals located in Australia. In C. E. J. Härtel, W. J. Zerbe, & N. M. Ashkanasy (Eds.), *Emotions in organizational behavior* (pp. 125–160). Mahwah, NJ: Lawrence Erlbaum Associates, Inc. eorge, J. M. (2000). Emotions and leadership: The role of emotional intelligence. *Human Relations*, *53*, 1027–1055. https://doi.org/10.1177/0018726700538001

Goetz, T., Frenzel, A. C., Stoeger, H., & Hall, N. C. (2009). Antecedents of everyday positive emotions: An experience sampling analysis. *Motivation and Emotion*, *34*(1), 49–62. https://doi.org/10.1007/s11031-009-9152-2

Gooty, J., Connelly, S., Griffith, J., & Gupta, A. (2010). Leadership, affect and emotions: A state of the science review. *The Leadership Quarterly*, *21*, 979–1004. https://doi.org/10.1016/j.leaqua.2010.10.005

Grandey, A. A. (2000). Emotional regulation in the workplace: A new way to conceptualizeemotional labor. *Journal of Occupational Health Psychology*, *5*, 59–100. https://doi.org/10.1037//1076-8998.5.1.95

Hall, N. C., Sampasivam, L., Muis, K. R., & Ranellucci, J. (2016). Achievement goals and emotions: The mediational roles of perceived progress, control, and value. British *Journal of Educational Psychology*, *86*(2), 313–330. Portico. https://doi.org/10.1111/bjep.12108

Härtel, C. E. J. (2008). How to build a healthy emotional culture and avoid a toxic culture. In C. L. Cooper & N. M. Ashkanasy (Eds.), *Research companion to emotion in organizations* (pp. 575–588). Cheltenham: Edwin Elgar. https://doi.org/10.4337/9781848443778.00049

Härtel, C. E. J., & Ashkanasy, N. M. (2011). Healthy human cultures as positive work environments. In N. M. Ashkanasy, C. E. P. Wilderom, & M. F. Peterson (Eds.), *The handbook of organizational culture and climate* (pp. 85–100). Thousand Oaks, CA: Sage. https://doi.org/10.4135/9781483307961.n6

Härtel, C. E. J., & Page, K. M. (2009). Discrete emotional crossover in the workplace: The role of affect intensity. *Journal of Managerial Psychology*, *24*, 237–253. https://doi.org/10.1108/02683940910939322

Hochschild, A. R. (1983). *The managed heart: Commercialization of human feeling*. Berkeley: University of California Press. https://doi.org/10.1002/pam.4050030365

Jordan, P. J., Ashkanasy, N. M., & Härtel, C. E. J. (2002). Emotional intelligence as a moderator of emotional and behavioral reactions to job insecurity. *The Academy of Management Review*, *27*, 361–372. https://doi.org/10.2307/4134384

Kluemper, D. H., Little, L. M., & DeGroot, T. (2009). State or trait: Effects of state optimism. On job-related outcomes. *Journal of Organizational Behavior*, *30*(2), 209–231. Portico. https://doi.org/10.1002/job.591

Krzeminska, A., Lim, J., & Härtel, C. E. J. (2018). Psychological capital and occupational stress in emergency services teams: Empowering effects of servant leadership and workgroup emotional climate. In L. Petitta, C. E. J. Härtel, N. M. Ashkanasy, & W. Zerbe (Eds.), *Research on emotion in organizations, Volume 14: Individual, relational, and contextual dynamics of emotions* (pp. 189–215). Bingley: Emerald Group Publishing. https://doi.org/10.1108/s1746-979120180000014017

Locke, E. A., & Latham, G. P. (2002). Building a practically useful theory of goal setting and task motivation: A 35-year odyssey. *American Psychologist*, *57*(9), 705–717. https://doi.org/10.1037//0003-066x.57.9.705

Luthans, F. (2002). The need for and meaning of positive organizational behavior. *Journal of Organizational Behavior*, *23*(6), 695–706. Portico. https://doi.org/10.1002/job.165

Luthans, F., Norman, S. M., Avolio, B. J., & Avey, J. B. (2008). The mediating role of psychological capital in the supportive organizational climate—Employee performance relationship. *Journal of Organizational Behavior*, *29*(2), 219–238. Portico. https://doi.org/10.1002/job.507

Mayer, J. D., & Salovey, P. (1997). What is emotional intelligence? In P. Salovey & D. Sluyter (Eds.), *Emotional development and emotional intelligence: Implications for educators* (pp. 3–31). New York: Basic Books.

Muse, L., Harris, S. G., Giles, W. F., & Feild, H. S. (2008). Work-life benefits and positive organizational behavior: Is there a connection? *Journal of Organizational Behavior*, *29*(2), 171–192. Portico. https://doi.org/10.1002/job.506

Norton, T, A., Ayoko, O. B., & Ashkanasy, N. M. (2021). A socio-technical perspective on the application of green ergonomics to open-plan offices: A review of the literature and recommendations for future research. *Sustainability, 13*(15), 8236, 1–22. https://doi.org/10.3390/su13158236

Ong, A. D., Bergeman, C. S., Bisconti, T. L., & Wallace, K. A. (2006). Psychological resilience, positive emotions, and successful adaptation to stress in later life. *Journal of Personality and Social Psychology*, *91*(4), 730–749. https://doi.org/10.1037/0022-3514.91.4.730

Pekrun, R. (2006). The control-value theory of achievement emotions: Assumptions, corollaries, and implications for educational research and practice. *Educational Psychology Review*, *18*(4), 315–341. https://doi.org/10.1007/s10648-006-9029-9

Petitta, L., Jiang, L., & Härtel, C. E. J. (2017). Emotional contagion and burnout among nurses and doctors: Do joy and anger from different sources of stakeholders matter? (SMI-2016-0125). *Stress and Health*, *33*, 358–369. https://doi.org/10.1002/smi.2724

Pizer, M. K., & Härtel, C. E. J. (2005). For better or for worse: Organizational culture and emotions. In C. E. J. Härtel, W. J. Zerbe, & N. M. Ashkanasy (Eds.), *Emotions in organizational behavior* (pp. 342–361). Mahwah, NJ: Lawrence Erlbaum Associates, Inc. https://doi.org/10.4324/9781410611895-30

Seligman, M. E. P., & Csikszentmihalyi, M. (2000). Positive psychology: An introduction. *American Psychologist*, *55*(1), 5–14. https://doi.org/10.1037//0003-066x.55.1.5

Schein, E. (1992). *Organizational culture and leadership*. San Francisco, CA: Jossey-Bass.

Schneider, B. (2000). The psychological life of organizations. In N. Ashkanasy, C. Wilderom, & M. Peterson (Eds.), *The handbook of organizational culture and climate* (pp. 23–30). Thousand Oaks, CA: Sage.

Sy, T., Côté, S., & Saavedra, R. (2005). The contagious leader: Impact of the leader's mood on the mood of group members, group affective tone, and group processes. *Journal of Applied Psychology*, *90*, 295–305. https://doi.org/10.1037/0021-9010.90.2.295

Troth, A. C., Lawrence, S. A., Jordan, P. J., & Ashkanasy, N. M. (2018). Interpersonal emotion regulation in the workplace: A conceptual and operational review and future research agenda. *International Journal of Management Reviews*, *20*, 523–543. https://doi.org/10.1111/ijmr.12144

Virtanen, T. (2000). Commitment and the study of organizational climate and culture. In N. M. Ashkanasy, C. P. M. Wilderom, & M. F. Peterson (Eds.), *Handbook of organizational culture and climate* (pp. 339–354). Thousand Oaks, CA: Sage Publications.

Watson, D., & Tellegen, A. (1985). Toward a consensual structure of mood. *Psychological Bulletin*, *98*, 219–235. https://doi.org/10.1037//0033-2909.98.2.219

Weiss, H. M., & Cropanzano, R. (1996). Affective events theory: A theoretical discussion of the structure causes and consequences of affective experiences at work. In B. M. Staw & L. L. Cummings (Eds.), *Research in organizational behavior* (vol. 18, pp. 1–74). Oxford: Elsevier Science.

West, B. J., Patera, J. L., & Carsten, M. K. (2009). Team level positivity: Investigating positive psychological capacities and team level outcomes. *Journal of Organizational Behavior, 30*(2), 249–267. Portico. https://doi.org/10.1002/job.593

Youssef, C. M., & Luthans, F. (2007). Positive organizational behavior in the workplace: The impact of hope, optimism, and resilience. *Journal of Management, 33*, 774–800. https://doi.org/10.1177/0149206307305562

Zaki, J., & Williams, W. C. (2013). Interpersonal emotion regulation. *Emotion, 13*, 803. https://doi.org/10.1037/a0033839

7

OPTIMIZING FREE WILL WITHIN THE GROUP MIND

A Hierarchical Extension of the Goal Breakthrough Model

Kennon M. Sheldon

Introduction and Overview

Good decisions require prolific initial idea generation, to increase the odds of finding the optimal course of action (Simonton, 2018). In other words, the decision space should be fully expanded before it is narrowed to a single track (Hopper & Sakuja, 2017). Unfortunately, human minds are not like chess-playing AIs, capable of explicitly considering all possible branches and options. Instead, we must *feel* our way, via implicit thought, toward the highest-quality options – i.e., the options that satisfy and integrate as many constraints as possible, that will bring us the objectively best results. How do we perform this deeply intuitive task, and how can we help ourselves to perform it even better?

Most pertinently for this book's theme, how can GROUPS of minds best optimize the collective goal selection task, and help themselves to perform it even better (Hopper & Sakuja, 2017)? And what insights from *individual*-level theories of innovative or optimal goal selection, if any, can generalize to *organizational*-level theories of optimal goal selection? In this chapter I'll try to address these interesting questions, by drawing from our recently proposed theory of free will, and its inner workings.

As an overview, in the first part of the chapter, I'll present the goal breakthrough model (GBM; Sheldon, et al., 2023; Sheldon, 2022, 2024). The GBM addresses the motivational tier of personality analysis, rather than the trait- or self-tiers of analysis (McAdams, 2015). Also, it is a personality *process* theory (about how all people function the same), rather than an individual difference theory (about how people vary). The GBM was designed to explain how people generate lifegoals, especially new or innovative ones. Lifegoals are the broader and longer-term initiatives that guide people in their daily strategizing, such as "get back to school,"

DOI: 10.4324/9781032619385-7

"work on controlling my temper," "stand up for myself in my relationships," "grow my career in marketing," or much else (Emmons, 1989; Klinger, 1977; Little et al., 2007). It can be very difficult to find, commit to, and attain meaningful lifegoals. Indeed, many people spend decades pursuing objectives they don't really want – meaning that they never find, or pursue, their deepest preferences (Sheldon, 2014). Instead, they remain "stuck" – hoping for some breakthrough that may never come. What can they do about this?

The GBM contends that people can best get unstuck when they start to *ask themselves new questions*. Such verbal activity typically occurs in response to perceived feelings of dissatisfaction, that the person wants to remedy. Although the posed new questions may not result in immediate answers, their mere posing can drive significant nonconscious activity during a subsequent incubation period. As a result, exciting new possibilities or creative solutions may begin to bubble up into the person's awareness. Ideally, such illumination experiences might improve or even transform the person's life and well-being, *if* they have the courage to follow their implications: to say, "I've found the best or (at least a good-enough) solution, so now I need to move forward!"

To support this dynamic process model of creative decision-making, I next describe relevant brain network research. Abstract or high-level decision-making involves characteristic sequential interactions between several high-level brain networks, especially the DMN, the SN, and the CCN (these acronyms will be defined later). I'll try to show that in the brain, good decision-making looks a lot like the GBM in action.

To complete the first part of the chapter, I'll consider the philosophical underpinnings of the GBM. I'll suggest that it provides a very plausible model of how psychological free will operates, which is fully consistent with current compatibilist philosophies. Such philosophies assert that free will (properly defined) is possible in a materialistic universe, and indeed, is more likely true than hard determinism. Finally, I'll show that the GBM is consistent with current evolutionary thinking on how human executive functioning differs from and probably exceeds all other primates. Only humans can cue themselves to envision multiple possible futures or destinies, then select one as their heartfelt goal, to pursue for decades. As a result of this capability, human wishes can (and do) shape worlds.

Of course, this is a book about positive organizational functioning, not positive personality functioning! To address this gap, in the second part of the chapter, I will wax speculative – extending the GBM analysis beyond the mind of the individual person, to the mind of the companies, organizations, and collectives in which individual people work (Islam, 2015; Theiner et al., 2010). I will ask: Can organizational "group minds" optimize their creative decision-making (i.e., their free will) in the same ways that individual minds optimize their own decision-making? Or does this metaphor fail, because are there fundamental differences between the two kinds of mental functioning? Differences seem likely, because the term "group mind" seems more of an analogy than a clearly recognizable fact (James et al., 1988). In a real human mind, the functional units (e.g., neurons, neuron-assemblies, brain regions, cognitive networks) are directly connected by wetware within a single brain and body. In contrast, for a "group mind," the functional units are located within physically separated brains and bodies. Thus, for the group mind, the interconnections between functional units (i.e., the various people) are far more tenuous and indirect.

Still, the collective cognition (Weick & Roberts, 1993) of a working group or organization can exhibit many properties analogous to the properties of individual minds (Bateson, 1972), as seen in ant colonies (Wilson, 1963) or eusocial rodent societies. First, as with individual minds, organizations contain informational units dedicated to memory and record-keeping; imaginal units dedicated to envisioning new possibilities; managerial units dedicated to executive functioning; and behavioral units dedicated to the enactment of goals provided by management. Second, both bottom-up and top-down processes take place within group minds, just as within individual minds. Yes, CEOs rule at the top of companies, but they are also constrained and influenced by what's newly emerging from the bottom ranks, just as people are constrained by feelings and emotions, emerging out of their own deeper organisms. Third, within group minds, just as within individual minds, there may be more (or less) willingness and capacity to notice and respond to dissatisfaction (the main instigator of the goal breakthrough process, as described below). Denial can hold sway for a long time. Fourth, executives within group minds may be reluctant to grant autonomy to lower-level decision-makers (Ryan & Deci, 2017), just as individual decision-makers may be reluctant to grant autonomy to their own intuitive solutions. Some organizations may be prone to rigidly control what workers do, especially when problems reign, whereas other organizations may grant their employees free rein to solve problems, as will be discussed.

In short: in the second part of the chapter, I'll push the analogy between individual versus organizational functioning as far as I can, to see where it leads. Now, let's return to the beginning!

Part I: Individual-Level Choice-Making and the GBM

Before considering how people select goals, it is helpful to consider the entire goal pursuit process, from start to finish. One useful lens is the well-known action phases or "Rubicon" model of goal pursuit, proposed by Gollwitzer and colleagues (Gollwitzer, 2012). This four-stage model (reproduced below) says that people start out in a deliberation phase ("what should I do?" Box 1). They usually have no trouble thinking of possibilities, so they simply pick the one that looks most valuable and doable (an expectancy-value model; Gollwitzer, 2012) – thereby "crossing the Rubicon" to a new goal or intention. Guided by the new goal, the person then commences planning (Box 2), then acting (Box 3), then evaluating afterwards (Box 4). Evaluation might lead to disengagement from the intention (either "I solved it!" or

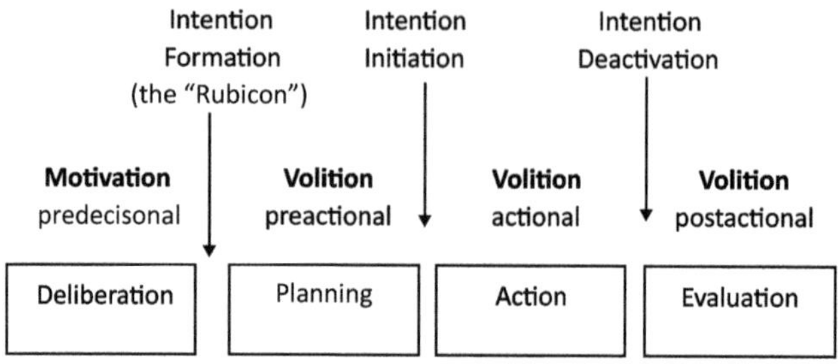

FIGURE 7.1 The Action Phases Model of Goal Pursuit

"I give up!"), or to reinvigoration of the intention ("I need to try harder/smarter!" Brandstätter & Bermann, 2022) (Figure 7.1).

Notably, most action phases research has focused on Boxes 2–4, that is the three *implementation*-related phases of action (Oettingen et al., 2001), after the Rubicon of decision is crossed, with relatively little attention devoted to Box 1, the *deliberation* phase. In other words, goal researchers in this (largely European) research tradition think much less about how people *select* goals in the first place, and much more about how they *enact* goals, after decisions have been made. Their general assumption, again, is that options are plentiful and that simple algorithms are sufficient to select between them.

However, many of us are familiar with the feeling of NOT knowing what to do, or of not being able to conjure any good options – the feeling of wanting, but not getting, promising new ideas or inspirations. The GBM, depicted below in Figure 7.2, is designed to explain how people can activate themselves within such "stuck" situations (Sheldon, 2022, 2024; Sheldon et al., 2022, in press). At the front end of the goal process, the GBM expands the Rubicon model's single deliberation stage into four substages, suggesting a way that people can operate their own minds in search of new action possibilities. At the back end of the goal process, the GBM condenses the Rubicon model's three implementational phases into one stage, called "elaboration" (although this stage could be re-expanded to include planning, action, and evaluation phases, yielding a full seven-stage model).

Background

The GBM is based on classic models of the creative process, going back to Wallas' influential four-stage model (1926) and continuing to present day research on the interactions between explicit and implicit cognition for creativity (Hélie & Sun, 2010). However, rather than addressing creative problem-solving in the moment or in a particular task, the GBM instead addresses creative goal selection, in life. Below I consider both levels of specificity simultaneously.

According to Wallas (1926), the would-be creator starts with a problem, to which they are trying to find an answer. In the GBM, this is represented as a state

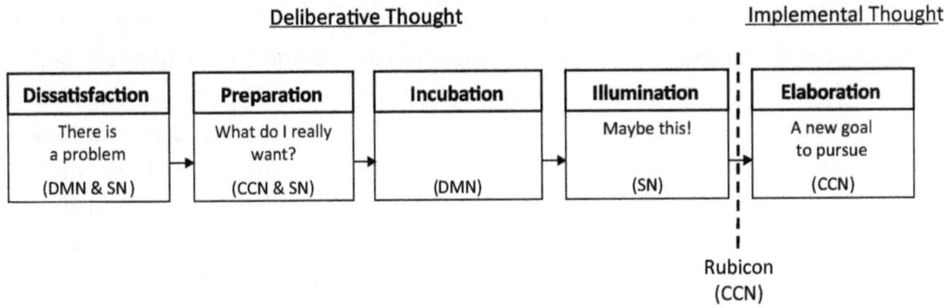

FIGURE 7.2 The Goal Breakthrough Model with Corresponding Brain Processes

of dissatisfaction with the status quo, at the far left of the Figure 7.2 diagram. Although a person may tolerate dissatisfaction for long periods of time, the GBM assumes that chronic dissatisfaction can eventually prompt the person to begin asking themselves questions – like "what do I really want?" and "what should I do, now?" In creative process theory, this is the "preparation" phase, as the would-be creator struggles, consciously, to solve the problem. When answers are not immediately forthcoming, the creator may stop trying, at least for a while. Similarly, a dissatisfied person may put aside, for now, the question of what to do next, or what to do differently. Next commences an incubation phase, in which nonconscious thought can occur. As set in motion by the preparation phase, the implicit mind may keep churning beneath the surface, or may be sensitized to recognize relevant analogies in the environment. Finally, at some fortuitous moment, new ideas or insights may rise to the creator's awareness – the "aha!" or illumination phase.

The classic example of illumination is Archimedes' realization that he could measure the volume of the king's golden crown via its water displacement, as he himself stepped into the bath. He knew the crown's weight, but did not know its volume, which was necessary to determine the gold's purity. His momentous insight was that the (easily measured) amount of water displaced by an irregular object (such as himself) provided a way to measure the crown's volume, and thus its purity! Supposedly, Archimedes leapt out of the bath and rushed to implement his new idea. Wallas called this the "elaboration" phase of the creative process, in which implementation replaces deliberation.

According to the GBM, entering the implementation phase requires the person to *speak*, or better yet, *write down*, a new goal or set of goals. They must impress the new goal upon themselves, in some way. This takes them "across the Rubicon" to action implementation, prompting them to start strategizing/making plans, emitting behaviors, and monitoring progress.

Empirical Test of the GBM

Sheldon et al. (2022) tested the GBM stage model directly, in repeated measures studies of both retrospective and prospective goal breakthroughs. In these studies, they found that rated initial preparation (i.e., intensity of self-questioning at time 1) predicted rated intensity of nonconscious thought during an incubation period (at time 2), which predicted the subsequent intensity of an illumination experience (at time 3). Intensity of illumination in return predicted enhanced psychological need-satisfaction, self-integration, and well-being (at time 4). In both studies, structural equation modeling supported the sequence of stages predicted by the GBM. Intensive self-questioning, the hypothesized critical executive function, led the way to stronger nonconscious thought, leading to greater new insights, finally leading to more impactful positive changes.

An Illustration

Consider a young corporate lawyer who, based on her excellent grades and record in law school, joined a large law firm after graduating, earning handsome compensation (Krieger & Sheldon, 2015). Although she is now (in her early 30s) rolling in money, she rarely has time to spend or enjoy it. What's more, her job is mostly about accumulating assets, securities, and wealth for her clients, rather than helping ordinary people solve real-life problems, as she pictured herself doing, back at the outset of law school. Despite her growing wealth, she feels rather stuck and miserable. What can change? How can she rediscover her youthful ideals?

According to the GBM, one transition-point may occur when she finally *notices* her misery, rather than shoving it aside – the point at which she really begins to question things ("what's wrong? What can I do differently?"). Another transition-point may occur when she doesn't immediately receive answers to these questions, and gives up the search, at least for now. This leads to incubation and nonconscious thought. Yet another transitional point may occur when a new idea pops into her mind – like "wait, what was that job opening I heard about recently, but dismissed? Financial director for a non-profit? Suddenly, that sounds intriguing!" A next transitional point may occur when she decides to make a change, by articulating a new goal ("I'll apply!"). A final transitional point may occur when she must either accept, or reject, the ensuing job offer. Maybe she gets cold feet, at the last moment? The breakthrough process could be derailed at any of these points.

At which transition points do people have the most potential efficacy, or even responsibility, for advancing their own breakthrough process? In other words, where (if anywhere) might they consciously take control? According to the GBM, the intentional and thinking self can be most involved and influential at two specific junctures. First, at the juncture of *starting to formulate verbal questions, after recognizing dissatisfaction* (commencement of the preparation phase). This transition may take considerable courage – to finally acknowledge a lingering problem, to the point of beginning to think about it. For the young lawyer described above, one Monday morning she realized she could hardly stand the thought of going to work – and started wondering: "is there a way out?" Second, the thinking self is also important at the juncture of *recognizing a good answer and turning it into a goal* (crossing the Rubicon to elaboration). Here, it may also take courage, to commit energy to a specific, effortful goal. For the young lawyer above, she immediately looked up the information about the newly remembered job opening, then resolved to apply for the job. In the end, this bold course of action led to many long-term benefits for her!

Brain Network Functioning and the GBM

To convince readers of the critical role of executive functioning at these two special junctures, it is useful to briefly consider the brain science underlying the GBM approach. Figure 7.2 shows the brain networks most active at various phases of the GBM, as discussed in detail by Sheldon et al. (2024). The first box contains the default mode network (DMN), which hosts intuitive, wide-ranging activity (Andrews-Hanna, 2012). DMN activity typically rules when we are musing or free-associating in an unguided way, and the DMN can stitch together many kinds of mental contents. When first discovered in the 1990s, the DMN was thought to be mere "mind-wandering," since it became inhibited during focused tasks, like counting backwards by 3s. But later the DMN was discovered to be quite relevant to much purposeful activity, as both a source of spontaneous new thoughts and feelings, and, as a resource for answering difficult questions. In the former guise, the DMN can yield the felt dissatisfaction that prompts the GBM (Box 1). In the latter guise, it can yield the creative new thinking that has been primed by self-questioning (Box 3).

Figure 7.2 also contains the Salience Network (SN), in Boxes 1, 2, and 4. The SN is in charge of recognizing the self-relevance of newly emerging information, within both the environment (via anterior cingulate cortex activity; Bush et al., 2000) and within the person (via anterior insula activity; Molnar-Szakacs & Uddin, 2022). The SN brings information to the person's attention, flagging it with a sense of importance – in both negative ("there is a problem!") and positive ("there is an opportunity!") cases. In the context of the GBM, the SN helps amplify negatively tinged activity within the DMN into fully felt dissatisfaction (Box 1), and furthermore, helps with the identification of the most pressing questions to ask oneself (Box 2). In addition, the SN is the brain network that helps recognize and amplify the significance of any "illuminations" which appear at the fringe of consciousness (Box 4).

Finally, Figure 7.2 contains the cognitive control network (CCN), which directs and focuses the flow of thought. The CCN works to retain information within working memory, including activated goals that regulate plan-making and behavioral enaction, even over long periods of time. The CCN also directs verbal processing, i.e., the person's "self-talk," as they engage with problems.

The CCN is critically involved during the elaboration/implementation stage of the GBM (Box 4; Niendam et al., 2012). After verbalizing the goal, the CCN should marshal energy and resources toward the goal's attainment. Nevertheless, the CCN is also important at the preparation phase of goal selection (Box 2), because it is a driver of verbal activity, including the activity of asking oneself new questions. And, as shown in Figure 7.2, the CCN is critically important for the crossing of the Rubicon, as it verbalizes and commits to the new goal. The latter are the two junctures or transition points discussed above, at which the conscious person might try to exert control.

It is important to state that the CCN isn't a mental homunculus or "lone executive," roaming the mind like a hero! The CCN requires and is informed and energized by input from both the DMN and the SN. Still, the CCN plays a particularly key role at the two junctures discussed above, befitting its role as the verbalizing, focalizing facet of the mind. This broad mental facet is sometimes referred to as "system 2," the step-by-step rational system, in contrast to "system 1," the more intuitive and automatic part of the mind (Kahneman, 2011). In GBM terms, system 2 corresponds with CCN, system 1 corresponds with DMN, and SN corresponds with (or connects) both.

Free Will, the GBM, and Evolution

Before completing this first part of the chapter, I'd like to consider the GBM in relation to the free will question, and in relation to key philosophical positions on the nature and functioning of free will. Why? Because the GBM well-formalizes these philosophical positions. Such a linkage will help better explain the "two critical junctures" discussed above, of (1) asking oneself new questions, and (2) verbalizing a new goal, thereby crossing the Rubicon. As I hope to show, self-directed activity at both junctures is necessary to successfully operate one's free will.

So, what is free will? The topic has engendered endless controversy and confusion. However, I believe this controversy is largely unnecessary, with some careful specification of definitions. Herein, I start with Wikipedia's definition of free will as "the capacity or ability to choose between different possible courses of action unimpeded." People can think about what they might want, then select their preference from among the options that appear. I take the position that the ability to query one's mind for future options, then pick one, is an evolved human capacity possessed by all mature and healthy humans (Sheldon, 2024). Of course, the operation of the innate capacity can be impeded (or depressed) by many factors including controlling authorities, highly constraining situations, and compromised brain functioning. Still, the capacity remains within healthy humans, no matter how limiting the situation. In extreme cases, we can choose to die for our principles, rather than give in to perceived evil around us (Frankl, 1946).

Notably, the wiki definition provided above exemplifies a *compatibilist* philosophical understanding of free will. Compatibilism holds that human agency is compatible (or consistent) with the existence of a brute material universe. By various possible means, extreme physical complexity can bring about a condition in which a conscious entity can cause its own behavior, somewhat (or in some way) independently of, or unpredictable from, underlying material forces and conditions. In contrast, deterministic perspectives assert that humans can never cause their own behavior; rather, their behavior is strictly determined by biological/physical and/or historical/situational forces over which conscious/deliberative processes have no control. Determinists insist that the feeling of choosing is always an illusion. Thus, what we really need to do, as scientists, is discover the bio-physical causes of such illusions, as well as the causes of behavior itself.

Reconciling these two perspectives is beyond the scope of this chapter. Suffice it to say that I side with the compatibilist view of philosopher Christian List in his book *Why free will is real* (2019). List advanced an emergentist argument for an inherent free will capacity, an argument which grants certain types of brain events irreducible causal force in the world. What kinds of brain events? List's specific definition pinpoints three sub-capacities: (1) the ability to conjure multiple options from one's mind, (2) the ability to choose one of them, and (3) the ability to enact that choice, behaviorally. People can imagine many different possible futures (i.e., they can conjure up multiple behavioral options), then they can decide which one they prefer, then they can start pursuing it as a goal.

Hopefully, readers can see that List's discussion of free will addresses the same choice processes that are addressed by the GBM, although List does not consider the mental activity underlying these stages, as I do. Thus, the GBM may provide a rather direct model of how free will works or can work.

Of course, the GBM is not the only model of this type. Related approaches include theories of prospective cognition (Seligman et al., 2016), mental time travel (Kellogg, 2023), future time perspective (Zimbardo & Boyd, 2008), and mental simulations (Zaleskiewicz et al., 2023). These approaches share the assumption that humans can intuit many paths toward many future landscapes, then pick one and work to bring it into existence. Our choices can create worlds. Free will evolved to allow humans to respond flexibly and creatively to the dazzling twists and turns of their intertwined personal and social landscapes (Sheldon, 2024). We do this by living within a story that has a narrative arc, in which the main character (i.e., us) has large degrees of freedom to make choices, within the moment.

Obviously, humans do not *always* choose in such an intentional way, nor do they always ask themselves probing questions about what they should do. There are cross-person and cross-time variations in these processes, as the longitudinal studies described earlier showed (Sheldon et al., 2022). Thus, often, people react much more automatically and mindlessly (although arguably, this is still their free will at work, in that they permitted the automatic behavior to proceed; Libet, 2005).

Part II: Extending the GBM to the Organizational Mind

How might the GBM help us to understand organizational choice-making, not just personal choice-making? Let's set up a point-by-point comparison. In considering an individual mind breaking through to new goals, the picture so far looks thus:

1. There is a person who feels stuck; they are pursuing goals that are not working for them, even if they are successful at those goals. Thus, they are perhaps reluctant to change course. The young lawyer discussed above is a case in point. According to the GBM, making a change first required her to notice her dissatisfaction (via spontaneous DMN activity) and then to recognize it as a problem (via SN activity).
2. This recognition moved her to start asking herself new questions, about what she wants or how to respond to the problem (via CCN activity).
3. Insightful answers took time in coming (via prompted DMN activity), but they were worth waiting for, because these integrative productions of her implicit mind satisfied many constraints at once.
4. During her "aha!" moment, she knew (via SN activity) that this new purpose was "it," so she crossed the Rubicon to the new goal – via verbal CCN activity. The CCN *sets* goals, not just enacts them.
5. Then her life changed! (via CCN-directed goal implementation). After her career shift, she derived much more satisfaction in life, because she was helping *worthy disadvantaged* people, rather than helping *unworthy advantaged* people. The former is much more happiness-conducive than the latter (Titova & Sheldon, 2022).

Repeated in narrative form: there was unsettling information which first had to be noticed by an executive process; which then had to shape and rebroadcast that information as a question for the deeper system; which then had to provide possible answers; which then had to be noticed (again) by an executive process; which then had to articulate and commit to a specific goal. There was back-and-forth between explicit and implicit (or conscious/nonconscious) parts of the mind, and the brain networks that implement these functions. There was a growing willingness to consider change, which led to increasingly novel ideas for change, which led, finally, to a brand-new direction for the person.

****

Can we extend the individual breakthrough process summarized above, to the efforts of an organizational group mind to solve its own difficult problems (Engel & Singer, 2008)? Let's start with a concrete example, analogous to the young lawyer. In 2012, Best Buy, an electronics retailer, was on the verge of bankruptcy. The on-line competition was taking too high a toll, and the big box store real estate wasn't pulling its weight. The CEO at that time, Richard Schulze, tried to leverage additional capital (and debt) to save the company. Perhaps fortunately, he was unable to close the deal.

Hubert Joly was brought in as the new CEO, an unusual choice because he had experience in hospitality but not in electronics. Dissatisfied with the company's current model, he asked everybody he could: "How can we turn this thing around?" His favorite suggestions came from front-line employees, much lower-down in the company. Some suggestions boiled down to this: "instead of us selling problems to the customer (i.e., hardware they don't know how to set up), how about us *solving* their problems?" (i.e., setting up their hardware). Joly recognized this as a promising solution to the brick-and-mortar conundrum (i.e., of why customers should drive to the store, instead of just shopping on-line). These conversations led to Best Buy's incorporation of "The Geek Squad," dedicated to solving buyers' technical issues. Arguably, the Geek Squad saved Best Buy (see Joly and Lambert's 2021 book, *The Heart of Business: Leadership Principles for the Next Era of Capitalism*).

With this example in mind, let's try to extend the five-point personal change process, outlined above, to the organizational mind, writ large.

1 There is an organization that seems stuck; it is pursuing goals that are not working for it, but it is perhaps reluctant to change course. Best Buy, discussed above, is a case in point. According to the GBM, making an organizational change requires the organization to first diagnose its dissatisfaction, and recognize it as a problem.

   Our first question in applying the GBM to the organizational case is: "where (or how or by whom) would dissatisfaction be recognized?" One location for such recognition is simply within the mind of the CEO, who is charged with making strategic choices for the company. Because the CEO's personal decisions are yoked to the company's decisions, the CEO's decisions (at least within their CEO role) ARE the company's decisions, perforce. If the CEO is skilled enough to recognize and interrogate their own dissatisfaction with the company's current course, then they may derive good solutions entirely from within their own minds. In this case, the GBM would apply only to the individual-level functioning of the CEO.

   Hubert Joly's contribution at Best Buy, of introducing a brand-new hospitality-based perspective, might seem to count in this regard. Maybe his genius and novel perspective alone lifted the company! Similarly, Shantanu Narayen, Adobe's current CEO, stated (in a 2023 Harvard Business Review article) that "Leaders must be dissatisfied with the status quo." Why? Because only then will they challenge their employees to do what they are truly capable of. Maybe what matters most is the CEO's personal dissatisfaction, and their drive to reduce it?

   Still, this may give too much credit to the CEO alone. Another possible source of dissatisfaction, besides "down in the ranks of the CEO's mind," is: *down in the ranks of the company*, i.e., in the company's "group mind." For example, employees or units with firsthand experience of the company's current problems might also be feeling dissatisfied with that status quo. They might try to register that dissatisfaction with their higher-ups, hoping (ultimately) to influence the CEO and the company's direction. Unfortunately, crossing this hierarchical gap, from low to high, can very be hard to do, as the night watchman on the Titanic discovered! (and as the young lawyer discovered, given how long it took for her to acknowledge and address her own growing personal dissatisfaction). As the new CEO at Best Buy, Joly didn't know what was wrong. To his credit, he invited his lower downs to tell him. And they were happy to!

This distinction between personal dissatisfaction and organizational dissatisfaction suggests an intriguing analogy: between *organizational* processes that operate beneath the attention of the CEO (as the only partly informed head of the company), and *nonconscious* processes that also operate beneath the attention of the CEO (as the only partly informed head of their own mind). In both cases, executive processes direct these lower-level processes, even if those processes are entirely ignorant of how such direction works (Engel & Singer, 2008). In either case, we would predict that CEOs who are open to *feeling and naming* dissatisfaction, will do better. Recognizing organizational dissatisfaction may be as simple as going out and talking to a few front-line employees, or as complex as creating a comprehensive survey system that monitors employee opinions.

2 Recognition of dissatisfaction should prompt the organization to start asking itself new questions, about what the organization wants or how to respond to the problem.

How does an "organizational mind" "ask itself questions?" This is a difficult issue. However, the simplest answer, already intimated above, is that the CEO's individual mind simply asks *itself* questions, in its role as decider for the company. Again, however, a better use of company resources might be for the CEO to ask questions of *the company* ("Here is the problem, who's got suggestions?"). The Hubert Joly case fits this model; he asked for every new perspective possible, not only from his own nonconscious mind but also from his company and its workers.

This model bespeaks a horizontal information stream, which directly connects all company units to problem statements, rather than a vertical hierarchized stream, surgically imposed by management. The latter approach is illustrated by a military hierarchy, where "need to know" is defined in a conservative and top-down way, such that most workers are kept in the dark. Such a structure may be required when the functional units are only loosely connected (in this case, as separate people within an organizational mind), and/or when not all units can be trusted with sensitive information (because they may reveal or sell the organization's secrets?).

Interestingly, such a hierarchical compartmentalization approach would NOT work well within an individual mind, because it would imply dissociation between the CCN and its DMN (i.e., between executive and imaginal processes). Obviously, people should not be trying to keep secrets from their own nonconscious minds! And arguably, CEOs shouldn't be keeping secrets from their own workers, either. That nondescript private or temp-pool worker might just have the answer to the problem, due to some fortuitous combination of experiences and circumstances – they just need to be asked (or be prompted to ask themselves). But what about the trust problem? Hopefully, if the organization treats and pays lower-level workers well enough, they won't want to sell out the organization. They will identify with the organizational mind, rather than feeling like an outsider to it. Interestingly, in his book, Joly insisted on drawing employees in, not pushing them out. People *like* to be part of effective organizational minds!

3 Insightful answers may take time in coming (via CEO-prompted organizational activity), but they are worth waiting for, because these integrative productions of the company's group mind (i.e., its collective cognition; Weick & Roberts, 1998) satisfy many constraints at once.

After the CEO broadcasts a call for work, many units and workers within the company begin responding, beneath the CEO's awareness (just as the young lawyer's nonconscious mind churned away, beneath her awareness). From the CEO's point of view, this all occurs during a mysterious "incubation" period, in which the company mind does its thing. From the GBM perspective, the important prerogative for the CEO is to step back and wait – to see what unpredictable new ideas will be inspired by their call for work. As Narayen (2023) stated, "your people will amaze you with their ingenuity!"

4 During the CEO's "aha!" moment, the CEO knew (via SN activity) that this new purpose was "it," so the CEO crossed the Rubicon to the new goal – via verbal CCN activity.

In other words, a good CEO, when presented with the novel answers bubbling up from the ranks below, should be able to recognize the best answer(s), in an "aha!" moment. Then they should use their decision-making power to cross the Rubicon to a new organizational goal or target. Again, this can take courage – as seen within the young lawyer who was willing to ditch everything, and as seen in any good CEO who is willing to take well-founded risks. Joly was ready to follow the new organizational intuition, to its conclusion: that the company should invest resources into training competent people to solve customers' IT problems. This decision eventually redefined Best Buy's brand, as the store that *solves* your problems, not just *sells* you problems.

5 Then the organization's life changed! After the company's directional shift, it derived much more profit from its operations.

Once deliberation is done and the new goal is set, then control passes to implementation, represented by the last three boxes of the action phases model depicted in Figure 7.1: planning, acting, and evaluating. Of course, the CEO remains responsible for ensuring that these activities unfold efficiently and effectively. But the main message of this chapter is that the CEO is also responsible for managing the delicate intuitive process of prompting oneself (or one's organization) to produce creative alternatives. This chapter has focused on that process.

Let's return to my narrative summary of the individual (young lawyer's) case, described above, and evaluate its generalizability to the organizational case.

Narrative Summary: There was unsettling information which first had to be noticed by an executive process; which then had to shape and rebroadcast that information as a question for the deeper system; which then had to provide possible answers; which again had to be noticed again by an executive process; which then had to articulate and commit to a specific goal. There was back-and-forth between implicit and explicit parts of the organization's mind, and between the organizational networks that implement these functions. There was a growing willingness to consider change, which led to increasingly novel ideas for change, which led, finally to a brand-new direction for the organization.

I suggest that the prior narrative summary of individual-level functioning also fits the organizational case. Group minds can work like individual minds! Thus, they can experience powerful breakthroughs if they function in the way outlined by the GBM. Although the CEO ideally leads the process, still, organizational (or nonconscious) processes can force the issue, to the benefit of the whole.

Chapter Summary

This concludes my attempt to create an analogy between the self-generated means by which *individual* free will may be optimized, and the ways by which *organizational* free will may be optimized. Hopefully the analogy will prove fruitful for interested scholars, despite the obvious disconnect between "individual" minds and "group" minds. Perhaps this gap is not as large as typically assumed?

References

Andrews-Hanna, J. (2012). The brain's default network and its adaptive role in internal mentation. *Neuroscientist, 18*(3), 251–270.

Bateson, G. (1972). *Steps to an ecology of mind: Collected essays in anthropology, psychiatry, evolution, and epistemology*. Chicago, IL: University of Chicago Press.

Brandstätter, V., & Bermann, K. (2022). Persistence and disengagement in personal goal pursuit. *Annual Review of Psychology, 73*, 271–299.

Bush, G., Luu, P., & Posner, M. I. (2000). Cognitive and emotional influences in anterior cingulate cortex. *Trends in Cognitive Sciences, 4*(6), 215–222.

Emmons, R. A. (1989). The personal striving approach to personality. In L. A. Pervin (Ed.), *Goal concepts in personality and social psychology* (pp. 87–126). Mahwah, NJ: Lawrence Erlbaum Associates.

Engel, C., & Singer, W. (Eds.) (2008). *Better than conscious? Decision making, the human mind, and implications for institutions*. Cambridge: MIT Press.

Frankl, V. (1946). *Man's search for meaning.* Boston, MA: Beacon Press.
Gollwitzer, P. M. (2012). Mindset theory of action phases. In P. A. M. Van Lange, A. W. Kruglanski, & E. T. Higgins (Eds.), *Handbook of theories of social psychology*. Vol. 1. (pp. 526–545). Thousand Oaks, CA: Sage Publications.
Hélie, S., & Sun, R. (2010). Incubation, insight, and creative problem solving: A unified theory and a connectionist model. Psychological Review, 117(3), 994–1024.
Hopper, P., & Sakuja, J. (2017). A 4-step process to help senior teams prioritize decisions. *Harvard Business Review.*
Islam, G. (2015). Extending organizational cognition: A conceptual exploration of mental extension in organizations. *Human Relations, 68*, 463–487.
James, L. R., Joyce, W. F., & Slocum, J. W. (1988). Comment: Organizations do not cognize. *Academy of Management Review, 13*(1), 129–132.
Joly, H., & Lambert, C. (2021). *The heart of business: Leadership principles for the next era of capitalism.* Boston, MA: Harvard Business Review Press.
Kahneman, D. (2011). *Thinking, fast and slow*. New York, NY: Farrar, Status, & Giroux.
Kellogg, R. T. (2023). More than language: Mental time travel, mentalizing, executive attention, and the left-hemisphere interpreter in human origins. *Psychological Review, 130*(6), 1592–1611.
Klinger, E. (1977). *Meaning and void: Inner experiences and the incentives in peoples' lives.* Minneapolis: University of Minnesota Press.
Krieger, L., & Sheldon, K. M. (2015). What makes lawyers happy? A data-driven prescription to redefine professional success. *George Washington Law Review, 83*(2), 554–627.
Libet, B. (2005). *Mind time: The temporal factor in consciousness.* Boston, MA: Harvard University Press.
List, C. (2019). *Why free will is real.* Boston, MA: Harvard University Press.
Little, B. R., Salmela-Aro, K., & Phillips, S. D. (Eds.) (2007). *Personal project pursuit: Goals, action, and human flourishing.* Mahwah, NJ: Lawrence Erlbaum Associates.
McAdams, D. P. (2015). Tracing three lines of personality development. *Research in Human Development, 12*(3–4), 224–228.
Molnar-Szakacs, I., & Uddin, L. Q. (2022). Anterior insula as a gatekeeper of executive control. Neuroscience & Biobehavioral Reviews, 139, 104736.
Narayen, S. (2023). Adobe's CEO on making big bets on innovation. https://hbr.org/2023/11/adobes-ceo-on-making-big-bets-on-innovation
Niendam, T. A., Laird, A. R., Ray, K. L., Dean, Y. M., Glahn, D. C., & Carter, C. S. (2012). Meta-analytic evidence for a superordinate cognitive control network subserving diverse executive functions. *Cognitive, Affective, & Behavioral Neuroscience, 12*(2), 241–268.
Oettingen, G., Pak, H., & Schnetter, K. (2001). Self-regulation of goal-setting: Turning free fantasies about the future into binding goals. *Journal of Personality and Social Psychology, 80*(5), 736–753.
Ryan, R. M., & Deci, E. L. (2017). *Self-determination theory: Basic psychological needs in motivation, development, and wellness.* New York: Guilford Press.
Seligman, M. E., Railton, P., Baumeister, R. F., & Sripada, C. (2016). *Homo prospectus.* Oxford: Oxford University Press.
Sheldon, K. M. (2014). Becoming oneself: The central role of self-concordant goal selection. *Personality and Social Psychology Review, 18*, 349–365.
Sheldon, K. M. (2022). *Freely determined: What the new psychology of the self tells us about how to live*. New York: Basic Books.
Sheldon, K. M. (2024, published electronically). The free will capacity: A uniquely human adaptation. *American Psychologist, 79*(7), 928–941.

Sheldon, K. M., Goffredi, R., & Titova, L. (2023, published electronically). The goal breakthrough model: Explicit questions drive implicit processes. *Journal of Research in Personality, 104*, 1110–1133.

Sheldon, K. M., Lee, W., & Reeve, J. (in press). How people find better lifegoals: The Goal Breakthrough Model and its neuroscientific underpinnings. *Social and Personality Psychology Compass, 18*(6), Article e12974. https://doi.org/10.1111/spc3.12974

Simonton, D. K. (2018). *The genius checklist: Nine paradoxical tips on how you can become a creative genius!* Boston: MIT Press.

Theiner, G., Allen, C., & Goldstone, R. L. (2010). Recognizing group cognition. *Cognitive Systems Research, 11*(4), 378–395.

Titova, L., & Sheldon, K. M. (2022). Happiness comes from trying to make others feel good, rather than oneself. *Journal of Positive Psychology, 17*, 1–15.

Wallas, G. (1926). *The art of thought*. London: Cape.

Weick, K. E., & Roberts, K. H. (1993). Collective mind in organizations: Heedful interrelating on flight decks. *Administrative Science Quarterly, 38* (3), 357–381.

Wilson, E. O. (1963). The socio biology of ants. *Annual Review of Entomology, 8*, 345–368.

Zaleskiewicz, T., Traczyk, J., & Sobkow, A. (2023). Decision making and mental imagery: A conceptual synthesis and new research directions. *Journal of Cognitive Psychology, 35*(5), 603–633.

Zimbardo, P., & Boyd, J. (2008). *The time paradox: The new psychology of time that will change your life*. New York, NY: Free Press.

8

RESILIENCE IN ORGANIZATIONAL SETTINGS

Thomas W. Britt and Chelsea LeNoble

The study of resilience in organizational settings has increased dramatically in recent years. Many factors have contributed to this increased interest in better understanding how employees, teams, and entire organizations function well under high levels of adversity. The COVID-19 pandemic provided a strong test for resilience within organizational contexts, as organizations attempted to respond to the effects of the pandemic in a way that would allow for continued functioning and survival. Although the study of resilience outside of organizations has a long history (see Masten, 2001), research on resilience by organizational scientists is relatively new (Raetze et al., 2022); and the field is still coming to consensus on key definitional issues and how best to study resilience. Furthermore, theoretical work on resilience in organizations has far outpaced empirical research on the topic.

This chapter highlights what we know about resilience in organizational settings. Space constraints prevent an exhaustive account of all the research done on resilience among employee samples. However, this chapter does address important developments in the field. The accomplishments made in the field are first discussed, followed by unresolved issues in the study of resilience in organizations. This chapter concludes with recommendations for future research focused on better understanding those attributes and processes in organizations that are important for positively adapting during and following adversity. Better understanding these determinants of resilience will result in more successful training and interventions designed to enhance organizational functioning under different types of adversity.

DOI: 10.4324/9781032619385-8

Accomplishments of the Field

Key Components of Resilience in Organizational Settings

Given that resilience is a somewhat nebulous construct that does not have definitive anchors to the objective world, it is probably not surprising that there have been over 100 proposed definitions of the construct (Meredith et al., 2011). Although many definitions of resilience exist, most emphasize an entity (e.g. individual or group) being exposed to some level of adversity and then demonstrating positive adaptation in response to that adversity (e.g., Britt & Sawhney, 2020; Fikretoglu & McCreary, 2012; Stoverink et al., 2020). Furthermore, researchers have generally agreed that it is useful to distinguish between resilience-promoting factors that reflect an entity's *capacity for resilience*, the *processes or enactment mechanisms* linking resilience-promoting factors to positive adaptation under adversity, and the *outcomes* important to examine as indicators of adaptation (Britt et al., 2016b; Fisher et al., 2019). In addition to distinguishing between these three components of resilience, organizational researchers have also noted these factors can be examined at the level of the employee, team, and entire organization. These three different components of resilience at multiple levels are depicted visually in Figure 8.1.

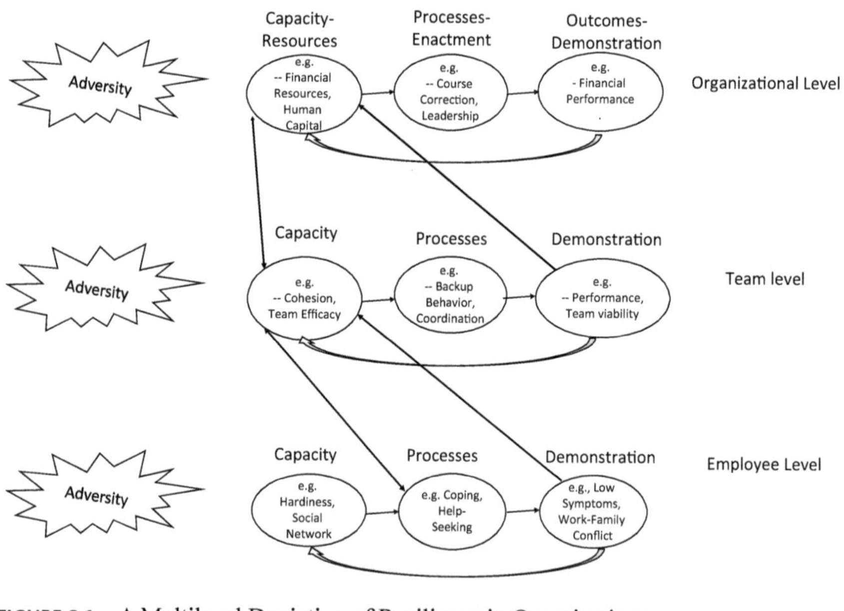

FIGURE 8.1 A Multilevel Depiction of Resilience in Organizations

Modified from Britt, T. W., & Sawhney, G. (2020). Resilience capacity, processes, and demonstration at the employee, team, and organizational levels: A multilevel perspective. In E. Powley, B. Caza, & A. Caza (Eds.), *Research handbook on organizational resilience* (pp. 10–24). Edward Elgar Publishing, United Kingdom.

This figure also shows the importance of the context of adversity for initiating the study of resilience, a topic we return to later in this section.

Resilience-promoting factors that make up an entity's capacity for resilience reflect all the resources possessed by an employee, team, or organization that can be utilized to address the adversity experienced on a given occasion. At the level of the individual employee, Britt et al. (2016b) used the domains of resources provided by Meredith et al. (2011) to highlight that employees have access to different personal, organizational, family, and community resources that can be utilized to respond to diverse types of adversity encountered in their lives. The construct of capacity for resilience is consistent with Hobfoll's Conservation of Resources (COR) Theory (see Hobfoll et al., 2018), which also highlights the structural access to resources possessed by individuals as a function of such factors as their socioeconomic status. Space constraints prevent a discussion of all the resilience-promoting factors that make up an employee's capacity for resilience, but researchers have noted the importance of personality traits such as hardiness (Bartone et al., 2012), the quality and strength of social connections that can provide social support (Britt et al., 2021), and the ability to flexibly apply coping strategies depending on demands that are present (Bonanno et al. 2011).

Figure 8.1 also highlights resilience-promoting factors contributing to the capacity for resilience at the Team level. Alliger et al. (2015) made the important point that a group of resilient employees do not necessarily make a resilient team, and multiple theoretical frameworks have been developed to identify the resilience-promoting factors for team resilience (Bowers et al., 2017; Chapman et al., 2018; Fisher et al., 2023; Gucciardi et al., 2018; Stoverink et al., 2020). Although there are some differences in the frameworks, notable team resilience-promoting factors include team cohesion, team potency, team psychology safety, team collective efficacy, and shared mental models. Furthermore, Gucciardi et al. (2018) made the important point that team resources important for resilience will vary depending on the context and nature of adversity encountered. Finally, resilience-promoting factors also come together to determine an organization's capacity for resilience. Models of organizational resilience tend to highlight the financial and human capital of the organization as contributors to the organization's capacity for resilience (Lengnick-Hall et al., 2011), but also note the importance of high-quality leadership (Stoverink et al., 2020).

The second major component of resilience in organizational settings includes the resilience-enacting mechanisms or processes that link promoting resource factors to positive adaptation during and following adversity. At the level of the individual employee, researchers have devoted a lot of attention to the ways in which adversity is appraised by employees and the coping strategies employees utilize when facing adversity (Britt et al., 2016b). Importantly, the ability to flexibly employ specific coping strategies depending on the adversity present has also been highlighted (Bonanno et al., 2011; Cheng et al., 2014). At the team level, different processes have been highlighted by different researchers; but processes such as communication and performance monitoring (Bowers et al., 2017) and coordination and backup behaviors (Stoverink et al., 2020) have been proposed as important for how a team responds to adversity. At the organizational level, the ability for organizations to relentlessly correct their course of direction when addressing adversity (Pulakos et al., 2019), and engagement in sense-making (Stoverink et al., 2020), have been highlighted as processes critical for positive adaptation to occur.

The final component in studies of resilience in organizational settings includes the outcomes important to examine as indicators of positive adaptation. One important contribution of organizational psychology to the study of resilience is recognizing the importance of multiple indices of adaptation. Researchers have emphasized not only the performance of employees, teams, and organizations but also indicators of well-being, including vitality, health symptoms, and work–family outcomes (Alliger et al., 2015; Bowers et al., 2017; Britt et al., 2016b). Different outcomes tend to be examined at different levels of analysis, with mental health symptoms often examined at the employee level, whereas performance is the primary outcome assessed at the team and organization levels. Researchers typically assess positive adaptation on a single outcome of interest, instead of examining whether a particular entity might adapt positively on one outcome, but not on another.

The Importance of Adversity

One other important accomplishment in the study of resilience in organizational settings is the recognition of the importance of examining the adversity that is present. As addressed in more detail in the next section, scholars have varied in how they have handled the construct of adversity in different models. Nevertheless, all agree that resilience must be studied in the context of an entity experiencing difficult conditions. In their seminal paper, Luthar and Cicchetti (2000) considered adversity to be one of the two critical components of resilience (the other being positive adaptation). According to Gucciardi et al. (2018), without adversity, resilience cannot be studied; in fact, they stated that adversity is "central to all definitions and conceptualizations of resilience" (p. 742). This emphasis on adversity helps distinguish resilience from related occupational health and well-being constructs. At the employee level, the experience of significant adversity helps distinguish the study of resilience from the related area of stress and coping within organizations. For example, military personnel who witness the death of a fellow soldier or firefighters seeing children being harmed experience traumatic events that reflect high levels of adversity (Britt et al., 2016b).

Considering the team level, the presence of adversity helps distinguish the study of team resilience from the related area of team adaptation, where teams are responding to relatively minor challenges that require a redirection of effort (Kennedy et al., 2016). Alliger et al. (2015) have noted such stressors as time pressure, hazardous work, and loss of a team member as indicators of adversity. Team resilience researchers (e.g., Alliger et al., 2015; Bowers et al., 2017) have also acknowledged that smaller stressors can accumulate to become as disruptive as a major crisis—thereby passing the threshold of significant adversity. Considering the organization level, the presence of adversity reflects broader crises and disruptive events that threaten the stability of the organization and the teams and employees within the organization. Organizational resilience research often focuses on severe contexts, like crises and disasters, as sources of adversity (e.g., Hällgren et al., 2018; Williams et al., 2017). In the section on unresolved issues in the field, we discuss the importance of characterizing adversity in organizational settings when studying resilience.

Multilevel Conceptualizations of Resilience

In addition to theorizing that resilience in organizational settings can be examined at different levels, researchers have also begun considering how dynamics at one level might influence another level (Britt & Sawhney, 2020; Fisher et al., 2023; Stoverink et al., 2020). These multilevel influences are depicted in Figure 8.1 through arrows at one level of analysis influencing resilience-related factors at a different level of analysis. Fisher et al. (2023) have provided the most explicit analysis of the multilevel nature of different components of resilience at the employee and team levels, including cross-level effects that may occur among components of resilience. Utilizing Hobfoll et al.'s (2018) notion of resource crossover, Fisher et al. (2023) argued that resources at the team level may cross over to employees who are part of the team, allowing those employees to positively adapt to adversity. For example, teams that are high in unit cohesion may transmit the resource of social support to individual team members, allowing them to better deal with adversity facing the employee as an individual.

Although Fisher et al. (2023) limited their discussion of cross-level influences to the employee and team levels, they argued that such influences likely occur at the organization level, too. Britt and Sawhney (2020) argued that organization-level resilience-promoting resources could have contextual influences on processes at a lower-level (e.g. the team; Bliese, 2000; Kozlowski & Klein, 2000). For example, an organizational-level culture of psychological safety may influence a team's level of resourcefulness when addressing challenges during a crisis. As discussed in the last section of this chapter, although theoretical discussions on multilevel influences on resilience in organizational settings have detailed the pathways through which such influences may occur, research is needed to identify which bottom-up and top-down processes are most likely when organizations face prolonged adversity.

Potential Dark Side to Resilience

Finally, researchers examining resilience in organizational settings have recognized that a directive to enhance employee resilience in the face of high levels of adversity has the potential to stigmatize those who fail to show resilience or develop mental health problems in response to occupational adversity exposure (Adler, 2013; Britt et al., 2016b). Often, such outcomes reflect reasonable responses to unsafe, exploitive working conditions (Kim et al., 2020; King et al., 2023). Consequentially, a focus on employees being resilient in the face of high levels of stressors at work can take responsibility away from employers to address controllable demands that place employees at risk for mental health problems. Researchers examining the resilience of healthcare professionals in the face of such adversity as the COVID-19 pandemic have emphasized the importance of system-level interventions that take responsibility away from employees for demonstrating resilience (National Academy of Medicine, 2019).

The recognition of a dark side to resilience has primarily focused on employees in high-risk occupations, as opposed to studying the dark side of resilience among teams and organizations. However, some work has expressed concerns at these levels as well (Fisher et al., 2023). In the case of teams, individual members may deplete resilience capacity resources at the team level when responding to their own adversity, preventing the team from having the resources it needs to respond to significant team-level stressors. Similarly, some teams may be forced to adapt positively to adversity at the expense of resources present within the team because of the organization withholding resources that would provide necessary support. Although this dynamic may result in short-term demonstrations of resilience by teams under adversity, the lack of additional resources from the organization could undermine resilience—for the team and the organization—in the long term. Kahn et al. (2018) have also noted how teams within an organization that are showing signs of strain may be cut off from necessary resources by the organization, which redirects resources to highly functioning teams. At the organizational level, mergers and layoffs are often considered ways of promoting resilience but may ultimately harm the organization in the long run (Datta et al., 2010).

Unresolved Issues in the Field

Although the study of resilience in organizations has made great strides in a relatively short amount of time, several unresolved issues remain in the field. These issues need to be addressed through improvements in theoretical arguments and the research designs used to understand resilience in organizational settings.

Resilience as Context Dependent

What resilience is or looks like is inherently dependent on the adversity being addressed, adapted to, or overcome. This means that resilience research should be highly context dependent. Context refers to a set of dynamic situational stimuli in the external environment that influences organizational behavior across multiple levels of analysis (Johns, 2018). Context-based theories like Affective Events Theory (Weiss & Cropanzano, 1996) and Event Systems Theory (EST; Morgeson et al., 2015) have been used to extend our understanding of how workers face and respond to adverse experiences in occupational settings. The resilience literature has yet to fully embrace the implications of context in its theories and frameworks. However, there are clear signs that context is at work in our very definitions.

For instance, Luthar and Cicchetti (2000) define resilience as "a dynamic process encompassing positive adaptation *within the context of significant adversity*" (p. 857, emphasis added). While most resilience research is not explicitly situated within organizational context research, researchers have begun to acknowledge and examine resilience from a context-specific lens (e.g., Hällgren et al., 2018). For example, Kossek and Perrigino (2016) argued that the occupational context (i.e., nature of tasks and demands) informs not only what resilience looks like in organizations but also how it can be enhanced. Similarly, Raetze et al. (2022) acknowledged that resilience is a construct rooted in context and stated that future research should focus more attention on describing organizational contexts in which resilience occurs. The lack of consideration of context could be one of multiple reasons why interventions involving resilience training among employees have received modest support for their effectiveness (Brassington & Lomas, 2021; Vanhove et al., 2016). For resilience training to be effective, the specific resources and processes beneficial for addressing specific sources of adversity need to be understood and targeted for intervention. A similar understanding is needed to enhance the effectiveness of training designed to assess teams and organizations' effectiveness.

In empirical research, a few papers have begun to consider how context informs our measurement of resilience. Todt et al. (2018) operationalized a "context-specific resilience construct" of innovator resilience potential, or the ability of innovators to overcome setbacks and continue producing innovation (p. 520). Fisher and Law (2021) developed and validated a framework for selecting a resilience measure based on the specific context in which the researcher is interested. Finally, to overcome the ways in which Likert-type resilience measures omit important information about the context of adversity, Teng et al. (2020) constructed a situation judgment test that assesses participant responses to a set of hypothetical scenarios reflecting adversity. While these empirical advances are helping move the literature forward, they still serve as indicators of how context remains an unresolved aspect of organizational resilience theory.

How Different Resources and Processes Are Combined When Examining Resilience

Related to the issue of the context dependence of resilience, there is a lack of theoretical or empirical consensus on combining the resources or attributes that are the most important at different levels of analysis, as well as the processes or enactment mechanisms that promote resilience. In terms of the resources or attributes that promote positive adaptation under adversity, little research has examined how different resources work together within a resilience framework, including whether there are particular types of resources best suited to addressing different types of adversity. Researchers typically assess only one or two resilience-promoting resources within the context of a given study and do not examine how a larger number of resources work to facilitate processes and adaptation.

At the level of the individual employee, researchers might examine hardiness (Bartone et al., 2012) or psychological capital (Luthans et al., 2006) as resilience-promoting resources. However, the extent to which these different resources come together to contribute to an employee's overall capacity for resilience has been under-investigated. Furthermore, it may be the case that some resources contribute to obtaining other resources necessary for addressing specific types of adversity, similar to the concept of resource caravans in Hobfoll's Conservation of Resources theory (Hobfoll et al., 2018). For example, the resource of a strong social network could facilitate the availability of social support during high levels of adversity. There may even be personal or energetic resource thresholds that must be met for critical resilience resources to be activated. For instance, all the social support in the world would be unable to help an employee who is too discouraged or exhausted to reach out to their social network. These concerns exist at the team and organizational levels as well. Although many resilience-promoting resources or attributes have been identified, how these resources influence each other or come together to define the capacity for resilience is not typically examined.

A similar lack of clarity exists with the most important resilience processes or enactment mechanisms that contribute to positive adaptation under adversity at different levels within the organization. At the employee level, researchers have emphasized a variety of appraisal and coping strategies for dealing with adversity (Dewe et al., 2010). However, the ability to flexibly use coping strategies depending on characteristics of the adversity has also been argued to be more important (Bonanno, et al. 2011; Britt et al., 2016a; Cheng et al., 2014). Looking at coping strategies dealing with adversity over time, Kleshinski et al. (2024) recently found that the depth or level at which coping strategies are used was more predictive of positive adaptation than the breadth of coping strategies.

Along similar lines, while some work has theorized that resilient coping typically may occur via forms of automatic and controlled processing (Tugade & Fredrickson, 2007), we are aware of no empirical research that tests whether resilience enactment tends to happen more automatically, like a reflex, or if it requires intentional effort—let alone whether automatic and controlled forms of resilience enactment result in different outcomes. Clearly, continued research on coping-related processes within the context of employee resilience is needed.

Similar questions emerge at the team and organization levels, as multiple processes have been identified as contributing to the ability of a team or organization to function positively under adversity. Furthermore, different processes have been argued to be effective for different types of adversity (Gucciardi et al., 2018). However, organizational scientists have not yet catalogued the most important processes for different types of adversity, or how multiple processes could be more beneficial than single processes.

The Importance and Assessment of Adversity

The treatment of adversity is one of the most important gaps in the current resilience literature. Indeed, adversity comprises the fundamental context under which resilience can be understood (Luthar et al., 2000). There is still lack of consensus on what constitutes adversity compared to what can be appraised as stressful but does not pass a threshold of being deemed severe enough to be labeled "adversity." In other words, we do not yet have agreement on the boundaries of what "significant adversity" is and what it is not.

Existing theories that already address adversity can be applied to enhance our understanding of resilience in organizations. While there is still disagreement about whether the experience of common occupational stressors such as high workload and role ambiguity constitute adversity (Britt et al., 2016b), models within the stressor–strain lineage have been applied to study resilience (e.g., Crane & Searle, 2016; Schilbach et al., 2021; Shoss et al., 2018). Specifically, these studies operationalize stressors as forms of adversity. Until we achieve greater consensus around a definition of adversity and stronger theory is developed for the role of adversity in the process of resilience in organizational settings (e.g., what does and what does not constitute adversity, how adversity is expected to trigger particular responses), the ability of such work to meaningfully advance the resilience literature is limited. If the field decides that occupational stressors do not constitute a level of adversity necessary for a resilience lens to be appropriate, what can we say of existing research that has operationalized adversity as occupational stressors? To resolve this issue, we must first settle on a definition and conceptualization of adversity before we move toward clarity in adversity measurement. Otherwise, we will continue to risk incorrectly categorizing whole swaths of research as fitting under a resilience umbrella.

Questions Regarding Measurement and Research Design

One challenge facing the study of resilience in organizations is the difficulty of conducting both multilevel and longitudinal studies with multiple organizations. The ideal research design for examining resilience in organizational settings would be to assess the resource-promoting factors that determine an entity's capacity for resilience prior to the experience of significant adversity, assess the resilience enactment mechanisms or processes at multiple points during the experience of adversity, and then assess multiple outcomes at multiple time points following the experience of adversity. This type of longitudinal design is challenging enough to conduct without the desirable addition of being able to examine employees embedded within teams embedded in organizations. There are also ethical considerations surrounding recruiting individuals and teams to participate in research when they are facing significant disruption, stressors, and crises.

Therefore, conducting these types of complex designs is difficult, which may explain why there are many studies conducted on resilience in organizational settings using cross-sectional designs, especially at the employee level. However, we would argue that it is very difficult, if not impossible, to study the resilience of employees, teams, and organizations, using cross-sectional designs, especially if the study models the primary components of resilience highlighted in the present chapter, which imply a process unfolding over time. The concern of cross-sectional designs in the study of resilience is further compounded by measures that claim to assess resilience or aspects of resilience. Self-report measures of resilience cannot be substituted for the empirical evaluation of whether resilience-promoting resources are linked to processes that result in positive adaptation following adversity.

Recommendations for Future Research in the Field

Given the unresolved issues identified above, we provide the following specific recommendations for future research on resilience in organizational settings:

1 **Integrate context into the study of resilience.** Our first recommendation is that resilience researchers should more explicitly consider context when studying resilience. Existing research has reinforced this notion, giving us a starting point for understanding that it is important to better integrate context into future resilience research (e.g., Cheng et al., 2020; Fisher et al., 2023; Raetze et al., 2022). Extending beyond these works, we believe that the best treatment of context in resilience research may involve not using a single "resilience" measure at all. Instead, effective resilience measurement might include resources existing prior to the emergence of adverse circumstances, the nature of the adversity in question, behaviors enacted, and resources mobilized in response to that adversity, context-relevant outcome measures, and how those outcomes change over time as a function of the other measured contextual features. Researchers should take care to apply this type of a priori integration of context into the empirical study and measurement of resilience whenever possible. When not possible, a post hoc integration of context can be achieved by thoroughly explaining the research setting and how adversity is expected to play a role in shaping the resilience phenomena of interest.

To move the resilience literature forward toward stronger context-based theory development and testing, we believe that future research should (1) more explicitly theorize and operationalize context in terms of omnibus (high-level features describing who, what, when, where, why) and discrete levels (proximal situational features driving organizational behavior; Johns, 2006) and (2) consider ways to incorporate process theorizing. Better integration of omnibus and discrete context can help researchers enhance the specificity of resilience construct conceptualizations and empirical measurement needed to resolve resilience research issues described above. Then, process theorizing can help clarify how resilience phenomena unfold over time and across various mechanisms, stages, or contingencies (Cloutier & Langley, 2020). Given that several resilience researchers have defined and conceptualized resilience as a process (e.g., Fisher et al., 2023; Hartmann et al., 2020; Luthar et al., 2000; Raetze et al., 2022), we find process theorizing to be a particularly important line of future work that can build upon and extend the contributions of existing context-based theoretical approaches.

2 **Explicitly characterize adversity.** Given the lack of consensus surrounding the level of adversity needed to be present to study resilience, future research should more intentionally integrate adversity into resilience theorizing. To understand the relationship between stress, adversity, and resilience, we can look back to the original conceptualization of these constructs. Hans Selye, credited as the founder of stressor–strain research, adopted the term "stress" from physics and engineering (Kültz, 2020; Robinson, 2018). If we look to physics, both stress and resilience play a role in the overall understanding of how materials respond when a force is placed upon them. Some more recent work has returned to the original physics model to conceptualize resilience as the area of a stressor—strain plot in which some "material" can bounce back from being deformed by stress to its original state, also known as the elasticity or flexibility (Den Hartigh & Hill, 2022).

If the stressor passes the threshold of the elastic limit, then there is a range of space referred to as the area of plasticity. Within the plasticity space, the material is still functional, but it cannot return to its original state. After plasticity, there is a point of fracture: the limit of bearing the load of a stressor before the material breaks. Finally, this concept of resilience in physics is distinct from the concept of stiffness, which refers to the amount of stress a material can withstand without ever experiencing deformation. By returning to the conceptual origins of stress, we may be able to better define the bounds of a stressor that constitute adversity. Perhaps a stressor can be considered to rise to the level of adversity if it threatens to "deform" an entity past its elastic limit; resilience might then be defined as the entity's ability to respond to the stressor so as to remain within its area of elasticity and not be pushed past the elastic limit. Under this perspective, there may be stressors against which individuals, teams, and organizations can exert "stiffness," or experience no "deformation." These stressors might therefore be excluded from a conceptualization of adversity, unless studies show that a prolonged duration of exposure for these stressors may "deform" an entity.

3 **Utilize more longitudinal and multilevel research designs**. Theoretical work on resilience in organizational settings has far outpaced empirical research on the topic. Most theories emphasize longitudinal components of the resilience process, including examining resources prior to adversity, processes during

adversity, and adaptation following adversity. Therefore, longitudinal designs with multiple time points are needed to answer relevant theoretical questions regarding how specific resources are connected to specific resources that promote positive adaptation under different types of adversity (Britt et al., 2021). The importance of longitudinal designs to understand the resilience process has also been emphasized by other researchers (Halbesleben et al., 2014).

In addition to longitudinal designs, multilevel designs will be necessary to examine how resilience-promoting resources and processes at one level within the organization are related to the demonstration of positive adaptation at other levels (Fisher et al., 2023). Although researchers have examined how particular resources at the unit level are related to adaptive functioning under adversity at the employee level (Campbell-Sills et al., 2022), multilevel research is rare in the study of resilience. Future research examining system-level influences on the responses of employees to adversity will require multilevel designs to highlight points for potential intervention (National Academy of Medicine, 2019).

4 **Explore narratives regarding the lived experience of resilience in organizational settings.**

One of the emphases of process theorizing is the importance of narratives and lived experience to provide deeper, richer understandings of organizational phenomena (Cloutier & Langley, 2020). Now that we generally agree on a process definition of resilience (e.g., Fisher et al., 2023; Raetze et al., 2022), future research should spend more time asking people what resilience actually looks like in their organizations, teams, and lives—across the work–life interface. Qualitative and mixed-methods research designs are needed that examine the narratives of employees positively adapting to different types of adversity experienced in the workplace. For example, King and her colleagues have assessed personal narratives of resilience in an employee selection context and open-ended accounts of Black employees overcoming the adversity of different types of race-based microaggressions (King et al., 2021, 2023). Additional narratives can be examined for teams and organizations showing resilience under adversity (Carden et al., 2018).

Conclusion

This chapter has attempted to highlight the current state of theory and research related to the study of resilience in organizational settings. There is general agreement on the different components involved in the study of resilience, the multilevel nature of the construct, the importance of significant adversity being present, and the potential negative outcomes of emphasizing resilience. Unresolved issues requiring additional research include the importance of studying resilience in situated contexts, characterizing the level of adversity in organizational settings, and understanding how best to integrate the different resources and mechanisms that promote positive adaptation to different types of adversity. Following the recommendations

provided in this chapter will hopefully result in more effective interventions and training to enhance the functioning of employees, teams, and organizations under difficult conditions.

References

Adler, A. B. (2013). Resilience in a military occupational health context: Directions for future research. In R. R. Sinclair & T. W. Britt (Eds.), *Building psychological resilience in military personnel: Theory and practice* (pp. 223–235). Washington, DC: American Psychological Association.

Alliger, G. M., Cerasoli, C. P., Tannenbaum, S. I., & Vessey, W. B. (2015). Team resilience: How teams flourish under pressure. *Organizational Dynamics, 44*(3), 176–184. https://doi.org/10.1016/j.orgdyn.2015.05.003

Bartone, P. T., Hystad, S. W., Eid, J., & Brevik, J. I. (2012). Psychological hardiness and coping style as risk/resilience factors for alcohol abuse. *Military Medicine, 177*(5), 517–524. https://doi-org.libproxy.clemson.edu/10.7205/MILMED-D-11-00200

Bliese, P. D. (2000). Within-group agreement, non-independence, and reliability: Implications for data aggregation and analysis. In K. J. Klein & S. W. J. Kozlowski (Eds.), *Multilevel theory, research, and methods in organizations: Foundations, extensions, and new directions* (pp. 349–381). San Francisco, CA: Jossey-Bass.

Bonanno, G. A., Pat-Horenczyk, R., & Noll, J. (2011). Coping flexibility and trauma: The Perceived Ability to Cope with Trauma (PACT) scale. *Psychological Trauma: Theory, Research, Practice, and Policy, 3*(2), 117–129. https://doi-org.libproxy.clemson.edu/10.1037/a0020921

Bowers, C., Kreutzer, C., Cannon-Bowers, J., & Lamb, J. (2017). Team resilience as a second-order emergent state: A theoretical model and research directions. *Frontiers in Psychology, 8*. https://doi.org/10.3389/fpsyg.2017.01360

Brassington, K., & Lomas, T. (2021). Can resilience training improve well-being for people in high-risk occupations? A systematic review through a multidimensional lens. *The Journal of Positive Psychology, 16*(5), 573–592. https://doi.org/10.1080/17439760.2020.1752783

Britt, T. W., Adler, A. B., & Fynes, J. (2021). Perceived resilience and social connection as predictors of adjustment following occupational adversity. *Journal of Occupational Health Psychology, 26*(4), 339–349. https://doi-org.libproxy.clemson.edu/10.1037/ocp0000286

Britt, T. W., Crane, M., Hodson, S. E., & Adler, A. B. (2016a). Effective and ineffective coping strategies in a low-autonomy work environment. *Journal of Occupational Health Psychology, 21*(2), 154–168. https://doi-org.libproxy.clemson.edu/10.1037/a0039898

Britt, T. W., & Sawhney, G. (2020). Resilience capacity, processes, and demonstration at the employee, team, and organizational levels: A multilevel perspective. In E. Powley, B. Caza, & A. Caza (Eds.), *Research handbook on organizational resilience* (pp. 10–24). Edward Elgar Publishing. https://doi.org/10.4337/9781788112215.00008

Britt, T. W., Shen, W., Sinclair, R. R., Grossman, M., & Klieger, D. (2016b). How much do we really know about employee resilience? *Industrial and Organizational Psychology: Perspectives on Science and Practice, 9*, 378–404.

Campbell-Sills, L., Flynn, P. J., Choi, K. W., Ng, T. H. H., Aliaga, P. A., Broshek, C., Jain, S., Kessler, R. C., Stein, M. B., Ursano, R. J., & Bliese, P. D. (2022). Unit cohesion during deployment and post-deployment mental health: Is cohesion an individual- or unit-level buffer for combat-exposed soldiers? *Psychological Medicine, 52*(1), 121–131. https://doi-org.libproxy.clemson.edu/10.1017/S0033291720001786

Carden, L. L., Maldonado, T., & Boyd, R. O. (2018). Organizational resilience: A look at McDonald's in the fast food industry. *Organizational Dynamics, 47*(1), 25–31. https://doi-org.libproxy.clemson.edu/10.1016/j.orgdyn.2017.07.002

Chapman, M. T., Lines, R. L. J., Crane, M., Ducker, K. J., Ntoumanis, N., Peeling, P., …, & Gucciardi, D. F. (2018). Team resilience: A scoping review of conceptual and empirical work. *Work & Stress*. https://doi-org.libproxy.clemson.edu/10.1080/02678373.2018.1529064

Cheng, S., King, D. D., & Oswald, F. (2020). Understanding how resilience is measured in the organizational sciences. *Human Performance, 33*(2–3), 130–163. https://doi.org/10.1080/08959285.2020.1744151

Cheng, C., Lau, H.-P. B., & Chan, M.-P. S. (2014). Coping flexibility and psychological adjustment to stressful life changes: A meta-analytic review. *Psychological Bulletin, 140*(6), 1582–1607. https://doi-org.libproxy.clemson.edu/10.1037/a0037913

Cloutier, C., & Langley, A. (2020). What makes a process theoretical contribution? *Organization Theory, 1*(1), https://doi.org/10.1177/2631787720902473.

Crane, M. F., & Searle, B. J. (2016). Building resilience through exposure to stressors: The effects of challenges versus hindrances. *Journal of Occupational Health Psychology, 21*(4), 468–479. https://doi.org/10.1037/a0040064

Datta, D. K., Guthrie, J. P., Basuil, D., & Pandey, A. (2010). Causes and effects of employee downsizing: A review and synthesis. *Journal of Management, 36*(1), 281–348.

Den Hartigh, R. J., & Hill, Y. (2022). Conceptualizing and measuring psychological resilience: What can we learn from physics? *New Ideas in Psychology, 66*, 100934.

Dewe, P. J., O'Driscoll, M. P., & Cooper, C. L. (2010). *Coping with work stress: A review and critique*. New York: Wiley.

Fikretoglu, D., & McCreary, D. R. (2012). Psychological resilience: A brief review of definitions, and key theoretical, conceptual, and methodological issues (Technical Report 2012-012). Toronto, Ontario, Canada: Defense R&D.

Fisher, D. M., & Law, R. D. (2021). How to choose a measure of resilience: An organizing framework for resilience measurement. *Applied Psychology, 70*(2), 643–673. https://doi.org/10.1111/apps.12243

Fisher, D. M., LeNoble, C. A., & Vanhove, A. J. (2023). An integrated perspective on individual and team resilience: Moving from multilevel structure to cross-level effects. *Applied Psychology, 72*(3), 1043–1074. https://doi.org/10.1111/apps.12419

Fisher, D. M., Ragsdale, J. M., & Fisher, E. C. S. (2019). The importance of definitional and temporal issues in the study of resilience. *Applied Psychology: An International Review, 68*(4), 583–620. https://doi-org.libproxy.clemson.edu/10.1111/apps.12162

Gucciardi, D. F., Crane, M., Ntoumanis, N., Parker, S. K., Thøgersen, N. C., Ducker, K. J., …, & Temby, P. (2018). The emergence of team resilience: A multilevel conceptual model of facilitating factors. *Journal of Occupational and Organizational Psychology*. https://doi-org.libproxy.clemson.edu/10.1111/joop.12237

Halbesleben, J. R. B., Neveu, J.-P., Paustian-Underdahl, S. C., & Westman, M. (2014). Getting to the "COR": Understanding the role of resources in conservation of resources theory. *Journal of Management, 40*(5), 1334–1364. https://doi.org/10.1177/0149206314527130

Hällgren, M., Rouleau, L., & De Rond, M. (2018). A matter of life or death: How extreme context research matters for management and organization studies. *Academy of Management Annals, 12*(1), 111–153. https://doi.org/10.5465/annals.2016.0017

Hartmann, S., Weiss, M., Newman, A., & Hoegl, M. (2020). Resilience in the workplace: A multilevel review and synthesis. *Applied Psychology, 69*, 1–47.

Hobfoll, S. E., Halbesleben, J., Neveu, J. P., & Westman, M. (2018). Conservation of resources in the organizational context: The reality of resources and their consequences. *Annual Review of Organizational Psychology and Organizational Behavior, 5*, 103–128.

Johns, G. (2006). The essential impact of context on organizational behavior. *Academy of Management Review, 31*(2), 386–408. https://doi.org/10.5465/amr.2006.20208687

Johns, G. (2018). Advances in the treatment of context in organizational research. *Annual review of Organizational Psychology and Organizational Behavior, 5*, 21–46.

Kahn, W. A., Barton, M. A., Fisher, C. M., Heaphy, E. D., Reid, E. M., & Rouse, E. D. (2018). The geography of strain: Organizational resilience as a function of intergroup relations. *The Academy of Management Review, 43*(3), 509–529. https://doi-org.libproxy.clemson.edu/10.5465/amr.2016.0004

Kennedy, D. M., Landon, L. B., & Maynard, M. T. (2016). Extending the conversation: Employee resilience at the team level. *Industrial and Organizational Psychology, 9*, 466–475.

Kim, J. Y., Campbell, T. H., Shepherd, S., & Kay, A. C. (2020). Understanding contemporary forms of exploitation: Attributions of passion serve to legitimize the poor treatment of workers. *Journal of Personality and Social Psychology, 118*(1), 121.

King, D. D., Fattoracci, E. S. M., Hollingsworth, D. W., Stahr, E., & Nelson, M. (2023). When thriving requires effortful surviving: Delineating manifestations and resource expenditure outcomes of microaggressions for Black employees. *Journal of Applied Psychology, 108*(2), 183–207. https://doi.org/10.1037/apl0001016

King, D. D., Lyons, B., & Phetmisy, C. N. (2021). Perceived resiliency: The influence of resilience narratives on attribution processes in selection. *Journal of Vocational Behavior, 131*. https://doi-org.libproxy.clemson.edu/10.1016/j.jvb.2021.103653

Kleshinski, C. E., Wilson, K. S., Stevenson-Street, J. M., & Rosokha, L. M. (2024). Coping with work–nonwork stressors over time: A person-centered, multi-study integration of coping breadth and depth. *Journal of Applied Psychology*. https://doi-org.libproxy.clemson.edu/10.1037/apl0001207

Kossek, E. E., & Perrigino, M. B. (2016). Resilience: A review using a grounded integrated occupational approach. *Academy of Management Annals, 10*(1), 729. https://doi.org/10.5465/19416520.2016.1159878

Kozlowski, S. W. J., & Klein, K. J. (2000). A multilevel approach to theory and research in organizations: Contextual, temporal, and emerging processes. In K. J. Klein & S. W. J. Kozlowski (Eds.), *Multilevel theory, research and methods in organizations: Foundations, extensions, and new directions* (pp. 3–90). San Francisco, CA: Jossey-Bass.

Kültz, D. (2020). Defining biological stress and stress responses based on principles of physics. *Journal of Experimental Zoology Part A: Ecological and Integrative Physiology, 333*(6), 350–358.

Lengnick-Hall, C. A., Beck, T. E., & Lengnick-Hall, M. L. (2011). Developing a capacity for organizational resilience through strategic human resource management. *Human Resource Management Review, 21*(3), 243–255. https://doi.org/10.1016/j.hrmr.2010.07.001

Luthans, F., Vogelgesang, G. R., & Lester, P. B. (2006). Developing the psychological capital of resiliency. *Human Resource Development Review, 5*(1), 25–44. https://doi-org.libproxy.clemson.edu/10.1177/1534484305285335

Luthar, S. S., & Cicchetti, D. (2000). The construct of resilience: Implications for interventions and social policies. *Development and Psychopathology, 12*(4), 857–885.

Luthar, S. S., Cicchetti, D., & Becker, B. (2000). The construct of resilience: A critical evaluation and guidelines for future work. *Child Development, 71*(3), 543–562. https://doi.org/10.1111/1467-8624.00164

Masten, A. S. (2001). Ordinary magic: Resilience processes in development. *American Psychologist, 56*(3), 227–238. https://doi.org/10.1037/0003-066X.56.3.227

Meredith, S., Sherbourne, C., Gaillot, S., J., Hansell, L., Ritschard, H. V., Parker, A. M., & Wrenn, G., (2011). *Promoting psychological resilience in the U.S. Military*, RAND Corporation (MG-966-OSD).

Morgeson, F. P., Mitchell, T. R., & Liu, D. (2015). Event system theory: An event-oriented approach to the organizational sciences. *Academy of Management Review, 40*(4), 515–537.

National Academies of Sciences, National Academy of Medicine, & Committee on Systems Approaches to Improve Patient Care by Supporting Clinician Well-Being. (2019). *Taking action against clinician burnout: A systems approach to professional well-being.*

Pulakos, E. D., Kantrowitz, T., & Schneider, B. (2019). What leads to organizational agility: It's not what you think. *Consulting Psychology Journal: Practice and Research, 71*(4), 305–320. https://doi-org.libproxy.clemson.edu/10.1037/cpb0000150.

Raetze, S., Duchek, S., Maynard, M. T., & Wohlgemuth, M. (2022). Resilience in organization-related research: An integrative conceptual review across disciplines and levels of analysis. *Journal of Applied Psychology, 107*(6), 867– 897. https://doi.org/10.1037/apl0000952

Robinson, A. M. (2018). Let's talk about stress: History of stress research. *Review of General Psychology, 22*(3), 334–342.

Schilbach, M., Baethge, A., & Rigotti, T. (2021). Do challenge and hindrance job demands prepare employees to demonstrate resilience? *Journal of Occupational Health Psychology, 26*(3), 155.

Shoss, M. K., Jiang, L., & Probst, T. M. (2018). Bending without breaking: A two-study examination of employee resilience in the face of job insecurity. *Journal of Occupational Health Psychology, 23*(1), 112.

Stoverink, A. C., Kirkman, B. L., Mistry, S., & Rosen, B. (2020). Bouncing back together: Toward a rhetorical model of work team resilience. *The Academy of Management Review, 45*(2), 395–422. https://doi.org/10.5465/amr.2017.0005.

Teng, Y., Brannick, M. T., & Borman, W. C. (2020). Capturing resilience in context: Development and validation of a situational judgment test of resilience. *Human Performance, 33*(2–3), 74–103.

Todt, G., Weiss, M., & Hoegl, M. (2018). Mitigating negative side effects of innovation project terminations: The role of resilience and social support. *Journal of Product Innovation Management, 35*(4), 518–542.

Tugade, M. M., & Fredrickson, B. L. (2007). Regulation of positive emotions: Emotion regulation strategies that promote resilience. *Journal of Happiness Studies, 8*, 311–333.

Vanhove, A. J., Herian, M. N., Perez, A. L. U., Harms, P. D., & Lester, P. B. (2016). Can resilience be developed at work? A meta-analytic review of resilience-building programme effectiveness. *Journal of Occupational and Organizational Psychology, 89*(2), 278–307. https://doi.org/10.1111/joop.12123

Weiss, H. M., & Cropanzano, R. (1996). Affective events theory: A theoretical discussion of the structure, causes and consequences of affective experiences at work. In B. M. Staw & L. L. Cummings (Eds.), *Research in organizational behavior: An annual series of analytical essays and critical reviews* (Vol. 18, pp. 1–74). Elsevier Science/JAI Press.

Williams, T. A., Gruber, D. A., Sutcliffe, K. M., Shepherd, D. A., & Zhao, E. Y. (2017). Organizational response to adversity: Fusing crisis management and resilience research streams. *Academy of Management Annals, 11*(2), 733–769. https://doi.org/10.5465/annals.2015.0134

9

EMERGING WORK WELLBEING CHALLENGES

Paula Brough and Jafar Akbari

Post-COVID Impacts on Workplace Wellbeing

In this chapter we discuss four of the major changes to our working lives experienced as a consequence of the COVID pandemic. The pandemic has profoundly impacted the organisation of work including systems relating to the health and wellbeing of workers. The pandemic has served as a catalyst for change, accelerating the adoption of remote work, digital transformation, and flexible working arrangements, particularly by specific groups of workers (Brough & Kinman, 2024b; Vyas-Doorgapersad, 2023). Organisational recognition of the value of providing healthy work environments, particularly environments fostering psychological as well as physical health, has also changed significantly. Thus, the term ‘psychosocial safety’ is now far more widely used as compared to its pre-pandemic usage. The recognition of the value of safeguarding employees’ health has also extended to increasingly recognise the issue of employee presenteeism and engagement. Working when unwell, or ‘not present’ is certainly discouraged significantly more now as compared to the pre-pandemic era. Finally, we also discuss how the pandemic has accelerated the adoption of digital transformation in our workplaces, particularly the use of artificial intelligence (AI) and how this will continue to impact our workplaces for the foreseeable future. Many of these changes have improved our working lives, but as always, these changes are also related to some negative impact for workers. We discuss the pros and cons of these major workplace changes below.

Remote, Hybrid, and Agile Work

One of the most obvious workplace changes widely experienced as a result of the COVID pandemic has been the widespread recognition and utilisation of hybrid or remote work arrangements. Rapid uptake in the flexibility of the physical location

DOI: 10.4324/9781032619385-9

of work occurred as a direct result of COVID lockdowns, when formal workplaces were inaccessible to many workers. Consequently, rapid technological utilisation by workers occurred to facilitate this remote work arrangement, thus software platforms such as Zoom and Microsoft Teams experienced widespread adoption. The benefits and challenges of both these remote work arrangements and rapid technological adoption, especially as applied to employee wellbeing, work engagement, and job performance, have been widely discussed (see for example, Brough & Kinman, 2024a; Brough et al., 2021a, 2021b). Remote work has been associated with mental health outcomes, both positive and negative. Positive outcomes include increased job satisfaction, decreased exhaustion, and reduced stress (Furuya et al., 2022; Shimura et al., 2021). A growing body of research has also documented associations between remote work and mental health challenges, including anxiety, depression, stress, headaches, and fatigue (Chirico et al., 2021). It is generally agreed, however, that remote working can benefit wellbeing, work–life balance and productivity provided key challenges are recognised and appropriate measures are in place to support workers (Mutebi & Hobbs, 2022).

It is pertinent to note here that for workers who have a choice of work location, the increased flexibility offered by remote working has endured post-COVID, often in spite of organisational policies calling for a blanket return to office working environments. Flexible remote working options have been primarily embraced by young workers, female employees, and workers with dependent children. Thus, remote working has addressed many of the difficulties associated with balancing work and non-work demands, for the workers most in need of this balance, and which have been discussed for many years within the work–life balance literature (e.g., Paula Brough et al., 2021a, 2021b; Brough et al., 2014).

Workplace Psychosocial Risks

Another major consequence of the pandemic has been the increased focus on employee's health and wellbeing per se. The marked increased interest in organisational wellbeing programmes and policies post-pandemic has taxed employers to look beyond the basic provision of yoga and massages for employees, to address more fundamental issues about the provision of healthy workplace environments, especially environments focused on psychosocial factors. Again, this is informed by decades long arguments prevalent within the occupational stress literature, which has argued for the responsibilities of employers to provide psychological (as well as physical) safe working conditions and cultures for their workers (e.g., Biggs et al., 2024; O'Driscoll & Brough, 2010). An important consequence highlighted by the pandemic was of the risks and adverse impacts caused by employees who attend work when they are unwell. Kinman et al. (2024) for example, recently discussed the importance of organisations adopting a 'healthy' sickness absence culture, highlighting the need for organisations' to ensure their attempts to reduce sickness absence do not inadvertently encourage dysfunctional presenteeism (discussed below). This is especially pertinent for workers experiencing symptoms related with long COVID and how these employees can be supported to return to work in an efficient but sustainable way.

Psychosocial risks (PRs) have gained recognition as significant factors affecting workers' health and safety. PRs are defined as aspects related to work design, organisation, and management, along with their social contexts, that can result in negative psychological, physical, and social effects when not properly managed (Leka et al., 2010). These risks include chronically high levels of job demands, low job control, inadequate rewards and social support, job insecurity, bullying, harassment, poor organisational justice, remote or isolated work, poor physical environment and interpersonal relationships in the workplace (Leka et al., 2015).

The transformation of work is evident in several aspects: increased workplace flexibility, advancements in technology, and shifts in the workforce demographics. These changes require the identification and integration of new risk factors into occupational safety and health (OSH) frameworks (Schulte et al., 2019). Moreover, the global impact of the COVID-19 pandemic, the growing digitalisation of work and the rising adoption of AI technologies have introduced new PRs, with potential implications for the health and wellbeing of workers. These developments necessitate further investigation and validation to understand their full impact. Different job resources, defined as social, physical, psychological, or organisational facets of the job, can be implemented to mitigate the adverse effects of PRs. For instance, in the context of job demands, job resources such as rewards, social support, interpersonal relations, feedback, and job control, can mitigate the adverse effects of chronically high demands (Johnson & Hall, 1988).

For example, a primary intervention directly addressing the control of PRs is psychosocial safety climate (PSC). PSC represents an organisation's genuine commitment to protect workers' psychological health (Dollard & Bakker, 2010), primarily manifested through its organisational policies, practices, and procedures. Specifically, PSC is defined as the policies, practices, and procedures aimed at protecting workers' psychological health and safety (Law et al., 2011; Dollard & Bakker, 2010). PSC embodies senior management's commitment, involvement, and consultation for employees' psychological health (Dollard & Bakker, 2010).

Employee Sickness Absence and Presenteeism

There is increasing concern post-COVID of the increased risk of presenteeism, especially for remote or agile workers, and the need for organisations to re-consider their mechanisms to better manage this risk and to target their supports. Presenteeism is commonly defined by two primary conceptualisations. *Sickness presenteeism* pertains to employees who work despite experiencing ill health (Aronsson et al., 2000). This definition is predominantly employed within European academic discourses and is quantitatively assessed based on the frequency of work attendance during periods of illness. The second definition of presenteeism is referred to as an impaired work function (J. Lerner et al., 2000). This conceptualisation is common in North American research to emphasise the productivity loss caused by presenteeism. On average between one third and one half of employees continue to work when unwell, although obviously this is very much influenced by the severity of the illness. The economic impact of presenteeism resulting from impaired work function, is typically larger than the economic consequences of sickness absence (Kigozi et al., 2017). For example, in the United States, presenteeism results in an annual economic cost of approximately US$312 million, compared to approximately US$176 million attributed to sickness absenteeism (Haque et al., 2019). Similarly, UK costs are cited as £6.6 billion for presenteeism compared to £3.7 billion for absenteeism (Cebr, 2023).

Employee presenteeism is significantly associated with decreased productivity, impaired work functions, and long-term negative effects on both physiological and psychological wellbeing. Presenteeism has been associated with chronic physical health conditions, including allergies, arthritis, chronic pain, diabetes, and musculoskeletal disorders (Schultz & Edington, 2007). Plus psychological conditions including depression (Kato et al., 2021), anxiety (Deady et al., 2022), and sleep disorders (Shimura et al., 2022). It is not really surprising that employees who have new or relatively minor symptoms of an illness may continue to work, at least partially, especially during the early stages of their illness. Many of these studies, especially the older ones, did not necessarily assess the type of work being conducted. Thus, working remotely answering emails when in the early stages of a virus infection (influenza, COVID, etc.), may be relatively 'easy' work to undertake and thus, may be considered generally acceptable. Other more complex work tasks or those requiring meeting with colleagues, would of course, be considered more unacceptable to perform when unwell. Thus, we suggest that these figures reporting the prevalence and costs of presenteeism should be considered with these more nuanced points in mind.

It is pertinent to note that rates of employee presenteeism are increasing across most industry sectors, and especially within public sector agencies, with presenteeism rates tripling since 2010 (CIPD, 2023). However, these increases are likely associated with an increased awareness of employee health and sickness, especially post-pandemic, as we noted above. Increased concerns about job security since the pandemic are also likely to have influenced increased rates of presenteeism (Kinman et al., 2024). Organisational culture has a strong impact on presenteeism rates, particularly managers' behaviours. Employees follow manager's role modelling behaviours, so a manager's attitude to sickness absenteeism, and/or their own behaviours of working while unwell, strongly influence their employee's subsequent presenteeism behaviours. The broader organisational culture which for example, may reward attendance and high work performance, and stigmatise absenteeism regardless of the cause, also serves to strongly influence employee's presenteeism behaviours (Kinman, 2019).

The healthcare industry appears to be especially prone to employee presenteeism, where the work culture of chronic high pressure, long hours, working shift-work, and a shortage of replacement staff serves to encourage this behaviour (Kinman & Grant, 2021). Presumably, this tendency for high rates of presenteeism amongst healthcare workers, has likely increased during and post-COVID, when the extreme high workloads and staff shortages would discourage even more staff to not attend work, and instead to work despite feeling unwell. The risks of illness contagion to colleagues and patients would be high and require careful employee management. For casual employees working when unwell may be essential in order to secure their pay. Thus, presenteeism rates are higher for workers in low socio-economic positions, compared to those in positions at higher levels who likely have more control over where and when they work (Kinman et al., 2024).

Workplace Digital and Technological Developments

Another consequence of the pandemic is the rapid 'digital transformation' of our workplaces now being experienced. Thus, multiple AI technologies are becoming increasingly prevalent in numerous industries, creating new working platforms, for example, via the development of work metaverses and digital twins of workers (Russell & Grant, 2024) for example, discussed how work technology and tools enable us to function as 'agile workers', which is a step beyond merely working in remote locations. The use of digital technology enables seamless communications between employers and workers, meaning that workers are (in theory) constantly available, accessible, and contactable: that is, agile. Importantly, the technology that facilitates agile working also enables employment to become more inclusive, offering increased work opportunities to sectors that have been traditionally marginalised, including workers with neurodivergence and/or disability and/or of a low socio-economic status. The potential drawbacks for employee wellbeing associated with this constant connectivity to work are, however, also acknowledged, echoing concerns about the need for careful boundary management between work and non-work domains.

Recently, AI has undergone significant development and has facilitated numerous improvements to create intelligence applications that can emulate human cognition and behaviour. This progress especially encompasses functions of speech recognition, natural language processing, and image recognitions. For instance, analyses using personal genetic data (Fang et al., 2020), images (Reece & Danforth, 2017), and text from social media (Chancellor & De Choudhury, 2020) can now predict health risks and mental disorders.

As the utilisation of AI continues to expand, researchers are increasingly exploring its potential to enhance mental health and wellbeing. With its capacity to analyse large datasets and make intricate decisions, AI holds promise in providing insights and support to individuals and communities striving to improve their health and wellbeing (D'Alfonso, 2020). Thus for example, AI-based applications are now being employed to assist with personalised sleep improvement (Jahrami & Pandi-Perumal, 2023), fatigue detection (Husom et al., 2022), analysing physical health data from wearable devices, and 'conversational agents' offering support for healthy eating habits or mental health issues (Maher et al., 2020). In our workplaces, AI is currently utilised to automate repetitive tasks, assist in decision-making processes, and provide personalised recommendations based on user preferences. The widespread adoption of digital technologies is also associated with new patterns of working including for example, the four-day working week (and the nine-day fortnight), hybrid and agile work as we discussed above, and the rise in community-based co-working hubs. This latter emergence of agile workers conducting their work from local or regional hubs has emerged primarily to address the isolation of agile workers. These community hubs can offer collaboration, psychological connectiveness, and community embeddedness, plus a lack of (long distance) commuting, and support for local communities and businesses (Russell & Grant, 2024). These capabilities may assist to reduce employee's occupational stress levels, and increase their efficiency and productivity, reportedly positively impacting workers' mental health (Gupta et al., 2023).

AI of course, also has disadvantages for some workers, serving to increase their stress experiences and reduce employee wellbeing. AI is associated with the loss of some job roles (partially offset by the development of new roles), a potential to destabilise labour markets, hinder wage growth, and lead to a long-term economic decline some estimated outcomes for example, indicate that approximately 47% of total US employment and 55% of Japanese employment are at risk of being computerised. The McKinsey Global Institute estimates that between 400 and 800 (David, 2017; Frey & Osborne, 2017) million workers will be replaced by AI by 2030 (Manyika et al., 2017). Additionally, the requirement for workers to 'keep up' with successive AI and software developments, increasingly integrate AI and digital technologies within their work roles, undergo training to sustain this digital technology adoption, and increase their knowledge of cyber-security prevention issues also increases the work demands (i.e., stress) for many workers. How much these additional work demands are offset by the benefits of workplace digital technologies will be pertinent to observe over the coming years.

Final Thoughts

This chapter has discussed four major changes to our workplaces which emerged from the COVID pandemic. It is apparent that the pandemic has changed the core meaning of the value of work for many employees, and these changes are already becoming firmly entrenched in some industries. It is likely of course, that further changes will emerge especially as our workplaces continue to adapt to the rapid uptake of digital technologies ensuring we hope, an increased meaningfulness of work accessible to a more diverse set of employees than we have experienced to date. We also hope that increasing recognition that inclusive workplace cultures – that promote equality, and value diversity in background, knowledge, skills, and experiences – have major benefits for employers and that this will encourage change in the future workplaces.

Finally, we note the pandemic has produced a widespread belief that a 'life beyond work' is valued highly by an increasing number of the younger generation of workers. These workers acutely experienced the pandemic lockdowns and its restrictions and physical health risks, at a key developmental stage in their lives. They have also witnessed the intense juggling act performed by their parents and older workers in an attempt to succeed in their work, family, and personal lives. The rise in experiences of work-related stress, mental ill health, and burnout amongst workers reported before the COVID-19 pandemic, attests to the damaging effects of this intense juggling of multiple life demands, and as is widely evidenced by the work–life balance literature (Brough et al., 2021a, 2021b). For many of our younger workers, therefore, the traditional 'masculine culture' of intense work hours and singular focus on career advancement, often undertaken at the expense of personal and family relationships, has an increasingly limited appeal (Brough et al., 2021a, 2021b). As these younger employees move through their working lives, we suggest it will be highly pertinent to observe how their attitudes and career expectations disrupt, shape, and transform the cultures within which they work. We foresee that major changes to how we work will, therefore, continue to occur over the next few years.

References

Aronsson, G., Gustafsson, K., & Dallner, M. (2000). Sick but yet at work. An empirical study of sickness presenteeism. *Journal of Epidemiology & Community Health*, *54*(7), 502–509.

Biggs, A., Brough, P., & Gai, S. (2024). Occupational stress, wellbeing, and burnout: Key considerations for improvements. In P. Brough & G. Kinman (Eds.), *Wellbeing at work in a turbulent era* (pp. 10–26). Cheltenham, UK: Edward Elgar Publishing, Incorporated.

Brough, P., & Kinman, G. (2024a). *Wellbeing at work in a turbulent era*. Cheltenham, UK: Edward Elgar Publishing, Incorporated.

Brough, P., & Kinman, G. (2024b). Will work ever be the same? Future trends for wellbeing at work. In P. Brough & G. Kinman (Eds.), *Wellbeing at work in a turbulent era* (pp. 1–9). Cheltenham, UK: Edward Elgar Publishing, Incorporated.

Brough, P., Kinman, G., McDowall, A., & Chan, X. W. (2021a). #MeToo' for work – Life balance. *British Psychological Society Work-Life Balance Bulletin*, *5*(1), 4–8.

Brough, P., Timms, C., O'Driscoll, M. P., Kalliath, T., Siu, O.-L., Sit, C., & Lo, D. (2014). Work–life balance: A longitudinal evaluation of a new measure across Australia and New Zealand workers. *The International Journal of Human Resource Management*, *25*(19), 2724–2744.

Brough, P., Wall, T., & Cooper, C. (2021b). Organizational wellbeing: An introduction and future directions. In T. Wall, C. L. Cooper, & P. Brough (Eds.), *The SAGE handbook of organizational wellbeing* (pp. 1–6). London, UK: Sage.

Cebr. (2023). *Financial wellbeing and productivity in the workplace; a Cebr report for Aegon*. Cebr.

Chancellor, S., & De Choudhury, M. (2020). Methods in predictive techniques for mental health status on social media: A critical review. *NPJ Digital Medicine*, *3*(1), 43.

Chirico, F., Zaffina, S., Di Prinzio, R. R., Giorgi, G., Ferrari, G., Capitanelli, I., & Ilesanmi, O. (2021). Working from home in the context of COVID-19: A systematic review of physical and mental health effects on teleworkers. *Journal of Health and Social Science, 6*(3), 319–332.

CIPD. (2023). *Health and wellbeing at work.* London: Chartered Institute of Personnel and Development.

D'Alfonso, S. (2020). AI in mental health. *Current Opinion in Psychology, 36*, 112–117.

David, B. (2017). Computer technology and probable job destructions in Japan: An evaluation. *Journal of the Japanese and International Economies, 43*, 77–87.

Deady, M., Collins, D., Johnston, D., Glozier, N., Calvo, R., Christensen, H., & Harvey, S. (2022). The impact of depression, anxiety and comorbidity on occupational outcomes. *Occupational Medicine, 72*(1), 17–24.

Dollard, M. F., & Bakker, A. B. (2010). Psychosocial safety climate as a precursor to conducive work environments, psychological health problems, and employee engagement. *Journal of Occupational and Organizational Psychology, 83*(3), 579–599.

Fang, Y., Scott, L., Song, P., Burmeister, M., & Sen, S. (2020). Genomic prediction of depression risk and resilience under stress. *Nature Human Behaviour, 4*(1), 111–118.

Frey, C. B., & Osborne, M. A. (2017). The future of employment: How susceptible are jobs to computerisation? *Technological Forecasting and Social Change, 114*, 254–280.

Furuya, Y., Nakazawa, S., Fukai, K., & Tatemichi, M. (2022). Health impacts with telework on workers: A scoping review before the COVID-19 pandemic. *Frontiers in Public Health, 10*, 981270.

Gupta, D., Singhal, A., Sharma, S., Hasan, A., & Raghuwanshi, S. (2023). Humans' emotional and mental well-being under the influence of artificial intelligence. *Journal for ReAttach Therapy and Developmental Diversities, 6*(6s), 184–197.

Haque, A., Fernando, M., & Caputi, P. (2019). Perceived human resource management and presenteeism: Mediating effect of turnover intentions. *Asia-Pacific Journal of Business Administration, 11*(2), 110–130.

Husom, E. J., Dautov, R., Nedisan Videsjorden, A., Gonidis, F., Papatzelos, S., & Malamas, N. (2022). Machine learning for fatigue detection using Fitbit fitness trackers. Proceedings of the 10th International Conference on Sport Sciences Research and Technology Support (icSPORTS 2022),

Jahrami, H., & Pandi-Perumal, S. R. (2023). Smart, personalized sleep: The benefits and risks of artificial intelligence and wearables in the consumer sleep technology market. *Sleep and Vigilance, 7*(1), 105–107.

Johnson, J. V., & Hall, E. M. (1988). Job strain, work place social support, and cardiovascular disease: A cross-sectional study of a random sample of the Swedish working population. *American Journal of Public Health, 78*(10), 1336–1342.

Kato, T., Baba, K., Guo, W., Chen, Y., & Nosaka, T. (2021). Impact of bipolar disorder on health-related quality of life and work productivity: Estimates from the national health and wellness survey in Japan. *Journal of Affective Disorders, 295*, 203–214.

Kigozi, J., Jowett, S., Lewis, M., Barton, P., & Coast, J. (2017). The estimation and inclusion of presenteeism costs in applied economic evaluation: A systematic review. *Value in Health, 20*(3), 496–506.

Kinman, G. (2019). Sickness presenteeism at work: Prevalence, costs and management. *British Medical Bulletin, 129*(1), 69–78.

Kinman, G., Clements, A., & Maher, K. (2024). Managing sickness absence, presenteeism & absence management. In P. Brough & G. Kinman (Eds.), *Wellbeing at work in a turbulent era,* (134–161). Cheltenham, UK: Edward Elgar Publishing, Incorporated.

Kinman, G., & Grant, C. (2021). Presenteeism during the COVID-19 pandemic: Risks and solutions. *Occupational Medicine, 71*(6–7), 243–244.

Law, R., Dollard, M. F., Tuckey, M. R., & Dormann, C. (2011). Psychosocial safety climate as a lead indicator of workplace bullying and harassment, job resources, psychological health and employee engagement. *Accident Analysis & Prevention, 43*(5), 1782–1793.

Leka, S., Jain, A., & Organization, W. H. (2010). Health impact of psychosocial hazards at work: An overview. Report for the World Health Organization. University of Nottingham.

Leka, S., Van Wassenhove, W., & Jain, A. (2015). Is psychosocial risk prevention possible? Deconstructing common presumptions. *Safety Science, 71*, 61–67.

Lerner, D., C. Amick III, B., Malspeis, S., & H. Rogers, W. (2000). A national survey of health-related work limitations among employed persons in the United States. *Disability and Rehabilitation, 22*(5), 225–232.

Maher, C. A., Davis, C. R., Curtis, R. G., Short, C. E., & Murphy, K. J. (2020). A physical activity and diet program delivered by artificially intelligent virtual health coach: Proof-of-concept study. *JMIR mHealth and uHealth, 8*(7), e17558.

Manyika, J., Lund, S., Chui, M., Bughin, J., Woetzel, J., Batra, P., Ko, R., & Sanghvi, S. (2017). Jobs lost, jobs gained: Workforce transitions in a time of automation. *McKinsey Global Institute, 150*(1), 1–148.

Mutebi, N., & Hobbs, A. (2022). *The impact of remote and hybrid working on workers and organisations*. UK Parliament POSTbrief, 49.

O'Driscoll, M. P., & Brough, P. (2010). Work organization and health. In S. Leka & J. Houdmont (Eds.), Occupational health psychology (pp. 57–87). Chichester: Wiley-Blackwell.

Reece, A. G., & Danforth, C. M. (2017). Instagram photos reveal predictive markers of depression. *EPJ Data Science, 6*(1), 15.

Russell, E., & Grant, C. (2024). Using digital tools to improve well-being and work performance in agile work. In P. Brough & G. Kinman (Eds.), *Wellbeing at work in a turbulent era*. Edward Elgar Publishing, Incorporated.

Schulte, P. A., Delclos, G., Felknor, S. A., & Chosewood, L. C. (2019). Toward an expanded focus for occupational safety and health: A commentary. *International Journal of Environmental Research and Public Health, 16*(24), 4946.

Schultz, A. B., & Edington, D. W. (2007). Employee health and presenteeism: A systematic review. *Journal of Occupational Rehabilitation, 17*(3), 547–579.

Shimura, A., Yokoi, K., Ishibashi, Y., Akatsuka, Y., & Inoue, T. (2021). Remote work decreases psychological and physical stress responses, but full-remote work increases presenteeism. *Frontiers in Psychology, 12*, 730969.

Shimura, A., Yokoi, K., Sugiura, K., Higashi, S., & Inoue, T. (2022). On workdays, earlier sleep for morningness and later wakeup for eveningness are associated with better work productivity. *Sleep Medicine, 92*, 73–80.

Vyas-Doorgapersad, S. (2023). A critical review of employee health, wellbeing programs, and organizational success: Navigating post-COVID-19 sustainable development. *International Journal of Research in Business and Social Science (2147–4478), 12*(6), 91–100.

10

EVOLUTIONARY PSYCHOLOGY FOR A POSITIVE WORKPLACE

Stephen M. Colarelli, Carter Vespi, and Mable E. Clark

Evolutionary Psychology

Evolutionary psychology is a meta-theoretical framework that applies the logic of natural selection to cognition, emotion, and behavior. However, before describing evolutionary psychology in more detail and how it can inform positive organizational behavior, it is important to say what it is not, given the many misconceptions about it (Confer et al., 2010). Perhaps the most prevalent misconception is that it implies biological determinism. This is nonsense. No serious evolutionary psychologist would support this notion. Although biology imposes rules that predispose the mind toward certain behaviors, behavior is a function of both nature *and* nurture (Lumsden & Wilson, 2005). Evolutionary psychology does, however, stand in sharp contrast to the standard social science model (SSSM). The SSSM posits that the human mind is a general, all-purpose learning mechanism, that biology plays a minimal role in human behavior, and that most human behavior is influenced by learning and culture. It remains a core assumption in much of the scholarship in organizational behavior and management (Colarelli & Arvey, 2015).[1]

Classical Evolutionary Psychology

Classical evolutionary psychology posits that the human mind contains multiple mechanisms that are the heritable products of natural selection. These mechanisms evolved over deep evolutionary time in response to recurrent challenges and problems faced by our ancestors. Consider human food preferences. People prefer foods containing fat, protein, carbohydrates, and salt.[2] These preferences come about because proteins (e.g., meat, nuts), carbohydrates (e.g., fruit), and minerals were critical for human health and development; therefore, people who had strong desires for these foods were more likely to survive and reproduce (Li, Van Vugt, &

DOI: 10.4324/9781032619385-10

Colarelli, 2018). Or consider mate preferences. Across cultures and time, people with a preference for mates with traits that signal high reproductive value are more likely to reproduce. Evidence of other evolved mechanisms – such as those that influence coalition partners, fairness perceptions, and pathogen avoidance (among many others) – has accumulated over the past several decades (Buss, 2019).

The concept of *mismatch* is critical in understanding applications of evolutionary psychology in modern contexts, particularly in the workplace (Li et al., 2018). Many human psychological mechanisms evolved during the Pleistocene epoch (from 2.8 million to 11,700 years ago). Because our biology evolves much slower than cultural changes, many of our psychological mechanisms are *mismatched* with modern environments. Conversely, much of our current environment is mismatched with human nature – particularly the modern work environment (Van Vugt, Colarelli, & Li, 2024; Van Vugt, Vespi, & Colarelli, in press). Returning to our food example, there is a mismatch between food availability in the modern world and our evolved food preferences. In our ancestral environment, food was difficult to get, so people could rarely overeat. Now, however, food with excessive fat and sugar content (i.e., junk food) is widely, easily, and inexpensively available. Because we still have strong evolved preferences for fats and sweets, we overconsume readily available junk food. A consequence of this mismatch is the current obesity epidemic and associated diseases (e.g., diabetes; Kessler, 2012).[3]

Cultural Evolution

Cultural evolution applies the logic of natural selection – variation, selection, and retention – to cultural products (e.g., artifacts, ideas, customs, institutions) (Campbell, 1975; Henrich, 2016). Cultural evolution is a useful way to account for both ephemeral fads and fashions as well as longer-lasting cultural (and organizational) practices and institutions. Cultural products are generated in a variety of ways (e.g., literature, art, science, happenstance). Those products that have appeal or utility are selected, and those that continue to be appealing or functional in given environments tend to be retained. Campbell (1975) argued that many social and religious practices are, in many ways, more effective than psychological interventions because the former had withstood the test of time through the crucible of cultural evolution. This is a functional view of cultural selection: cultural practices that serve a useful function (whether people are aware of the function or not) tend to be retained.[4] More recently, Henrich (2016) has gone further and argued that much of human progress can be accounted for by the mechanism of cultural evolution – that culture is a cumulative process that is smarter than any individual. Colarelli (1998, 2003) has applied the ideas of cultural evolution to understanding and explaining common practices that occur in organizations.

Coevolution

Coevolution, or dual inheritance theory, posits an interaction between genes and culture. Strong cultural innovations, such as agriculture, can become environmental pressures influencing the genetic traits that are likely to be adaptive and spread throughout a population. Conversely, genes have an influence on the development and acceptance of cultural innovations. Genes constrain the evolution of culture, but only to an extent (Lumsden & Wilson, 2005). Culturally driven selection processes are faster and can produce stronger selection pressures than purely biological ones because culture is shared among groups and therefore spreads rapidly (Laland et al., 2010). Thus, many traits are targeted for selection. An example of culture influencing genes is lactose tolerance. In most human populations, only children can digest lactose within milk, meaning that adult humans are largely lactose intolerant. However, in northern-European populations, humans developed the ability to digest lactose because of culturally driven selection pressures (dairy farming) within the last 5,000–10,000 years (Bersaglieri et al., 2004). Other examples of genes influencing culture include with whom and how people form cooperative alliances, leadership preferences, and common disgust and avoidance reactions (Van Vugt et al., in press).

Evolutionary Psychology and a Positive Workplace

Now that we have outlined the major principles of evolutionary psychology, we turn our focus to how these principles can create more positive organizations. Positive psychology is the study of the conditions and processes that contribute to the flourishing or optimal functioning of people, groups, and institutions. It counterbalances psychology's historical focus on human suffering and languishment. In this way, positive psychology strives toward a more complete understanding of the human condition (Gable & Haidt, 2005). A greater overall emphasis on employee happiness and health can improve employee well-being and is a much needed contrast to the traditional, utilitarian perspective of human resource management.

Ideas from evolutionary psychology can contribute to a positive workplace in several ways. First, evolutionary psychology provides a realistic understanding of human nature. Thus, interventions – including positive interventions – based on a realistic understanding of human nature are more likely to be effective than those that are not (Colarelli & Arvey, 2015).[5] Second, the concept of mismatch serves as an important framework for developing positive workplace interventions. This framework can help organizational scientists and managers make relatively straightforward changes by altering the workplace environment so that it is more compatible with evolved human nature. Finally, the broader concepts from natural and cultural selection are useful for interventions that increase the diversity of ideas and people in organizations as well as for designing more effective change processes.

Four Simple, Effective, and Positive Workplace Interventions

Here we describe four simple evolutionary psychological interventions that are (mostly) straightforward to implement: increasing exposure to nature, allowing employees to bring a companion animal to work, facilitating the development of workplace friendships, and implementing changes that enable employees to stand, move, and walk more during their workday.

Exposure to Natural Elements

There is a substantial body of literature on the positive effects of exposure to natural elements on physical and mental health (e.g., Bergefurt et al., 2022). Much of this empirical literature follows from evolutionary theories about responses to environments (van Esch et al., 2019). Orians' (1986) savanna hypothesis argues that people have an affinity for savanna-like environments that we evolved in on the savannahs of East Africa, which were relatively resource rich and secure environments. Thus, we developed psychological adaptations that draw us to views of undulating grasslands, scattered trees and copses, and bodies of water. We still respond positively to landscape and savanna-like settings, which also reduce stress responses (Ulrich, 1983). Attention restoration theory (ART; Kaplan, 1995) suggests that natural scenes are restorative because they provide a respite from cognitively effortful tasks. Most modern environments require sustained, prolonged, and directed attention, resulting in mental fatigue. Natural views, on the other hand, use involuntary or effortless attention (fascination) – which is restorative. Thus, nature can exert positive influences on human emotions and cognition.

However, it was not until recently that researchers began examining whether exposure to nature would be comparably beneficial in workplace settings as well, where direct exposure to nature is limited or nonexistent. Several studies have found that images of nature (paintings, window views) have similar effects as direct exposure to nature. An and colleagues (2016) found that exposure to natural elements (potted plants, window views, sunlight, photos or paintings of natural landscapes) were positively associated with job satisfaction and organizational commitment, and negatively associated with depressed mood. They also found that exposure to nature acted as a buffer against role stressors: the negative association between role stressors and job satisfaction (as well as organizational commitment) was smaller for employees who experienced more exposure to nature at work. Van Esch and colleagues (2019) examined the effects of office window views on employee well-being by comparing the effects of nature versus urban views, as well as the effects of view features. They found that natural elements in office window views were associated with greater job satisfaction and feelings of restoration, as well as lower turnover intentions, emotional exhaustion, and feelings of apprehension. In addition, some view features – particularly coherence and refuge – were associated with beneficial outcomes regardless of whether they were from natural or urban views.

There are a variety of nature exposure interventions that organizations can consider. One relatively simple intervention would be to hang photographs, paintings, or posters depicting natural settings in common areas (hallways, break rooms, restrooms, entryways, foyers, etc.), or give employees photos or paintings of nature for their workspaces. Thus, providing employees with exposure to natural elements, even if the elements are artificial (e.g., photographs), can allow them to reap some of the benefits of having nature in their workspaces. Live plants are another good option. Organizations could allow – and encourage – employees to bring potted plants into their office spaces. Organizations could also bring nature indoors by constructing interior natural settings in common areas, which could be large plants, wall plants, or, if the organization is so inclined, indoor waterfalls.[6] If an organization desires a more encompassing intervention, it might also consider the addition of real – as opposed to simulated – forms of nature at work, given that real natural elements are likely more effective than simulated ones. For example, organizations could expand their office windows (or add more of them) to allow more sunlight to enter their offices. Many studies have demonstrated numerous psychological and physiological benefits of sunlight exposure (An et al., 2016; Holick, 2004), so adding more space for windows would likely be effective in promoting employee health, well-being, and overall performance. More windows could provide the additional benefit of enabling workers to view the natural landscapes, if there are natural views to see. To the extent that there are grounds surrounding workplace facilities, an organization could engage a landscape architect to turn them into attractive natural settings, with paths and ponds so employees can visit and enjoy the area. This would expose employees to both sunlight and natural elements – as well as provide an area for walking (an excellent exercise) perhaps even with a favorite four-legged companion that is welcome at work.

Companion Animals in the Workplace

Dogs and humans have had a unique and psychologically meaningful bond for at least 15,000 years, when dogs were thought to be first domesticated (Vilà et al., 1997). Humans have been burying dogs in rituals (similar to those used for family members) since dogs were domesticated. Unlike most animals, dogs use eye contact to communicate with humans and are attentive to body language cues (Savalli, Resende, & Gaunet, 2016), possibly to strengthen communication and social bonds. Thus, it is not surprising that the presence of companion dogs has positive psychological and physiological benefits on humans. For example, the presence of a dog improves mood and decreases stress (Machová et al., 2020). In addition, a companion dog increases friendly interactions with strangers (McNicholas & Collis, 2000). Companion dogs have also been shown to exert beneficial influences on individuals and groups in workplace settings (Junça-Silva, 2022). For instance, Colarelli and colleagues (2017) found that having a companion dog nearby enhanced the cooperation, physical intimacy, and verbal cohesion of small groups. Furthermore, the same groups who had a companion dog present were rated by observers as being more friendly, cooperative, active, attentive, and enthusiastic than control groups who did not have a companion dog. Organizations appear to be increasingly amenable to having pets in their workspaces (Janowitz, 2023; Quan & Schabram, 2023). Companion dogs are environmental stimuli that trigger – in most people – psychological mechanisms that evoke positive emotions and behavior. Thus, allowing companion dogs in the workplace may serve as another simple and low-cost yet effective intervention for increasing communication, cooperation, and trust.[7] A dog-friendly workplace can also be an unobtrusive and effective way for organizations to get their employees to get out of their chairs and move periodically, as employees will need to take their dogs outside for a bathroom break and possibly a short walk.

There are a number of ways by which organizations can integrate pet ownership (or even simply the presence of a pet) into their workplaces in a practical manner. Although most employees believe that pets create a more positive environment to work in, there are still those who disagree. Because of this, organizations should be judicious about how they craft their policies around pets in the workplace. For example, organizations should make it clear that, if pets are to be brought to work, they should be properly socialized. Organizations should also be aware of local health and safety guidelines and restrict the presence of pets to certain areas accordingly, or to even restrict certain kinds of pets to prevent company liability for accidents. Organizations may start the process incrementally, limiting the presence of pets to certain days of the week and, if more skeptical employees say they are comfortable, gradually expanding the times allowed for pets at work. As with most interventions, transitions from one workplace arrangement to another should be sensitive to feedback from affected stakeholders, especially those who express initial discomfort with the change.

Facilitating Workplace Friendships

If companionship between humans and dogs is conducive to a more positive workplace, then the positive effects of companionship among humans themselves are likely to be even stronger. Human friendships have been one of the most crucial manifestations of cooperation throughout human evolutionary history (Hruschka, 2010). People with close friends tend to live longer, healthier, and happier lives (Waldinger & Schulz, 2023) and are at much lower risk of mortality than individuals with very few or no close friends (Dunbar, 2021). It would not be a great leap to infer, therefore, that the physical and psychological health benefits of friendships would also extend to workplace settings, which is indeed what recent research by Mirando and colleagues (2024) found. Furthermore, this same study found that workplace friendships contribute positively to knowledge sharing, innovative behaviors, and job performance. The authors argue that these benefits are largely attributable to the increase in psychological resources that strong social connections confer to individuals within organizations and beyond. However, this raises the more ultimate question of *why* friends increase psychological resources in the first place. This is likely because friendships were evolutionarily adaptive throughout human history, contributing greatly to human survival and reproductive success.

Considering the evidence that workplace friendships are beneficial for employees, we would recommend that organizational leaders attempt to facilitate the formation of close social bonds among their employees. For instance, organizations might implement attractive break rooms, game rooms, or exercise rooms that allow employees to socialize with one another and develop friendships. They might also use onboarding practices for new employees that allow for the formation of social relationships with organizational insiders or plan informal get-togethers or activities that involve disclosure of personal information, which will likely foster trust between employees. We believe that interventions such as these, although perhaps requiring more effort than previously mentioned interventions, are nonetheless very feasible and are made worth the effort by the benefits conferred by workplace friendships.

As a counterpoint, some researchers have argued that workplace friendships can be a distraction and can create conflicts of interest that should be avoided in the workplace (Pillemer & Rothbard, 2018), reinforcing the trope that the workplace should strictly be reserved for business, with no room for friendships. More recent research, however, suggests that the benefits of workplace friendships are likely to outweigh the costs (e.g., Mirando et al., 2024). Therefore, we would also encourage organizations to combat popular misconceptions about friendships in the workplace by facilitating an organizational climate that promotes the formation of friendships at work.

Facilitating Movement and Exercise

Exercise is an evolutionary conundrum. On the one hand, most people do not exercise and do not enjoy exercise. Indeed, a majority of the general population does not meet general health guidelines for weekly physical activity, largely because of lack of intrinsic motivation to do so (Teixeira et al., 2012). On the other hand, exercise is essential to human health. Muscles and bones will atrophy without regular and sufficient exercise (Lieberman, 2015). Lack of exercise – particularly in the modern world – contributes to a variety of maladies, including heart disease, diabetes, and obesity. Exercise has also been shown to have positive effects on mental health. Therefore, it might seem counterintuitive that humans appear to be inherently averse to exercise, considering that the physical and psychological benefits of engaging in regular exercise are so substantial.

Research in human evolution can help us understand and deal with this conundrum. Humans evolved to avoid excessive physical activity because engaging in physical activity expends valuable calories (Lieberman, 2015), which were far scarcer in ancestral times than they are today (Li et al., 2018). Nevertheless, our hunter-gatherer ancestors, who did not like exercise any more than we do, had no choice: they had to exert themselves to survive (to get food and water, build shelters, and visit friends and relatives). Not so with humans in the modern world. We have easy access to calories and conveniences (automobiles, elevators, the internet) that allow us to go through our days with minimal movement and exercise. And because most of us dislike exercise, we take advantage of opportunities and conveniences to avoid it.

Because of people's evolved antipathy toward exercise, the results of physical exercise interventions in workplaces are mixed at best (Groeneveld et al., 2010). However, we believe that an evolutionary psychological understanding may help refine the focus of exercise-based interventions and, in turn, make them more effective. For one, it is difficult to convince employees to engage in exercise, even when organizations provide exercise facilities (Groeneveld et al., 2010). Thus, a more indirect approach is necessary that reverses modern mismatch to a situation more like our ancestors, where they had little choice but to move. Organizations should use interventions that give people little or no choice to exercise. Evolutionary interventions pertaining to exercise are unique in that they address humans' innate propensity to *avoid* doing something (in this case, exercise), rather than to actively seek something out (e.g., gravitating toward nature, making friends). So, rather than simply facilitating an activity that employees will then naturally carry out themselves, interventions for physical exercise require the organization to implement activities, structures, or policies that require employees to be more physically active during the workday. Although this may sound coercive or paternalistic, we believe that the long-term benefits of having healthier employees far outweigh the more immediate costs of imposing them.

We suggest three types of movement/exercise interventions, ranging from simple and least disruptive to those that are more complex. First, organizations might consider limiting how much able-bodied employees can use movement-saving devices, such as elevators and escalators. For instance, organizations might consider restricting elevator use for small distances (two or three floors) to individuals who need them (e.g., people with physical disabilities), making it necessary for most employees to take the stairs. Second, organizations can install office furniture that facilitates physical movement, such as standing or treadmill desks. At a minimum, organizations could make this type of furniture a default option. Treadmill desks have been shown to be effective in improving physical health, although the evidence regarding their psychological effects is more uncertain (MacEwen, MacDonald, & Burr, 2015). Furthermore, people who stand more tend to have lower rates of obesity than people who sit for longer durations during the day, attesting to the potential efficacy of simply having employees use standing desks instead of sitting ones (Levine et al., 2005). Third, a more elaborate intervention might be to purposefully extend the walking distances between places that employees regularly go – for example, between the parking lot and the work facility, or between workspaces and bathrooms and cafeterias. In doing so, employees would have no choice but to walk more during their daily activities at work, which can cumulatively expend a surprisingly large number of calories throughout the workday.

Common Threads

Common to all four of these interventions are core elements of the evolutionary psychological perspective: evolved psychological adaptations guiding preferences for and comfort with particular stimuli, a mismatch between human nature and the stimuli typically found in modern organizations, and modifying organizational environments so that they are more matched with human nature. These interventions have significant advantages. First, after they are implemented, they operate on a continuous basis – no further maintenance needs to be done to maintain the effects of these interventions. Second, these interventions do not require motivation, continuous effort, and repetition by employees. They provide stimuli or affordances that – by their very presence – create positive workplace outcomes.[8] This contrasts with most organizational interventions, which require continuous and conscious employee effort (e.g., stress reduction exercises, working out at employee fitness centers). Third, organizations have options on how to implement these interventions, ranging from simple and inexpensive to more involved and costly. Moreover, these interventions (except those for increasing movement and exercise) are unlikely to engender strong employee resistance. This is because they tap into fundamental human mechanisms that drive positive responses.

We urge organizations to conduct an audit to assess their current state with respect to these four interventions (nature, companion animals, workplace friendship, and exercise affordances). Organizations should develop appropriate metrics to continue to track progress in these areas and monitor the effects of these four factors on important organizational outcomes.

A Cautionary Tale: Why Interventions Are Difficult But Are Still Worth Trying

While the above four interventions should be easier to implement than many others, implementing any intervention is easier said than done. Interventions are difficult to implement for several reasons. Self-interest is a primary human motivation. Thus, managers and employees (and consultants) often view interventions from the perspective of their own interests. Because organizations (and social systems more generally) consist of self-interested individuals and groups, conflicts of interest are inevitable, which limit a smooth adoption of a new intervention.[9] For example, when there is tension between productivity and the well-being of workers, management typically favors the former because it serves their self-interest to a larger degree. In addition, many practices and procedures are routinized and deeply embedded in an organization's structure – ossified by structural inertia – making any change difficult (Hannan & Carroll, 1995). Most psychological interventions in organizations also require constant motivation and effort on the part of managers and employees. Who has the time for this? People are busy doing their jobs, keeping their heads above water. Thus, most people will not have the motivation or interest to engage in psychological interventions that require additional attention, time, and effort.

However, even if interventions were easy to implement, many would still fail (Dewar & Keller, 2009) because they produce small effects. They barely move the needle. One reason for their small effects is that the science behind organizational interventions, particularly psychological interventions, is often problematic: replicability problems, statistical limitations, methodological and measurement limitations, and so on. Even scientifically solid interventions have limited impact. This is because organizations are complex systems consisting of many interacting parts that impinge on an intervention, reducing intended effects.

Yet, interventions are still worth trying because they are crucial elements of cultural variation, which organizations need to adapt to new circumstances. Rather than viewing interventions as devices to solve specific organizational problems, they should be regarded as cultural variations, subjected to the crucible of cultural evolution (variation, selection, retention). Although some interventions will be beneficial while others will not, it is the existence of a *variety of interventions* that is important. Variation drives evolution. Organizations that experiment with multiple interventions (particularly those that are evidence-based and have a theoretical foundation compatible with human nature) are more likely to experience success with interventions than organizations that do not. Still, although we can estimate probabilities of success of an intervention, any intervention only can be considered effective to the extent that it has been tested in the crucible of cultural evolution (Campbell, 1975; Colarelli, 1998; Wilson, 2016).

Future Directions

In this chapter, we have outlined some implementable and effective interventions for creating a more positive workplace. In this section we would like to suggest more ambitious evolutionary interventions. One intervention that could be explored pertains to the size of organizations. Organizations that are extremely large and span multiple countries are severely mismatched with how social units were traditionally structured throughout human evolutionary history (Hill & Dunbar, 2003). Organizational researchers may therefore wish to investigate the effects of limiting the number of employees that can comprise a department, unit, or team, ensuring that employees do not feel alienated or disconnected from other employees. Future researchers may also wish to examine how other mismatches can be reduced with flexible work schedules and greater work–life integration. For example, flexible start and end times, compressed workweeks, or hybrid work arrangements may allow employees to work during the time of day at which they are the most productive, which can vary among individuals based on circadian rhythms and energy levels. Flexible scheduling would have the additional benefit of creating greater integration between employees' personal and professional lives. This is more aligned with humans' natural approach to work–life balance, in which most adults cared for children and elderly kin throughout the workday, as opposed to modern work arrangements, in which organizations typically expect employees to be entirely devoted to the organization while they are at work. Other potentially fruitful interventions for a more positive workplace might involve shifting organizational cultures to make them more collaborative and communal, rather than individualistic and competitive. This could potentially resolve the mismatch between our ancestral work cultures – which were largely cooperative and involved team efforts to complete tasks (Narayanan et al., 2022) - and modern work cultures, which mostly emphasize competition and individual performance.

Conclusion

In this chapter, we discussed the various ways by which an evolutionary psychological perspective can be brought to bear on the development of a more positive workplace. We described evolutionary psychology as a general framework for understanding human behavior and discussed how evolutionary theory and research can be applied as a means of creating a more positive workplace via organizational interventions. We believe that an evolutionary perspective can be useful – perhaps even indispensable – in determining the kinds of interventions that are long-lasting and most likely to result in happier, healthier, and more productive employees.

Notes

1. This may be why programs to change people – training, development, socialization – are among the most recommended (Lambert et al., 2022) and commonly used (Nielsen et al., 2010) interventions in organizations.
2. Human food preferences are a good example of the interaction of nature and nurture. On the one hand, humans have evolved preferences for fats, protein, salt, and carbohydrates. On the other hand, culture influences – within these broad biological parameters – particular preferences. For example, pork is the most widely consumed meat in China. However, in much of the middle east, because pork is forbidden by Jewish and Islamic dietary laws, poultry and lamb are widely consumed. However, in neither China nor the middle east do people consume grass or hay (except perhaps when facing starvation) as do ungulates.
3. It would be hard to argue that the obesity epidemic, resulting in large part from over consumption of foods high in sugar and fats, is strictly due to learning. While marketing and learning play a part, it is more likely that the marketing of junk food taps into existing psychological mechanisms. Efforts to teach people about the negative impact of junk food and the beneficial effects of healthful foods have had little effect, and may even be counterproductive (Memon et al., 2020).
4. The variation in spice preferences throughout the world is a product of cultural evolution (Sherman & Flaxman, 2001). Many spices and seasonings (e.g., onions and garlic) have antimicrobial properties. Through cultural evolution, the frequency with which people prepared and ate spicy food increased in hotter climates because foods are more likely to

go bad (rot) quicker in these climates, and the use of food spices slows this down. Thus, by using spices in hotter climates, food would spoil more slowly, and people would become ill less frequently from eating spoiled food. This was undoubtedly a process of blind variation and selection where a cultural practice evolved over time and users typically could not explain the (scientific) reasons for it. See Henrich (2016) for other examples.

5 Bruno Bettelheim's prescription for treating autism is a classic example of the harm that interventions can cause when they are based on incorrect assumptions about human nature (Severson & Aune, 2008). Bettelheim believed that lack of maternal warmth and bonding causes autism. Thus, he recommended that autistic children be isolated from their mothers in a treatment facility. Bettelheim's wrongheaded ideas about the causes of and treatment for autism were responsible for the myth of the "refrigerator mother," additional anguish for mothers with autistic children, and wasted time and resources on an ineffective treatment regimen.

6 Government regulations or incentives may also increase health promoting views at work. Currently in the United States, natural lighting is mandated in spaces occupied by humans, and the total window area must be at least as large as 8% of the floor area of a room.

7 Dogs are now being used in some courtroom settings. The presence of a friendly companion dog helps to reduce witness anxiety and facilitate more open communication (Ramey, 2024).

8 We are not describing "nudges." Nudges are a choice situation that predisposes people to choose one alternative over another (Thaler & Sunstein, 2008). For example, placing healthy food at the beginning of a buffet counter and unhealthy food at the end, people are more likely to choose more healthy foods because of its location in the buffet line. Evolutionary psychological interventions involve creating an environment that presents positive stimuli similar to that which was encountered during the environment of evolutionary adaptedness and for which our minds are still adapted. These stimuli correspond to specific psychological mechanisms associated with positive emotions and behaviors.

9 Although consultants engaged in change efforts encourage aligning interests, complete alignment is impossible in systems composed of self-interested individuals.

References

An, M., Colarelli, S. M., O'Brien, K., & Boyajian, M. E. (2016). Why we need more nature at work: Effects of natural elements and sunlight on employee mental health and work attitudes. *PLoS One*, *11*(5), e0155614. https://doi.org/10.1371/journal.pone.0155614

Bergefurt, L., Weijs-Perrée, M., Appel-Meulenbroek, R., & Arentze, T. (2022). The physical office workplace as a resource for mental health—A systematic scoping review. *Building and Environment*, *207*, 108505. https://doi.org/10.1016/j.buildenv.2021.108505

Bersaglieri, T., Sabeti, P. C., Patterson, N., Vanderploeg, T., Schaffner, S. F., Drake, J. A., Rhodes, M., Reich, D. E., & Hirschhorn, J. N. (2004). Genetic signatures of strong recent positive selection at the Lactase gene. *The American Journal of Human Genetics*, *74*(6), 1111–1120. https://doi.org/10.1086/421051

Buss, D. (2019). *Evolutionary psychology: The new science of the mind* (6th ed.). New York: Routledge.

Campbell, D. T. (1975). On the conflicts between biological and social evolution and between psychology and moral tradition. *American Psychologist*, *30*, 1103–1126. https://doi.org/10.1111/j.1467-9744.1976.tb00277.x

Colarelli, S. M. (1998). Psychological interventions in organizations: An evolutionary perspective. *American Psychologist*, *53*(9), 1044. https://doi.org/10.1037//0003-066x.53.9.1044

Colarelli, S. M. (2003). *No best way: An evolutionary perspective on human resource management*. Westport, CT: Praeger.

Colarelli, S. M., & Arvey, R. D. (Eds.) (2015). *The biological foundations of organizational behavior*. Chicago, IL: University of Chicago Press. https://doi.org/10.7208/chicago/9780226127293.001.0001

Colarelli, S. M., McDonald, A. M., Christensen, M. S., & Honts, C. (2017). A companion dog increases prosocial behavior in work groups. *Anthrozoös, 30*(1), 77–89. https://doi.org/10.1080/08927936.2017.1270595

Confer, J. C., Easton, J. A., Fleischman, D. S., Goetz, C. D., Lewis, D. M., Perilloux, C., & Buss, D. M. (2010). Evolutionary psychology: Controversies, questions, prospects, and limitations. *American Psychologist, 65*(2), 110. https://doi.org/10.1037/a0018413

Dewar, C., & Keller, S. (2009, April 1). The irrational side of change management. *McKinsey Quarterly, 2*(10), 100–109. https://www.mckinsey.com/capabilities/people-and-organizational-performance/our-insights/the-irrational-side-of-change-management

Dunbar, R. (2021). *Friends: Understanding the power of our most important relationships.* London: Little Brown.

Gable, S. L., & Haidt, J. (2005). What (and why) is positive psychology? *Review of General Psychology, 9*(2), 103–110. https://doi.org/10.1037/1089-2680.9.2.103

Groeneveld, I. F., Proper, K. I., van der Beek, A. J., Hildebrandt, V. H., & van Mechelen, W. (2010). Lifestyle-focused interventions at the workplace to reduce the risk of cardiovascular disease—A systematic review. *Scandinavian Journal of Work, Environment & Health*, 202–215. https://doi.org/10.5271/sjweh.2891

Hannan, M. T., & Carroll, G. R. (1995). An introduction to organizational ecology. In G. R. Carroll and M. T. Hannan (Eds.), *Organizations in industry: Strategy, structure, and selection* (pp. 15–31). New York, NY: Oxford University Press.

Henrich, J. (2016). *The secret of our success: How learning from others drove human evolution, domesticated our species, and made us smart*. Princeton, NJ: Princeton University Press.

Hill, R. A., & Dunbar, R. I. (2003). Social network size in humans. *Human Nature, 14*(1), 53–72. https://doi.org/10.1007/s12110-003-1016-y

Holick, M. F. (2004). Sunlight and vitamin D for bone health and prevention of autoimmune diseases, cancers, and cardiovascular disease. *The American Journal of Clinical Nutrition, 80*(6), 1678S–1688S. https://doi.org/10.1093/ajcn/80.6.1678s

Hruschka, D. J. (2010). *Friendship: Development, ecology, and evolution of a relationship* (Vol. 5). Berkeley, CA: University of California Press.

Janowitz, K. (2023) Pet-friendly workplaces are on the rise. Here's why Fuse said yes to pets. *California Business Journal*. https://calbizjournal.com/pet-friendly-workplaces-are-on-the-rise-heres-why-fuse-said-yes-to-pets

Junça-Silva, A. (2022). Friends with benefits: The positive consequences of pet-friendly practices for workers' well-being. *International Journal of Environmental Research and Public Health, 19*(3), 1069. https://doi.org/10.3390/ijerph19031069

Kaplan, S. (1995). The restorative benefits of nature: Toward an integrative framework. *Journal of Environmental Psychology, 15*(3), 169–182. https://doi.org/10.1016/0272-4944(95)90001-2

Kessler, D. A. (2012). *Your food is fooling you: How your brain is hijacked by sugar, fat, and salt*. New York, NY: Roaring Brook Press.

Laland, K. N., Odling-Smee, J., & Myles, S. (2010). How culture shaped the human genome: Bringing genetics and the human sciences together. *Nature Reviews Genetics, 11*(2), 137–148. https://doi.org/10.1038/nrg2734

Lambert, B., Caza, B. B., Trinh, E., & Ashford, S. (2022). Individual-centered interventions: Identifying what, how, and why interventions work in organizational contexts. *The Academy of Management Annals*, *16*(2), 508–546. https://doi.org/10.5465/annals.2020.0351

Levine, J. A., Lanningham-Foster, L. M., McCrady, S. K., Krizan, A. C., Olson, L. R., Kane, P. H., Jensen, M. D., & Clark, M. M. (2005). Interindividual variation in posture allocation: Possible role in human obesity. *Science*, *307*(5709), 584–586. https://doi.org/10.1126/science.1106561

Li, N. P., Van Vugt, M., & Colarelli, S. M. (2018). The evolutionary mismatch hypothesis: Implications for psychological science. *Current Directions in Psychological Science*, *27*(1), 38–44. https://doi.org/10.1177/0963721417731378

Lieberman, D. E. (2015). Is exercise really medicine? An evolutionary perspective. *Current Sports Medicine Reports*, *14*(4), 313–319. https://doi.org/10.1249/jsr.0000000000000168

Lumsden, C. J., & Wilson, E. O. (2005). *Genes, mind, and culture-the coevolutionary process*. World Scientific. https://doi.org/10.1142/5786

MacEwen, B. T., MacDonald, D. J., & Burr, J. F. (2015). A systematic review of standing and treadmill desks in the workplace. *Preventive Medicine*, *70*, 50–58. https://doi.org/10.1016/j.ypmed.2014.11.011

Machová, K., Procházková, R., Vadroňová, M., Součková, M., & Prouzová, E. (2020). Effect of dog presence on stress levels in students under psychological strain: A pilot study. *International Journal of Environmental Research and Public Health*, *17*(7), 2286. https://doi.org/10.3390/ijerph17072286

McNicholas, J., & Collis, G. M. (2000). Dogs as catalysts for social interactions: Robustness of the effect. *British Journal of Psychology*, *91*(1), 61–70. https://doi.org/10.1348/000712600161673

Memon, A. N., Gowda, A. S., Rallabhandi, B., Bidika, E., Fayyaz, H., Salib, M., & Cancarevic, I. (2020). Have our attempts to curb obesity done more harm than good? *Cureus*, *12*(9). https://doi.org/10.7759/cureus.10275

Mirando, T., Colarelli, S. M., Han, K., Vespi, C. (2024). Friends with workplace benefits. Unpublished manuscript. Department of Psychology, Central Michigan University, Mt. Pleasant, Michigan, USA.

Narayanan, J., Puranam, P., & Van Vugt, M. (2022). Human-centric organizing: A perspective from evolutionary psychology. *INSEAD*. https://ssrn.com/abstract=3959703

Nielsen, K., Randall, R., Holten, A. L., & González, E. R. (2010). Conducting organizational-level occupational health interventions: What works? *Work & Stress*, *24*(3), 234–259. https://doi.org/10.1080/02678373.2010.515393

Orians, G. (1986). An ecological and evolutionary approach to landscape aesthetics. In E. C. Penning-Rowsell & D. Lowenthal (Eds.), *Landscape meanings and values* (pp. 3–25). London: Allen & Unwin. https://doi.org/10.4324/9781003270270-2

Pillemer, J., & Rothbard, N. P. (2018). Friends without benefits: Understanding the dark sides of workplace friendship. *Academy of Management Review*, *43*(4), 635–660. https://doi.org/10.5465/amr.2016.0309

Quan, S. X., & Schabram, K. (2023, No. 13). Research: The benefits of a pet-friendly workplace. *Harvard Business Review*. https://hbr.org/2023/11/research-the-benefits-of-a-pet-friendly-workplace

Ramey, C. (April 24, 2024). Who let the dogs in? Courthouse canines are having a moment. *Wall Street Journal*. https://www.wsj.com/us-news/dogs-courthouses-courts-lawyers-9c882f0b?mod=mhp

Savalli, C., Resende, B., & Gaunet, F. (2016). Eye contact is crucial for referential communication in pet dogs. *PLoS One*, *11*(9), e0162161. https://doi.org/10.1371/journal.pone.0162161

Severson, K. D., & Aune, J. A. (2008). Bruno bettelheim, autism, and the rhetoric of scientific authority. In M. Osteen (Ed.), *Autism and representation* (pp. 65–76). New York: Routledge.

Sherman, P. W., & Flaxman, S. M. (2001). Protecting ourselves from food. *American Scientist*, *89*, 142–151. https://doi.org/10.1511/2001.18.142

Teixeira, P. J., Carraça, E. V., Markland, D., Silva, M. N., & Ryan, R. M. (2012). Exercise, physical activity, and self-determination theory: A systematic review. *International Journal of Behavioral Nutrition and Physical Activity*, *9*, 1–30. https://doi.org/10.1186/1479-5868-9-78

Thaler, R., & Sunstein, C. (2008). *Nudge: Improving decisions about health, wealth and happiness*. New Haven, CT: Yale University Press.

Ulrich, R. S. (1983). Aesthetic and affective response to natural environment. In I. Altman & J. F. Wohlwill (Eds.), *Behavior and the natural environment* (pp. 85–125). New York: Plenum Press. https://doi.org/10.1007/978-1-4613-3539-9_4

van Esch, E., Minjock, R., Colarelli, S. M., & Hirsch, S. (2019). Office window views: View features trump nature in predicting employee well-being. *Journal of Environmental Psychology*, *64*, 56–64. https://doi.org/10.1016/j.jenvp.2019.05.006

Van Vugt, M., & Colarelli, S. M., & Li, N. (2024). Virtually (mis)matched: Evolved human minds operating in the digital workplace. *Organizational Psychology Review*, 1–22. https://doi.org/10.1177/20413866241232138

Van Vugt, M., Vespi, C., & Colarelli, S. M. (in press). Evolutionary approaches to industrial and organizational psychology: Working with human nature. In M. L. Fisher (Ed.), *APA handbook of evolutionary psychology* (3rd ed.). New York: Wiley.

Vilà, C., Savolainen, P., Maldonado, J. E., Amorim, I. R., Rice, J. E., Honeycutt, R. L., Crandall, K. A., Lundeberg, J., & Wayne, R. K. (1997). Multiple and ancient origins of the domestic dog. *Science*, *276*(5319), 1687–1689. https://doi.org/10.1126/science.276.5319.1687

Waldinger, R., & Schulz, M. (2023). *The good life: Lessons from the world's longest scientific study of happiness*. New York, NY: Simon and Schuster.

Wilson, D. S. (2016). Intentional cultural change. *Current Opinion in Psychology*, *8*, 190–193. https://doi.org/10.1016/j.copsyc.2015.12.012

11

CROSS-CULTURAL POSITIVE ORGANIZATIONAL BEHAVIOR

Sharon Glazer and Catherine T. Kwantes

Cross-Cultural Positive Organizational Behavior

Positive organizational behavior (OB) and positive organizational psychology (OP) are partner disciplines; both focus, in part, on factors that can enhance and promote employee well-being and positive affect. Work can provide an avenue for meaning and fulfillment (Rosso et al., 2010). However, it has not been until around 2015 when international organizations began to pay attention to employee wellness. Indeed, the International Organization for Standardization (The parenthetical could be (ISO 34003:2021; https://www.iso.org/news/ref2677.html), The United Nations (UN) through its Sustainable Development Goals (SDGs; https://sdgs.un.org/goals), and the International Labor Organization (International Labor Organization [ILO], 2022) in collaboration with the World Health Organization (WHO) have all come to recognize that experiences at work can either adversely or positively affect mental health and well-being. For example, ISO standard 45003 presents guidelines for managing psychosocial risks to promote employee well-being. Additionally, of the 17 UNSDGs, Goals 3 (i.e., ensure healthy lives and improve well-being), 5 (i.e., achieve gender equality), and 8 (i.e., focused on decent work and productive employment) are likely most related to the works conducted by professionals in OB and organizational psychology.

The fields of OB and OP share the same foundational roots and, through the present, the fields share the same body of literature and complement scholarship to the point that they are indistinguishable at times. The fields' foundations are situated in the period of scientific assessments of efficiency, led by Frederick Taylor and Frank and Lillian Moller Gilbreth, followed by safety and training research led by Hugo Münsterberg and selection and placement as guided by James Cattell and Walter D. Scott. Around the 1940s, there was a group of scholars at the

DOI: 10.4324/9781032619385-11

Tavistock Institute focusing on Quality of WorkLife (QWL). The QWL initiative focused on interpersonal relationships and group behaviors. However, by the 1960s scholars became increasingly interested in occupational stress, leadership, and new approaches to motivation. The focus was turning toward identifying problems in the organization and implementing interventions to improve the situation, mitigate individual and organizational strains and enhance individual well-being. Scholars began to recognize that healthy and thriving people are necessary to have healthy and thriving organizations. Thus, it is not enough to attract, select, train, and retain the right people (Schneider, 1987), organizations today are tasked with creating a positive experience for employee prospects, recruits, incumbents, and even those who attrit. The concept used to describe this movement to focus on positive experiences was first termed positive psychology.

Positive psychology is not a domain that began in the world of work. Clinical psychologist Martin Seligman's presidential address to the American Psychological Association in 1998 is often cited as the official start to the positive psychology movement. For this he is known as the Father of Positive Psychology. Seligman focused on topics including learned helplessness, depression, well-being, resilience, and optimism. These are all topics that, in one way or another, are studied by organizational psychologists with a focus on experiences of the workplace.

The positive psychology movement draws from the humanistic movement (in which the QWL program can be categorized) to focus on factors that help individuals achieve eudaimonia, well-being, and purpose. It is from this lens that we focus our chapter on positive OB[1] across cultures. To begin, we present some background on factors often studied to understand culture, including values, norms, and beliefs. We take these concepts into consideration and use them as *tools* to understand results from studies conducted in different countries around the world on well-being and positive OBs.

Culture

Geert Hofstede, a social psychologist and one of the eminent scholars of the field of cross-cultural psychology, recognized that culture is complex and hard to define (operationally and conceptually). To make the concept accessible to engineers, he depicted culture as the "software of the mind," suggesting that culture is in the mind of the person. We do not disagree with this, but we also recognize that culture is outside the person too, such that different people, institutions, and artifacts shape and refine the "software." In this sense, culture is both inside and outside the person. Individuals know culture when they experience something that is "not normal." Like a fish that does not know it needs water to survive until it is taken out of it, often people do not realize how much their day-to-day thinking, feelings, and behaviors are shaped by their environment until they are taken out of the environment. At that point a person might adopt or reject the new cultural presses (e.g., in the United States, a child calling a friend's parent "Ms. Sally" or "Mr. Darren" rather than "Sally" or "Darren" or adopting or rejecting a dominant view, such as Culture X is evil). A natural question that follows is how would social scientists operationalize culture in order to assess its implications, particularly (for the purposes of this book), positive OBs?

Values

In the late 1960s, Hofstede (1980) set out to study employee engagement amongst IBM employees and managers in all countries where IBM had an office. In so doing, he fed his curiosity about country differences by testing the items at the culture level of analysis. In other words, rather than 117,000 individuals in his dataset, Hofstede's culture-level database consisted of 40 countries, for which responses to items were a country's average on each given item. From here he went on to test the relationships amongst country-level means on items and discovered four clear factors that he labeled: Individualism and Collectivism (INDCOL), Power Distance (PD), Masculinity–Femininity (Masc–Fem), and Uncertainty Avoidance (UA). These four cultural values were discovered at the cultural level of analysis.

INDCOL has to do with how an individual and a group relate to one another, with individuals being distinct from the group representing individualism and individuals being a part of the group representing collectivism. PD reflects the hierarchy from the subordinates' perspective. The more distant subordinates perceive themselves from the supervisor(s) the greater the PD. Masc–Fem reflects roles people may have in a society. Countries that are characterized as masculine tend to have clear roles and people rarely cross the lines to fulfill other roles. For example, in a highly masculine country, a professor would not also engage in financial account management of their travel expenses. It is also sometimes expressed in terms of what work roles a woman can take and those a man can take. For example, Japan is a high masculine society. This does not mean that women cannot be business executives. In fact, there are some women working in such a capacity, however they are typically not also mothers. Finally, UA has to do with the extent to which rules and policies are established, implemented, and reinforced to reduce ambiguity. The more rules the more uncertainty avoidant the country, the fewer the rules (i.e., the greater the flexibility), the more uncertainty tolerant the country. For example, if norms include children using a title for an adult, and referring to a friend's parent as Darren, rather than Mr. Darren, results in stern disciplinary actions, the culture is likely higher on UA. However, if an adult expresses a simple chuckle and makes no mention of the transgression, the country is low on UA.

Since Hofstede's original works were published, a small, but significant advancement has been made. The Chinese Culture Connection (1987) conducted their research from an East Asian lens and identified an additional cultural variable, referred to as Confucian Dynamism. Hofstede (2001) claimed that the term, and its definition, would be too difficult for most Western scholars to remember (since most are not deeply familiar with Confucian philosophy) that he termed the concept long-term vs. short-term orientation (LTO vs. STO). The idea of LTO is that cultures reinforce long-term planning and saving for the future, whereas cultures reinforcing STO do not plan strategically beyond what can be clearly forecasted (as evident in the plethora of credit cards US residents can have).

For over 50 years, Hofstede's (1980, 2001) cultural values have been heavily relied upon to help characterize and explain differences in OBs. His cultural values were identified *post hoc* and based on (primarily) men in IBM. Moreover, while he labeled his factors as cultural values, the items reflected practices and based on how the items related to one another when analyzed at the cultural level of analysis, he affixed labels that reflected the grouping of items and then claimed they reflected cultural values. In reality, none of the items were motivational states reflecting values.

Recognizing this shortcoming, Shalom Schwartz systematically studied values of students and teachers. Drawing on the works of Rokeach (1973), Schwartz (1992) defined values as principles that guide people's lives. At the heart of his values survey were 56 or 57 items reflecting different principles which respondents would rate as very important (or of supreme importance) to not important (or opposed to one's values). His studies originated at the individual level of analysis (e.g., Schwartz, 1992; Schwartz & Bilsky, 1987), samples of teachers (those who socialize a country's next generation) and university students (the people who will define the culture in the coming years). Aggregating items into ten value types, Schwartz and colleagues found that the order of preference for each of the ten value types was mostly consistent across countries. He and his team also noted that healthy values (reflecting openness to change and self-transcendence values) relate to worker well-being (Schwartz & Sortheix, 2017). However, when he realized that researchers were erroneously applying the mean group scores of value types as characteristics of a whole culture, he followed Hofstede's (1980) procedures to identify cultural values, for which he found seven (Schwartz, 1999).

The seven cultural values are intellectual autonomy and affective autonomy which oppose conservatism, egalitarianism vs. power distance, and harmony vs. mastery. Unlike Hofstede's (1980) cultural values, Schwartz's (1999) cultural values are based on responses to values (principles that guide people's decisions, responses, and actions). While there is growing popularity in the use of Schwartz's cultural values (e.g., Glazer & Beehr, 2005; Morales et al., 2019) to contextualize cultures, scholars in business continue to categorize countries most heavily on INDCOL (Oyserman et al., 2002), ignoring other factors that characterize a country or culture and ignoring Schwartz's more refined approach to identifying cultural values. Both Hofstede's culture scores (https://www.hofstede-insights.com/country-comparison-tool) and Schwartz's measures and scores (Schwartz, 2021) are handy tools to use to explain cultural differences *post hoc*, and, if doing research, they are handy tools for *a priori* making and testing hypotheses.

Beliefs and Norms

Another way to characterize cultures is through beliefs and norms. This approach began with the introduction of social axioms or generalized social beliefs. These represent beliefs that are pervasive in a societal culture and passed down from generation to generation as well as taught to newcomers (Bond et al., 2004; Leung & Bond, 2008). Research on social axioms were gaining ground in the early 2000s, but after the untimely passing of Kwok Leung, the main champion of the measure, fewer have continued to study social axioms (e.g., Kwantes & Karam, 2009; Kwantes & Bond, 2019). The cross-culturally validated measure, Social Axioms Survey (SAS), is openly available in multiple languages, which enhances its utility for cross-cultural comparative work.

Cultural tightness and looseness (CTL) reflect adherence to or deviations from cultural norms (Gelfand et al., 2011). Tight cultures tend to be homogenous, and people are strongly reinforced to follow others, whereas loose cultures tend to be heterogenous, and people are encouraged to do what they please. CTL has been gaining a great deal of traction in the literature, particularly after Gelfand's (2019) publication of *Rule Makers, Rule Breakers*. As with cultural values, CTL scores and measure can be used to make and test predictions and explain findings about cultural differences on variables of interest.

Role of Culture in Positive OB

Throughout this chapter we will demonstrate how the aforementioned values, norms, and beliefs can be used as tools to develop and test hypotheses that explain similarities or differences between cultures. As more researchers are using these tools *a priori,* we will review the state of cross-cultural positive OB research.

Eudaimonic and Hedonic Well-Being

In this section, we highlight an important summary of findings from Sonnentag et al.'s (2023) review of the state of health and well-being research, which mentions the importance of culture, and acknowledges that more scholarship on the role of culture is needed. In particular, we focus on the central variables of eudaimonic and hedonic well-being. Eudaimonia literally refers to the experience of being in good spirits, but in psychological research it is conceptualized as the experience of flourishing. Sonnentag et al. (2023) summarize the state of literature around organizational predictors and outcomes of eudemonia and hedonia (i.e., a kind of joy or state of happiness). In their review of the field of health and well-being at work, it was clear that more research focused on hedonic well-being (measured with instruments assessing a state of arousal, vigor, and affect) than on eudaimonic (measured with instruments capturing meaning in work tasks and use of one's skills) well-being. Sonnentag et al. characterize research on eudaimonic well-being as focused on "experiences of meaningfulness" (p. 477), particularly at work.

Predictors of Eudaimonia and Hedonia

Sonnentag et al. (2023) organize predictors of eudaimonic and hedonic states of well-being in terms of workplace and organizational factors, on the one hand, and individual behavioral factors, on the other hand. Work and organizational-related factors predicting hedonic and eudaimonic states of well-being include job resources, such as autonomy, feedback skill variety, and task identity and significance (Sonnentag et al., 2023). These results suggest that having resources make people happier and more engaged with their work. Social support, which some might categorize as a resource, and positive interpersonal interactions with team members positively relate with hedonic and eudaimonic well-being. Several other works suggest that culture may moderate the extent to which social support affects stress and buffers the stressor–strain relationship (Beehr & Glazer, 2001). For example, Glazer (2006) found that reports of receiving supervisor social support was greater in Anglo and Western European countries than East Asian and Eastern European countries, with no differences for Latin American countries with the other regions. Glazer and Amren (2018) found that supervisor or organizational social support sometimes mitigated the stressor–strain relationship (in the United States and Canada), sometimes it intensified it (in Latin European and Germanic countries), and often had no impact at all (Nordic Europe, Latin America, Southern Asia, Confucian Asia, Australia/New Zealand, and Anglo Europe). Moreover, a leader having a transformational, change-oriented, service- or task-oriented leadership style may also positively relate to subordinates' hedonic (e.g., job satisfaction) and eudaimonic (i.e., meaning at work) well-being, whereas the opposite may occur with abusive leadership style (Sonnentag et al., 2023).

Behavioral factors that appear to increase hedonic and eudaimonic well-being include proactive (e.g., job crafting) and prosocial (e.g., providing support) behaviors (Sonnentag et al., 2023). Rest breaks and socializing with others at work are also linked to increased hedonic well-being, whereas active recovery activities, such as engaging in hobbies may lead to increased eudaimonic well-being. For example, with respect to hedonic well-being, psychological detachment indirectly related to life satisfaction in a general sample of Argentinian workers (Medrano & Trógolo, 2018). It also related to generally good health and high positive affectivity, but also to negative affect among Italian workers (Gaudiino & Di Stefano, 2023). Finally, in a 12-country study eudaimonia was more strongly related with life satisfaction than was hedonia (Gaston-Breton et al., 2021).

Interventions to Achieve Eudaimonic and Hedonic Well-Being

Scholarly research on primary (e.g., job redesign), secondary (e.g., cognitive appraisal), and tertiary (e.g., mindfulness, relaxation) interventions shows promise in positively influencing hedonic well-being, whereas few studies linked interventions to eudaimonic well-being (Sonnentag et al., 2023). In fact, through a meta-analysis, Monzani et al. (2021) found that mindfulness increased hedonic well-being more so than eudaimonic well-being. However, in their follow-up experimental study of nurses in Spain, mindfulness training might also improve eudaimonic well-being. More research across cultures is still warranted to support this finding. In a study conducted with Brazilian police, however, it was clear that a person's disposition to reframe stressors so that they are not as noxious (i.e., having high meaningfulness in life) buffered the adverse relationship between role stressors and strains (Torres et al., 2022).

In the next section we delve into literature on positive OBs that may develop as a direct or indirect outcome of organizational and work resources and demands. The review attends to (1) commonalities and (2) differences in these positive OBs across cultures, as well as (3) constructs which may be universally endorsed, but may be conceptualized differently across cultures, and connect these concepts to decent work and positive organizational climate. Finally, (4) we wish to acknowledge blind spots that remain in a full understanding of the relationship between societal culture and positive OB. The literature continues to lack inclusivity of many voices, and there may well be other aspects of the relationship that have yet to be explored, such as Indigenous perspectives (cf. Blume, 2020) and the African philosophy of *ubuntu*[2] (cf. Mangaliso et al., 2022).

Positive OBs

Commonalities

It has been suggested that the foundation of human dignity is the freedom to make choices, or free will (Jafari et al., 2023). Self-determination theory (Deci & Ryan, 2000) takes this a step further and suggests that the satisfaction of three basic psychological needs, autonomy, relatedness, and competence, is universally essential for humans to thrive (Chen et al., 2015). When these three needs have been fulfilled, higher psychological health results (Ntoumanis et al., 2021). They have been posited as fundamentally universal for eudemonia, as they are reflected in the ability to pursue self-chosen or intrinsic goals, the ability to behave autonomously, having a sense of mindfulness, and the ability to act in ways that promote fulfillment of basic psychological needs (Ryan et al., 2008).

Although, as noted above, well-being consists of both eudaimonia and hedonia, much of the cross-cultural work on positive OB has focused on eudemonic rather than hedonic well-being (Sonnentag et al., 2023). Hedonic well-being focuses on intraindividual factors, whereas eudemonic well-being focuses more on interpersonal factors, which puts it squarely in the realm of social behavior and most affected by cultural behavioral norms. Thus, the process of work and the context of work are key to understanding well-being. Ample evidence suggests that multiple aspects of organizations are affected by culture. For example, organizational culture often reflects the societal culture in which it is embedded (Glazer, 2021; Kwantes & Dickson, 2011), with social norms of interacting and behavioral expectations impacting how work is conducted in a given context. Yet commonalities are found across national contexts in what types of organizational culture support positive employee outcomes (Szumal & Cooke, 2019). Employees who described the organizational culture they work in as a good fit for the way they prefer to interact with their work and colleagues indicate better teamwork and communication in their organization across six countries, including Australia, Canada, Germany, South Africa, United Kingdom, and United States (Kwantes et al., 2007). Positive individual outcomes were also perceived across six countries (Canada, Hong Kong, New Zealand, South Africa, United Kingdom, and the United States) in what aspects of organizational culture support effectiveness (Kwantes & Boglarsky, 2007), suggesting there may be universals across culture in what behavioral norms in the workplace have positive outcomes and reflect positive OB.

Similarly, the concept of "decent work" (Ghai, 2003) has been proposed as comprising the minimum necessary requirements for human dignity in the workplace. The International Labour Organization defines decent work as involving

> opportunities for work that is productive and delivers a fair income, security in the workplace and social protection for all, better prospects for personal development and social integration, freedom for people to express their concerns, organize, and participate in the decisions that affect their lives and equality of opportunity and treatment for all women and men.
>
> *(Decent work|International Labour Organization (ilo.org))*

Fundamental to both positive organizational cultures and the provision of decent work is the concept of trust. The importance of trust is universal, and it has been termed "a basic fact of social life" (Luhmann, 2017, p. 5). Trust has been described as "the single most important ingredient for the development and maintenance of happy, well-functioning relationships" (Simpson, 2007, p. 264). Its importance in a positive work environment has been well documented, with trust linked to various positive outcomes such as job satisfaction (Jones et al., 2023), job involvement and organizational commitment (Lambert et al., 2023), and job performance (Clément et al., 2020).

The concept of trust and its related concept of trustworthiness provide an interesting venue to examine how a construct that is universally important may yet have different bases in different cultural contexts. Trust reflects the willingness to be vulnerable to another with the expectation of positive outcomes while trustworthiness indicates an assessment of how risky such vulnerability would be. Or, as Hardin (2002) indicated, "trusting someone in some context is simply to be explained as merely the expectation that the person will most likely be trustworthy" (p. 31). Note the importance of contextual factors in this definition. While trust remains critical to positive interactions, how trust develops and how it plays out can differ based on culture. Similarly, trustworthiness may, by definition, be a universal phenomenon, yet cultural differences impact expectations of trustworthy behaviors and attributes (Kwantes & McMurphy, 2021). In a study across ten countries, for example, descriptions of trustworthy supervisors and trustworthy colleagues uniformly indicated the importance of integrity in trustworthiness (Kartolo et al., 2021) yet varied considerably with differences in participants' ratings of ability and benevolence as important to establishing trustworthiness (Kwantes & Kartolo, 2021).

Differences

Some positive organizational concepts such as effective organizational cultures, decent work, and trust have commonalities across cultures. As noted above, for some of these concepts while the meaning may be universally consistent, how the concepts are enacted can vary across cultural contexts (Kwantes & Glazer, 2017). There are also some positive organizational concepts that are conceptualized differently in different contexts.

Organizational identity is one such topic that has been linked to positive OBs, such as teamwork and organizational citizenship behaviors (Evans & Davis, 2014; Xiang & Yang, 2020). Organizational identity, rests in large part on Social Identity Theory, which stipulates that individual identity is, at least in part, informed by and defined by membership in various (in- vs. out-) groups (Tajfel, 1978). Moreover, the development of social identity differs across cultures (Feitosa et al., 2012), in part, because culture shapes what is defined as an "in-group," which, inevitably, differs in different societal contexts (Brewer & Chen, 2007). Consequently, it can be deduced that societal culture would also influence positive OBs.

Leadership also serves as an example of a universal construct, in which culture has a clear impact on how leaders develop and maintain positive leadership. Williams et al.'s (2022) findings, for example, indicate that leaders in multiple countries in Africa, Asia, Australia, Europe, and South America consider sharing power with subordinates as important positive leadership while leaders from the United States highlighted the strategical use of power themselves to achieve important goals as a positive leadership behavior.

Similarly, organizational commitment is a construct linked with job satisfaction (Ndlovu et al., 2021; Tran, 2023) and human values (Glazer et al., 2004) in many contexts. Indeed, the three-component model of organizational commitment, including affective, continuance, and normative commitment (Meyer & Allen, 1991), has been globally validated (e.g., Meyer et al., 2007; Pinho et al., 2024). Although the three-component model is invariant across cultures, antecedents and outcomes of each of the components differ across cultures (Kwantes, 2003; Wasti, 2003).

Organizational citizenship behaviors (OCBs) have also been examined in several cultural contexts with both commonalities and differences found (Fischer et al., 2019; Kadam et al., 2021). OCBs are voluntary behaviors that employees engage in to help individuals in their workplace (OCB-I) or to help the organization as a whole (OCB-O). OCBs are important prosocial behaviors as they have significant correlations with positive employee outcomes, such as job satisfaction and organizational commitment (LePine et al., 2002), however research suggests that it is important to consider context in understanding these behaviors (Jiao et al., 2013; Karam & Kwantes, 2011). For example, the dimensions of helping, civic virtue, and sportsmanship were found to be common dimensions in a study across Canada, Iran, Turkey (Kabasakal et al., 2011). Job satisfaction was also related to OCB in all cultural contexts, but culture impacted the relative importance of each dimension. Some research suggests that there may be unique factors of OCB depending on cultural context. For example, Farh et al. (1997) found some different dimensions of OCB in the Chinese context than have been reported in the western literature (e.g., social welfare participation emerged in the Chinese context). Other research has suggested that OCB interpretation may differ across cultures. Kwantes and colleagues (2008) found that internalized social axioms impacted whether employees viewed specific behaviors as in-role or extra-role, effectively resulting in different criteria for what constitutes an OCB.

Absent Voices

Any discussion of cross-cultural positive OB would be remiss in not pointing out that our knowledge base is skewed as most of the topics covered have been theorized and researched in Western, Educated, Industrialized, Rich, and Democratic (WEIRD) countries (Henrich et al., 2010), including the United States, Canada, and Anglo, Western, and Nordic Europe. Thus, even if tested in non-WEIRD countries, the concepts are derived from the mindset of a scholar from a WEIRD background. Likewise, some manifestations occurring in non-WEIRD countries may not even be documented in mainstream English language journals (Nichols et al., 2020). An exception may be the pan-African philosophy of *ubuntu* (Mangaliso et al., 2022), which has broken through in OB discourse. This concept emphasizes the community and relationships. In cultures where the community is prioritized over individuals, positive OBs are likely to yield collective benefits. Furthermore, much of the knowledge base has been built on for-profit corporate contexts and may not generalize beyond that to other types of work contexts, such as non-profit organizations and the informal economy. As Saxena (2021) points out, over half of the world's population works in the informal economic sector. As such, those voices are absent from discourse and research set out to understand what makes for positive OB.

Conclusion

Positive OBs, as most, if not all OBs, are culturally relative. This chapter has demonstrated that although there are commonalities in the desire for hedonic and eudemonic well-being, and commonalities in positive OBs, context matters with respect to how these concepts are conceptualized and operationalized, and the factors that affect them. More cross-cultural positive OB research is desperately needed to include the currently absent voices: populations from non-WEIRD countries and from the informal economy. We close this chapter with a call for more research with these populations and for a systematic discovery of factors considered positive OBs in these contexts.

Notes

1 Organizational behavior is, in essence, the business discipline for organizational psychology, with a focus on bridging behavioral science theory to practice. Many of the achievements in theory, research, and practice in the domains of organizational psychology and organizational behavior are indistinguishable as to their origins; scholars in organizational behavior are often coming from organizational psychology programs (though rarely the reverse).

2 Ubuntu has a focus on human dignity, a harmonious coexistence, a commitment to the collective, and humility (Mangaliso et al., 2022).

References

Beehr, T. A., & Glazer, S. (2001). A cultural perspective of social support in relation to occupational stress. In P. Perrewé, D. C. Ganster, & J. Moran (Eds.), *Exploring theoretical mechanisms and perspectives: Vol. 1. Research in occupational stress and well-being* (pp. 97–142). Bingley, UK: Emerald Group.

Blume, A. W. (2020). *A new psychology based on community, equality, and care of the Earth: An Indigenous American perspective*. Santa Barbara, CA: Praeger.

Bond, M. H., Leung, K., Au, A., Tong, K., de Carrasquel, S. R. Murakami, F., et al. (2004). Culture-level dimensions of social axioms and their correlates across 41 cultures. *Journal of Cross-Cultural Psychology, 35*, 548–570.

Brewer, M. B., & Chen, Y. (2007). Where (who) are collectives in collectivism? Toward conceptual clarification of individualism and collectivism. *Psychological Review, 114*(1), 133–151. https://doi.org/10.1037/0033-295X.114.1.133

Chen, B., Assche, J., Vansteenkiste, M., Soenens, B., & Beyers, W. (2015). Does psychological need satisfaction matter when environmental or financial safety are at risk? *Journal of Happiness Studies, 16*(3), 745–766.

Chinese Culture Connection. (1987). Chinese values and the search for culture-free dimensions of culture. *Journal of Cross-Cultural Psychology, 18*, 143–164.

Clément, L., Fernet, C., Morin, A. J. S., & Austin, S. (2020). In whom college teachers trust? On the role of specific trust referents and basic psychological needs in optimal functioning at work. *Higher Education, 80*(3), 511–530. https://doi.org/10.1007/s10734-019-00496-z

Deci, E. L., & Ryan, R. M. (2000). The "what" and "why" of goal pursuits: Human needs and the self-determination of behavior. *Psychological Inquiry, 11*(4), 227.

Evans, W. R., & Davis, W. (2014). Corporate citizenship and the employee: An organizational identification perspective. *Human Performance, 27*(2), 129–146. https://doi.org/10.1080/08959285.2014.882926

Farh, J. L., Earley, P. C., & Lin, S. C. (1997). Impetus for action: A cultural analysis of justice and organizational citizenship behavior in Chinese society. *Administrative Science Quarterly, 42*(3), 421–444.

Feitosa, J., Salas, E., & Salazar, M. R. (2012). Social Identity: Clarifying its dimensions across cultures. *Psychological Topics/Psihologijske Teme, 21*(3), 527–548.

Fischer, R., Ferreira, M. C., Van Meurs, N., Gok, K., Jiang, D.-Y., Fontaine, J. R. J., Harb, C., Cieciuch, J., Achoui, M., Mendoza, M. S. D., Hassan, A., Achmadi, D., Mogaji, A., & Abubakar, A. (2019). Does organizational formalization facilitate voice and helping organizational citizenship behaviors? It depends on (national) uncertainty norms. *Journal of International Business Studies, 50*, 125–134.

Gaston-Breton, C., Lemoine, J. E., Voyer, B. G., & Kastanakis, M. N. (2021). Pleasure, meaning or spirituality: Cross-cultural differences in orientations to happiness across 12 countries. *Journal of Business Research, 134*, 1–12. https://doi.org/10.1016/j.jbusres.2021.05.013

Gaudiino, M., & Di Stefano, G. (2023). To detach or not to detach? The role of psychological detachment on the relationship between heavy work investment and well-being: A latent profile analysis. *Current Psychology, 42*(8), 6667–6681. https://doi.org/10.1007/s12144-021-01958-3

Gelfand, M. (2019). *Rule makers, rule breakers: Tight and loose cultures and the secret signals that direct our lives*. New York, NY: Scribner.

Gelfand, M. J., Raver, J. L., Nishii, L., Leslie, L. M., Lun, J., Lim, B. C., Duan, L., Almaliach, A., Ang, S., Arnadottir, J., Aycan, Z., Boehnke, K., Boski, P., Cabecinhas, R., Chang, D., Chhokar, J., D'Amato, A., Ferrer, M., Fischlmayr, I. C,…, & Yamaguchi, S. (2011). Differences between tight and loose cultures: A 33-nation study. *Science, 332*(6033), 1100–1104. https://www.jstor.org/stable/27977953

Ghai, D. (2003). Decent work: Concept and indicators. *International Labour Review, 142*(2), 113–145.

Glazer, S. (2006). Social support across cultures. *International Journal of Intercultural Relations, 30*(5), 605–622. https://doi.org/10.1016/j.ijintrel.2005.01.013

Glazer, S. (2021). Organizational role ambiguity as a proxy for uncertainty avoidance. *International Journal of Intercultural Relations, 85*, 1–12. https://doi.org/10.1016/j.ijintrel.2021.08.011

Glazer, S., & Amren, M. A. (2018). Culture's implications on support as a moderator of the stressor-outcome relationship. *International Journal of Stress Management, 25*(S1), 7–25. https://doi.org/10.1037/str0000087

Glazer, S., & Beehr, T.A. (2005). Consistency of the implications of three role stressors across four countries. *Journal of Organizational Behavior, 26*, 467-487. https://doi.org/10.1002/job.326

Glazer, S., Daniel, S. C., & Short, K. M. (2004). A study of the relationship between organizational commitment and human values in four countries. *Human Relations, 57*, 323–345. https://doi.org/10.1177/0018726704043271

Hardin, R. (2002). *Trust & trustworthiness*. New York, NY: Russell Sage Foundation.

Henrich, J., Heine, S. J., & Norenzayan, A. (2010). The weirdest people in the world?. *Behavioral and Brain Sciences, 33*(2-3), 61–83. https://doi.org/10.1017/S0140525X0999152X

Hofstede, G. (1980). *Culture's consequences: International differences in work-related values*. Beverly Hills, CA: Sage.

Hofstede, G. (2001). *Culture's consequences: Comparing values, behaviors, institutions, and organizations across nations* (2nd ed). Thousand Oaks, CA: Sage.

International Labour Organization. (2022). *Mental health at work: Policy brief*. World Health Organization. https://www.ilo.org/media/370016/download.

Jafari, S. A., Araminia, B., Tavasoli, H., Tavasoli, N., Abedi, S., & Bakhshe, A. F. (2023). Examining the criteria of human dignity. *Journal of Medical Ethics & History of Medicine, 16*(14), 1–14.

Jiao, C., Richards, D. A., & Hackett, R. D. (2013). Organizational citizenship behavior and role breadth: A meta-analytic and cross-cultural analysis. *Human Resource Management, 52*, 697–714.

Jones, J., Abeita, A. J., Murray, S. R., & Bell, M. (2023). An investigatory research on organizational trust and its relationship with job satisfaction and psychological contract breach. *Administrative Issues Journal: Education, Practice & Research, 13*(1), 1–12.

Kabasakal, H., Dastmalchian, A., & Imer, P. (2011). Organizational citizenship behaviour: A study of young executives in Canada, Iran, and Turkey. *International Journal of Human Resource Management, 22*(13), 2703–2729.

Kadam, R., Balasubramanian, S., Kareem Abdul, W., & Jabeen, S. S. (2021). Predicting organizational citizenship behavior in a multicultural environment: The role of cultural intelligence and cultural distance. *International Journal of Cross-Cultural Management, 21*(3), 602–624.

Karam, C. M., & Kwantes, C. T. (2011). Contextualizing cultural orientation and organizational citizenship behavior. *Journal of International Management, 17*(4), 303–315. https://doi.org/10.1016/j.intman.2011.05.007

Kartolo, A., Kwantes, C. T., & Townsend, A. (2021). The stereotype content of trustworthy colleagues and supervisors across 11 nations. Presented at the 2021 SIOP Annual Conference. [Virtual].

Kwantes, C. T. (2003). Organizational citizenship and withdrawal behaviors in the USA and India: Does commitment make a difference? *International Journal of Cross-Cultural Management, 3*(1), 5–26.

Kwantes, C. T., Arbour, S., & Boglarsky, C. A. (2007). Fit and outcomes in six national contexts: An organizational level analysis. *Journal of Organizational Culture, Communication, and Conflict, 11*, 95–112.

Kwantes, C. T., & Bond, M. H. (2019). Organizational justice and autonomy as moderators of the relationship between social and organizational cynicism. *Personality and Individual Differences, 151*, [Article 109391]. https://doi.org/10.1016/j.paid.2019.04.046

Kwantes, C. T., & Boglarsky, C. A. (2007). Perceptions of organizational culture, leadership effectiveness, and personal effectiveness across six countries. *Journal of International Management, 13*, 204–213.

Kwantes, C. T., & Dickson, M. W. (2011). Organizational culture in a societal context: Lessons from GLOBE and beyond. In N. N. Ashkanasy, C. Wilderom, & M. F. Peterson (Eds.), *The handbook of organizational culture and climate* (2nd ed; pp. 494–514). Thousand Oaks, CA: Sage.

Kwantes, C. T., & Glazer, S. (2017). Culture, organizations, and work: Clarifying concepts. In S. Glazer & C. T. Kwantes (Series Eds.), *Springer briefs in culture, organizations, & work*. Cham, Switzerland: Springer.

Kwantes, C. T., & Karam, C. M. (2009). Social axioms and organizational behaviors. In K. Leung, & M. Bond (Eds.), *Psychological aspects of social axioms: Understanding global belief systems*. New York, NY: Springer.

Kwantes, C. T., & McMurphy, S. (2021). Contextual influences on trust and trustworthiness: An etic perspective. In C. T. Kwantes & B. C. H. Kuo (Eds.), Trust and Trustworthiness across Cultures: Implications for Societies and Workplaces. Cham, Switzerland: Springer.

Kwantes, C. T., Karam, C. M., Kuo, B. C. H., & Towson, S. (2008). Organizational citizenship behaviours: The influence of culture. *International Journal of Intercultural Relations, 32*(3), 229–243.

Kwantes, C. T., & Kartolo, A. (2021). A 10-nation exploration of trustworthiness in the workplace. *Interpersona: An International Journal on Personal Relationships, 15*(2), 146–166. https://doi.org/10.5964/ijpr.5639

Lambert, E. G., Qureshi, H., & Frank, J. (2023). Exploring the effects of different workplace trust variables on the work attitudes of police officers. *Police Practice and Research, 24*(2), 164–175. https://doi.org/10.1080/15614263.2022.2113787

LePine, J. A., Erez, A., & Johnson, D. E. (2002). The nature and dimensionality of organizational citizenship behavior: A critical review and meta-analysis. *Journal of Applied Psychology, 87*(1), 52–65.

Leung, K., & Bond, M. H. (2008). Psycho-logic and eco-logic: Insights from Social Axioms dimensions. In F. J. R. van de Vijver, D. A. Van Hemert, Y. H. Poortinga (Eds.), *Multilevel Analysis of Individuals and Cultures (*pp. 199–222). New York, NY: Taylor & Francis.

Luhmann, N. (2017). *Trust and power.* Cambridge, UK: Polity Press.

Mangaliso, M. P., Mangaliso, N. A., Ndanga, L. Z. B., & Jean-Denis, H. (2022). Contextualizing organizational change management in Africa: Incorporating the core values of ubuntu. *Journal of African Business, 23*(4), 1029–1048.

Medrano, L. A., & Trógolo, M. A. (2018). Employee well-being and life satisfaction in Argentina: The contribution of psychological detachment from work. *Revista de Psicología del Trabajo y de las Organizaciones, 34*(2), 69–81.

Meyer, J. P., & Allen, N. J. (1991). A three-component conceptualization of organizational commitment. *Human Resource Management Review, 1*(1), 61–89.

Meyer, J. P, Srinivas, E. S., Lal, J. B., & Topolnytsky, L. (2007). Employee commitment and support for an organizational change: Test of the three-component model in two cultures. *Journal of Occupational & Organizational Psychology, 80*(2), 185–211.

Monzani, L., Escartín, J., Ceja, L., & Bakker, A. B. (2021). Blending mindfulness practices and character strengths increases employee well-being: A second-order meta-analysis and a follow-up field experiment. *Human Resource Management Journal, 31*(4), 1025–1062. https://doi.org/10.1111/1748-8583.12360

Morales, C., Holtschlag, C., Masuda, A. D., & Marquina, P. (2019). In which cultural contexts do individual values explain entrepreneurship? An integrative values framework using Schwartz's theories. *International Small Business Journal, 37*(3), 241–267. https://doi.org/10.1177/0266242618811890

Ndlovu, T., Quaye, E. S., & Saini, Y. K. (2021). Predicting organisational commitment: The role of line manager communication, employee trust and job satisfaction. *South African Journal of Business Management, 52*(1), 1–11.

Nichols, A. L., Glazer, S., Ion, A., & Moukarzel, R. (2020). The global impact of North American journal prestige: Understanding its effects on faculty life throughout the world. *Industrial & Organizational Psychology: Perspectives on Science and Practice, 13*, 339–344. https://doi.org/10.1017/iop.2020.54

Ntoumanis, N., Ng, J. Y. Y., Prestwich, A., Quested, E., Hancox, J. E., Thøgersen-Ntoumani, C., Deci, E. L., Ryan, R. M., Lonsdale, C., & Williams, G. C. (2021). A meta-analysis of self-determination theory-informed intervention studies in the health domain: Effects on motivation, health behavior, physical, and psychological health. *Health Psychology Review, 15*(2), 214–244.

Oyserman, D., Coon, H. M., & Kemmelmeier, M. (2002). Rethinking individualism and collectivism: Evaluation of theoretical assumptions and meta-analyses. *Psychological Bulleting, 128*(1), 3–72. https://doi.org/10.1037//0033-2909.128.1.3

Pinho, A. P. M., Meyer, J. P., Espinoza, J. A., & Oliveira, E. R. S. (2024). HRM practices and organizational commitment profiles in Brazil. *Current Psychology, 43*(14), 13051–13071.

Rokeach, M. (1973). *The nature of human values*. Free Press.

Rosso, B. D., Dekas, K. H., & Wrzesniewski, A. (2010). On the meaning of work: A theoretical integration and review. *Research in Organizational Behavior, 30*, 91–127. https://doi.org/10.1016/j.riob.2010.09.001

Ryan, R. M., Huta, V., & Deci, E. L. (2008). Living well: A self-determination theory perspective on eudaimonia. *Journal of Happiness Studies, 9,* 139–170. https://doi.org/10.1007/s10902-006-9023-4

Saxena, M. (2021). Cultural skills as drivers of decency in decent work: An investigation of skilled workers in the informal economy. *European Journal of Work & Organizational Psychology, 30*(6), 824–836.

Schneider, B. (1987). The people make the place. *Personnel Psychology, 40,* 437–453.

Schwartz, S. H. (1992). Universals in the content and structure of values: Theoretical advances and empirical tests in 20 countries. *Advances in Experimental Social Psychology, 25*, 1–65. https://doi.org/10.1016/S0065-2601(08)60281-6

Schwartz, S. H. (1999). Some theoretical and practical implications. *Applied Psychology: An International Review, 48*(1), 23–47. https://doi.org/10.1017/cbo9780511620799.007

Schwartz, S. H. (2021). A repository of Schwartz value scales with instructions and an introduction. *Online Readings in Psychology and Culture, 2*(2). https://doi.org/10.9707/2307-0919.1173

Schwartz, S. H., & Bilsky, W. (1987). Toward a universal psychological structure of human values. *Journal of Personality and Social Psychology, 53*(3), 550–562.

Simpson, J. A. (2007). Psychological foundations of trust. *Current Directions in Psychological Science, 16*(5), 264–268.

Sonnentag, S., Tay, L., & Nesher Shoshan, H. (2023). A review on health and well-being at work: More than stressors and strains. *Personnel Psychology, 76*, 473–510. https://doi.org/10.1111/peps.12572

Sortheix, F. M., & Schwartz, S. H. (2017). Values that underlie and undermine well-being: Variability across countries. *European Journal of Personality, 31*, 187–201. https://doi.org/10.1002/per.2096

Szumal, J. L., & Cooke, R. A. (2019). *Creating constructive cultures.* Plymouth, MI: Human Synergistics International.

Tajfel, H. (1978). *Differentiation between social groups: Studies in the social psychology of intergroup relations*. Academic Press.

Torres, C. V., Glazer, S., Macedo, F. G. L., & Nascimento, T. G. (2022). Why stay with the police? How meaningfulness in life moderates the mediated effects of role stressors' appraisals on anxiety and intention to leave the State Brazilian police. *International Journal of Police Science and Management, 24*(4), 339–355. https://doi.org/10.1177/14613557221089564

Tran, Q. H. N. (2023). Exploring relationships among overload stress, work-family conflict, job satisfaction, person–organisation fit and organisational commitment in public organizations. *Public Organization Review, 23*(2), 759–775.

Wasti, S. A. (2003). The influence of cultural values on antecedents of organisational commitment: An individual-level analysis. *Applied Psychology: An International Review, 52*(4), 533–554.

Williams, E. N., Grande, S., Nakamura, Y. T., Pyle, L., & Shaw, G. (2022). The development and practice of authentic leadership: A cultural lens. *European Journal of Training & Development, 46*(9), 937–952.

Xiang, L., & Yang, Y.-C. (2020). Factors influencing green organizational citizenship behavior. *Social Behavior & Personality: An International Journal, 48*(9), 1–12. https://doi.org/10.2224/sbp.8754

12

HEAL

Defining a New POB Construct

Vishal Gupta and Anmol Basant

> All this is full. All that is full.
> From fullness, fullness comes.
> When fullness is taken from fullness,
> Fullness still remains.
>
> —The Brihadaranyaka Upanishad (5.1)
> (translated by Eknath Easwaran)

Introduction

A study released in August 2023 exploring attitudes toward the world of work of 32,000 employees in 17 countries reported that globally about two-thirds (65%) employees report being stressed at work and close to 47% report mental health issues (Bhattacharya, 2023). What was surprising to note in the study was that almost six out of ten employees reported that their leaders, managers or colleagues lack the necessary tools and training to engage in mental health conversations without preconceived notions.

Emphasizing the importance of acknowledging the issue of stress and taking steps to reduce it, the report observed,

> Numerous employers showed tremendous support for mental health and stress during the pandemic, but it is crucial for them to continue their vigilance… A compassionate workplace culture holds immense value for both employers and employees. When individuals feel safe and supported, they are significantly more likely to perform better in their roles, require fewer sick leaves, and develop a positive outlook toward the company.

DOI: 10.4324/9781032619385-12

Stress is a phenomenon that includes an individual getting exposed to a stressor (external challenge or demand), perceptual processing of the stressor by the individual and finally the behavioral and physiological response. Stress has been referred to as an internal state that

> ...reflects the subject's inability to forestall or diminish perception, recall, anticipation, or imagination of disvalued circumstances, those that in reality or fantasy signify great and/or increased distance from desirable (valued) experiential states, and consequently, evoke a need to approximate the valued states.
>
> *(Hobfoll, 2001, p. 339)*

Stress has the potential to influence psychological and physiological health that, in turn, impact an individual's well-being (Edwards, 1992). While terms like well-being, happiness, or life satisfaction are used interchangeably in literature and literature shows that there is significant correlation between these terms (Bartels, 2015), well-being has been referred to as an umbrella term that represents a broad category of phenomena that includes people's emotional responses, domain satisfaction and global judgments of life satisfaction (Diener et al., 1999).

Developing better ways to tackle stress is important for individuals as well as organizations. Work-related stress has been reported to be an important determinant of cardiovascular diseases and mortality (Fishta & Backé, 2015). In a study that reviewed organizational research and collated economic valuations of work-related stress in Australia, Canada, Denmark, France, Sweden, Switzerland, the United Kingdom, the United States and the EU-15, it was found that at a national level and pan-European level, the estimated cost of work-related stress ranged from US$221.13 million to $187 billion (Hassard et al., 2018). Productivity losses contributed between 70% and 90% to the total costs related to stress while healthcare and medical costs constituted the remaining 10%–30%.

The Conservation of Resources (COR) theory posits that the depletion of resources is the primary factor driving the stress process and that in order to restore well-being, the individual engages in a process of coping by either developing new resources or through the replenishment of depleted resources (Hobfoll, 2001). Resources encompass objects, personal attributes, circumstances, or energies esteemed for their intrinsic value or for their role as facilitators in obtaining or safeguarding other valued resources (Diener & Fujita, 1995; Hobfoll, 2001). Further, resources are indispensable, and stress arises when they are endangered, diminished, perceived as unstable, or when individuals struggle to envision a means of nurturing and safeguarding their resources through collective or individual endeavors (Hobfoll, 2001). Expanding upon this notion, Hobfoll (2011) additionally suggested that resources do not exist independently but rather travel collectively, akin to packs or caravans, both for individuals and organizations. Possessing a significant resource may also lead to the development of other resources.

In this chapter, we propose a set of three first-order psychological capacities (or resources), namely, harmony (H), equanimity (E) and authentic living (AL), along with the second-order construct of 'HEAL', that can be developed and can help cope with stress, improve well-being and eventual performance at the workplace. Our conceptualization of HEAL, a second-order developmental construct, can also be understood as an extension of the work around positive organizational behavior (POB) and positive psychological capital done by Luthans and colleagues (Luthans, 2002; Luthans, Youssef & Avolio, 2006). We define the HEAL construct as an 'individual's developmental capacity that drives harmonious thoughts, develops an equanimous outlook toward life situations, and encourages one to live according to one's true self (core values) and lead a life of meaning and purpose'. For inclusion as a psychological resource in the context of POB, HEAL must meet specific criteria, such as being positive, measurability, a state-like or developmental nature, relevance to organizational outcomes (behavioral, attitudinal and performance) and adherence to scientific standards encompassing both theory and research (Luthans, 2002; Luthans, Youssef & Avolio, 2015). The remainder of this chapter summarizes the background and POB criteria fit of each of the three HEAL capacities, relevant research to date and potential implications for stress, well-being and the field of OB in general.

Harmony (H): The Source of Positive Cognitive Health

Defining Harmony

Harmony can be understood as a combination of *spiritual oneness*, *loving-kindness* and *compassion.* Spiritual Oneness has been defined as 'belief in the spiritual interconnectedness and essential oneness of all phenomena, both living and non-living; and a belief that happiness depends on living in accord with this understanding' (Garfield et al., 2014, p. 357). Oneness has also been defined as a sense of non-duality and a transcendent unity that is beyond all qualification (Fry & Kriger, 2009) and as 'never losing the awareness that we are all connected to each other, and that we live for the universe through our choices and actions' (Thakadipuram, 2010, p. 464). Cho et al. (2018) defined the loving–kindness–compassion combine as 'a feeling of being touched by a person's suffering, wanting to help them (compassion), and wishing them to be happy (loving-kindness), which arises from a deep insight that all beings are connected (universality)' (p. 141). Building on the positive definitions of oneness, loving–kindness and compassion, we define harmony as 'a thought based on oneness and loving-kindness'.

Harmony stands as one of the most revered ideals in the Indian and Chinese cultures (Chang & Celik, 2018; Fry & Kriger, 2009; Li, 2006). Hindu philosophy explicitly uses the term 'oneness' and 'harmony' in its scriptures and advocates the development of a 'selfless mindset' (Kjell et al., 2016). In the Upanishad, one of the oldest and most revered Indian scriptures, unity with the ultimate (super) consciousness is considered to be the essence of *moksha* (liberation) (Easwaran, 2017). The Eastern philosophy posits that harmony is inherently relational (Chang & Celik, 2018; Fry & Kriger, 2009) and that things flourish through mutual support and dependence. The notion of harmony fosters a holistic perspective emphasizing balance and adaptability in personal well-being, considering social and environmental factors (Kjell et al., 2016). Embracing a harmonious attitude cultivates a greater willingness to participate in negotiation and compromise while diminishing the inclination toward confrontation and conquest. This thought process enables individuals to consider the broader context and offer peaceful resolutions to both individual and global challenges (Li, 2006).

The 21st quantum physics has provided support to the notion that there is no duality. The discovery of the Higgs Boson in 2012 and with it the realization that matter and energy are one and the same thing led to many scientists realize that there is in effect only one force that binds everything and that there is an invisible energy that manifests itself in terms of matter and then converts back into energy (Sarker, 2021). Quantum physicists today believe that our universe is made up of one unified field and that all subatomic (or quantum) particles exhibit a dual nature and behave both as particle and wave (Hollick, 2011; Sarker, 2021). Many renowned scientists talk about this equivalence (oneness or harmony) in different ways. Erwin Schrödinger, an Austrian physicist who developed fundamental results in quantum theory and won the Nobel Prize famously observed, 'The total number of minds in the universe is one. In fact, consciousness is a singularity phasing within all beings' (Wintjen, 2018).

Development and Impact of Harmony

Despite its potential significance to individuals and organizations, harmony is arguably one of the most under-researched topics in OB literature (Chang & Celik, 2018). We outline some of the key results from literature that points toward its developmental as well as positive nature. Kjell et al. (2016) discovered a significant correlation between harmony in life and well-being, which explained a greater amount of unique variation than life satisfaction in several well-being surveys. Fry and Kriger (2009) argued that leaders who have a 'non-dual' mindset and view a 'transcendent unity beyond all qualification' manifest unconditional regard for others, are able to intuit the needs of their group members more quickly and foster equality at workplace. The authors go on to observe that

> the manifestation of unconditional regard for the other as oneself and the immediate intuition of the needs of the group as a result of the merging of 'self' and 'other' are likely to be rarely observed in organizational settings. Thus, the non-dual level of being and awareness is to be aspired to and realized usually via much inner work and provides a vision of what leadership can become at the highest level.
>
> *(Fry & Kriger, 2009, p. 1685)*

According to Dambrun and Richard (2011), authentic and lasting well-being is based on selflessness, while self-centeredness produces unstable and fluctuating well-being. Chaskalson and Teasdale (2011) highlighted that a prevalent source of suffering occurs when the mind contrasts its perceptions of its current state with its ideals of where it believes it should be. If the disparity between these two is unresolved, dwelling on the gap can intensify suffering. Chang and Celik (2018) mentioned that oneness (harmony) exhibits itself at three levels: individual, interpersonal and transpersonal. When there is harmony between an individual's mind, body and energy systems, well-being results, which in turn can enable the individual to work better and develop his/her competencies. Harmony at the interpersonal level pertains to developing strong relationships at work, being a good citizen and being cooperative and ethical in one's dealings with others. And harmony at the transpersonal level can motivate an individual to think not just about his/her own organization but also about how the organization is impacting stakeholders outside its boundary, thereby encouraging ethical behaviors.

Mindfulness as well as yoga-based practices can aid in the development of harmony. In separate meta-analyses, Galante et al. (2014) and Reilly and Stuyvenberg (2023) showed that loving–kindness mediation improves self-compassion, health and well-being. Luberto et al. (2018) that meditation can improve empathy, compassion and prosocial behaviors. Also, a combination of loving–kindness and mindfulness meditations can have stronger benefits on reducing anxiety (Zheng et al., 2023). Emphasizing the importance of combining yoga-based and mindfulness-based practices in order to align cognitive, psychological, physiological as well as energetic systems, Chang and Celik (2018) argued that such a combination can lead to the development of a sense of harmony and oneness with all living and non-living beings. We, thus, believe that 'harmony' is a core capacity that can be developed and enables positive mental (cognitive) health. While initial results are encouraging, more research is needed to explore how harmony can be developed in work contexts and also examine its impact on individual-, group- and organization-level outcomes.

Equanimity (E): Enabling Emotional Stability

Defining Equanimity

Emotions usually emerge as reactions to an internal or external events that holds a positive or negative significance for the individual (Salovey & Mayer, 1990). The state of equanimity refers to 'a balanced reaction to joy and misery, which protects one from emotional agitation' (Bodhi, 2005, p. 154). Building on the definition of equanimity given by Desbordes et al. (2015) as 'an even-minded mental state or dispositional tendency toward all experience or objects, regardless of their valence (pleasant, unpleasant, or neutral) or source' (p. 357), we conceptualize it as 'staying neutral and calm toward all outcomes, irrespective of their valence or source'.

Although equanimity as a concept has not been discussed much in the Western psychological context (Desbordes et al., 2015), it has been widely discussed in Eastern wisdom traditions (especially Hinduism and Buddhist) (Jijina & Biswas, 2022). Within the Buddhist tradition, the concept of equanimity is a complex and diverse idea that has been defined in several ways during the course of the development of Buddhist philosophy. The term 'equanimity' in the Theravadan Buddhist literature has two specific usages. The first definition pertains to the concept of 'neutral feeling' which denotes a mental experience devoid of both pleasantness and unpleasantness and entails neither amplifying nor diminishing the current mental state (Bodhi, 2000, p. 34). Another definition of equanimity denotes a mental state 'unaffected by biases or preferences', characterized by maintaining an 'impartial attitude' toward all experiences and beings (Bodhi, 2000; Jijina & Biswas, 2022).

In the Bhagavad Gita, one of the oldest and most sacred scripture of the Hindus, the concept of *stithpragya* (stable wisdom) holds a central place. *Sthithpragya* in the Bhagavad Gita (Śrīmad Bhagavadgītā, 2008) denotes the practice of maintaining balance amidst life's diverse experiences, including pleasure and agony, honor and humiliation and gain and loss (Jijina & Biswas, 2022). Describing an individual of stable wisdom, Krishna[1] mentions 'he who is unattached to everything, and meeting with good and evil, neither rejoices nor recoils, his mind is stable' (Śrīmad Bhagavadgītā, 2008, verse 2.57).

Development and Impact of Equanimity

Cultivating equanimity can be advantageous for managing stress, well-being and performance. Thoughts and emotions, whether real or perceived, prompt a synchronized array of bodily reactions (Desbordes et al., 2015). These responses involve the interplay between the neurological, endocrine and immunological systems (Sternberg, 2000). Under normal scenarios, these coordinated bodily reactions enable effective stress coping, facilitating a gradual return to a regular state after stress subsides. However, failure in coping or recovery can lead to long-term damage (Karatsoreos & McEwen, 2011; Desbordes et al., 2015). Equanimity can facilitate the recovery from mental or physical stress, assisting the individual in swiftly returning to a state of equilibrium (Desbordes et al., 2015).

Equanimity has largely been ignored in the OB literature and has been replaced by terms such as 'acceptance' or 'being non-judgmental' (Weber, 2021). Although empirical evidence regarding the relationship between equanimity and individual outcomes is somewhat limited, a few recent studies have indicated a negative association between equanimity and psychological distress. Smyth et al. (2024) proposed a few mechanisms through which a state of equanimity can help one deal with stress effectively. They first posited that by adopting an impartial attitude toward all experiences, individuals with elevated measures of equanimity may be less inclined to perceive challenges as inherently unfortunate and may even view them as integral aspects of life, circumstances for personal growth, or even crucial components of a meaningful existence. Secondly, they also proposed that equanimity may diminish automatic mental and behavioral reactivity when faced with stressors and obstacles (Desbordes et al., 2015; Lindsay et al., 2018). Nickerson and Hinton (2011) discussed the importance of equanimity in anger regulation by adopting a healthy distance from oneself and emotion thereby enabling one to 'stay in the middle'.

Limited evidence suggests that it is possible to develop equanimity through dedicated practices such as Yoga and meditation. In a review of research on equanimity, Weber (2021) showed that equanimity can be developed using a distinct and dedicated meditation practice. Researchers have argued that 'decentering' or 'self-distancing' could be effective techniques in developing equanimity. Decentering is a mental state characterized by three interrelated metacognitive processes, namely, meta-awareness, disidentification from internal experience and reduced reactivity to thought content (Shoham et al., 2017). It is possible to develop equanimity through mindfulness as well as Yoga-based practices that emphasize experiencing the present moment situations without self-referentiality (self-distancing or decentering) (Desbordes et al., 2015; Hadash, Plonsker, et al., 2016).

Mindfulness practices can emphasize the decoupling of desire from the tone of the current experience and develop an intentional attitude of acceptance (Hadash, Segev, et al., 2016). By practicing mindfulness, individuals can develop and enhance capacity to monitor conscious experiences as they arise in awareness and practice shifting to an 'observing' perspective thereby developing a broad contextual awareness of mental events as subjective, transient events, rather than accurate reflections of reality, or oneself (Shepherd et al., 2016). In a qualitative study of 30 experts from various contemplation traditions of Yoga, Buddhism and Indian psychology, Jijina and Biswas (2022) developed a detailed map of cultivation equanimity through contemplative practices such as mediation and yoga and through non-contemplative practice of taking regulated diet.

Authentic Living (AL): Giving Voice to Inner Values

Defining Authentic Living

Authenticity is conceptualized as the state of being true to oneself and entails both self-awareness and self-expression (Harter, 2002; Kernis & Goldman, 2006). Being authentic pertains to the degree of consistency between external expressions and internal values and beliefs (Lehman et al., 2019). Gardner et al. (2005) described authentic leaders as individuals who 'display actions that are guided by the leaders' true self as reflected by core values, beliefs, thoughts and feelings, as opposed to environmental contingencies or pressures from others' (p. 347). Using a person-centered conception of authenticity, Wood et al. (2008) proposed a tripartite definition of authenticity that involved self-alienation, authentic living and accepting external influence as underlying components. Self-alienation was defined as the 'extent to which the person experiences self-alienation between conscious awareness and actual experience (the true self)', authentic living as 'behaving and expressing emotions in such a way that is consistent with the conscious awareness of physiological states, emotions, beliefs, and cognitions', and accepting external influence as 'the extent to which one accepts the influence of other people and the belief that one has to conform to the expectations of others' (p. 386).

Viktor Frankl, in his famous book titled *Man's Search for Meaning*, argued that the quest for meaning and purpose is inherent in human beings. Recognizing that meaning is something that one discovers by working toward a bigger cause than one's own self-gratification, he noted

> For success, like happiness, cannot be pursued; it must ensure, and it only does so as the unintended side-effect of one's dedication to a cause greater than oneself or as the by-product of one's surrender to a person other than oneself.
>
> *(Frankl, 2008, p. 12)*

Work that is meaningful incorporates 'cognitively meaningful tasks, but it is also about work that creates a sense of joy, which connects workers to a larger good and to things viewed by the worker as important in life' (Duchon & Plowman, 2005, p. 814). Combining the above definitions of authenticity and meaningful work, we define authentic living as 'deploying one's strengths and/or values in the larger interests of the society'.

The essence of these different conceptualizations of authenticity revolves around whether an individual is aligning their actions with their inner, true self. Hindu philosophy advocates that an individual should act according to *Dharma* without being attached to the fruits or personal consequences. *Dharma* can be a complex concept to understand comprehensively but in simple words it can be defined as 'actions that are done to drive sustainability in the society in the long run' (Ganatra, 2021). The Bhagavad Gita advocates that individuals must live according to *sāttvika* (true and excellent) values which enable one to connect to the inner self. In the Gita, Krishna mentions, 'that by which man perceives one imperishable divine existence as undivided and equally present in all individual beings, know that knowledge to be *sāttvika* [of excellent quality]' (Śrīmad Bhagavadgītā, 2008, verse 18.20). Further, reminding individuals to act according to values of selflessness, harmony and equanimity, he proclaims, 'that action which is ordained by the scriptures and is not accompanied by the sense of doership, and has been done without any partiality or prejudice by one who seeks no return, is called *sāttvika*' (Śrīmad Bhagavadgītā, 2008, verse 18.23) and that which is 'free from attachment, unegoistic, endowed with firmness and zeal and unswayed by success and failure – such a doer is said to be *sāttvika*' (Śrīmad Bhagavadgītā, 2008, 19.26).

Development and Impact of Authentic Living

Happiness is said to emerge when an individual authentically expresses one's virtues and strengths. Making deliberate choices and taking responsibility for them is said to lead to well-being and engagement in life (Sutton, 2020). Individuals with high levels of authenticity have the capacity to align their actions with their personal interests and values. As a result, these behaviors contribute to an overall enhancement of well-being (Medlock, 2012). On the other hand, individuals with low authenticity frequently find themselves compelled to behave in a manner inconsistent with their inner experiences, resulting in heightened psychological disagreements and diminished well-being (Goldman & Kernis, 2002).

Chalofsky and Krishna (2009) argued that employees with high levels of productivity are intrinsically motivated by the work (i.e., find their work meaningful), view themselves as inseparables from their work (authenticity) and are therefore more likely to be engaged and committed at work. We thus argue that authentic living is likely to be a positive contributor to workplace outcomes. In support of the above observation, Sutton (2020) conducted a meta-analysis of research studies done on the topic of authenticity, well-being and engagement and reported positive relationships between authentic expression of self with well-being as well as engagement at work. Based on the findings of the study, Sutton concluded that 'authenticity has positive implications for individual well-being and work engagement and could provide an important path to building healthy work organisations'.

Meaningful work predicts work engagement, commitment and job satisfaction, which in turn predict employee performance, organizational citizenship behavior and withdrawal intentions (Allan et al., 2019). Bailey et al. (2019), in a review of research on meaningful work, found that apart from commitment, engagement and job satisfaction, meaningful work is also positively related to job enjoyment, feelings of accomplishment and growth, motivation, positive self-concept, career commitment, creativity, knowledge sharing behavior, happiness and performance perceptions. In an interesting study done within teams, Leroy et al. (2021) showed that when team members are authentic in putting forward their unique perspectives and are also willing to listen to and understand other team members' perspectives, there results a positive impact on the overall team performance. Such teams are better able to assimilate information shared, thereby leading to positive overall performance.

While there exists limited research on the development of authenticity, substantial evidence exists for the development of meaningfulness. Demonstrating both the possibility of developing authentic living as well as its impact on individual outcomes, Lin and Park (2023) demonstrated that mindfulness is positively related to authentic living which in turn is positively related to individuals' anti-consumption behavior. Through a quasi-experimental intervention conducted with business students in Switzerland, Kipfelsberger et al. (2022) showed that the authentic living and non-acceptance of external influence dimensions of authenticity can be strengthened through a career and personal development program that comprised of coaching sessions, group workshops that provided an opportunity for self-reflection, develop interpersonal skills, and finally an opportunity to express one's true self in a safe relational context.

Meaningfulness at work has been found to be positively influenced by multiple factors. Hackman and Oldham (1975) showed that meaningfulness at work can be developed by consciously working on job design, specifically skill variety, task significance and task identity. Leadership styles such as transformational leadership, spiritual leadership, leader–member exchange and supervisory support has also been shown to have positive effects on meaningfulness at work (Bailey et al., 2019). Spiritual, and learning-focused workplace climate, as well as positive workplace relationships have also been found to lead to a sense of meaningfulness at work (Bailey & Madden, 2017; Duchon & Plowman, 2005).

HEAL: A New Resource for Coping, Well-Being and Performance

Adopting a POB approach, this chapter proposes for today's workforce a new resource to cope with stress, have better well-being and thus be more productive at work. This chapter introduces three core strengths of harmony, equanimity and authentic living which together make up the second-order positive psychological capacity HEAL. Box 1 briefly summarizes these three capacities and we argue in this chapter that these capacities meet the specific criteria of POB namely, being positive, measurable, capable of being developed and having a positive impact on performance (Luthans, 2002; Luthans et al., 2015). Using the arguments from Eastern philosophy (primarily Hinduism and Buddhism), we advocate that developing harmony, equanimity and authentic living can enable individuals cope with stress better, enhance their well-being, and ultimately their performance.

Our conceptualization of HEAL are also in alignment with the core tenets of cognitive behavioral therapy (CBT) that argues that any psychological problem arises from one's thoughts, emotions or behaviors (Tolin, 2024). We position stress as a psychological problem that needs to be dealt with at all three levels of cognition, emotion and behavior. The dimensions of HEAL target each of these three elements proposed by the CBT. At the level of cognition, we advocate developing harmonious thoughts. The notion of harmony encourages a holistic perspective emphasizing balance and flexibility with social and environmental factors instead of keeping oneself at the center in the grand scheme of things. At the level of emotions, we argue for developing equanimity – a balanced and even-minded mental state toward life experiences, irrespective of their emotional valence or origin. Finally, at the level of behavior, we advocate authentic living – being true to one's core values and living a life of meaning and purpose.

While the research on each of the three concepts in mainstream organizational behavior literature is limited, the preliminary evidence that exists supports the contention that these three core capacities of HEAL can be developed as well as

BOX 1 AN OVERVIEW OF HEAL

1 **Harmony (H)** – 'A thought based on oneness and loving-kindness'

- Oneness, loving–kindness and compassion – closely aligned with revelations of quantum physics
- Measurable, found to be related to well-being, life satisfaction and highest quality of leadership
- Development through mindfulness meditation and yoga-based practices

2 **Equanimity (E)** – 'Staying neutral and calm toward all outcomes, irrespective of their valence or source'

- Neutral mindset, *stithpragya* (stable wisdom)
- Measurable, related to reduced automatic mental and behavioral reactivity, and better emotional health
- Development through practice of decentering, self-distancing, staying in the middle and regulated diet

3 **Authentic Living (AL)** – 'Deploying one's strengths and/or values in the larger interests of the society'

- Acting according to one's virtues and strengths, finding meaning and purpose at work and in life
- Measurable, related to engagement at work, subjective well-being and performance
- Can be developed through mindfulness practices, coaching and training sessions, working on job characteristics and developing an authentic (spiritual) workplace culture

have a positive impact on individual's well-being and performance. By presenting theoretical arguments as well as specific evidence from literature, we believe that mindfulness-based as well as Yoga-based practices can enable the development of the three HEAL capacities, as can dedicated training as well as coaching programs. Using the notion that resources do not exist in isolation but instead work collectively, we also advocate that the practice of mindfulness and Yoga-based practices, which themselves can be seen as positive resources, can aid the development of HEAL. Definitely, more focused research is needed in this direction.

We believe that the three HEAL capacities can act as positive resources that can help an individual with stress effectively. Furthermore, our conceptualization of HEAL extends the research on POB and positive psychological capital. While psychological capacities discussed in literature so far have primarily focused on work performance, we position HEAL as a construct that has the potential to not just improve performance by enabling better coping with stress, and improving well-being.

Note

1 One of the most revered Hindu Gods who is said to have spoken the Gita to his disciple Arjuna.

References

Allan, B. A., Batz-Barbarich, C., Sterling, H. M., & Tay, L. (2019). Outcomes of meaningful mork: A meta-analysis. *Journal of Management Studies, 56*(3), 500–528.

Bailey, C., & Madden, A. (2017). Time reclaimed: Temporality and the experience of meaningful work. *Work, Employment and Society, 31*(1), 3–18.

Bailey, C., Yeoman, R., Madden, A., Thompson, M., & Kerridge, G. (2019). A review of the empirical literature on meaningful work: Progress and research agenda. *Human Resource Development Review, 18*(1), 83–113.

Bartels, M. (2015). Genetics of wellbeing and its components satisfaction with life, happiness, and quality of life: A review and meta-analysis of heritability studies. *Behavior Genetics, 45*(2), 137–156.

Bhattacharya, R. (2023, August 17). Mental health: 76% of Indian workers say stress negatively impacting work, shows survey—The Economic Times. *The Economic Times.* https://economictimes.indiatimes.com/jobs/hr-policies-trends/76-of-indian-workers-say-stress-negatively-impacting-work-shows-survey/articleshow/102810905.cms?from=mdr

Bodhi, B. (2000). *A comprehensive manual of Abhidhamma: The philosophical psychology of Buddhism*. Buddhist Publication Society, Kandy (Sri Lanka).

Bodhi, B. (2005). *In the Buddha's words: An anthology of discourses from the Pali Canon.* Wisdom Publications, Somerville (USA).

Chalofsky, N., & Krishna, V. (2009). Meaningfulness, commitment, and engagement: The intersection of a deeper level of intrinsic motivation. *Advances in Developing Human Resources, 11*(2), 189–203.

Chang, T. F., & Celik, D. A. (2018). From mindfulness to oneness: "Inner engineering" of the complex adaptive human system. *Academy of Management Proceedings, 2018*(1), 11819.

Chaskalson, M., & Teasdale, J. D. (2011). How does mindfulness transform suffering? I: The nature and origins of dukkha. *Contemporary Buddhism: An Interdisciplinary Journal, 12*(1), 89–102.

Cho, H., Noh, S., Park, S., Ryu, S., Misan, V., & Lee, J. S. (2018). The development and validation of the lovingkindness-compassion scale. *Personality and Individual Differences, 124*, 141–144.

Dambrun, M., & Ricard, M. (2011). Self-centeredness and selflessness: A theory of self-based psychological functioning and its consequences for happiness. *Review of General Psychology, 15*(2), 138–157.

Diener, E., & Fujita, F. (1995). Resources, personal strivings, and subjective well-being: A nomothetic and idiographic approach. *Journal of Personality and Social Psychology, 68*(5), 926.

Diener, E., Suh, E. M., Lucas, R. E., & Smith, H. L. (1999). Subjective well-being: Three decades of progress. *Psychological Bulletin, 125*(2), 276–302.

Desbordes, G., Gard, T., Hoge, E. A., Hölzel, B. K., Kerr, C., Lazar, S. W., Olendzki, A., & Vago, D. R. (2015). Moving beyond mindfulness: Defining equanimity as an outcome measure in meditation and contemplative research. *Mindfulness, 6*(2), 356–372.

Duchon, D., & Plowman, D. A. (2005). Nurturing the spirit at work: Impact on work unit performance. *The Leadership Quarterly*, *16*(5), 807–833.

Easwaran, E. (2017). *The Upanishads*. Jaico Publishing, Mumbai (India).

Edwards, J. R. (1992). A cybernetic theory of stress, coping, and well-being in organizations. *The Academy of Management Review*, *17*(2), 238–274.

Fishta, A., & Backé, E.-M. (2015). Psychosocial stress at work and cardiovascular diseases: An overview of systematic reviews. *International Archives of Occupational and Environmental Health*, *88*(8), 997–1014.

Frankl, V. E. (2008). *Man's search for meaning*. Rider, London (UK).

Fry, L., & Kriger, M. (2009). Towards a theory of being-centered leadership: Multiple levels of being as context for effective leadership. *Human Relations*, *62*(11), 1667–1696.

Galante, J., Galante, I., Bekkers, M.-J., & Gallacher, J. (2014). Effect of kindness-based meditation on health and well-being: A systematic review and meta-analysis. *Journal of Consulting and Clinical Psychology*, *82*(6), 1101–1114.

Ganatra, A. (2021). *Mahabharata unravelled: Lesser-known facets of a well-known history*. Bloomsbury, New Delhi (India).

Gardner, W. L., Avolio, B. J., Luthans, F., May, D. R., & Walumbwa, F. (2005). "Can you see the real me?" A self-based model of authentic leader and follower development. *The Leadership Quarterly*, *16*(3), 343–372.

Garfield, A. M., Drwecki, B. B., Moore, C. F., Kortenkamp, K. V., & Gracz, M. D. (2014). The oneness beliefs scale: Connecting spirituality with pro-environmental behavior. *Journal for the Scientific Study of Religion*, *53*(2), 356–372.

Goldman, B. M., & Kernis, M. H. (2002). The role of authenticity in healthy psychological functioning and subjective well-being. *Annals of the American Psychotherapy Association*, *5*(6), 18–20.

Hackman, J. R., & Oldham, G. R. (1975). Development of the job diagnostic survey. *Journal of Applied Psychology*, *60*(2), 159.

Hadash, Y., Plonsker, R., Vago, D. R., & Bernstein, A. (2016). Experiential self-referential and selfless processing in mindfulness and mental health: Conceptual model and implicit measurement methodology. *Psychological Assessment*, *28*(7), 856–869.

Hadash, Y., Segev, N., Tanay, G., Goldstein, P., & Bernstein, A. (2016). The decoupling model of equanimity: Theory, measurement, and test in a mindfulness intervention. *Mindfulness*, *7*(5), 1214–1226.

Harter, S. (2002). Authenticity. In C. R. Snyder & S. J. Lopez (Eds.), *Handbook of positive psychology* (pp. 382–394). Oxford University Press, Oxford (UK).

Hassard, J., Teoh, K. R. H., Visockaite, G., Dewe, P., & Cox, T. (2018). The cost of work-related stress to society: A systematic review. *Journal of Occupational Health Psychology*, *23*(1), 1–17.

Hobfoll, S. E. (2001). The influence of culture, community, and the nested-self in the stress process: Advancing conservation of resources theory. *Applied Psychology: An International Journal*, *50*(3), 337–421.

Hobfoll, S. E. (2011). Conservation of resource caravans and engaged settings. *Journal of Occupational and Organizational Psychology*, *84*(1), 116–122.

Hollick, M. (2011). *The science of oneness: A world view for our age*. John Hunt Publishing, Alresford (UK).

Jijina, P., & Biswas, U. N. (2022). Various pathways for cultivation of equanimity: An exploratory study. *Psychological Studies*, *67*(1), 28–42.

Karatsoreos, I. N., & McEwen, B. S. (2011). Psychobiological allostasis: Resistance, resilience and vulnerability. *Trends in Cognitive Sciences*, *15*(12), 576–584.

Kernis, M. H., & Goldman, B. M. (2006). A multicomponent conceptualization of authenticity: Theory and research. *Advances in Experimental Social Psychology, 38*, 283–357.

Kipfelsberger, P., Braun, S., Fladerer, M. P., & Dragoni, L. (2022). Developing authenticity: A quasi-experimental investigation. *Personality and Individual Differences, 198*, 111825.

Kjell, O. N. E., Daukantaitė, D., Hefferon, K., & Sikström, S. (2016). The harmony in life scale complements the satisfaction with life scale: Expanding the conceptualization of the cognitive component of subjective well-being. *Social Indicators Research, 126*, 893–919.

Lehman, D. W., O'Connor, K., Kovács, B., & Newman, G. E. (2019). Authenticity. *Academy of Management Annals, 13*(1), 1–42.

Leroy, H., Hoever, I. J., Vangronsvelt, K., & Van Den Broeck, A. (2021). How team averages in authentic living and perspective-taking personalities relate to team information elaboration and team performance. *Journal of Applied Psychology, 106*(3), 364–376.

Li, C. (2006). The Confucian ideal of harmony. *Philosophy East and West, 56(4)*, 583–603.

Lin, L. M., & Park, H. J. (2023). Mindfulness and anti-consumption behavior: The role of authentic living. *Asia Pacific Journal of Marketing and Logistics, 35*(9), 2110–2121.

Lindsay, E. K., Young, S., Smyth, J. M., Brown, K. W., & Creswell, J. D. (2018). Acceptance lowers stress reactivity: Dismantling mindfulness training in a randomized controlled trial. *Psychoneuroendocrinology, 87*, 63–73.

Luberto, C. M., Shinday, N., Song, R., Philpotts, L. L., Park, E. R., Fricchione, G. L., & Yeh, G. Y. (2018). A systematic review and meta-analysis of the effects of meditation on empathy, compassion, and prosocial behaviors. *Mindfulness, 9*(3), 708–724.

Luthans, F. (2002). Positive organizational behavior: Developing and managing psychological strengths. *Academy of Management Perspectives, 16*(1), 57–72.

Luthans, F., Youssef, C. M., & Avolio, B. J. (2006). *Psychological capital: Developing the human competitive edge*. Oxford University Press, Oxford (UK).Luthans, F., Youssef, C. M., & Avolio, B. J. (2015). *Psychological capital and beyond.* Oxford University Press, Oxford (UK).

Medlock, G. (2012). The evolving ethic of authenticity: From humanistic to positive psychology. *The Humanistic Psychologist, 40*(1), 38–57.

Nickerson, A., & Hinton, D. E. (2011). Anger regulation in traumatized Cambodian refugees: The perspectives of Buddhist monks. *Culture, Medicine and Psychiatry, 35*(3), 396–416.

Reilly, E. B., & Stuyvenberg, C. L. (2023). A meta-analysis of loving-kindness meditations on self-compassion. *Mindfulness, 14*(10), 2299–2310.

Salovey, P., & Mayer, J. D. (1990). Emotional intelligence. *Imagination, Cognition and Personality, 9*(3), 185–211.

Sarker, C. R. (2021). Consciousness in quantum physics and meaning in the advaita philosophy of Adi Sankaracharya. *Ultimate Reality and Meaning, 38*(1–2), 73–81.

Shepherd, K. A., Coifman, K. G., Matt, L. M., & Fresco, D. M. (2016). Development of a self-distancing task and initial validation of responses. *Psychological Assessment, 28*(7), 841–855.

Shoham, A., Goldstein, P., Oren, R., Spivak, D., & Bernstein, A. (2017). Decentering in the process of cultivating mindfulness: An experience-sampling study in time and context. *Journal of Consulting and Clinical Psychology, 85*(2), 123–134.

Smyth, A., Juneau, C., Hong, S., Ilagan, M. J., & Knäuper, B. (2024). Facing obstacles with equanimity: Trait equanimity attenuates the positive relations between values obstruction and symptoms of depression, anxiety, and stress. *Mindfulness, 15*(4), 945–957.

Śrīmad Bhagavadgītā (Sixth Reprint) (2008). Gita Press, Gorakhpur (India).
Sternberg, E. (2000). *The balance within: The science connecting health and emotions.* Freeman, London (UK).
Sutton, A. (2020). Living the good life: A meta-analysis of authenticity, well-being and engagement. *Personality and Individual Differences, 153*, 109645.
Thakadipuram, T. (2010). Leadership wholeness: A human resource development model. *Human Resource Development International, 13*(4), 463–475.
Tolin, D. F. (2024). *Doing CBT.* Guilford Press, New York (US).
Weber, J. (2021). A systematic literature review of equanimity in mindfulness based interventions. *Pastoral Psychology, 70*(2), 151–165.
Wintjen, H. (2018, September 14). Erwin Schrödinger: There is only one mind. *Hendrik Wintjen.* https://www.hendrik-wintjen.info/consciousness/erwin-schroedinger-one-mind/
Wood, A. M., Linley, P. A., Maltby, J., Baliousis, M., & Joseph, S. (2008). The authentic personality: A theoretical and empirical conceptualization and the development of the authenticity scale. *Journal of Counseling Psychology, 55*(3), 385–399.
Zheng, Y., Yan, L., Chen, Y., Zhang, X., Sun, W., Lv, J., Zhou, J., Gu, X., Zhao, X., Luo, W., Chen, Y., Lang, Y., Wang, Z., Gao, C., Jiang, Y., Li, R., Deng, Y., & Zeng, X. (2023). Effects of loving-kindness and compassion meditation on anxiety: A systematic review and meta-analysis. *Mindfulness, 14*(5), 1021–1037.

13

GAME, SET AND MATCH! CREATING AN ORGANIZATIONAL GROWTH MINDSET AND POSITIVE ORGANIZATIONAL BEHAVIOUR THROUGH COMMON-GOOD HRM

Brian Matthews, Michael Muller-Camen, and Jennifer Wieland

Introduction

Because of growing pressures to become more sustainable, organizations are searching for effective ways to incorporate socio-ecological concerns into existing economic strategic goals, and where possible, at the same time, to utilize sustainable 'green' employee behaviour to enhance organizational innovation and performance (Paulet, Holland and Morgan, 2021). The discipline of human resource management (HRM) is often allocated the task of convincing workers of the need for change, of positively influencing desired organizational citizenship behaviour and implementing green agendas (Baldassari et al., 2023). However, changing behaviour and moving away from an established single strategic purpose (i.e., profit, market share) towards multi-purpose (i.e., social and ecological) has proved a major challenge and this has initiated a debate about the suitability of current business models and the fixed mindsets behind them – at least within the Sustainable HRM academic community (Podgorodnichenko, Edgar and McAndrew, 2020).

One difficulty is that many companies interpretate organizational sustainability as mainly an opportunity to use the challenge of climate change to a, optimize the sustainable use of material resources and save costs, to b, improve their 'green' image and legitimacy and c, to increase market share and gain new environmentally aware customers (Mukonza and Swarts, 2020). However, this market-centric, strategic frame of thought and mindset is lacking in both an employee perspective and any commitment towards creating wider social or ecological value (Richards, 2022). A central challenge is the assumed inherent conflict between business and societal needs and the necessity to always create a 'win–win', which often paradoxically results in a continued bias of shareholder and economic priorities at the

DOI: 10.4324/9781032619385-13

expense of the wider common good. We argue in order to overcome this impasse and initiate a change in behaviour a switch in mindset will be first required.

A second, but related issue is a narrow focus (especially by HRM as a managerial function) on influencing the individual performance of internal stakeholders rather than recognizing the broader nature of sustainability as a complex multi-stakeholder dilemma of collective action, involving wider interrelated concerns of transparency, compliance and participation (Ostrom, 1990; Yoder, Wagner, Sullivan-Wiley and Smith, 2022). We assert therefore that a stubbornness towards the primacy of economic interests, hierarchical managerial systems of control and a defensive harm-avoiding 'fixed mindset' (Athota and Athota, 2021) often obscures the need for HRM to proactively interact with internal and external stakeholders (including employees) and provide the necessary structural support, agency and opportunities for them to fully engage with organizational green and sustainable agendas (Aust, Matthews and Müller-Camen, 2020; Matthews, Obereder, Aust and Müller-Camen, 2018). HRM now faces the dilemma of motivating employees towards new strategic environmental targets to which they are often very mistrustful, and where HR managers often lack the necessary mindset, awareness, skills, resources and theoretical frameworks to change counterproductive sensibilities and actions.

Generally however, and regarding our specific topic of sustainability, people with a 'growth mindset' have been found to be more open to sustainable agendas and to exhibit pro-environmental behavioural tendencies (Duchi, Lombardi, Paas and Loyens, 2020). And recently, there has been an increased interest in how HRM can enhance job satisfaction, employee engagement and workplace relations through developing a 'growth mindset' (Han and Stieha, 2020) where competence and behaviour are positively changed by influencing attitudes and self-beliefs (Dweck and Molden, 2005). This is backed up by research showing a positive relationship between this positive mentality and desired individual-level (motivation, engagement, satisfaction) and organizational (relationships with management, citizenship behaviour) outcomes (Han and Stieha, 2020). For instance, developing an awareness that personal flaws and limitations can be worked on and overcome (with the required training and structural support), has been shown to positively influence workers perceptions (Forsythe and Johnson, 2017) and plays an important role in fostering worker engagement (Caniëls, Semeijn and Renders, 2018).

On the other hand, the concept of a growth mindset although well established in the fields of education and psychology is less well known in the domains of management and HRM (Hochanadel and Finamore, 2015). In this chapter, we suggest that the growth mindset approach, which is based on empowering people and developing trust, on supporting and rewarding collaboration, and reframing challenges as opportunities, could be particularly relevant and useful in enabling HR managers to regain trust and to cultivate a culture more abetting to sustainable employee behaviour. A shift to a positive mindset (beginning with management) could also help address specific and persistent organizational level hurdles to change and improve wider common-good progress, for example, by counteracting the negative impact of greenwashing and a loss of legitimacy on psychological climate, workplace relations and employee behaviour (Tahir, Athar and Afzal, 2020). We argue therefore that while, on the one hand, the development of a growth mindset is a necessary requirement for authentic management commitment to sustainable change, an increased sense of common-good purpose and a culture of shared sustainable purpose can help a more positive and healthier mindset to develop.

The sustainable HRM paradigm which has slowly but steadily gained ground over the past 20 years or so demands quite a radical (but we argue, viable) change in managerial mindset or thinking (Ehnert, 2013). This is particularly true of the more recent relational Common-Good HRM (CGHRM) type (Aust et al., 2020). From this stakeholder-centric, multidimensional perspective, developing a positive organizational culture which motivates and empowers employees (and provides opportunities for personal development), is just as important for long-term sustainability as technological investments or improving HR processes (King and Cohen, 2023). Rather than viewing HRs role as one to utilize employees' innate talents and strengths for corporate benefit, a sustainable, CGHRM works on the premise that skills and abilities can be improved and developed in a holistic sense, and importantly, that HRM as a social actor, has a fundamental responsibility to support this through the utilization of all available resources (Aust et al., 2020).

To date however, this appeal for a HRM characterized by a commitment to stakeholder empowerment, self-efficacy, self-management and proactive learning (i.e., a growth mindset) has faced strong resistance especially from practitioners who still measure success purely in terms of organizational efficiency, economic performance and shareholder value (Kaufman, 2020). At the same time, other (more critical and 'commons' orientated) scholars, have long argued that sustainability needs to be considered a collective problem which can only be solved collectively (Ostrom, 2009). For example, by establishing the optimal conditions for institutions of collective action to develop (Ostrom, 1990), and where the concerns of internal and external stakeholders are incorporated into business and HR sustainable strategies (Albareda and Sison, 2020; Aust, Cooke, Müller-Camen and Wood, 2024).

We argue as a result, that while a shift to a 'growth mindset' is to be welcomed and indeed necessary, the collectivist and collaborative elements of growth mind set theory also need to be strengthened and emphasized. We suggest that instead of trying to modify individual mindsets mainly with strategic organizational performance and growth outcomes as the focal point (Athota and Athota, 2021), a shift towards a 'common-good mindset' and from a 'me-thinking' to 'we-thinking' (Tavanti and Wilp, 2021), will be required at both an individual and organizational level if acceptance is be won for more socially responsible solutions which require a radical break with tradition and entrenched norms and patterns of behaviour.

We therefore draw on Sustainable HRM literature, especially the new CGHRM approach (Aust et al., 2020), on the one hand, and on the concept of 'growth mindset', on the other hand (Dweck, 2006), in the search for a human-centric solution to the challenge of sustainability. Our chapter has seven main parts. First, we follow our introduction by (2) discussing how a strategic HRM with a 'fixed mindset' has long played the *game* to achieve reputation power and status and is *set* in its ways, but now is challenged to transform its 'me-thinking' understandings of self-interest. We then (3) explore how the development of a specific growth or 'common-good mindset' (such as CGHRM), and a move in the direction of 'we-thinking' can help HRM to better align or *match* shareholder and stakeholder expectations. In our next section (4), we compare strategic HRM with common-good HRM characteristics with a focus on mindset, HRM leadership, organizational culture and employee behaviour. We then move on to (5) discuss CGHRM implementation, and (6) CGHRM outcomes. Finally, (7) we draw our conclusions.

Strategic HRM and Fixed Mindset

According to mindset theory people with a fixed mindset regard abilities and skills as immutable and as a result view challenges and change as a risk rather than an opportunity (Dweck, 2006). HRM has long been associated (or rather dominated) by a strategic model based on the 'fixed mindset' assumption that HR practices should be aimed at utilizing the given talents and abilities of internal actors, for example by matching tasks with given skill. As a result, the discipline has become narrow-minded and overtly occupied with firm-centric individual antecedents of success and therefore resistant to change (Kaufman, 2020). At the same time, the implicit assumptions and personal dispositions of HR managers have been shown to impact procedural justice and the fairness of performance appraisals and consequently future employee behaviour (Heslin and VandeWalle, 2011). Therefore, context is important. Apart from continued bias, one side affect has been a disconnect from the fundamental socio-psychological needs and perceptions of employees as reflected in concerns about a lack of workplace fairness and opportunities to grow both professionally and personally as well as with the wider community and the concerns of broader stakeholders. As a result, HRM has had a limited success in improving ever-deteriorating employee relations and has even less impact on addressing deeper societal challenges such as racial discrimination, gender inequality, unemployment and social justice (Stahl, Brewster, Collings and Hajro, 2020). However, in growth-orientated organizational cultures employees have been shown to develop innovative growth-orientated behaviours and be open to change and accept new challenges (Pavlatos and Ioakimidis, 2024).

Therefore, in the search for viable solutions, in this chapter, we contend that despite the decontextualized and deterministic nature of strategic business (and HRM) models, that a change in mindset is both possible and desirable (Schumann and Dweck, 2014) and that organizations can choose between a fixed closed mindset of constraining control or a more open and innovative mindset of collaborative growth (Murphy and Reeves, 2019). Whether HRM as an operative function has the power to question policy and influence established business norms and thinking is a matter of debate. It is however safe to say that the dominating psychological mindset has consequences not only for individual belief and motivation but also for policies and practices, and thus an organizations and HRs ability to become sustainable. For example, in a 'fixed mindset' culture which is characterized by an understanding that talent and ability is static, and which encourages people to be defensive, to compete for recognition, to grandstand and to show off their skills, a shift to organizational citizen behaviour and enhanced cooperation for societal benefit will be difficult to achieve (Özduran and Tanova, 2017). On the other hand, in organizations with a culture of growth which sends signals that intelligence and talent are malleable and can be developed encourages employees to be more optimistic, trustful and open and to develop new skills and collective ways of acting, a change towards more positive 'other-orientated' behaviour will be much easier (Rogers, Christian, Jennings and Lanaj, 2023).

However, to achieve this transition, we argue that HRM will need to drop the selfish *'game'* of me-thinking and its focus on normative promotionalism (Kaufman, 2020), to build a new common-good purpose and thus overcome mistrust, improve management–employee relations and engage with both internal and external stakeholders. This open and socially engaged communal approach is particularly important when addressing the complex multi-level challenge of sustainability.

Sustainable CGHRM and Growth Mindset

Tavanti and Wilp (2021) have put forward the idea of a common-good mindset towards sustainability which moves from 'me-thinking' to a more communal 'we-thinking' (which we suggest can be considered an example of a growth mindset). To enable this shift, they call for an integrated form of management training, a focus on building cooperative capabilities and importantly, the development of a mindset centred on achieving human and societal flourishing. Derived from the long tradition of the common good, as expressed in the humanistic and philosophical writings of Aristotle, Aquinas, Rousseau (and even Marx), this conceptualization of sustainability goes beyond single-purpose (materialistic, business) understandings to include the public benefit and wider happiness or eudaimonia, achieved through cooperation and congruence rather than competition and divergence. More recently in the domain of economics, Ostrom's principles of governing the commons (1990), provided a valuable framework of open dialogue stakeholder participation, self-management and democratic governance. Despite a renewed interest, support for a holistic and integrated commons standpoint has so far been weak in management circles. Even within the Sustainable HRM debate distinctly inward focused fixed mindset 'inside-out' models have tended to dominate (Matthews and Müller-Camen, 2025). As a result, more sweeping issues of inequality, societal justice, citizenship and empowerment which impact employee's quality of life and general well-being are seldom included in organizational sustainability agendas.

On the other hand, by encouraging a more integrated common-good mindset (Tavanti and Wilp, 2021) HRM gains a legitimate reason (and purpose) for example, to redirect resources towards the development and growth of worker capabilities and not just immediate job-related skills, in providing coaching to develop resilience against the difficulties of life and not just work-stress, and to support democratic processes to enhance efficacy and confidence and not just self-management aimed at improving efficiency and productivity. To reflect the need for a higher goal and more 'we' communality within the sustainable HRM paradigm, a CGHRM was developed. This is a critical-pragmatic and relational multi-stakeholder approach to work and employment relations, characterized by an outside-in perspective that emphasizes the importance of common-good values and the societal purpose of HRM in enabling maximum stakeholder empowerment. This approach aims to enhance an organization's socio-ecological impact by encouraging and developing individual and collective engagement and action (Matthews and Müller-Camen, 2025).

A core argument of this chapter is however that although CGRHM can be considered a contemporary example of a growth mindset towards (HR) sustainability, in order to be adopted it requires a managerial commitment to more societal and ethical HRM responsibility, and an openness to increased stakeholder participation and deliberate workplace democracy. Importantly, synchronically and in the face of increasing disengagement, loss of voice and HR–employee mistrust, Pham et al. (2023) have recently suggested that a CGHRM could indeed act as a driver of employee motivation and positive behavioural change. Others argue that CGHRM can help change attitudes and behaviours towards sustainability by creating a positive organizational culture based for example, on co-creation and collaboration (Aust, Cooke, Müller-Camen and Wood, 2024). Building on these propositions, and by introducing and further developing CGHRM within the narrative of positive organizational behaviour, we show how by questioning hierarchical assumptions and creating the right conditions, i.e., a community orientated mindset, opportunities for collective action, HR can positively contribute to reaching the goal of sustainability. And this without relying on or trying to accommodate single-purpose, market-based ideologies and restrictive mentalities. To underline the transformative nature of this model and to further strengthen our case for a HRM with a deeper societal purpose, we analyse the CGHRM-Mindset nexus with regard to characteristics, implementation and outcomes.

CGHRM Characteristics

As a sub-type of SustHRM, CGHRM has the same goal of human, economic and societal sustainability. It also has similar characteristics, such as a recognition of a lack of ethical values within business and an awareness of the negative impact of certain HRM norms and practices (Kramar, 2022). It has also been shown to have positive sustainable behavioural impacts, for example, to influence individual ethical behaviour via value commitment (Pham et al, 2023), build resilience to deal with uncertainty related to digitalization (Cooke, Dickmann and Parry, 2022) and increase the trustworthiness of sustainable reporting (Järlström, Saru, Viitasaari and Akrivou, 2024). From this worldview, CGHRM could be regarded as a type of SustHRM with simply a stronger focus on external stakeholders, and sustainable governance such as the United Nations sustainability goals, SDGs (Aust et al., 2020). At the same time, the strategic-sustainable HRM discussion is particularized by a number of inherent (e.g., efficiency vs capabilities, social legitimacy vs profitability, short-term success vs long-term sustainability) tensions (Kramar, 2022).

We argue that, through its intensity of engagement with these tensions that CGHRM has set its own a distinctive tone. As a result, its latest conceptualization (Matthews and Müller-Carmen, 2025), CGHRM has a gained a specific industrial relations profile and can be now considered a critical-pragmatic, relational and pluralistic answer to a HRM lacking in awareness of a need for investing in employee capabilities, workplace democracy and employee voice. This further development is important when considering the need to change established mindsets.

To illustrate our point, and to emphasize the necessity of a more collectivist framework, we compare (in Table 13.1) strategic and common-good HR approaches regarding differences in HR mindset, leadership, culture and behaviour.

A core characteristic of a CGHRM perspective is how organizational sustainability is inherently linked to the wider communal good. A *common-good HRM mindset* equates personal well-being with societal flourishing or collective happiness (eudaimonia). In comparison with strategic HRM, the inclusion of external stakeholders has therefore a higher priority, and HR needs to adopt practices to reflect this – for example, by developing a culture of 'we-thinking' and strengthening the societal and ecological dimensions of sustainable HRM strategies. As we show in Table 13.1, such a major reframing of business purpose means a new form of *values-based HRM leadership* will be required. Although questions of economics remain strategically important, more space is given to the ethical and socio-ecological impact (e.g., unemployment, gender equality, social justice and human rights) of decisions. This means that future HRM leaders will need an enhanced awareness of the grand challenges facing a diverse range of stakeholders and will be obliged to develop the necessary leadership styles and skills to (better) address them. Here, socio-relational concepts of global citizenship leadership (Torres and Bosio, 2020), and collective leadership (Eva, Cox, Herman and Lowe, 2021), which transcend traditional business-societal mind-frames and boundaries could gain more weight. Strong leadership commitment to broader responsibility for the commons could be reflected in a new and less-hierarchical *human-centric organizational culture* and empowering working environment which is both more sensitive to worker perceptions, feelings and beliefs, and also supportive of employee demands for agency, recognition and respect. As a result of opportunities for personal improvement

TABLE 13.1 SHRM – CGHRM Comparative Characteristics

Organizational Factors	*Strategic HRM*	*Sustainable CGHRM*
Mindset	'**Me**-thinking' Focus is mainly on **individual behaviour** and performance. **Fixed mindset**, focus on skill not development. Ability is a given, difficult if impossible to change. Implicit bias and explicit discrimination are reflected in HR practices, e.g., performance appraisals. Results in passive, mistrustful and disengaged employees. Employees act competitively, prioritize personal advantage.	'**We**-thinking' Focus on **collective behaviour** for collect common-good impact. **Growth mindset**. Abilities can be changed over time. Dependent on situational and contextual factors. Positive reflection and openness reduce bias and improves inclusion. Results in active, trusting and engaged employees. Employees act collaborative, more willing to support others.
Leadership	Based on the assumption that one type of **strong, top-down managerial leadership** is required to ensure behaviour is congruent with organizational goals. Leadership decisions driven mainly by strategic (share value) considerations.	Based on the assumption that better organizational performance is encouraged by **inclusive and shared leadership** which encourages enhanced participation, workplace democracy and diversity of opinion. Leadership decisions (also) driven by considerations of ethical societal and ecological impact.
Culture	**Hierarchical**, Firm-centric, Inside-out, Top-down. Organizational culture of efficiency, damage and risk avoidance and competitiveness. HRM focused on matching given skills with task requirements. Employees feel undervalued and utilized. Disengagement and resignation results.	**Empowering**, Human-centric, Outside-in, Bottom-up. Organizational culture of learning from mistakes, knowledge sharing and collaboration. HRM invests in personal development and ability enhancement. Employees feel understood and valued. A positive perception of HRM interventions develops.
Employee behaviour	HR strategy driven by an understanding that people are mainly extrinsically **motivated by self-interest**, are passively compliant, critic-sensitive and generally sceptic of change. Increased alienation and deviant behaviour.	HR strategy driven by the belief that people when intrinsically **motivated by shared meaning** and increased voice, become actively engaged, react positively to feedback, are more innovative and open to change. Increased org. identification and OCB.

employees would feel respected and valued, gain confidence and engage more. In turn, a CGHRM inspired ethical paradigm shift and *organizational citizenship behaviour* amongst employees contributes to combined individual, team and organizational success (Pham et al., 2023).

Despite a seemingly unbridgeable conflict of interest, we argue that, although a new mindset of collective responsibility requires a rethinking of current firm-centric HR approaches to sustainability and a compromise from a number of stakeholders, a win–win situation can still be created on the path to sustainability. Whereas the adoption of a CGHRM approach supports a working environment of trust, solidarity, respect and openness and will improve organizational performance, the resulting growth mindsets at multiple levels (Han and Stieha, 2020), will enable employees to perceive the challenge of sustainability as an opportunity to learn, change behaviour sustainably, find meaning in collective responsibility, grow as engaged members of their (team, organization, society) community and create common-good value. This positive orientation and optimism can only be in the long-term strategic interests of firms dependent on innovation and creativity. A major concern remains however, amongst scholars and practitioners alike, is whether and how a CGHRM can be implemented in an organizational landscape still dominated by fixed mainstream strategic shareholder considerations. In Table 13.2 we use the lens of growth mindset to make a few suggestions and explore CGHRM implementation across the dimensions of purpose, policy, processes and practice.

CGHRM Implementation

One of the main concerns related to collective action solutions in general and in our case CGHRM in particular is how to implement such an alternative model in practice. Especially, as a multi-level appeal for stakeholder-governance, it requires a totally new mindset and a very strong strategic-openness towards participation, dialogue and transparency. Presently, although multiple stakeholders (workers, customers, suppliers, distributors), are known to contribute to the process of firm value creation and appropriation (Tantalo and Priem, 2016), non-economic (societal, ecological) stakeholders are often sidelined in asymmetric economic strategies, including HRM, especially when profits or market share are in danger (Ritala, Albareda and Bocken, 2021). However, from a 'commons' perspective, complex global grand challenges require decisive, deeper and more democratic solutions based on a strong values-driven commitment to change but also clearly defined and negotiated social rules of engagement and the inclusion of civil society (Ferraro, Etzion and Gehman, 2015; Ostrom, 1990). Others argue for managers to have the courage for deeper change (Ergene, Banerjee and Hoffman, 2021) and perhaps adopt more participatory forms of organizing (Albareda and Sison, 2020). It is these calls to incorporate broader conceptualizations of purpose and into organizational strategy and to integrate workers, customers and suppliers in decision-making processes (which again involves a thinking reset), which provide a foundation for our suggestions for CGHRM implementation.

TABLE 13.2 CGHRM Implementation

Growth Mindset Attributions	*CGHRM Purpose*	*CGHRM Policy*	*CGHRM Processes*	*CGHRM Practices*
Learning	Shared common-good purpose and vision results in co-creation and reciprocal supportive learning.	A policy directed towards common-good impact encourages the development of skills and competencies to achieve sustainable change.	HR processes are designed to support a positive growth demeanor amongst managers and employees and an atmosphere of transparent communication.	HR practices are aimed at developing capabilities, for example by incorporating a growth mindset in training programs, recognizing the innovative value of experimentation, trial and error and learning from experience.
Motivation	Employee engagement is enhanced through a shared new social identity, workplace meaning and common purpose directed at sustainable change.	HR policy reflects an understanding that mindsets can be changed to positively influence human and organizational potential.	A growth mindset is embedded in all areas of HR policy with the aim of motivating and encouraging employee engagement.	HR practices such as recruiting training and career development are designed to motivate and support employees from day one in the organization. e.g., Coaching and mentoring, conflict resolution. Collective and intrinsic forms of motivation are prioritized to develop collective self-esteem and optimism.
Self-efficacy	A multi-stakeholder purpose enables HR managers to redefine their role as facilitators of self-efficacy.	HR policy and important strategic decisions are pro-active, courageous and based on the power of self-efficacy and belief in one's skills, talent and abilities.	HR processes are aimed at creating self-management and experiences of affirmative self-efficacy rather than demotivating control and command.	HR practices incorporate elements of democracy, job-ownership and self-management wherever possible.

Skills/capabilities	The purpose of HR is reframed in terms of developing capabilities rather than managing resources.	Policy mirrors an understanding that job-related skills alone are inadequate to equate people with the means to address barriers to flourishing and well-being.	HR processes are directed at building capabilities and a growth mindset to view challenges and difficulties as opportunities.	HR practices of training designed at developing competencies for personal growth. Recruiting practices are focused on future potential and values rather than current skills.
Trust/openness	A HR common-good purpose connects people in an atmosphere of collective responsibility, respect for each other and openness.	A CGHRM mindset influencing a policy of transparency and openness increases the authenticity of Org. sustainable reports.	HR processes are characterized by CGV´s of solidarity, dignity, trust and reciprocity.	CGHRM practices such as performance appraisal and career development are developed and refined through a democratic process of constant feedback and adjustment.
Altruism	HR adopts a multi-stakeholder purpose aimed at increasing common-good value and the benefit of all.	HR policy Prioritizes cooperation over competition and collective interests over self-interest.	HR processes and structures encourage an altruistic mindset and establish common-good norms as the ethical standard.	Practices of pay and compensation offer incentives and reward for cooperation and selflessness.
Action/ engagement	A new CG mindset enables HR to adopt a purpose of pro-active sustainable engagement.	A managerial commitment to worker participation, polycentricity and collective action is visible in HR policy.	HR processes are supportive of active worker solidarity. Ample space and opportunity is provided for collective voice.	HR practices are designed to compensate for rather than mirror social inequalities and a lack of voice. E.g., through positive discrimination, flatter and more transparent pay systems.

By redefining the role of HRM and moving from single to multi- (common-good) purpose HRM is freed of the deterministic shackles of economic performance and shareholder value. This has several advantages with regard to mindset related behavioural attributions such as learning, motivation, skills, self-efficacy, trust and altruism. For example, a shared common-good purpose and vision centred on the societal value of work and collective well-being enables an atmosphere of co-creation and reciprocal supportive learning to emerge. Furthermore, from the perspective of a growth mindset, HR policy and practices encourage rather than hinder employees to make mistakes through trial and error and be creative and innovative. As a result, HRM policies can be redesigned, and resources reallocated to the task of developing the necessary skills and competencies to strengthen personal resilience and also achieve sustainable change while maintaining competitive advantage. Compared to earlier approaches here a truly integrative win–win situation can be created. To fortify this argument, we now discuss individual, team and organizational level CGHRM outcomes.

CGHRM Outcomes

Scholars argue that there is still a lack of understanding as to whether and if a CGHRM can support the (often considered contractionary) aims of sustainability and performance (Lu, Zhang, Yang and Wang, 2023). The traditional mindset has tended to be that any investment in sustainability (human, societal or ecological) benefit needs to produce also measurable benefits in economic (profit, market share) terms. Although there is evidence that in certain companies which are not primarily driven by profit, e.g., B-corps, this balance is easier to achieve (Aust et al., 2020), a solution needs to be found for mainstream (i.e. profit-driven) firms.

By approaching the issue from an alternative 'commons' direction, in Table 13.3 we show how by developing a positive growth mindset and adopting a CGHRM framework HRM can make a number of contributions to both enhanced sustainability and performance at an individual, team and organizational level. For example, at an individual level, increased opportunities for job-ownership, participation in decision making can lead to an increased sense of belonging and organizational identification and thus enhanced pride, quality of work and performance. CGHRM has indeed been shown to be a facilitator of organizational citizenship behaviour and positive reciprocal conduct (Pham et al., 2023).

At the level of the team, heightened productivity and effectiveness results from a more communal 'we' culture, collective efficacy and a CGHRM leadership which encourages shared success and collective well-being. Finally, at the organizational level, a new growth mindset reduces institutional resistance to change and enables HRM to better implement sustainable strategic goals. In addition, a HRM with a multi-level economic-socio-ecological purpose combined with fluid boundaries and increased responsibility for grand challenges enables HRM to access and utilize the knowledge and resources of external stakeholders to the benefit of all.

TABLE 13.3 CGHRM Outcomes

	Organizational Performance	*Organizational Sustainability*
Individual	Individual productivity is increased by a positive attitude and belief in ability to reach set goals. Increased self-efficacy and confidence results in hope, resilience, well-being and job-satisfaction. Self-management, task-ownership and organizational identification leads to increases in pride, quality of work and performance.	Individual pro-societal and sustainable behaviour is strengthened by a common-good growth mindset. CGV organizational embeddedness strengthens the acceptance of HR sustainable and green agendas at an individual level – and fosters a willingness to adapt behaviour accordingly.
Team	Team identity and performance is enhanced by a culture of trust, reciprocity and collaboration. A shared CG purpose deepens team motivation engagement and cohesion.	The shift to a 'we-mind-frame' supports a strong team identity and builds support for green and common-good initiatives. The boundaries between internal and external stakeholders become more fluid and increases understanding for more collective socially responsible involvement.
Organizational	A CGHRM mindset results in increased cooperation, a positive culture of mistakes, leading to innovation and creativity. An organizational growth mindset lowers institutional resistance to change and makes it easier to implement and meet new strategic goals.	Increased communication, transparency and trust results in enhanced legitimacy for Org. level Sustainability interventions. Opportunities for debate, participation and collective action limits the danger of greenwashing. A common-good mindset which enables CGHRM improves the trustworthiness of Sustainability reporting.

Conclusions

The goal of sustainability remains a major strategic challenge for organizations. Failure on the part of HRM to convince employees of the need to positively change behaviour is undermining the legitimacy of HRM as contributor to organizational success and to reach the aim of sustainability. A historical and systemic disconnect between a (perceived managerial and shareholder centric) strategic HRM and (the rapidly shifting) needs and interests of workers has made this task more difficult.

Driven by a fixed mindset of single purpose, and by conventions of individual performance, HRM is unable to overcome resistance to change, attitudes of mistrust nor to positively influence behaviour. A mindset revision and new conceptualization of HRM is therefore indispensable if progress is to be achieved. By allocating HRM a new multi-stakeholder purpose orientated towards societal benefit (incorporating individual and collective flourishing), a human-centric CGHRM involving a shift from a 'me' to 'we' culture can help a growth mindset develop, create new norms of collaboration and facilitate the emergence of new forms of (desired, organizational citizenship) behaviour.

References

Albareda, L., & Sison, A. J. G. (2020). Commons organizing: Embedding common good and institutions for collective action. Insights from ethics and economics. *Journal of Business Ethics*, *166*(4), 727–743.

Athota, V. S. (2021). *Mind over matter and artificial intelligence: Building employee mental fitness for organisational success*, Palgrave MacMillan: Singapore .

Aust, I., Matthews, B., & Müller-Camen, M. (2020). Common good HRM: A paradigm shift in sustainable HRM? *Human Resource Management Review*, *30*(3), 100705.

Aust, I., Cooke, F. L., Müller-Camen, M., & Wood, G. (2024). Achieving sustainable development goals through common-good HRM: Context, approach and practice. *German Journal of Human Resource Management*, *38*(2), 93–110.

Baldassari, P., Eberhard, S., Jiang, Y., Muller-Camen, M., Obereder, L., Schiffinger, M., & Thiele, R. (2023). Looking up and fitting in: Team leaders' and members' behaviors and attitudes toward the environment in an MNC. *Human Resource Management*, *62*(3), 267–282.

Caniëls, M. C., Semeijn, J. H., & Renders, I. H. (2018). Mind the mindset! The interaction of proactive personality, transformational leadership and growth mindset for engagement at work. *Career Development International*, *23*(1), 48–66.

Cooke, F. L., Dickmann, M., & Parry, E. (2022). Building sustainable societies through human-centred human resource management: Emerging issues and research opportunities. *The International Journal of Human Resource Management*, *33*(1), 1–15.

Duchi, L., Lombardi, D., Paas, F., & Loyens, S. M. (2020). How a growth mindset can change the climate: The power of implicit beliefs in influencing people's view and action. *Journal of Environmental Psychology*, *70*, 101461.

Dweck, C. S. (2006). *Mindset: The new psychology of success*. Random House.

Dweck, C. S., & Molden, D. C. (2005). Self-Theories: Their Impact on Competence Motivation and Acquisition. In A. J. Elliot & C. S. Dweck (Eds.), *Handbook of competence and motivation* (pp. 122–140). Guilford Publications.

Ehnert, I. (2013). Paradox as a lens for theorizing sustainable HRM: Mapping and coping with paradoxes and tensions. In I. Ehnert, H. Wes, & K. J. Zink (Eds.), *Sustainability and human resource management: Developing sustainable business organizations* (pp. 247–271). Springer: Berlin Heidelberg.

Eva, N., Cox, J. W., Herman, H. M., & Lowe, K. B. (2021). From competency to conversation: A multi-perspective approach to collective leadership development. *The Leadership Quarterly*, *32*(5), 101346.

Ergene, S., Banerjee, S. B., & Hoffman, A. J. (2021). (Un) sustainability and organization studies: Towards a radical engagement. *Organization Studies*, *42*(8), 1319–1335.

Ferraro, F., Etzion, D., & Gehman, J. (2015). Tackling grand challenges pragmatically: Robust action revisited. *Organization Studies*, *36*(3), 363–390.

Forsythe, A., & Johnson, S. (2017). Thanks, but no-thanks for the feedback. *Assessment & Evaluation in Higher Education*, *42*(6), 850–859.

Han, S. J., & Stieha, V. (2020). Growth mindset for human resource development: A scoping review of the literature with recommended interventions. *Human Resource Development Review*, *19*(3), 309–331.

Heslin, P. A., & VandeWalle, D. (2011). Performance appraisal procedural justice: The role of a manager's implicit person theory. *Journal of Management*, *37*(6), 1694–1718.

Hochanadel, A., & Finamore, D. (2015). Fixed and growth mindset in education and how grit helps students persist in the face of adversity. *Journal of International Education Research*, *11*(1), 47–50.

Järlström, M., Saru, E., Viitasaari, M., & Akrivou, K. (2024). Integrating 'common good' authenticity for sustainable human resource management reporting. *German Journal of Human Resource Management*, 23970022241229035.

Kaufman, B. E. (2020). The real problem: The deadly combination of psychologisation, scientism, and normative promotionalism takes strategic human resource management down a 30-year dead end. *Human Resource Management Journal*, *30*(1), 49–72.

King, D., & Cohen, E. (2023). Human resources management: Developing a sustainability mindset. In P. Moltan-Hill (Ed.), *Sustainable management* (pp. 265–291). Routledge: Abdington.

Kramar, R. (2022). Sustainable human resource management: Six defining characteristics. *Asia Pacific Journal of Human Resources*, *60*(1), 146–170.

Lu, Y., Zhang, M. M., Yang, M. M., & Wang, Y. (2023). Sustainable human resource management practices, employee resilience, and employee outcomes: Toward common good values. *Human Resource Management*, *62*(3), 331–353.

Matthews, B. Obereder, L., Aust, I., & Müller-Camen, M. (2018). Competing paradigms: Status-quo and alternative approaches in HRM. In D. Renwick (Ed.), *Green HRM* (pp. 116–134). Routledge: London.

Matthews, B., & Müller-Camen, M. (2025). Sustainable HRM – A critical and commons-centric perspective. In Collins, D., Wood, G., & Szamosi (Eds.), *Human resource management—A critical approach* (3rd ed.). Routledge. (Conditionally accepted)

Mukonza, C., & Swarts, I. (2020). The influence of green marketing strategies on business performance and corporate image in the retail sector. *Business Strategy and the Environment*, *29*(3), 838–845.

Murphy, M. C., & Reeves, S. L. (2019). Personal and organizational mindsets at work. *Research in Organizational Behavior*, *39*, 100121.

Ostrom, E. (1990). *Governing the commons: The evolution of institutions for collective action*. Cambridge University Press.

Ostrom, E. (2009). A general framework for analyzing sustainability of social-ecological systems. *Science*, *325*(5939), 419–422.

Özduran, A., & Tanova, C. (2017). Manager mindsets and employee organizational citizenship behaviours. *International Journal of Contemporary Hospitality Management*, *29*(1), 589–606.

Paulet, R., Holland, P., & Morgan, D. (2021). A meta-review of 10 years of green human resource management: Is Green HRM headed towards a roadblock or a revitalisation? *Asia Pacific Journal of Human Resources*, *59*(2), 159–183.

Pavlatos, O., & Ioakimidis, M. (2024). Management accountants with a growth mindset and changes in the design of costing systems: The role of organisational culture. *Accounting & Finance*, *64*(2), 2085–2110.

Pham, N. T., Jabbour, C. J. C., Pereira, V., Usman, M., Ali, M., & Vo-Thanh, T. (2023). Common good human resource management, ethical employee behaviors, and organizational citizenship behaviors toward the individual. *Human Resource Management Journal, 33*(4), 977–1000.

Podgorodnichenko, N., Edgar, F., & McAndrew, I. (2020). The role of HRM in developing sustainable organizations: Contemporary challenges and contradictions. *Human Resource Management Review, 30*(3), 100685.

Richards, J. (2022). Putting employees at the centre of sustainable HRM: A review, map and research agenda. *Employee Relations, 44*(3), 533–554.

Ritala, P., Albareda, L., & Bocken, N. (2021). Value creation and appropriation in economic, social, and environmental domains: Recognizing and resolving the institutionalized asymmetries. *Journal of Cleaner Production, 290*, 125796.

Rogers, B. A., Christian, J. S., Jennings, R. E., & Lanaj, K. (2023). The growth mindset at work: Will employees help others to develop themselves? *Academy of Management Discoveries, 9*(1), 67–92.

Schumann, K., & Dweck, C. S. (2014). Who accepts responsibility for their transgressions? *Personality and Social Psychology Bulletin, 40*(12), 1598–1610.

Stahl, G. K., Brewster, C. J., Collings, D. G., & Hajro, A. (2020). Enhancing the role of human resource management in corporate sustainability and social responsibility: A multi-stakeholder, multidimensional approach to HRM. *Human Resource Management Review, 30*(3), 100708.

Tahir, R., Athar, M. R., & Afzal, A. (2020). The impact of greenwashing practices on green employee behaviour: Mediating role of employee value orientation and green psychological climate. *Cogent Business & Management, 7*(1), 1781996.

Tantalo, C., & Priem, R. L. (2016). Value creation through stakeholder synergy. *Strategic Management Journal, 37*(2), 314–329.

Tavanti, M., & Wilp, E. A. (2021). Common good mindset: The public dimensions of sustainability. In A. A. Ritz & I. Rimanoczy (Eds.), *Sustainability mindset and transformative leadership: A multidisciplinary perspective*, 241–265, Palgrave Macmillan: Cham.

Torres, C. A., & Bosio, E. (2020). Global citizenship education at the crossroads: Globalization, global commons, common good, and critical consciousness. *Prospects, 48*(3), 99–113.

Yoder, L., Wagner, C. H., Sullivan-Wiley, K., & Smith, G. (2022). The promise of collective action for large-scale commons dilemmas. *International Journal of the Commons, 16*(1), 47–63.

14

METHODOLOGICAL DEVELOPMENTS AND CHALLENGES IN POSITIVE TRAIT ASSESSMENT

Gloria Liou, Andy Jiang, and Louis Tay

With substantial and growing interest in positive organizational scholarship, positivity assessment has become a key research area in both organizational behavior and positive psychology. While positivity assessment can cover an extensive range of constructs that span both types and levels (e.g., purpose, subjective well-being, positive relationships) (Allen & McCarthy, 2015; Seligman, 2011; Seligman & Csikszentmihalyi, 2000), we focus on individual attributes in this chapter as we believe the assessment of positive individual attributes has particularly unique challenges and recent methodological developments. Furthermore, the domain of positive individual attributes is one of the three issues positive psychology seeks to address according to the founders of positive psychology (Seligman & Csikszentmihalyi, 2000) as well as leading positive psychologists today (Feraco et al., 2022; Fowers et al., 2021; McGrath, 2023).

Assessing positive individual attributes—often called *strengths and virtues* (Peterson & Seligman, 2004) in the literature—is of interest to individuals, organizations, and societies. Individuals may be interested in identifying positive traits and learning how to activate them, as positive traits have been shown to improve work and life outcomes (Littman-Ovadia et al., 2014; Schutte & Malouff, 2019). For organizations, there is increasing evidence that positive individual attributes are valuable for predicting key organizational outcomes, such as job performance, work engagement, job satisfaction, and prosocial behavior (Freidlin & Littman-Ovadia, 2020; Harzer & Ruch, 2014; Heintz & Ruch, 2020; Hou et al., 2020; van Woerkom et al., 2016; van Woerkom & Meyers, 2015). Unsurprisingly, organizations have begun assessing these positive traits (Crossan et al., 2013; Matthews et al., 2006; Offstein & Dufresne, 2007; Wang & Hackett, 2016). For societies, there is a need to cultivate these positive attributes in their members, and more educational institutions are implementing ways to conduct such assessments

DOI: 10.4324/9781032619385-14

TABLE 14.1 The Virtues and Strengths in the Character Strengths and Virtues (CSV) Handbook

Virtues	*Strengths*
Wisdom	Creativity, curiosity, judgment, love of learning, perspective
Courage	Bravery, perseverance, honesty, zest
Humanity	Love, kindness, social intelligence
Justice	Teamwork, fairness, leadership
Temperance	Forgiveness, humility, prudence, self-regulation
Transcendence	Appreciation of beauty and excellence, gratitude, hope, humor, spirituality

within the education domain (Climie & Henley, 2016). There is even ongoing discussion on how economic models can incorporate and assess virtues (Heckman et al., 2023).

A key concern then is our ability to measure positive traits well, as their assessment yields important theoretical implications and real-world consequences. To successfully study and implement positivity assessment, we believe it is critical to have an understanding of the measures used today and the challenges they bring. To this end, we begin by reviewing dedicated measures that have been developed for positive trait assessment and other related measures used in the field. Next, we discuss recent developments and challenges of popular approaches to positivity trait measurement—as well as strategies to overcome these challenges. We conclude with future research directions.

Positive Trait Measures

The Character Strengths and Virtues (CSV) handbook (2004) is the foundation on which positive trait measures were developed (Peterson & Seligman, 2004). In their handbook, Peterson and Seligman used a top-down theoretical approach to identify a set of positive traits. These traits included six virtues under which 24 character strengths were classified (see Table 14.1); the character strengths represented measurable expressions of the virtues that people could cultivate (Peterson & Seligman, 2004). This proposed six-factor structure of positivity has been partly supported by some research (Giuliani et al., 2020; Ruch et al., 2020; Ruch & Proyer, 2015), but most studies found three or four factors to be a better fit, and there is a recognition that more work needs to ascertain the underlying structure.

The Values in Action Inventory of Strengths (VIA-IS)

The Values in Action Inventory of Strengths (VIA-IS) is a positive trait measure used to assess CSV in both general positive psychology and positive organizational psychology (Linley et al., 2007). The VIA-IS consists of 240 Likert-style, self-report items designed to measure the CSV's 24 character strengths (ten items per strength) in adults. Respondents rate each item from 1 (very much unlike me) to 5 (very much like me) based on whether the statement describes what they are like (Linley et al., 2007). Sample items include "at least once a day, I stop and count my blessings," an item measuring gratitude, and "I know that I will succeed with the goals I set for myself," an item measuring hope.

In recent years, several adaptations of the VIA-IS have been developed—reduced and revised measures, a measure for adolescents, and VIA-IS translations in other (not English) languages. The VIA-120 was developed by taking the five (of ten total) scale items with the highest total-item correlations for each character strength, reducing the assessment from 240 to 120 items while maintaining good validity and reliability (VIA Institute, 2024). Similarly, the VIA-72 was developed by taking the three items with the highest total-item correlations; validity and reliability were lower than the original VIA-IS but still acceptable (VIA Institute, 2024).

In 2017, the VIA Institute released the VIA-IS-R, a substantially revised version of the VIA-IS. The VIA-IS-R consists of 192 scale items selected based on content validity, internal consistency reliability, differential correlation with other scales, and reading level (VIA Institute, 2024). In addition to incorporating the CSV model and VIA-IS items, the VIA-IS-R seeks to represent McGrath's model of three virtues (McGrath, 2015)—caring (heart), inquisitiveness (mind), and self-control (gut)—into the assessment. Two reduced versions of the VIA-IS-R have been developed. The VIA-IS-M was developed by taking the four scale items with the highest total-item correlation for each character strength in the VIA-IS-R, resulting in 92 items (VIA Institute, 2024). The VIA-IS-P was developed with the same strategy but only with VIA-IS-R items keyed in the positive direction (VIA Institute, 2024).

As with the VIA-IS, the Values in Action Inventory for Youth (VIA-Youth) measures the CSV's 24 character strengths but uses different scale items that are more suitable for youth ages 10–17 (Park & Peterson, 2006). Although the workforce primarily consists of adults, there are adolescent workers who may find the VIA-Youth items to be more relevant and results to be more usable. Identifying and developing character strengths may also influence adolescents' vocational interests and decisions regarding future employment. For organizations seeking to assess positive traits in their adolescent workers, the VIA-Youth could serve as an addition or alternative to the VIA-IS. Finally, the (original) VIA-IS has been translated into 40 languages, and those translations with sufficient respondents have been evaluated for reliability (VIA Institute, 2024); the reduced and revised VIA-IS versions have also been translated into several, but fewer, languages.

The Comprehensive Inventory of Virtuous Instantiations of Character (CIVIC)

Recently, there has been increased interest in a more data-driven, bottom-up approach to the assessment of positive traits. The Comprehensive Inventory of

Virtuous Instantiations of Character (CIVIC) was developed using this approach, with a focus on psychometric properties and appropriate modeling of trait items using exploratory structural equation modeling (ESEM) (Ng et al., 2018). Through an iterative process of item selection and refinement, Ng and colleagues (2018) created a measure of positive traits—conceptualized as *character* rather than strengths and virtues—with a consistent factor structure across multiple samples. The CIVIC factor structure revealed eight higher-order *character cores* of appreciation, intellectual engagement, fortitude, interpersonal consideration, sincerity, temperance, transcendence, and empathy. Additionally, Ng and colleagues (2018) examined the relationship between these character cores and personality and found that although they were moderately to highly associated, character and personality predicted outcomes differently. While personality dimensions explained more variance in mental ill-being (i.e., depression and anxiety), character dimensions explained more variance in a range of well-being and flourishing constructs (e.g., subjective well-being, physical health, social support, basic psychological needs) and moral constructs (e.g., moral identity, moral foundations).

Related Measures

In addition to assessments dedicated to positive traits, there are existing measures for several traditionally "descriptive" traits that are acknowledged by positive psychologists as having qualities of positive traits. For example, studies have found that agreeableness is strongly and positively related to both character (Ng et al., 2018) and well-being (Castellani et al., 2016). Studies have also found relationships with other Five-Factor personality traits, including extraversion, conscientiousness, and emotional stability (Anglim et al., 2020; Castellani et al., 2016; Cosentino & Castro Solano, 2017; Ng et al., 2018). This is not surprising given that developing the qualities of agreeableness, conscientiousness, and emotional stability are signs of maturity as we age (Hogan & Roberts, 2004).

Furthermore, Honesty-Humility—the sixth factor of HEXACO personality (Lee & Ashton, 2008)—has conceptual overlap with positive trait measures and can constitute a positive trait as well. *Honesty* and *humility* are both character strengths in the CSV classification, and the Honesty-Humility trait measures "the tendency to be fair and genuine in dealing with others, in the sense of cooperation with others even when one might exploit others without suffering retaliation" (Ashton & Lee, 2007, p. 156), touching on additional character strengths of *fairness* and *kindness*. Although there has been little empirical research on the relationship between HEXACO personality traits and character, studies have found that Honesty-Humility to be strongly and positively related to well-being (Anglim et al., 2020). Therefore, we argue that traditional personality traits can also constitute measures of positive trait assessments.

Challenges with Self-Report Surveys

The current paradigm often utilizes self-report measures to assess positive traits. Self-report measures have been shown to produce numerous methodological challenges (Podsakoff et al., 2003; Schwab, 2004), and there are several challenges that are especially salient in positivity assessment—social desirability, global positivity factor, and transient states. Additionally, there are concerns about measuring "too much of a good thing" as there is evidence that, in some cases, a moderate amount of a positive trait may be more effective than higher degrees of that trait (Vergauwe et al., 2017a, 2017b).

Social Desirability

Social desirability refers to the tendency of some people to respond to items more as a result of their desire for social acceptability than their true feelings (Podsakoff et al., 2003). In the case of positivity and general trait assessment, people may choose responses that represent higher levels of socially desired traits, especially in selection contexts when there is an assumed "correct" answer (Morgeson et al., 2007; Osin, 2009; Roulin & Krings, 2020; Wood et al., 2022). This type of faking behavior has been found in other individual difference assessments in high-stakes situations (e.g., personnel selection contexts), such as in assessments of Five-Factor personality (i.e., extraversion, conscientiousness, agreeableness, emotional stability, openness to experience), competitiveness, and innovativeness (Morgeson et al., 2007; Roulin & Krings, 2020).

Researchers have proposed several strategies to overcome social desirability, many of which are drawn from the faking literature. For example, some studies have found that the use of warnings during the assessment to answer truthfully has reduced instances of faking—both negative warnings that dishonest responding will invalidate assessment scores and positive warnings providing encouragement that honest responding leads to usable scores (Converse et al., 2008; Oswald & Hough, 2011). Others have found that forced-choice procedures, where the respondent is forced to select from statements that were already made rather than creating their own statements, may reduce faking (Ng et al., 2021; Oswald & Hough, 2011; Ryan & Ployhart, 2014). Measuring social desirability and controlling its effect can also mitigate some of the effects when conducting analyses on self-report measures (Larson, 2019).

Global Positivity Factor

The global positivity factor is a hypothetical general factor of positive traits—the idea that a single underlying factor can account for the positive correlations among the different positive traits (Ng et al., 2017). This general factor may be a higher-order latent trait or the result of a one-factor structure underlying a given model. Alternatively, the global positivity factor could be a result of socially desirable responses applied across assessment items (Macdonald et al., 2008).

Ng and colleagues (2017) proposed bifactor modeling as an approach to mitigating this methodological challenge. Unlike other approaches (e.g., second-order modeling), bifactor modeling allows for (easy) detection of group factors when group factors are not independent of the general factor (Chen et al., 2006; Ng et al., 2017). Bifactor modeling also has fewer restrictions in the variance accounted for by the general factor in lower-order factor loadings (Chen et al., 2006; Ng et al., 2017). With these two features, bifactor modeling can provide a representative factor structure of positive traits in spite of the global positivity factor, as well as a nuanced understanding of the impact of that general factor. More generally, this points conceptually to whether there is a global positive trait factor (i.e., good–bad) that needs to be accounted for in all positive trait assessments.

Impact from Transient States

Transient state effects refer to the influence of recent events (e.g., interaction with a disgruntled customer, a bad day at the office, receiving a compliment from a boss or co-worker) on the manner in which people view themselves and the world around them (Podsakoff et al., 2003). Transient states are a particular concern for positivity assessment. As an example, one can easily imagine how a recent negative event (e.g., a death in the family, getting fired) could change a person's response to "at least once a day, I stop and count my blessings," a sample VIA-IS item from above. A person's response to "I know that I will succeed with the goals I set for myself," the other sample item, may be (temporarily) lowered for someone who worked hard for and expected a promotion but recently learned they did not get it.

To reduce the effect of transient states, global self-reports usually include words such as "in general" in the question to help respondents think more broadly about the construct being measured, shifting their attention away from their current mood to reduce the effect of transient mood. Another approach is through the experience sampling method (ESM) to limit the effect of transient mood on self-report measures by asking the same questions multiple times between different time intervals. With such data, one could aggregate multiple instances to obtain estimates of positive traits over time, or use latent state-trait (LST) theory, which helps to separate traits from transient state and situation influences (Steyer et al., 1999). Furthermore, a revised version of LST (LST-R) contains more formally defined theoretical concepts that are useful for the formation of statistical analysis models; models derived from this theory help to separate traits from situational effects, method effects, and measurement errors in longitudinal and intervention studies (Steyer et al., 2015, 2023).

Too Much of a Good Thing

The core idea of Too Much of a Good Thing (TMGT) in organizational research is that too much of a good thing—particularly positive traits—is ultimately bad

(Grant & Schwartz, 2011; Pierce & Aguinis, 2013; cf. Ng & Tay, 2020). In other words, the optimal level of a predictor variable is less likely to be found at the high (or low) end of the continuum but closer to the middle; more is not always better, and there is an inflection point after which further increases of a desirable trait become counterproductive. Researchers have found evidence of this curvilinear effect in a number of positive traits, including charisma (Vergauwe et al., 2017b), work passion (Astakhova, 2015), and extraversion (Blickle et al., 2015).

Although these curvilinear TMGT effects are challenging to identify, Vergauwe and colleagues (2017a) developed an alternative rating scale methodology—the too little/too much (TLTM) scale—that allows for a more direct test of curvilinear associations and is aligned with the TMGT philosophy. Studies found that using the TLTM response format added incremental validity over Likert-style ratings for several predictor variables and improved the detection of curvilinear predictor–criterion relationships (Vergauwe et al., 2017a).

Developments and Challenges with Other-Reports

In addition to self-report measures, researchers have used other-report methods in positivity assessment. The study of well-being in particular has relied on other-report measures for decades (Diener, 1994; Lepper, 1998), including reports from spouses, relatives, and close friends (e.g., Fritz et al., 2010; Koydemir & Schütz, 2012; Lepper, 1998). There have been developments in other-reports of positive traits as well. Researchers have examined a peer-rating form (i.e., perspective change) of the VIA-IS and found high convergence between self- and peer-ratings (Buschor et al., 2013; Ruch et al., 2020). Other studies have developed their own other-report instruments to measure character strengths particularly pertinent in a given organization (e.g., the military; Bang et al., 2016). While there are unique strengths associated with other-reports, such as overcoming self-report biases and impression management, they have their own unique set of challenges. As a type of survey reporting, they share some similar challenges with self-reports (Podsakoff et al., 2003; Schwab, 2004), and issues such as halo effects, rater leniency effects, and rater severity effects, are particularly salient in positivity assessment.

Halo Effects

Halo or halo error is a psychological process in which a rater forms an overall impression of the merit or standing of a ratee prior to assigning ratings; the overall rater impression leads to unrealistically large correlations between scores for different positive traits given by the rater to the ratee (i.e., halo effect) (Stanley, 1961; Thorndike, 1920; Viswesvaran et al., 2005). Due to the idiosyncratic rater impressions, halo effect produces psychometric issues by inflating within-rater reliabilities and deflating between-rater reliabilities. Recent research shows that there is a global positivity effect when people rate others' traits (Rau et al., 2021), which will particularly affect the assessment of positive traits.

Although they all result in large correlations between scores, halo effect is conceptually and empirically distinct from effects of general factors in ratings and true interdimensional correlations (Viswesvaran et al., 2005). From a measurement standpoint, it is critical to separate halo effect from these other effects, and there has been research on methods to isolate and statistically account for (i.e., reduce) halo (Harvey, 1982; Hulin, 1982; Landy et al., 1982; Viswesvaran et al., 2005). Additionally, researchers have suggested that focusing on specific, observable behaviors rather than global judgments and using objective and standardized criteria for evaluations may reduce halo effect (e.g., for humility; Van Tongeren et al., 2023a, 2023b).

Rater Leniency and Severity Effects

Rater leniency and severity errors occur when a rater gives consistently high or low ratings to all ratees, regardless of evidence for high or low levels of a trait or trait dimension (Podsakoff et al., 2003; Schwab, 2004). Rater leniency and severity errors have detrimental effects on the validity of ratings as the ratings no longer reflect true scores and differences. In extreme cases, identical ratings across all ratees effectively render the assessment useless for decision making.

These rater errors may be a result of the rater's personal beliefs, interpersonal dynamics, culture, and ability (Mishra & Roch, 2013; Ng et al., 2011; Tanaka & Ross, 2023; Varma et al., 2005). The mitigation strategies for leniency and severity effects overlap with those for halo effects, including focus on behaviors, use of objective criteria, and statistical methods to remove error (Brown et al., 2017; Maul, 2013; Myford & Wolfe, 2004). In addition, researchers should seek to obtain multiple raters, ideally from diverse backgrounds, in order to reduce these idiosyncratic effects pertaining to rater biases.

Developments and Challenges with Data Science Methods

Data science methods continue to grow in psychology, and an emerging amount of positivity assessment research uses these methods. For example, several researchers have used text mining analysis of social media language to study human flourishing (Cebral-Loureda et al., 2023) and well-being (Li et al., 2023; Sametoğlu et al., 2023). For positive traits specifically, Pang and colleagues (2020) found that Twitter (now X) posts can be used to characterize and predict the 24 character strengths of VIA-IS (Pang et al., 2020). Additionally, Leutner and colleagues (2020) investigated the use of chatbot-based and game-based assessments, which aggregate numerous unconventional behavioral data points (e.g., response time, ability to adapt to changing scenarios), to study emotion management and emotional recognition (Leutner et al., 2020), associated with the character strengths of *self-regulation* and *judgment*. As data science methods are increasingly used to assess positive traits, it is important to understand the challenges of these methods.

In this section, we focus on the challenges of organic data, ground truth measures, and machine learning measurement bias—see Liou et al. (2022) for an overview of psychometric issues in technology-based assessments.

Challenges with Organic Data

Data science methods often rely on *organic data*—data that are not generated through intentional research design (e.g., surveys, lab experiments). Instead, organic data are typically "incidental outputs" of technology systems, including social media platforms, search engines, and traffic cameras (Liou et al., 2022). These technology systems provide large and constantly increasing amounts of data, which is critical for performing data science methods that rely on data quantity.

A primary challenge with organic data comes from the technology systems themselves, which are controlled by external parties. These external parties frequently make substantial changes to their systems, which have downstream effects on the data generated. For example, a social media platform changing its word limit on posts would affect what users write and subsequently, what social media text data is available to collect and analyze (Boot et al., 2019; Cao et al., 2022). These changes are particularly concerning for test–retest reliability, which would be difficult if not impossible to assess as there are different features and data available at each time point. Additionally, organic data reflect factors unique to the technology systems (Liou et al., 2022). For example, while the use of (im)polite language on social media may reflect individual differences in positive traits, it likely also reflects social media policies on harassment and hate speech.

Range restriction is another challenge with organic data, and there have been several studies examining personality and social media data in particular. Research has found that openness and extraversion predict technology acceptance (Svendsen et al., 2013) and extraversion predicts the frequency of social media use (there have been results in both positive and negative directions; e.g., Blackwell et al., 2017; Moore & McElroy, 2012). Given the relationship between personality and positive traits (e.g., Anglim et al., 2020; Castellani et al., 2016; Cosentino & Castro Solano, 2017; Ng et al., 2018), it is reasonable to assume that positive traits may play some role in the availability of social media and other organic data (e.g., search engine data), introducing a potential confound. Furthermore, there are known racial, gender, class, and educational differences in technology use (Garg & Sengupta, 2019; Jackson et al., 2008; Yardi & Bruckman, 2012) that impact the availability of organic data.

Social desirability, discussed in Challenges with Self-Report Surveys, is worth noting in this section as well, especially regarding social media data. Many studies have found that people present an idealized (and inaccurate) version of themselves online (e.g., Möller et al., 2022; Zhao et al., 2008). Because people generally want to have—or at least pretend to have—strengths and virtues, it is likely that levels of positive traits will be inflated when using social media data.

Challenges with Ground Truth Measures

Data science methods often rely on a *ground truth measure* (or labeled data) that a model is trained to predict. For example, researchers building a model using Internet searches to assess curiosity, a character strength for wisdom, would need some other measure of curiosity to determine whether or not their model is accurate at predicting curiosity. Unfortunately, this ground truth measure is typically a self-report survey or other-report, so any issues from that measure would carry over into the model since the model is being evaluated on convergence with that specific measure rather than objective reality (Tay et al., 2020).

Another related methodological challenge is the (over-)emphasis on predictability that accompanies such models. With VIA-IS, CIVIC, and other individual difference scales, items are selected based on whether they sufficiently load onto the intended construct but also whether they do not load onto other irrelevant constructs (Liou et al., 2022; Tay et al., 2020). However, with data science methods, because the focus is on predictability, models optimize for maximizing convergence with measures of a given trait without minimizing convergence with irrelevant traits, creating issues around validity.

Machine Learning Measurement Bias

The models used in data science methods are increasingly machine learning (ML) based, and there is evidence that ML-based models in resume screening and interview assessments have led to bias with real-world consequences (Booth et al., 2021; Dastin, 2018). Measurement bias in ML-based models can occur when models yield different predictions (e.g., individual scores, group means) for different subgroups (e.g., race, gender) despite having the same ground truth score (Liou et al., 2022; Tay, Woo, et al., 2021). For example, if a man and a woman had the same score for kindness on the self-report survey the model was developed to predict, but the model assigned a higher score to the man than the woman, there would be measurement bias. Measurement bias can also occur when the model has different predictive accuracies for different groups, meaning that the model has a poorer fit for certain groups (Cheung & Rensvold, 2002; Tay et al., 2015), leading to poorer decision making for those groups and inequitable outcomes.

Measurement bias in ML-based models can be a result of biased data and/or biased model training (Liou et al., 2022). Biased data from the ground truth measure (e.g., using a biased self-report survey) and/or from the technology system (e.g., using provided posts from a social media company that is nonequivalent between subgroups) inevitably lead to bias in the model. On the other hand, biased model training occurs when the model uses different mechanisms to assign scores. For example, to maximize predictive accuracy for courage, a model might use two predictors (bravery, perseverance) for one subgroup and two different predictors (honesty, zest) for another subgroup. Even if a model used the same predictors, measurement bias can still occur if the predictors are weighted differently between subgroups (Liou et al., 2022)—for example, 50% bravery and 50% perseverance for one group, and 90% bravery and 10% perseverance for another group. See Tay, Woo, et al. (2021) for more information on investigating and mitigating machine learning measurement bias in psychological assessment.

Future Directions

The field of positive trait assessment is exciting, and we elaborate on four areas of future research directions among many different possibilities.

Within-Person Methods

Experience sampling methodology (ESM) (Csikszentmihalyi & Larson, 1987) is a within-person measurement technique developed by one of the founders of positive psychology, Mihaly Csikszentmihalyi. ESM has increasingly become relevant for assessing positive traits, particularly as psychology moves toward capturing the within-person variation of affect, personality, and other individual traits (Can, 2020; Conner et al., 2009; Dimotakis et al., 2011; Gabriel et al., 2019). Through ESM, researchers can better understand the temporal properties of positive feelings, behaviors, and actions related to positive traits. For example, ESM can be used to understand the ebb and flow of daily gratitude behaviors on a momentary basis and if it further differs among individuals (Nezlek et al., 2017). Moreover, with the advancement of technology, such methods are increasingly paired with passive sensor data collection that enables the capture of objective behaviors (e.g., GPS location, phone use) (Anderl et al., 2023; Müller et al., 2020; Thapa et al., 2021). It is critical to better understand how positive traits are related to different objective behaviors, particularly in light of the limitations of self-reports.

Multi-Level Methods

While individual positive traits form the basis of our understanding of positive attributes, we believe it is important to develop the assessment of positive traits and positive attributes more broadly at higher levels of analysis (e.g., teams, organizations, societies). While typical aggregation approaches (e.g., means) are often the standard ways of analyzing such data (Prewett et al., 2009), researchers should explore other distributional characteristics (e.g., variance, skewness) at higher levels of analysis (see Tay, Jebb, & Scotney, 2021). This allows us to determine the effects of how positivity may change group dynamics (e.g., skewness could reveal the extent to which a small group of individuals high on courage can change aspects of society). In addition, researchers can explore "referent-shift" rating methods (Chan, 1998) where individuals rate the positive attributes of their team, organization, or society (e.g., "my organization is humble") to determine if discrepancies between these views and self-views affect various valued outcomes.

Cultural Perspectives

While a tremendous amount of exciting work has focused on positive traits being universal (e.g., CSV), we believe that there are incredible cultural nuances. Tracking the decades of research in more "descriptive" human traits (i.e., personality), there has been both a recognition of the universality and the cultural specificity of these trait dimensions (Heine & Buchtel, 2009; Kubokawa & Ottaway, 2009). It appears that most of the current work on positive trait assessments emphasizes universality and takes an imposed etic approach assuming that all assessed dimensions are similar across cultures and languages. From such an etic approach, more work on cultural measurement equivalence—the extent to which positive trait measures developed in one culture can generalize to people in other cultures (Trimble, 2010)—should be conducted. Beyond etic approaches, we believe there needs to be more emic approaches to examine how different cultures understand and assess a variety of character traits and virtues. It may be that different taxonomies, emphases, or configurations are found with such approaches. Personality measures developed with consideration for certain contexts (e.g., culture) is an example of an emic approach as the measure accounts for individual differences that are more important for the considered culture (Burtaverde & Iliescu, 2019).

Automated Video Interviews

From a data science standpoint, there is emerging work using machine-learned automated behavioral techniques to assess human traits. These techniques help overcome limitations of self-reports and allow scaling of assessments to a large number of individuals at once. One technique that has been examined is automated video interviews which assess people on a given trait from their verbal, paraverbal, and nonverbal behaviors. Research shows that automated video interviews may be able to assess some dimensions of personality traits and can generalize to different interview questions (Hickman et al., 2022). We propose that future research explore automated video interviews for positive traits as a new form of positive trait assessment.

Conclusion

In this chapter, we discussed the importance of positive traits in key work and life outcomes and the development and use of the major positive trait measures used in the field. Additionally, we presented recent developments, challenges, mitigation strategies, and future research directions of positive trait assessment. We believe that our overview of the methodological developments and challenges in positive trait assessments will allow both researchers and practitioners to better understand why and how to assess positive individual attributes.

References

Allen, M., & McCarthy, P. (2015). Be happy in your work: The role of positive psychology in working with change and performance. *Journal of Change Management, 16*, 1–20. https://doi.org/10.1080/14697017.2015.1128471

Anderl, C., Hofer, M. K., & Chen, F. S. (2023). *Directly-measured smartphone screen time predicts well-being and feelings of social connectedness*. https://doi.org/10.25384/SAGE.22147820.v1

Anglim, J., Horwood, S., Smillie, L. D., Marrero, R. J., & Wood, J. K. (2020). Predicting psychological and subjective well-being from personality: A meta-analysis. *Psychological Bulletin, 146*(4), 279–323. https://doi.org/10.1037/bul0000226

Ashton, M. C., & Lee, K. (2007). Empirical, theoretical, and practical advantages of the HEXACO model of personality structure. *Personality and Social Psychology Review, 11*(2), 150–166. https://doi.org/10.1177/1088868306294907

Astakhova, M. N. (2015). The curvilinear relationship between work passion and organizational citizenship behavior. *Journal of Business Ethics, 130*(2), 361–374. https://doi.org/10.1007/s10551-014-2233-5

Bang, H., Eilertsen, D. E., Boe, O., & Nilsen, F. A. (2016). Development of an observational instrument (obscif) for evaluating character strengths in army cadets. *EDULEARN16 Proceedings*, 7803–7808. https://doi.org/10.21125/edulearn.2016.0711

Blackwell, D., Leaman, C., Tramposch, R., Osborne, C., & Liss, M. (2017). Extraversion, neuroticism, attachment style and fear of missing out as predictors of social media use and addiction. *Personality and Individual Differences, 116*, 69–72. https://doi.org/10.1016/j.paid.2017.04.039

Blickle, G., Meurs, J. A., Wihler, A., Ewen, C., Merkl, R., & Missfeld, T. (2015). Extraversion and job performance: How context relevance and bandwidth specificity create a non-linear, positive, and asymptotic relationship. *Journal of Vocational Behavior, 87*, 80–88. https://doi.org/10.1016/j.jvb.2014.12.009

Boot, A. B., Tjong Kim Sang, E., Dijkstra, K., & Zwaan, R. A. (2019). How character limit affects language usage in tweets. *Palgrave Communications, 5*(1), 1–13. https://doi.org/10.1057/s41599-019-0280-3

Booth, B. M., Hickman, L., Subburaj, S. K., Tay, L., Woo, S. E., & D'Mello, S. K. (2021). Bias and fairness in multimodal machine learning: A case study of automated video interviews. *Proceedings of the 2021 International Conference on Multimodal Interaction*, 268–277. https://doi.org/10.1145/3462244.3479897

Brown, A., Inceoglu, I., & Lin, Y. (2017). Preventing rater biases in 360-degree feedback by forcing choice. *Organizational Research Methods, 20*(1), 121–148. https://doi.org/10.1177/1094428116668036

Burtaverde, V., & Iliescu, D. (2019). Emic vs etic frame of reference personality assessment in the prediction of work-related outcomes. *Career Development International, 24*(7), 686–701. https://doi.org/10.1108/CDI-10-2018-0273

Buschor, C., Proyer, R. T., & Ruch, W. (2013). Self- and peer-rated character strengths: How do they relate to satisfaction with life and orientations to happiness? *The Journal of Positive Psychology, 8*(2), 116–127. https://doi.org/10.1080/17439760.2012.758305

Can, O. (2020). Experience sampling methodology: A systematic review and discussion for organizational research. *Electronic Journal of Business Research Methods, 18*(2), Article 2. https://doi.org/10.34190/JBRM.18.2.005

Cao, J., Hochmair, H. H., & Basheeh, F. (2022). The effect of Twitter app policy changes on the sharing of spatial information through Twitter users. *Geographies*, *2*(3), Article 3. https://doi.org/10.3390/geographies2030033

Castellani, V., Perinelli, E., Gerbino, M., & Caprara, G. V. (2016). Positive orientation and interpersonal styles. *Personality and Individual Differences*, *98*, 229–234. https://doi.org/10.1016/j.paid.2016.04.048

Cebral-Loureda, M., Hernández-Baqueiro, A., & Tamés-Muñoz, E. (2023). A text mining analysis of human flourishing on Twitter. *Scientific Reports*, *13*(1), 3403. https://doi.org/10.1038/s41598-023-30209-7

Chan, D. (1998). Functional relations among constructs in the same content domain at different levels of analysis: A typology of composition models. *Journal of Applied Psychology*, *83*(2), 234–246. https://doi.org/10.1037/0021-9010.83.2.234

Chen, F. F., West, S. G., & Sousa, K. H. (2006). A comparison of bifactor and second-order models of quality of life. *Multivariate Behavioral Research*, *41*(2), 189–225. https://doi.org/10.1207/s15327906mbr4102_5

Cheung, G. W., & Rensvold, R. B. (2002). Evaluating goodness-of-fit indexes for testing measurement invariance. *Structural Equation Modeling: A Multidisciplinary Journal*, *9*(2), 233–255. https://doi.org/10.1207/S15328007SEM0902_5

Climie, E., & Henley, L. (2016). A renewed focus on strengths-based assessment in schools. *British Journal of Special Education*, *43*(2), 108–121. https://doi.org/10.1111/1467-8578.12131

Conner, T. S., Tennen, H., Fleeson, W., & Barrett, L. F. (2009). Experience sampling methods: A modern idiographic approach to personality research. *Social and Personality Psychology Compass*, *3*(3), 292–313. https://doi.org/10.1111/j.1751-9004.2009.00170.x

Converse, P. D., Oswald, F. L., Imus, A., Hedricks, C., Roy, R., & Butera, H. (2008). Comparing personality test formats and warnings: Effects on criterion-related validity and test-taker reactions. *International Journal of Selection and Assessment*, *16*(2), 155–169. https://doi.org/10.1111/j.1468-2389.2008.00420.x

Cosentino, A. C., & Castro Solano, A. (2017). The high five: Associations of the five positive factors with the big five and well-being. *Frontiers in Psychology*, *8*. https://doi.org/10.3389/fpsyg.2017.01250

Crossan, M., Mazutis, D., Seijts, G., & Gandz, J. (2013). Developing leadership character in business programs. *Academy of Management Learning & Education*, *12*(2), 285–305. https://doi.org/10.5465/amle.2011.0024a

Csikszentmihalyi, M., & Larson, R. (1987). Validity and reliability of the experience-sampling method. *Journal of Nervous and Mental Disease*, *175*(9), 526–536. https://doi.org/10.1097/00005053-198709000-00004

Dastin, J. (2018). *Amazon scraps secret AI recruiting tool that showed bias against women.* Reuters. https://www.reuters.com/article/us-amazon-com-jobs-automationinsight/amazon-scraps-secret-ai-recruiting-tool-that-showed-bias-against-womenidUSKCN1MK08G/

Diener, E. (1994). Assessing subjective well-being: Progress and opportunities. *Social Indicators Research*, *31*(2), 103–157. https://doi.org/10.1007/BF01207052

Dimotakis, N., Scott, B. A., & Koopman, J. (2011). An experience sampling investigation of workplace interactions, affective states, and employee well-being. *Journal of Organizational Behavior*, *32*(4), 572–588. https://doi.org/10.1002/job.722

Feraco, T., Casali, N., Menenghetti, C., Greiff, S., & Cona, G. (2022). *Is good character all that counts? A comparison between the predictive role of specific strengths and a general factor of "good character" using a bifactor model.* OSF. https://doi.org/10.31234/osf.io/ab9tp

Fowers, B. J., Carroll, J. S., Leonhardt, N. D., & Cokelet, B. (2021). The emerging science of virtue. *Perspectives on Psychological Science*, *16*(1), 118–147. https://doi.org/10.1177/1745691620924473

Freidlin, P., & Littman-Ovadia, H. (2020). Prosocial behavior at work through the lens of character strengths. *Frontiers in Psychology*, *10*. https://doi.org/10.3389/fpsyg.2019.03046

Fritz, C., Yankelevich, M., Zarubin, A., & Barger, P. (2010). Happy, healthy, and productive: The role of detachment from work during nonwork time. *Journal of Applied Psychology*, *95*(5), 977–983. https://doi.org/10.1037/a0019462

Gabriel, A. S., Podsakoff, N. P., Beal, D. J., Scott, B. A., Sonnentag, S., Trougakos, J. P., & Butts, M. M. (2019). Experience sampling methods: A discussion of critical trends and considerations for scholarly advancement. *Organizational Research Methods*, *22*(4), 969–1006. https://doi.org/10.1177/1094428118802626

Garg, R., & Sengupta, S. (2019). "When you can do it, why can't I?": Racial and Socioeconomic differences in family technology use and non-use. *Proceedings of the ACM on Human-Computer Interaction*, *3*(CSCW), 63:1–63:22. https://doi.org/10.1145/3359165

Giuliani, F., Ruch, W., & Gander, F. (2020). Does the excellent enactment of highest strengths reveal virtues? *Frontiers in Psychology*, *11*. https://doi.org/10.3389/fpsyg.2020.01545

Grant, A. M., & Schwartz, B. (2011). Too much of a good thing: The challenge and opportunity of the inverted U. *Perspectives on Psychological Science*, *6*(1), 61–76. https://doi.org/10.1177/1745691610393523

Harvey, R. J. (1982). The future of partial correlation as a means to reduce halo in performance ratings. *Journal of Applied Psychology*, *67*(2), 171–176. https://doi.org/10.1037/0021-9010.67.2.171

Harzer, C., & Ruch, W. (2014). The role of character strengths for task performance, job dedication, interpersonal facilitation, and organizational support. *Human Performance*, *27*(3), 183–205. https://doi.org/10.1080/08959285.2014.913592

Heckman, J. J., Galaty, B., & Tian, H. (2023). *The economic approach to personality, character and virtue* (Working Paper 31258). National Bureau of Economic Research. https://doi.org/10.3386/w31258

Heine, S. J., & Buchtel, E. E. (2009). Personality: The universal and the culturally specific. *Annual Review of Psychology*, *60*, 369–394. https://doi.org/10.1146/annurev.psych.60.110707.163655

Heintz, S., & Ruch, W. (2020). Character strengths and job satisfaction: Differential relationships across occupational groups and adulthood. *Applied Research in Quality of Life*, *15*(2), 503–527. https://doi.org/10.1007/s11482-018-9691-3

Hickman, L., Bosch, N., Ng, V., Saef, R., Tay, L., & Woo, S. E. (2022). Automated video interview personality assessments: Reliability, validity, and generalizability investigations. *The Journal of Applied Psychology*, *107*(8), 1323–1351. https://doi.org/10.1037/apl0000695

Hogan, R., & Roberts, B. W. (2004). A socioanalytic model of maturity. *Journal of Career Assessment*, *12*(2), 207–217. https://doi.org/10.1177/1069072703255882

Hou, J., He, Y., Zhao, X., Thai, J., Fan, M., Feng, Y., & Huang, L. (2020). The effects of job satisfaction and psychological resilience on job performance among residents of the standardized residency training: A nationwide study in China. *Psychology, Health & Medicine*, *25*(9), 1106–1118. https://doi.org/10.1080/13548506.2019.1709652

Hulin, C. L. (1982). Some reflections on general performance dimensions and halo rating error. *Journal of Applied Psychology*, *67*(2), 165–170. https://doi.org/10.1037/0021-9010.67.2.165

Jackson, L. A., Zhao, Y., Kolenic, A., Fitzgerald, H. E., Harold, R., & Von Eye, A. (2008). Race, gender, and information technology use: The new digital divide. *Cyber Psychology & Behavior*, *11*(4), 437–442. https://doi.org/10.1089/cpb.2007.0157

Koydemir, S., & Schütz, A. (2012). Emotional intelligence predicts components of subjective well-being beyond personality: A two-country study using self- and informant reports. *The Journal of Positive Psychology*, *7*(2), 107–118. https://doi.org/10.1080/17439760.2011.647050

Kubokawa, A., & Ottaway, A. (2009). Positive psychology and cultural sensitivity: A review of the literature. *Graduate Journal of Counseling Psychology*, *1*(2).

Landy, F. J., Vance, R. J., & Barnes-Farrell, J. L. (1982). Statistical control of halo: A response. *Journal of Applied Psychology*, *67*(2), 177–180. https://doi.org/10.1037/0021-9010.67.2.177

Larson, R. B. (2019). Controlling social desirability bias. *International Journal of Market Research*, *61*(5), 534–547. https://doi.org/10.1177/1470785318805305

Lee, K., & Ashton, M. C. (2008). The HEXACO personality factors in the indigenous personality lexicons of English and 11 other languages. *Journal of Personality*, *76*(5), 1001–1054. https://doi.org/10.1111/j.1467-6494.2008.00512.x

Lepper, H. S. (1998). Use of other-reports to validate subjective well-being measures. *Social Indicators Research*, *44*(3), 367–379. https://doi.org/10.1023/A:1006872027638

Leutner, F., Codreanu, S.-C., Liff, J., & Mondragon, N. (2020). The potential of game- and video-based assessments for social attributes: Examples from practice. *Journal of Managerial Psychology*, *36*(7), 533–547. https://doi.org/10.1108/JMP-01-2020-0023

Li, W., Tang, L., Montayre, J., Harris, C., West, S., & Antoniou, M. (2023). Investigating health and wellbeing challenges facing an ageing workforce in the construction and nursing industries: Computational linguistic analysis of Twitter data (Preprint). *Journal of Medical Internet Research*. https://doi.org/10.2196/49450

Linley, P. A., Maltby, J., Wood, A. M., Joseph, S., Harrington, S., Peterson, C., Park, N., & Seligman, M. E. P. (2007). Character strengths in the United Kingdom: The VIA Inventory of Strengths. *Personality and Individual Differences*, *43*(2), 341–351. https://doi.org/10.1016/j.paid.2006.12.004

Liou, G., Bonner, C. V., & Tay, L. (2022). A psychometric view of technology-based assessments. *International Journal of Testing*, *22*(3–4), 216–242. https://doi.org/10.1080/15305058.2022.2070757

Littman-Ovadia, H., Lazar-Butbul, V., & Benjamin, B. A. (2014). Strengths-based career counseling: Overview and initial evaluation. *Journal of Career Assessment*, *22*(3), 403–419. https://doi.org/10.1177/1069072713498483

Macdonald, C., Bore, M., & Munro, D. (2008). Values in action scale and the Big 5: An empirical indication of structure. *Journal of Research in Personality*, *42*(4), 787–799. https://doi.org/10.1016/j.jrp.2007.10.003

Matthews, M. D., Eid, J., Kelly, D., Bailey, J. K. S., & Peterson, C. (2006). Character strengths and virtues of developing military leaders: An international comparison. *Military Psychology*, *18*(sup1), S57–S68. https://doi.org/10.1207/s15327876mp1803s_5

Maul, A. (2013). Method effects and the meaning of measurement. *Frontiers in Psychology*, *4*. https://doi.org/10.3389/fpsyg.2013.00169

McGrath, R. E. (2015). Integrating psychological and cultural perspectives on virtue: The hierarchical structure of character strengths. *The Journal of Positive Psychology*, *10*(5), 407–424. https://doi.org/10.1080/17439760.2014.994222

McGrath, R. E. (2023). A summary of construct validity evidence for two measures of character strengths. *Journal of Personality Assessment*, *105*(3), 302–313. https://doi.org/10.1080/00223891.2022.2120402

Mishra, V., & Roch, S. G. (2013). Cultural values and performance appraisal: Assessing the effects of rater self-construal on performance ratings. *The Journal of Psychology, 147*(4), 325–344. https://doi.org/10.1080/00223980.2012.694377

Möller, T., Doms, B., & Stel, M. (2022). Online deceptive impression management: Self-admission and other estimates of false Facebook-selves. *The Open Psychology Journal, 15*(1). https://doi.org/10.2174/18743501-v15-e2206090

Moore, K., & McElroy, J. C. (2012). The influence of personality on Facebook usage, wall postings, and regret. *Computers in Human Behavior, 28*(1), 267–274. https://doi.org/10.1016/j.chb.2011.09.009

Morgeson, F. P., Campion, M. A., Dipboye, R. L., Hollenbeck, J. R., Murphy, K., & Schmitt, N. (2007). Reconsidering the use of personality tests in personnel selection contexts. *Personnel Psychology, 60*(3), 683–729. https://doi.org/10.1111/j.1744-6570.2007.00089.x

Müller, S. R., Peters, H., Matz, S. C., Wang, W., & Harari, G. M. (2020). Investigating the relationships between mobility behaviours and indicators of subjective well-being using smartphone-based experience sampling and GPS tracking. *European Journal of Personality, 34*(5), 714–732. https://doi.org/10.1002/per.2262

Myford, C., & Wolfe, E. (2004). Detecting and measuring rater effects using many-facet rasch measurement: Part II. *Journal of Applied Measurement, 5*, 189–227.

Nezlek, J. B., Newman, D. B., & Thrash, T. M. (2017). A daily diary study of relationships between feelings of gratitude and well-being. *The Journal of Positive Psychology, 12*(4), 323–332. https://doi.org/10.1080/17439760.2016.1198923

Ng, K.-Y., Koh, C., Ang, S., Kennedy, J. C., & Chan, K.-Y. (2011). Rating leniency and halo in multisource feedback ratings: Testing cultural assumptions of power distance and individualism-collectivism. *Journal of Applied Psychology, 96*(5), 1033–1044. https://doi.org/10.1037/a0023368

Ng, V., Cao, M., Marsh, H. W., Tay, L., & Seligman, M. E. P. (2017). The factor structure of the Values in Action Inventory of Strengths (VIA-IS): An item-level exploratory structural equation modeling (ESEM) bifactor analysis. *Psychological Assessment, 29*(8), 1053–1058. https://doi.org/10.1037/pas0000396

Ng, V., Lee, P., Ho, M.-H. R., Kuykendall, L., Stark, S., & Tay, L. (2021). The development and validation of a multidimensional forced-choice format character measure: Testing the Thurstonian IRT approach. *Journal of Personality Assessment, 103*(2), 224–237. https://doi.org/10.1080/00223891.2020.1739056

Ng, V., & Tay, L. (2020). Lost in translation: The construct representation of character virtues. *Perspectives on Psychological Science, 15*(2), 309–326. https://doi.org/10.1177/1745691619886014

Ng, V., Tay, L., & Kuykendall, L. (2018). The development and validation of a measure of character: The CIVIC. *The Journal of Positive Psychology, 13*(4), 346–372. https://doi.org/10.1080/17439760.2017.1291850

Offstein, E. H., & Dufresne, R. L. (2007). Building strong ethics and promoting positive character development: The influence of HRM at the United States Military Academy at West Point. *Human Resource Management, 46*(1), 95–114. https://doi.org/10.1002/hrm.20147

Odin, P. (2009). Social desirability in positive psychology: Bias or desirable sociality? In T. Freire (Ed.), Understanding positive life research and practice on positive psychology (pp. 407–428). Lisbon, Portugal: Climepsi.

Oswald, F., & Hough, L. (2011). Personality and its assessment in organizations: Theoretical and empirical developments. *APA Handbook of Industrial and Organizational Psychology, 2*, 153–184. https://doi.org/10.1037/12170-005

Pang, D., Eichstaedt, J. C., Buffone, A., Slaff, B., Ruch, W., & Ungar, L. H. (2020). The language of character strengths: Predicting morally valued traits on social media. *Journal of Personality*, *88*(2), 287–306. https://doi.org/10.1111/jopy.12491

Park, N., & Peterson, C. (2006). Moral competence and character strengths among adolescents: The development and validation of the Values in Action Inventory of Strengths for Youth. *Journal of Adolescence*, *29*(6), 891–909. https://doi.org/10.1016/j.adolescence.2006.04.011

Peterson, C., & Seligman, M. E. P. (2004). *Character strengths and virtues: A handbook and classification*. Washington, United States: American Psychological Assoc.

Pierce, J. R., & Aguinis, H. (2013). The too-much-of-a-good-thing effect in management. *Journal of Management*, *39*(2), 313–338. https://doi.org/10.1177/0149206311410060

Podsakoff, P. M., MacKenzie, S. B., Lee, J.-Y., & Podsakoff, N. P. (2003). Common method biases in behavioral research: A critical review of the literature and recommended remedies. *The Journal of Applied Psychology*, *88*(5), 879–903. https://doi.org/10.1037/0021-9010.88.5.879

Prewett, M. S., Walvoord, A. A. G., Stilson, F. R. B., Rossi, M. E., & Brannick, M. T. (2009). The team personality–team performance relationship revisited: The impact of criterion choice, pattern of workflow, and method of aggregation. *Human Performance*. https://doi.org/10.1080/08959280903120253

Rau, R., Carlson, E. N., Back, M. D., Barranti, M., Gebauer, J. E., Human, L. J., Leising, D., & Nestler, S. (2021). What is the structure of perceiver effects? On the importance of global positivity and trait-specificity across personality domains and judgment contexts. *Journal of Personality and Social Psychology*, *120*(3), 745–764. https://doi.org/10.1037/pspp0000278

Roulin, N., & Krings, F. (2020). Faking to fit in: Applicants' response strategies to match organizational culture. *Journal of Applied Psychology*, *105*(2), 130–145. https://doi.org/10.1037/apl0000431

Ruch, W., Heintz, S., & Wagner, L. (2020). Co-occurrence patterns of character strengths and measured core virtues in German-speaking adults. *Frontiers in Psychology*, *11*. https://doi.org/10.3389/fpsyg.2020.599094

Ruch, W., & Proyer, R. T. (2015). Mapping strengths into virtues: The relation of the 24 VIA-strengths to six ubiquitous virtues. *Frontiers in Psychology*, *6*. https://doi.org/10.3389/fpsyg.2015.00460

Ryan, A. M., & Ployhart, R. E. (2014). A century of selection. *Annual Review of Psychology*, *65*, 693–717. https://doi.org/10.1146/annurev-psych-010213-115134

Sametoğlu, S., Pelt, D. H. M., Eichstaedt, J. C., Ungar, L. H., & Bartels, M. (2023). Comparison of wellbeing structures based on survey responses and social media language: A network analysis. *Applied Psychology: Health and Well-Being*, *15*(4), 1555–1582. https://doi.org/10.1111/aphw.12451

Schutte, N. S., & Malouff, J. M. (2019). The impact of signature character strengths interventions: A meta-analysis. *Journal of Happiness Studies*, *20*(4), 1179–1196. https://doi.org/10.1007/s10902-018-9990-2

Schwab, D. P. (2004). *Research methods for organizational studies* (2nd ed.). Psychology Press. https://doi.org/10.4324/9781410611284

Seligman M. E. P. (2011). *Flourish: A visionary new understanding of happiness and well-being* (pp. xii, 349). New York, NY: Free Press.

Seligman, M. E. P., & Csikszentmihalyi, M. (2000). Positive psychology: An introduction. *American Psychologist*, *55*(1), 5–14. https://doi.org/10.1037/0003-066X.55.1.5

Stanley, J. C. (1961). Analysis of unreplicated three-way classifications, with applications to rater bias and trait independence. *Psychometrika*, *26*(2), 205–219. https://doi.org/10.1007/BF02289715

Steyer, R., Geiser, C., & Loßnitzer, C. (2023). Latent state–trait models. In *APA handbook of research methods in psychology: Data analysis and research publication* (Vol. 3, 2nd ed., pp. 297–316). American Psychological Association. https://doi.org/10.1037/0000320-013

Steyer, R., Mayer, A., Geiser, C., & Cole, D. A. (2015). A theory of states and traits—Revised. *Annual Review of Clinical Psychology, 11*, 71–98. https://doi.org/10.1146/annurev-clinpsy-032813-153719

Steyer, R., Schmitt, M., & Eid, M. (1999). Latent state–trait theory and research in personality and individual differences. *European Journal of Personality, 13*(5, Spec Issue), 389–408. https://doi.org/10.1002/(SICI)1099-0984(199909/10)13:5<389::AID-PER361>3.0.CO;2-A

Svendsen, G. B., Johnsen, J.-A. K., Almås-Sørensen, L., & Vittersø, J. (2013). Personality and technology acceptance: The influence of personality factors on the core constructs of the Technology Acceptance Model. *Behaviour & Information Technology, 32*(4), 323–334. https://doi.org/10.1080/0144929X.2011.553740

Tanaka, M., & Ross, S. J. (2023). Impact of self-construal on rater severity in peer assessments of oral presentations. *Assessment in Education: Principles, Policy & Practice, 30*(2), 203–220. https://doi.org/10.1080/0969594X.2023.2189564

Tay, L., Jebb, A. T., & Scotney, V. S. (2021). Assessments of societal subjective well-being: Ten methodological issues for consideration. In M. T. Lee, L. D. Kubzansky, & T. J. VanderWeele (Eds.), *Measuring well-being: Interdisciplinary perspectives from the social sciences and the humanities* (p. 0). Oxford University Press. https://doi.org/10.1093/oso/9780197512531.003.0004

Tay, L., Meade, A. W., & Cao, M. (2015). An overview and practical guide to IRT measurement equivalence analysis. *Organizational Research Methods, 18*(1), 3–46. https://doi.org/10.1177/1094428114553062

Tay, L., Woo, S. E., Hickman, L., Booth, B. M., & D'Mello, S. (2021). *A conceptual framework for investigating and mitigating Machine Learning Measurement Bias (MLMB) in psychological assessment*. OSF. https://doi.org/10.31234/osf.io/mjph3

Tay, L., Woo, S. E., Hickman, L., & Saef, R. M. (2020). Psychometric and validity issues in machine learning approaches to personality assessment: A focus on social media text mining. *European Journal of Personality, 34*(5), 826–844. https://doi.org/10.1002/per.2290

Thapa, S., Tay, L., & Hou, D. (2021). Experience sampling methodology: Conceptual and technological advances for understanding and assessing variability in well-being research. In P. D. Harms, P. L. Perrewé, & C.-H. (Daisy) Chang (Eds.), *Examining and exploring the shifting nature of occupational stress and well-being* (Vol. 19, pp. 137–154). Emerald Publishing Limited. https://doi.org/10.1108/S1479-355520210000019007

Thorndike, E. L. (1920). A constant error in psychological ratings. *Journal of Applied Psychology, 4*(1), 25–29. https://doi.org/10.1037/h0071663

Trimble, J. E. (2010). Cultural measurement equivalence. In C. S. Clauss-Ehlers (Ed.), *Encyclopedia of cross-cultural school psychology* (pp. 316–318). Springer US. https://doi.org/10.1007/978-0-387-71799-9_112

Van Tongeren, D. R., Ng, V., Hickman, L., & Tay, L. (2023a). Behavioral measures of humility: Part 1. Theoretical and methodological review. *The Journal of Positive Psychology, 18*(5), 711–721. https://doi.org/10.1080/17439760.2022.2109202

Van Tongeren, D. R., Ng, V., Hickman, L., & Tay, L. (2023b). Behavioral measures of humility: Part 2. Conceptual mapping and charting ways forward. *The Journal of Positive Psychology, 18*(5), 722–732. https://doi.org/10.1080/17439760.2022.2109201

van Woerkom, M., & Meyers, M. C. (2015). My strengths count! *Human Resource Management, 54*(1), 81–103. https://doi.org/10.1002/hrm.21623

van Woerkom, M., Oerlemans, W., & Bakker, A. B. (2016). Strengths use and work engagement: A weekly diary study. *European Journal of Work and Organizational Psychology*, *25*(3), 384–397. https://doi.org/10.1080/1359432X.2015.1089862

Varma, A., Pichler, S., & Srinivas, E. S. (2005). The role of interpersonal affect in performance appraisal: Evidence from two samples – The US and India. *The International Journal of Human Resource Management*, *16*(11), 2029–2044. https://doi.org/10.1080/09585190500314904

Vergauwe, J., Wille, B., Hofmans, J., Kaiser, R. B., & De Fruyt, F. (2017a). The too little/too much scale: A new rating format for detecting curvilinear effects. *Organizational Research Methods*, *20*(3), 518–544. https://doi.org/10.1177/1094428117706534

Vergauwe, J., Wille, B., Hofmans, J., Kaiser, R., & De Fruyt, F. (2017b). The double-edged sword of leader Charisma: Understanding the curvilinear relationship between charismatic personality and leader effectiveness. *Journal of Personality and Social Psychology*, *114*. https://doi.org/10.1037/pspp0000147

VIA Institute. (2024). *VIA assessments*. https://www.viacharacter.org/researchers/assessments

Viswesvaran, C., Schmidt, F. L., & Ones, D. S. (2005). Is there a general factor in ratings of job performance? A meta-analytic framework for disentangling substantive and error influences. *Journal of Applied Psychology*, *90*(1), 108–131. https://doi.org/10.1037/0021-9010.90.1.108

Wang, G., & Hackett, R. D. (2016). Conceptualization and measurement of virtuous leadership: Doing well by doing good. *Journal of Business Ethics*, *137*(2), 321–345. https://doi.org/10.1007/s10551-015-2560-1

Wood, J. K., Anglim, J., & Horwood, S. (2022). Effect of job applicant faking and cognitive ability on self-other agreement and criterion validity of personality assessments. *International Journal of Selection and Assessment*, *30*(3), 378–391. https://doi.org/10.1111/ijsa.12382

Yardi, S., & Bruckman, A. (2012). Income, race, and class: Exploring socioeconomic differences in family technology use. *Proceedings of the SIGCHI Conference on Human Factors in Computing Systems*, 3041–3050. https://doi.org/10.1145/2207676.2208716

Zhao, S., Grasmuck, S., & Martin, J. (2008). Identity construction on Facebook: Digital empowerment in anchored relationships. *Computers in Human Behavior*, *24*(5), 1816–1836. https://doi.org/10.1016/j.chb.2008.02.012

15

PERMA+4 AND POSITIVE ORGANIZATIONAL PSYCHOLOGY 2.0

Opportunities for Embracing Methodological and Technological Advances

Stewart I. Donaldson and Scott I. Donaldson

The Science and Practice of Positive Psychology

At the turn of the century, the late Mihaly Csikszentmihalyi and Martin Seligman provided a clear vision for how to develop a body of empirical evidence that "would promise to improve quality of life and prevent the pathologies that arise when life is barren and meaningless" (Seligman & Csikszentmihalyi, 2000, p. 5). This new science of positive subjective experience, positive individual traits, and positive institutions, most often referred to as "Positive Psychology," has provided a better understanding the factors that allow individuals, groups, teams, leaders, organizations, communities, and societies to flourish (Donaldson, Csikszentmihalyi, & Nakamura, 2020).

Donaldson, Dollwet, and Rao (2015) took stock of the first 15 years of the peer-reviewed literature linked to the vision for a science of positive psychology in their widely cited article "Happiness, excellence, and optimal human functioning revisited: Examining the peer-reviewed literature linked to positive psychology." More than 1,300 peer-reviewed publications on positive psychology topics, and with more than 750 of these articles including empirical tests of positive psychology theories, principles, and interventions realized the initial vision. It was found well-being was by far the most investigated topic and that the science of positive psychology had become a growing sub-area within the broader discipline of psychology and was using the scientific methods of psychology to better understand well-being, excellence, and optimal human functioning.

Donaldson, Gaffaney, and Cabrera (2023) provided a more recent review of the field and found that more than two decades of peer-reviewed science on positive psychology topics supports a thriving evidence-based positive psychology practice. Thousands of undergraduates, graduate students, and professionals

DOI: 10.4324/9781032619385-15

across the globe have now been trained in the science and practice of positive psychology. Many practitioners have the tools needed to assess, develop, and manage the building blocks of well-being and positive functioning, and to promote human flourishing at multiple levels of analysis and across many domains. There is also sound experimental evidence showing that multicomponent positive psychology interventions (MPPIs) are efficacious on average, and work well under specific conditions (Donaldson, Cabrera, & Gaffaney, 2021; Donaldson & Chen, 2021; Donaldson, Lee, & Donaldson, 2019). For example, Donaldson et al. (2019) in one of the first meta-analyses of POP interventions found that five types of interventions appeared to be the most effective:

- Employee well-being
- Psychological capital (PsyCap)
- Job crafting
- Employee strengths
- Employee gratitude

The next generation of MPPIs are being designed to reach beyond western, educated, industrialized, rich, and democratic countries, and to focus more on enhancing diversity, equity, and inclusion and to reach more marginalized and underserved populations (Donaldson, Cabrera, & Gaffaney, 2021).

Kim et al. (2018) in their article "The International Landscape of Positive Psychology Research: A Systematic Review" showed that the science of positive psychology quickly became an international endeavor after its early beginnings in the United States. It is now estimated that the majority of scholarly contributions to positive psychology are from outside the United States. The International Association of Positive Psychology (IPPA) was established in 2007 has been a catalyst for the rapid development of national and regional positive psychology associations and societies to support practitioners, scientists, scientific journals, book series, grants and contracts, undergraduate courses, and graduate programs across the world (Donaldson et al., 2023).

The Science and Practice of Positive Organizational Psychology

Perhaps the most popular and fruitful application of the science of positive psychology has been to improve the quality of work life and the effectiveness of organizations (see Donaldson & Chen, 2021; Donaldson & Dollwet, 2013; Donaldson, van Zyl, & Donaldson, 2022). Inspired by the original vision for positive psychology, Luthans (2002) expanded the ideas to the workplace and coined the term positive organizational behavior (POB). He defined POB as the study and application of positively oriented human resource strengths and psychological capacities that can be measured, developed, and effectively managed for performance in today's workplace. Cameron and colleagues (2003) pursued a similar path and described their new approach as positive organizational scholarship (POS). POS was defined as the study of that which is positive, flourishing, and life-giving in organizations. Donaldson and Ko (2010) examined the peer-reviewed empirical research that had resulted from studies of positive psychology in the workplace and offered the umbrella term positive organizational psychology (POP) to connect and consolidate the extensive literature and empirical database that had emerged. POP is defined as the scientific study of positive subjective experiences and traits in the workplace and positive organizations and its application to improve the effectiveness and quality of life in organizations (Donaldson & Ko, 2010, p. 177).

Today POP continues to thrive in terms of scientific study, university courses and degree programs, and has provided a wide range of evidence-informed practices and interventions to help workers, teams, leaders, and organizations thrive and reach their potential (Donaldson & Chen, 2021; Donaldson et al., 2022; van Zyl et al., 2023). One of the most robust findings across many POP research studies is that well-being is strongly linked to positive functioning at work (Donaldson et al., 2022; Moscoso & Salgado, 2021; Lester et al., 2021). The US Surgeon General makes this link even more clear and important (especially in post-pandemic times) in his recent National Report on "Workplace Mental Health & Well-being (2022)." Work and careers are important aspects of our lives, and for many, most of our waking hours are spent on work or work-related activities. Workplaces are often the engine of our well-being and positive functioning in life and powerfully influence our health, wealth, and well-being. Research has now made it clear that efforts to foster workplace well-being can have great public health as well as organizational productivity and effectiveness benefits (US Surgeon General, 2022).

More recently, Walsh, Boz, and Lyubomirsky (2023) reviewed and updated the available evidence on the topic and concluded well-being causes positive functioning and success rather than the other way around. They based this claim on cross-sectional, longitudinal, and experimental studies that persuasively and robustly showed that relative to their less happy peers, happy people experience superior success on a host of outcomes, including job satisfaction, performance, productivity, work engagement, burnout, supervisor evaluations, income, negotiations, and creativity. They concluded that rather than pressuring employees to act happy – an approach that has previously led to both legal problems and backlash – organizations may foster greater worker well-being by measuring it, building thriving corporate cultures, and deploying positive activities in the workplace.

PERMA+4 Well-Being and Positive Functioning

More than 25 years of studying and applying positive psychology in the workplace has resulted in an evidence-based framework that can guide assessments, practices, activities, interventions, and programs to enhance worker well-being and positive functioning. Donaldson et al. (2022) described the holistic PERMA+4 framework in detail showing how it developed from synthesizing and summarizing the science of positive psychology and POP since their inception. Simply put, there are at least nine building blocks that can be developed and cared for to enhance well-being and positive functioning at work and in life more generally:

Seligman (2011) proposed the first five measurable elements, which can be actively developed, and called them PERMA:

1 **Positive Emotions**. Experiencing happiness, joy, love, gratitude, etc. in the here and now.
2 **Engagement**. Being highly absorbed, emersed, or experiencing flow while engaged in activities of one's life.
3 **Relationships**. Having the ability to establish and maintain positive, mutually beneficial relationships with others characterized by experiences of love and appreciation.
4 **Meaning**. The experience of being connected to something larger than the self or serving a greater purpose.
5 **Accomplishment**. Experiencing a sense of mastery over a particular domain of interest or achieving important or challenging life/work goals.

Seligman (2018) encouraged the scientific positive psychology community to search for additional building blocks which may enhance or strengthen the PERMA framework. Donaldson (2019) and Donaldson et al. (2020) conducted an extensive systematic literature review, meta-analysis, and a range of qualitative assessments in order to determine if and how the framework could be extended into work-related contexts. They found that four additional building blocks could explain additional variance in work-related wellbeing and performance, and many workers and leaders concurred that they were good candidates for expanding and making the PERMA framework more comprehensive and holistic. Donaldson (2019), Donaldson and Donaldson (2021a, 2021b), Donaldson et al. (2020, 2023, 2024a, 2024b) have found empirical evidence supporting the addition of these four elements:

1 **Physical Health**. Operationalized as a combination of high levels of biological, functional, and physical health assets.
2 **Mindset**. Adopting a growth mindset characterized by an optimistic, future-oriented view of life, where challenges or setbacks are seen as opportunities to grow. This may also be a function of psychological capital, perseverance or grit.
3 **Work Environment**. The quality of the physical work environment (which includes spatiotemporal elements, such as access to natural light, fresh air, physical safety and a positive psychological climate) aligned to the preferences of the individual
4 **Economic Security**. Perceptions of financial security and stability required to satisfy individual needs (see Figure 15.1).

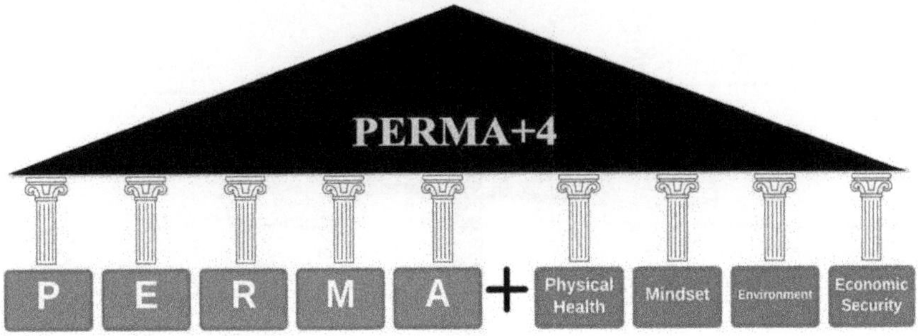

FIGURE 15.1 PERMA+4 Building Blocks of Well-being and Positive Functioning

Cabrera and Donaldson (2023) recently reviewed 111 peer-reviewed empirical articles based on responses from a total of 170,544 participants. Most of the participants were healthy adults working across a wide range of professions and industries. Overall, the relationship between PERMA and its variants (e.g., PERMA+4, PERMAH) with well-being and positive functioning was found to be exceptional strong. Nine of the studies provided evidence related to the efficacy of PERMA-based interventions.

Positive Organizational Psychology 2.0 (POP 2.0)

The first two decades of POP have been very productive and resulted in new evidence-based theories and frameworks to guide workplace activities and interventions (Donaldson et al., 2022; Donaldson & Chen, 2021; van Zyl et al., 2023). Van Zyl et al. (2023) pointed out that the discipline is now on the cusp of a new wave of research and intervention, and described these new and upcoming efforts as POP 2.0. Simply put, POP 2.0 will be an "evidence-based, data-driven field that utilizes technological advancements and human-centered design to understand and enhance positive characteristics of individuals, organizations, and society for optimal psychological functioning, wellbeing, and performance" (van Zyl et al., 2023, p. 7). One purpose of this chapter is to review some of the opportunities for improving future POP research in light of methodological and technological advances, and to contribute to the vision of a more precise science and practice of POP 2.0 in the years ahead. Some of the opportunities explored will include:

- Understanding and reducing self-report bias
- Learning from longitudinal designs
- Better understanding POP topics in virtual and hybrid workplaces
- Embracing rapidly advancing technologies
- Using checklists to design POP 2.0 interventions and future research

The science of positive psychology over the first two decades, including POP research, has been criticized extensively. One of the important foundational

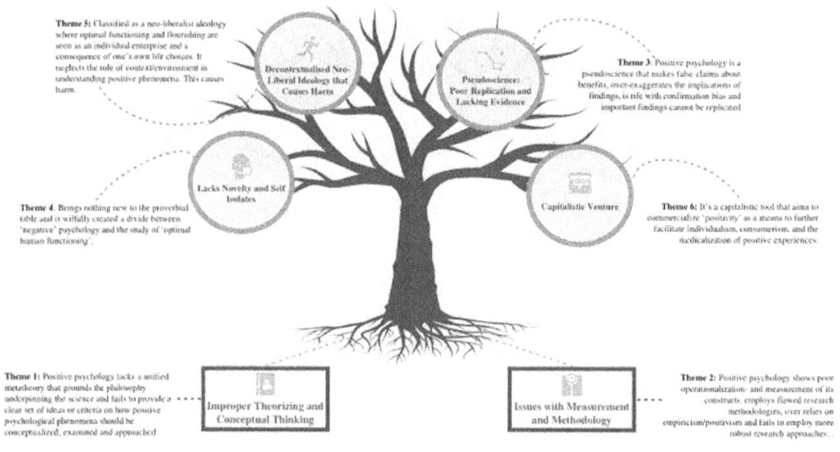

FIGURE 15.2 Summary of Main Criticisms and Critiques of Positive Psychology

criticisms is of how we define and measure our concepts. For example, van Zyl et al. (2023) in a systematic review 117 unique critiques and criticisms of positive psychology six overarching themes including (a) lacked proper theorizing and conceptual thinking, (b) was problematic as far as measurement and methodologies were concerned, (c) was seen as a pseudoscience that lacked evidence and had poor replication, (d) lacked novelty and self-isolated itself from mainstream psychology, (e) was a decontextualized neo-liberalist ideology that caused harm, and (f) was a capitalistic venture. See Figure 15.2.

Some possible solutions to address the first three themes is to develop POP 2.0 in a way that better addresses self-report bias, learns more from longitudinal designs, and that uses more rigorous efficacy and effectiveness evaluations. Furthermore, to address Theme 4 – lacks novelty and self isolates – developing a more in-depth understanding of new topics informed by other fields, such as systems analysis, working virtually, artificial intelligence, social media analytics, big data analysis and machine learning, and commercial determinates of health and well-being, holds great promise for building a more robust and relevant field poised to dramatically improve its applications and expand its impact. While themes 5 and 6 are beyond the scope of this paper, they should also be considered and avoid replicated in POP 2.0.

Understanding and Reducing Self-Report Bias

Reliable and valid measurement is foundational for building a strong science. The development of science of positive psychology and POP 2.0 rests on accurate tests of theories, frameworks, principles, practices, and interventions. Ackerman, Warren, and Donaldson (2018) found in a systematic review of the positive psychology research literature that while there are some reliability analyses and validations occurring within the field, the creation of new measures for the purpose of a specific study far outpaces the validation of existing measures. In addition to the general need for more scale validation work, they also found a predominant use of self-report measurement scales – 78% of empirical articles used some type of self-report measurement scale, with 68% using *only* self-report measurements.

Donaldson and Grant-Vallone (2002) clearly described the problem of solely or over relying on self-report measures in workplace research. Workers often believe that reporting honest answers to sensitive questions can have devastating consequences, even when researchers claim their responses will be anonymous or confidential. Given the continued wide-spread use of surveys based on self-reports there is growing concerns that psychological research conducted in the workplace can be highly misleading (see Donaldson & Donaldson, 2021a, 2021b).

There are four general factors that often lead employees to bias their answers to researchers' questions about their personal and work behavior, as well as their thoughts about their supervisors, co-workers, and organizational climate and culture. As shown in Figure 15.3, these motivational factors include whether there actual thoughts or behaviors are socially undesirable, the sensitivity of the question asked, the participants propensity to give social desirable answers, and the situational pressure to give socially desirable answers.

Several POP studies have attempted to understand how significant a problem this may be in POP research to date. A multitrait multimethod (MTMM) research design with 220 knowledgeable co-worker pairs (N = 440) showed that the 9 PERMA+4 building blocks of well-being (positive emotions, engagement, relationships, meaning, accomplishment, physical health, mindset, environment, and

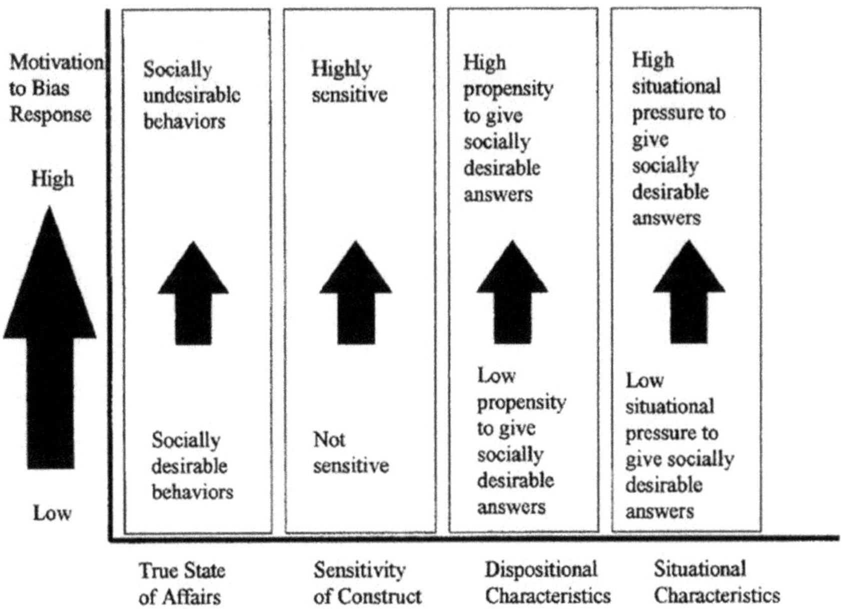

FIGURE 15.3 Motivation to Bias Responses Factors

economic security) significantly predicted well-being above and beyond self-report bias and mono-method bias (Donaldson et al., 2021a). A second MTMM study of PERMA+4 predicting work role performance (Donaldson & Donaldson 2021b) and a third MTMM study of PsyCap (hope, efficacy, resilience, optimism; Donaldson et al., 2021b) revealed essentially the same patterns. However, these MTMM studies also revealed that you get substantially higher correlations between variables when they are all measured by self-reports (or the same method), in contrast to using knowledgeable co-worker reports of well-being and work role performance (or using different methods). This type of information can be used to better interpret future POP 2.0 research that is limited by cross-sectional self-report designs, and to motivate researchers to go beyond relying solely on self-report measures (or just one method of measurement) when possible in POP 2.0. Better operationalization and measurement (Theme 2 above) should be a high priority for POP 2.0.

Learning from Longitudinal Studies

Another important methodological limitation to date is that much of our POP empirical knowledge is based only on cross-sectional studies. For example, in a recent systematic review of all of the PERMA and PERMA+4 empirical research to date (Cabrera & Donaldson, 2023), approximately 85% of 111 empirical studies used cross-sectional survey designs open to the problems of self-report and mono-method bias discussed above. They concluded that the next generation of research in this area would benefit greatly from designs that assessed relationships over time (more than at just one time point) as well as more experimental designs when appropriate. It is very difficult to understand potential causal pathways (including reciprocal causation) and potential confounding factors when the evidence is based only on correlations collected at one time point.

Some researchers have begun to answer the call for more longitudinal research on well-being, positive functioning, and human flourishing. For example, Cabrera (2024) recently found that the PERMA+4 building blocks strongly predict well-being and positive functioning at work over multiple time points. There is also a very large multi-year research effort under way known as the Global Flourishing Study (GFS). The GFS is a large, longitudinal and multinational panel study that aims to explore the distribution, determinants, and interrelations of various concepts related to human well-being and human flourishing with more than 200,000 people across a geographically and culturally diverse set of countries around the world (Padget et al., 2024).

This is a five-year longitudinal data collection and research collaboration between researchers at Baylor University and Harvard University, in partnership with Gallup and the Center for Open Science (COS), and with the support of a consortium of funders. As part of this project, COS is making the data from the study an open access resource so researchers, journalists, policymakers, and educators worldwide can access detailed information about what makes for a flourishing life

(GFS 2024: https://www.cos.io/gfs). The longitudinal data collected and analyzed as part of this study focused on work and work life promises to deepen our understanding human flourishing as it relates to work and workers across cultures.

Evaluations of PERMA+4 and POP 2.0 interventions is another type of longitudinal design that promises to yield rich information about the workplace of tomorrow. A recent systematic review analyzed the findings from 25 meta-analyses, 42 review papers, and the high-quality RCTs of positive psychology interventions (PPIs) designed to generate well-being that were included within those studies (Donaldson et al., 2021). Findings revealed that PPIs have the potential to generate well-being even during a global pandemic, with even larger effect sizes in non-Western countries. Four exemplar PPIs – that have been tested with a high-quality RCT have positive effects on well-being and could be implemented during a global pandemic – were presented and discussed. It is important to point out that activities to build the PERMA+4 building blocks were found as key ingredients in the exemplar PPIs. The components of a general strategy to enhance the PERMA+4 building blocks or well-being, are presented in Table 15.1.

TABLE 15.1 Five Components That Can Be Incorporated into Positive Psychology Intervention Design

PPI Component	*Objective*	*Description*
Learn	Knowledge and awareness	Develop an awareness and understanding of topics and oneself.
Practice	Behavioral skills	Practice simple skills and exercises that can be incorporated into daily life.
Reflect	Sense-making and reinforcement	Practice reflection after exercises to encourage sense-making and reinforcement of new skills.
Relate	Engagement and accountability	Clarify understanding with experts and relate to peers to amplify effects and reinforce accountability.
Plan	Sustainability	Set goals and create a plan to practice new skills in daily life to encourage long-term sustainability.

In addition to using the highest quality experimental longitudinal designs to determine the efficacy of PPIs in the workplace, more effectiveness evaluations in organizational settings (versus controlled laboratory settings) using mixed-method approaches also hold great promise for advancing POP 2.0 (Donaldson, 2022; Donaldson et al., 2019, 2021). Theory-driven effectiveness evaluations using rigorous mixed-method longitudinal designs offer many advantages for understanding how POP interventions work under "real-world" conditions (Donaldson, 2022; Donaldson & Chen, 2021). The new enhanced Centers for Disease Control (CDC) Enhanced Evaluation Framework offers POP 2.0 researchers and evaluators an approach to conduct and learn from more participatory effectiveness evaluations (see CDC Enhanced Evaluation Framework, 2024; Figure 15.4).

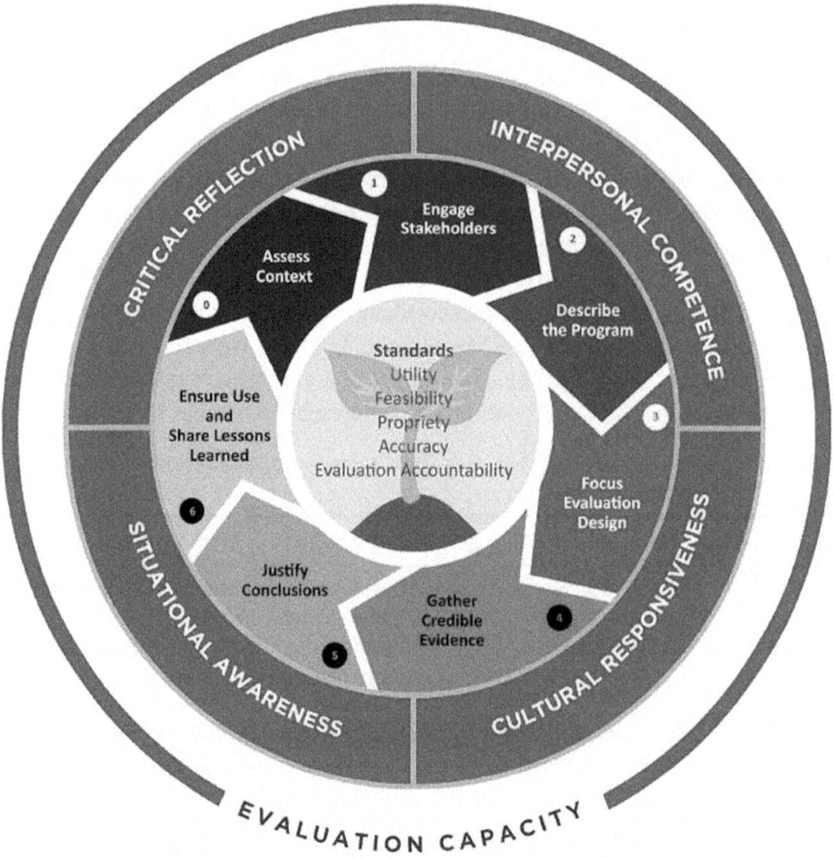

FIGURE 15.4 Enhanced CDC Evaluation Framework

Virtual and Hybrid Workplaces

The US Surgeon General (2022) recently published a national report on "Workplace Mental Health and Well-being," and discussed how the global pandemic has provided us an opportunity to rethink how we work. Most people spend the majority of their waking hours engaged in work or work-related activities (such as education and job preparation). The Surgeon General highlights how important it is post-pandemic to design work environments (including digital, remote, and hybrid work) that support well-being, optimal experience, and positive functioning:

> There are more than 160 million people who are a part of the US workforce today. Work is one of the most vital parts of life, powerfully shaping our health, wealth, and well- being. At its best, work provides us the ability to support ourselves and

our loved ones, and can also provide us with a sense of meaning, opportunities for growth, and a community. When people thrive at work, they are more likely to feel physically and mentally healthy overall, and to contribute positively to their workplace. This creates both a responsibility and unique opportunity for leaders to create workplace environments that support the health and well-being of workers.

(Surgeon General, 2022)

The massive shift toward more virtual workplaces and flexible working arrangements both challenges some of our basic understandings of work and organizational behavior, and provides POP 2.0 a wonderful opportunity to contribute to the design of virtual and hybrid work environments that enhance well-being and positive functioning. The POP and PERMA+4 knowledge we have gathered to date provides a timely and useful evidence base that can be used to achieve the five essentials for workplace mental health and well-being in POP 2.0:

- Protection from harm
- Connection and community
- Work–life harmony
- Mattering at work
- Opportunity for growth

These essential elements of a healthful work environment in 2024 and beyond center on worker voice and equity, and offer POP researchers and practitioners an exciting opportunity to focus its knowledge and resources on in POP 2.0 (U.S. Surgeon General, 2022; see Figure 15.5).

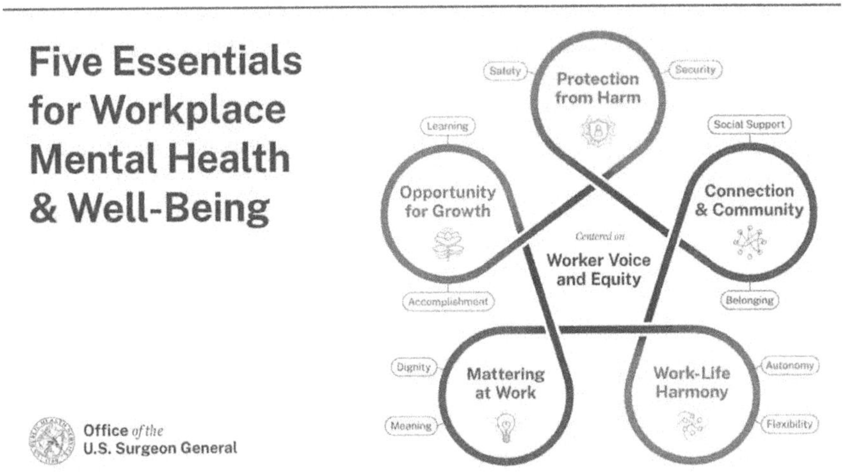

FIGURE 15.5 Five Essential for Workplace Mental Health and Well-Being

Embracing Rapidly Advancing Technologies

Not only are rapidly advancing technologies enabling us to function well in virtual and hybrid work environments, they are also changing the way we work, and have the potential to dramatically improve productivity and quality of work life. van Zyl et al. (2023) suggested POP 2.0 must embrace this technological revolution to remain relevant in the future, and identified important trends we should pay attention to:

- **Decentralization of work**: the rise of remote work and the gig economy has created challenges for traditional organizational structures and dynamics that POP has long investigated.
- **Increases in data-driven approaches to assessment and development initiatives:** This growing emphasis on using big data to inform organizational decision-making, from hiring to retention and succession planning, has posed new challenges for POP. While data-driven approaches can provide valuable insights, they risk reducing complex human phenomena to mere numbers, which is antithetical to the human-centered approach promoted by positive psychology.
- **Automation of human processes**: Technological advancements have become ubiquitous in organizations seeking to leverage these technologies as both competitive advantage and cost-saving mechanisms. This proliferation of accessible technology has led to innumerable tasks that were once done by humans now being done by automated systems. The effects on worker well-being are a growing concern as the implementation of automated systems – although linked to efficiency – creates disruption of other organizational systems, including workplace dynamics, organizational structure, and aspects of organizational culture.
- **Artificial intelligence, social robots, and virtual workspaces:** The burgeoning science and application of AI, robots, and virtual work technologies have similarly upended traditional models of how workers interact, collaborate, and perform their tasks; the implications of which are barely beginning to be researched and understood.

Other technological advances and topics that POP 2.0 researchers might study and pay close attention to include big data analyses, machine learning, social media analytics, the commercial determinants of health and well-being the like (see Donaldson et al., 2022; van Zyl et al., 2023). The main point is that technologically enhanced remote and hybrid workplaces of the future will offer many new opportunities for leaders, managers, and PERMA+4 and POP 2.0 researchers and practitioners.

Using Checklists to Design POP 2.0 Interventions, Publications, and Future Research

One of the recent trends in the science positive psychology is to move beyond the individual level of analysis, and to take a systems-informed approach to enhancing well-being and positive functioning at work (see Kern et al., 2019). For example, recent research has shown that PERMA+4 predicts well-being and work performance at the employee, team, and supervisor levels of analysis (Donaldson et al., 2024a), and that psychological safety moderators some of those relationships (Donaldson et al., 2024b). This raises the question of how do we design and evaluate systems-informed PERMA+4 and POP 2.0 interventions.

Gaffaney (2024) designed and validated the *Systems-Informed Well-Being Initiative Design Checklist*. Using state-of-the-art Checklist Design Methodology, she has created a checklist to guide our future intervention design efforts in POP 2.0. The six high level steps she recommends we follow in future design efforts include:

1 Lay the foundation
2 Diagnose and define focus
3 Design the initiative
4 Plan the evaluation
5 Implement and evaluate
6 Sustain and scale

An important opportunity for POP 2.0 is to design and use evidence-based checklists like this one in an effort to make our interventions, programs, and practices more effective. For a more detailed understanding of this process, please see Gaffaney (2024).

Another application illustrating the value of using clear criteria and checklists to guide POP 2.0 is for publishing in the top tier peer-reviewed literature. Now that positive psychology and POP research has matured over the past 25 years, many of the top journals in these fields have adapted their criteria and checklists. For example, some of the latest criteria POP 2.0 researchers should aim to meet if the plan to publish in the *Journal of Positive Psychology* (Emmons, 2024) include:

1 The paper reports more than a single study and shows that the major finding can be replicated
2 Multiple measures were used, including measures in addition to self-report assessment
3 Sophisticated and/or ambitious methodologies were employed
4 The paper is theory driven
5 The manuscript presents creative new ideas or methods
6 The paper is of such importance within positive psychology that it is likely to substantially influence an area of research
7 The paper is well-written and free of technical and grammatical errors

POP 2.0 and PERMA+4 researchers might greatly benefit by knowing and following criteria like these as they attempt to advance the peer-reviewed science in the years to come.

Our final example of using checklists to guide the future work of positive organizational psychologists and POP 2.0 focuses on an approach to mitigating some of the critiques and criticisms of positive psychology research to date (see van Zyl et al., 2023). In an effort to help future researchers to design better research studies, Gaffaney and Donaldson (2024) have offered a new checklist.

The examples of clear criteria and checklists provided above are meant to be illustrative of this overall approach to improving positive psychology research and practice. Developing clear criteria for defining high-quality POP 2.0 and evidence-based checklists to guide our processes and content hold great promise for improving PERMA+4 and POP 2.0 research and practice in the years ahead.

Conclusion

This chapter describes how POP has evolved significantly as a science and practice over the past 25 years, with numerous evidence-based applications for contemporary workplaces. At the same time there is growing societal recognition that POS 2.0 is needed to help reach both public health goals and organizational success in today's and tomorrow's evolving workplaces, which aligns with the US Surgeon General's Report on Workplace Mental Health and Well-being (US Surgeon General, 2022). It is our hope that PERMA+4 and POP 2.0 researchers and practitioners continue to stay highly engaged and relevant by taking advantage of least some of the methodological and technological opportunities explored in this paper.

References

Ackerman, C., Warren, M. A., & Donaldson, S. I. (2018). Scaling the heights of positive psychology: A systematic review of measurement scales. *International Journal of Well-being*, *8*(2), 1–21.

Cabrera, V. (2024). PERMA+4 building blocks of well-being: A mixed methods exploration of mechanisms and conditions that enable the subjective well-being of workers. Doctoral Dissertation, Claremont Graduate University.

Cabrera, V. & Donaldson, S. I. (2023). PERMA to PERMA+4 building blocks of well-being: A systematic review of the empirical literature. *Journal of Positive Psychology*, *19*(1), 1–20 https://doi.org/10.1080/17439760.2023.2208099.

Cameron, K. S., Dutton, J. E., & Quinn, R. E. (2003). *Positive organizational scholarship: Foundations for a new discipline.* San Francisco, CA: Berrett-Koehler.

CDC Enhanced Evaluation Framework (2024). Center for Disease Control: CDC.GOV.

Donaldson, S. I. (2019). Evaluating employee positive functioning and performance: A positive work and organizations approach. Doctoral Dissertation, Claremont Graduate University.

Donaldson, S. I. (2022). *Introduction to theory-driven program evaluation: Culturally responsive and strengths-focused* applications (2nd edition). New York: Routledge.

Donaldson, S. I., Cabrera, V., & Gaffaney, J. (2021). Following the science to generate well-being: Using the highest quality experimental evidence to design interventions. *Frontiers in Psychology.* https://doi.org/10.3389/fpsyg.2021.739352.

Donaldson, S. I., & Chen, C. (Eds.) (2021). *Positive organizational psychology interventions: Design & evaluation.* Hoboken, NJ: Wiley-Blackwell.

Donaldson, S. I., Chen, C., & Donaldson, S. I. (2021). Designing positive organizational psychology interventions. In S. I. Donaldson & C. Chen (Eds.), *Positive organizational psychology interventions: Design & evaluation.* Hoboken, NJ: Wiley-Blackwell.

Donaldson, S. I., Csikszentmihalyi, M., & Nakamura, J. (Eds.) (2020). *Positive psychological science: Improving everyday life, well-being, work, education, and societies across the globe.* New York: Routledge Academic.

Donaldson, S. I., & Dollwet, M. (2013). Taming the waves and wild horses of positive organizational psychology. *Advances in Positive Organizational Psychology, 1,* 1–21.

Donaldson, S. I., Dollwet, M., & Rao, M. (2015). Happiness, excellence, and optimal human functioning revisited: Examining the peer-reviewed literature linked to positive psychology. *Journal of Positive Psychology, 9*(6), 1–11.

Donaldson, S. I., & Donaldson, S. I. (2021a). The positive functioning at work scale: Psychometric assessment, validation, and measurement invariance. *Journal of Well-Being Assessment, 4*(2), 181–215.

Donaldson, S. I., & Donaldson, S. I. (2021b). Examining PERMA+4 and work role performance beyond self-report bias: Insights from multitrait-multimethod analyses. *Journal of Positive Psychology.* https://doi.org/10.1080/17439760.2021.1975160.

Donaldson, S. I., Donaldson, S. I. & Chen, C. (2021). Evaluating positive organizational psychology interventions. In S. I. Donaldson & C. Chen (Eds.), *Positive organizational psychology interventions: Design & evaluation.* Hoboken, NJ: Wiley-Blackwell. pp. 1–38.

Donaldson, S. I., Donaldson, S. I., Chan, L., & Kang, K. W. (2021b). Positive psychological capital (PsyCap) meets multitrait-multimethod analysis: Is PsyCap a robust predictor of well-being and performance controlling for self-report bias? *International Journal of Applied Positive Psychology.* https://doi.org/10.1007/s41042-021-00060-0.

Donaldson, S. I., Donaldson, S. I., McQuaid, M. L., & Kern, M. L. (2023). The PERMA+4 short scale: A cross-cultural empirical validation using item response theory. *International Journal of Applied Positive Psychology, 8,* 555–569.

Donaldson, S. I., Donaldson, S. I., McQuaid, M. L., & Kern, M. L. (2024a). Systems-informed PERMA+4: Measuring well-being and performance at the employee, team, and supervisor levels of analysis. *International Journal of Applied Positive Psychology,* 9, 1153–1166.

Donaldson, S. I., Donaldson, S. I., McQuaid, M. L., & Kern, M. L. (2024b). Systems-informed PERMA+4 and psychological safety: Predicting work-related and performance across an international sample. *Journal of Positive Psychology.* https://doi.org/10.1080/17439760.2024.2387341.

Donaldson, S. I., Gaffaney, J., & Cabrera, V. (2023). The science and practice of positive psychology: From a bold vision to PERMA+4. In C. Markey & H. S. Friedman (Eds.), *The 3rd edition of the encyclopedia of mental health.* Cambridge, MA: Academic Press. Vol 3, pp. 79–93.

Donaldson, S. I., & Grant-Vallone, E. J. (2002). Understanding self-report bias in organizational behavior research. *Journal of Business and Psychology, 17*(2), 245–262.

Donaldson, S. I., Heshmati, S., Young, J. Y., Donaldson, S. I. (2021a). Examining building blocks of well-being beyond PERMA and self-report bias. *Journal of Positive Psychology.* https://doi.org/10.1080/17439760.2020.1818813.

Donaldson, S. I., & Ko, I. (2010). Positive organizational psychology, behavior, and scholarship: A review of the emerging literature and evidence base. *Journal of Positive Psychology*, *5*(3), 177–191.

Donaldson, S. I., Lee, J. Y, & Donaldson, S. I. (2019). The effectiveness of positive psychology interventions in the workplace: A theory-driven evaluation perspective. In S. Rothman, L. E. van Zyl, & I. Rothman (Eds.), *Theoretical approaches to multi-cultural positive psychology interventions*. New York: Springer. pp. 115–159

Donaldson, S. I., van Zyl, L. E., & Donaldson, S. I. (2022). PERMA+4: A framework for work-related well-being, performance and positive organizational psychology 2.0. *Frontiers in Psychology*, *2*, 817244. https://doi.org/10.3389/fpsyg.2021.817244.

Emmons, R. (2024). *Editor of the Journal of Positive Psychology*. Email communication.

Gaffaney, J. (2024). A checklist to design and evaluate systems-informed wellbeing initiatives: A mixed methods validation. Doctoral Dissertation, Claremont Graduate University.

Gaffaney, J., & Donaldson, S. I. (2024). Evaluating criticisms and critiques. Recommendations for improving the science and practice of positive psychology. Manuscript under review. Global Flourishing Study (GFS) 2024. https://www.cos.io/gfs.

Kern, M. L., Williams, P., Spong, C., Colla, R., Sharma, K., Downie, A., Talyor, J. A., Sharp, S., Siokou, C., & Oades, L. G. (2019). Systems informed positive psychology. *The Journal of Positive Psychology*, *15*(6), 705–715.

Kim, H., Doiron, K., Warren, M. A., & Donaldson, S. I. (2018). The international landscape of positive psychology research: A systematic review. *International Journal of Wellbeing*, *8*(1), 50–70.

Lester, P. B., Stewart, E. P., Vie, L. L., Bonett, D. G., Seligman, E. P., & Diener, E. (2021). Happy soldiers are highest performers. *Journal of Happiness Studies*, 1–22. https://doi.org/10.1007/s10902-021-00441-x.

Luthans, F. (2002a). The need for and meaning of positive organizational behavior. *Journal of Organizational Behavior: The International Journal of Industrial, Occupational and Organizational Psychology and Behavior*, *23*(6), 695–706.

Moscoso, S., & Salgado, J. F. (2021). Meta-analytic examination of a suppressor effect on subjective wellbeing and job performance relationship. *Journal of Work Organizational Psychology*, *37*, 119–131. https://doi.org/10.5093/jwop2021a13.

Padget, R. N., Bradshaw M., Chen Y., Cowden, R. G., Jang S. J., Kim, E. S., Shiba, K., Johnson, B. R., & VanderWeele, T. J. (2024). Analytic methodology for demographic variation analyses for wave 1 of the Global Flourishing Study. Manuscript submitted for publication.

Seligman, M. (2018). PERMA and the building blocks of well-being. *The Journal of Positive Psychology*, *13*(4), 333–335. https://doi.org/10.1080/17439760.2018.1437466.

Seligman, M. E. P. (2011). *Flourish: A visionary new understanding of happiness and well-being*. New York, NY: Free Press.

Seligman, M. E. P., & Csikszentmihalyi, M. (2000). Positive psychology: An introduction. *American Psychologist*, *55*, 5–14. https://doi.org/10.1037/0003-066X.55.1.5.

US Surgeon General (2022). Framework for workplace mental health & well-being. https://www.hhs.gov/surgeongeneral/priorities/workplace-well-being/index.html.

van Zyl, L. E., Dik, B. J., Donaldson, S. I., Klibert, J. J., di Blasi, Z., van Wingerden, J., & Salanova, M. (2023). Positive organisational psychology 2.0: Embracing the technological revolution. *The Journal of Positive Psychology*. https://doi.org/10.1080/17439760.2023.2257640.

Walsh, L. C., Boz, S. G., & Lyubomirsky, S. (2023). *Well-being and career success*. Washington, DC: American Psychological Association.

INDEX

Note: **Bold** page numbers refer to tables; *italic* page numbers refer to figures and page numbers followed by "n" denote endnotes.

For Product Safety Concerns and Information please contact our EU
representative GPSR@taylorandfrancis.com
Taylor & Francis Verlag GmbH, Kaufingerstraße 24, 80331 München, Germany

www.ingramcontent.com/pod-product-compliance
Ingram Content Group UK Ltd.
Pitfield, Milton Keynes, MK11 3LW, UK
UKHW020147200926
475702UK00016B/2599
9781032612416